Beyond Sexual Abuse

WILEY SERIES ON
PSYCHOTHERAPY AND COUNSELLING

Series Editors

Franz Epting
Department of Psychology
University of Florida

Glenys Parry
Department of Psychiatry
University of Southampton

Personal Construct Counseling and Psychotherapy
Franz R. Epting

Self, Symptoms and Psychotherapy
Edited by
Neil Cheshire and Helmut Thomae

Beyond Sexual Abuse
Therapy with Women who were Childhood Victims
Derek Jehu

Further titles in preparation

Beyond Sexual Abuse

Therapy With Women Who Were Childhood Victims

DEREK JEHU

Department of Psychology
University of Leicester

in association with
Marjorie Gazan and Carole Klassen

JOHN WILEY & SONS

Chichester · New York · Brisbane · Toronto · Singapore

Library of Congress Cataloging in Publication Data:

Jehu, Derek.
    Beyond sexual abuse : therapy with women who were childhood
victims / Derek Jehu, in association with Marjorie Gazan and Carole
Klassen.
        p.   cm. — (Wiley series on psychotherapy and counseling)
    Bibliography: p.
    Includes indexes.
    ISBN 0 471 91913 6
    1. Adult child abuse victims—Treatment.   2. Women—Mental health.
3. Psychotherapy.   I. Gazan, Marjorie.   II. Klassen, Carole.
III. Title.   IV. Series.
RC569.5.C55J44 1988
616.85′83—dc19   88–17081
                                                                              CIP

British Library Cataloguing in Publication Data:

Jehu, Derek
    Beyond sexual abuse : therapy with women
    who were childhood victims.
    1. Sexual abuse victims. Psychotherapy
    I. Title   II. Gazan, Marjorie   III. Klassen,
    Carole
    616.89′14

    ISBN 0 471 91913 6

Typeset by Inforum Ltd, Portsmouth
Printed and bound in Great Britain by Bath Press Ltd, Bath

Contents

Part 5: Conclusion

Preface

It has become apparent in recent years that the sexual abuse of children is neither a rarity nor a fantasy. Among those children who are abused some grow up to experience psychosocial problems in adulthood that appear to be related to the abuse and its surrounding circumstances, and that are sufficiently distressing for the victims to seek therapeutic help. The literature on the treatment of these problems in this client group is extremely sparse and most of the reports that are available do not include any systematic evaluation of the intervention.

My interest in this area arose when I was Director of the University of Manitoba (U. of M.) Sexual Dysfunction Clinic where many women patients were found to have a history of sexual abuse. One of my graduate students at that time, Marjorie Gazan, became especially interested in the treatment of these women and despite my cautions concerning the virtually complete lack of previous work and literature she very successfully investigated this topic in her Master's thesis (Gazan, 1985). With the aim of broadening and extending this innovative inquiry I submitted a proposal to the Department of National Health and Welfare, Canada, and was subsequently awarded a National Welfare Grant (No. 4556-1-12) for a three-year study to be conducted in the Psychological Service Center at the U. of M. The major objectives of the study were to increase knowledge of the problems experienced by previously sexually abused women who seek therapy and to develop and evaluate a treatment program to alleviate these problems. The empirical findings and clinical experience gained in piloting and conducting the study are the main bases for this book and supplementary sources in the literature are cited whenever these are available. Thus, in addition to contributing to the sparse knowledge base in the field, a major aim of the book is to provide a treatment manual for therapists who wish to draw upon the U. of M. program in their own practices.

A series of 51 women was treated in the program. During an initial assessment information was gathered about their demographic characteristics, families of origin, sexual abuse experiences, and psychosocial problems. These problems could be categorized as mood disturbances, interpersonal difficulties, and sexual dysfunctions. The mood disturbances included feelings of guilt, low self-esteem, and depression. The general themes of isolation, insecurity, discord, and inadequacy appeared to permeate the clients' interpersonal relationships. The commonest sexual dysfunctions were phobias, aversions, and sexual dissatisfaction.

An assessment and treatment package was developed for each major category of problems. Treatment was conceptualized as consisting of certain general therapeutic conditions, such as the therapist–client relationship, and more specific treatment procedures for particular problems. Thus, the predominant procedure for mood disturbances was cognitive restructuring. Interpersonal problems were treated with a range of procedures including cognitive restructuring and training in the skills of communication, problem solving, assertiveness, and coping with stress. Mood disturbances and interpersonal problems often contributed to the clients' sexual dysfunctions in which case the procedures just listed were deployed, and a stress management approach was adopted when sexual stresses appeared to be contributary factors. The main treatment formats were individual or couple therapy, the latter when the victim had a partner and both were willing for him to attend sessions. These were conducted by one therapist, in most cases a woman. Additionally, an assertiveness training group for some victims, and a situation/transition group for some partners were provided, in each case conducted by a male–female, co-therapy team.

All the problems and treatment procedures mentioned in this brief overview are discussed much more extensively throughout the book wherever the particular topic seems likely to be most appropriate and helpful for practitioners who may wish to draw upon our findings and experience.

DEREK JEHU

Series Preface

This series of texts on psychotherapy and counselling is written for practitioners, teachers and advanced students. Some books will offer original thinking on theory and technique, others an authoritative account of a single approach. The series also includes books, like this one, which focus on a particular problem area and give psychotherapists the benefit of specialist experience.

Recent years have seen quite remarkable changes in our awareness of childhood sexual abuse. We now know that it is far from being a rare phenomenon; a dismaying number of men use children for sexual purposes, often but not always girls, both within and outside the family. Because of the difficulty in identifying victims, the true prevalence of such abuse will probably never be known—it could be more widespread than even current estimates suggest. Therapists working with child victims and their families now have a number of articles and texts to help them. However, the psychological effects of such abuse often reach into adulthood, and almost nothing is available to help the practitioner faced with an adult survivor of childhood abuse.

Many psychotherapists and counsellors now *routinely* consider the possibility of a client's psychological difficulty being grounded in such an experience. They know that this possibility is not confined to those with sexual problems or phobias about gynaecological examinations. Prior sexual abuse can also be implicated in eating disorders, depression, low self esteem, agoraphobia and recurrent relationship difficulties.

In this book, Professor Jehu draws on his experience at the University of Manitoba Sexual Dysfunction Clinic, where many women patients were found to have a history of sexual abuse. He and his colleagues worked with 51 women, gathering information about their problems and experiences and developing a treatment approach within a cognitive behavioural framework. The book will be invaluable to such therapists, providing detailed information about how to plan and evaluate a comprehensive intervention. It uses many concrete clinical examples; by far the best way for practising clinicians to learn its application. As a coherent account of one group's approach, it will be informative and useful to many other practitioners, giving them a deeper insight into the relationship between childhood sexual abuse and adult difficulties.

This is not an easy topic to write about—it arouses strong feelings in the reader. In presenting such a careful and well researched account, Derek Jehu has done us a great service.

GLENYS PARRY
Series Editor

Acknowledgments

My associates and I owe an immense debt to the women and their partners who participated in the U. of M. program. They helped us to understand the longer term consequences of child sexual abuse and collaborated fully and actively in their own treatment. Inevitably, this was at times a distressing process and the fortitude and persistence displayed by these clients was a constant source of admiration and encouragement for their therapists. Quotations from the records written by several clients are cited throughout the book but the requirements of confidentiality prevent me from identifying those who provided this illuminating and valuable material. My sincere thanks are extended to these necessarily pseudonymous contributors.

Marjorie Gazan and Carole Klassen were employed as research therapists throughout the program. In these positions they demonstrated great clinical skill and exceptional commitment to the welfare of the clients and the success of the study. In this book, the illustrative case material from the clients whose pseudonyms are Eileen and Marc, Elaine, Jackie, Maureen, Ruth and Doug, and Sara is based on reports provided by Marjorie, and the material from Amanda and Steve, Dawn, Roberta and Brian, and Sharon and Dick, is based on reports by Carole. I am grateful to them for their perceptive observations and excellent records on the problems and progress of these clients in particular, as well as more generally for their invaluable clinical contribution and wholehearted devotion to the study.

Several graduate students also made valuable and much appreciated contributions to the program. Rosemary Popescul and Gisele Rouillard undertook individual or couple therapy (Popescul and Rouillard, 1986). Ann Doige and her co-therapist Reid Hartry conducted the group for partners that is described in Chapter 15 (Doige, 1985). David Schwab and his co-therapist Marjorie Gazan provided the assertiveness training group described in Chapter 19 (Schwab, 1986).

My heartfelt thanks to Jane McCallum who relieved me of all the administrative chores associated with the program, not to mention typing the mountains of material that culminated in the final report and treatment manual as well as this book. Her calm, pleasant, efficient, and dedicated presence has been a constant support to me throughout the study. I was delighted that her interest in and commitment to helping the victims of abuse led her to extend the U. of M. program by exploring its delivery in a group format as the topic for her own graduate work (McCallum, 1987).

Very generous financial support for the study was provided by the Department of National Health and Welfare, Canada. I am most grateful to the successive Ministers of Health, the Honorable Monique Begin and the Honorable Jake Epp, and to the taxpayers of Canada, without whose aid it would not have been possible to offer the program. The Director of the National Welfare Grant program, Ester Kwavnick, and successive Regional Consultants, Gilda Good, Len Epp, and David Allen, have all been unfailingly constructive and helpful. It has been a great pleasure to work with them.

Last, but by no means least, I would like to thank the successive Directors of the Psychological Service Center, Morgan Wright and Walter Driedger, for facilitating and supporting the program as one component of the Center's services to the community of Manitoba.

DEREK JEHU

PART 1

Introduction

CHAPTER 1

Prevalence of Child Sexual Abuse

Until quite recently the sexual abuse of children was generally regarded as a rare occurrence and reports of it happening tended to be attributed to Oedipal fantasies (Masson, 1984; Rush, 1980). We know now that it is not uncommon and that many reports are only too real rather than imagined. The purpose of this chapter is not to review the evidence on the prevalence of sexual abuse in detail (see Peters, Wyatt, & Finkelhor, 1986; Russell, 1986) but to present some of the best established findings on its occurrence among females in the United States of America, Canada, and Great Britain, as contextual background for later discussion of the nature of sexual abuse, the psychosocial problems that are sometimes associated with it, and the treatment of these problems in adult women.

Prevalence in the USA

The only study based on a random sample of the population of the entire United States was conducted by Lewis (1985). The knowledge, attitudes, and personal experiences of 1374 females concerning child sexual abuse were surveyed in a telephone interview lasting half an hour. Some form of sexual abuse during childhood was reported by 27% of these subjects.

Two other studies have been conducted with random samples drawn from more restricted populations. In San Francisco, Russell (1983, 1986) obtained a sample of 930 women which represented a 50% response rate. A face-to-face interview lasting an average of 1 hour 20 minutes was conducted with each respondent. In Los Angeles County, Wyatt (1985) obtained a sample of 248 women which represented a response rate of 55%. Each respondent was interviewed on a face-to-face basis for between 3 and 8 hours.

In Russell's study 'extrafamilial child sexual abuse was defined as one or more unwanted sexual experiences with persons unrelated by blood or marriage, ranging from petting (touching of breasts or genitals or attempts at such touching) to rape, before the victim turned 14 years, and completed or attempted forcible rape experiences from the ages 13 to 17 years (inclusive)

3

Table 1.1.   *Prevalence of Child Sexual Abuse in San Francisco (Russell, 1983) and Los Angeles (Wyatt and Peters, 1986a)*

	San Francisco		Los Angeles	
	n	%	n	%
Contact abuse				
Intrafamilial:				
Up to age 13	108	12	42	17
Up to age 17	152	16	51	21
Extrafamilial:				
Up to age 13	189	20	57	23
Up to age 17	290	31	69	29
Intrafamilial and/or extrafamilial:				
Up to age 13	258	28	89	36
Up to age 17	357	38	104	42
Contact and non-contact abuse combined				
Up to age 13	450	48	117	47
Up to age 17	594	54	131	53

Note   The data in columns 1 to 4 are from 'Issues in the definition of child sexual abuse in prevalence research' by G.E. Wyatt and S.D. Peters, 1986, *Child Abuse and Neglect*, **10**, p. 237. Copyright 1986 by the Pergamon Press. Adapted by permission.

. . . *intrafamilial child sexual abuse* was defined as any kind of exploitive sexual contact that occurred between relatives, no matter how distant the relationship, before the victim turned 18 years old. Experiences involving sexual contact with a relative that were wanted *and* with a peer were regarded as nonexploitive, for example, sex play between cousins or siblings of approximately the same ages. An age difference of less than five years was the criterion for a peer relationship' (1983, pp. 135–136). Originally, Wyatt used a slightly different definition of extrafamilial abuse but she has recalculated her prevalence rates according to Russell's definition and has reported the rates for both studies (Wyatt & Peters, 1986a) as shown in Table 1.1.

Thus, in summary, the prevalence rates for all forms of child sexual abuse among females in the United States are variously reported as 54% by Russell, 53% by Wyatt and Peters, and 27% by Lewis. Some possible reasons for this variation in rates are discussed in the conclusion to this chapter but it seems clear that sexual abuse is experienced by a substantial proportion of American women.

Prevalence in Canada

A random sample of 1006 women drawn from the national population of

Canada completed a questionnaire that was delivered and collected by a member of the survey staff. These respondents constituted a response rate of approximately 94%. An unwanted touching of a 'sex part' of their body was reported by 23% of the respondents and 22% said that someone had tried to have sex with them when they did not want this or that they had been sexually attacked. The unwanted sexual acts in both these categories occurred in approximately two-thirds of cases when the victims were aged under 18 years, and in one-third when they were aged under 14 years (*Sexual Offences Against Children in Canada*, 1984). Thus, sexual abuse involving physical contact was experienced during childhood by a substantial proportion of Canadian women.

Prevalence in Great Britain

In Britain, Baker and Duncan (1985) studied a nationally representative sample of 1049 women each of whom was interviewed on a face-to-face basis. They were asked if they had ever been sexually abused according to the following definition: 'A child (anyone under 16 years) is sexually abused when another person, who is sexually mature, involves the child in any activity which the other person expects to lead to their sexual arousal. This might involve intercourse, touching, exposure of the genital organs, showing pornographic material or talking about sexual things in an erotic way' (Baker & Duncan, 1985, p. 458). An affirmative reply was given by 12% of the respondents and another 12% refused to answer the question. Among those who reported sexual abuse this had involved physical contact in 40% of cases, and it was intrafamilial in 14% of cases. These prevalence rates appear to be generally lower than those reported in the United States and Canada but even so child sexual abuse is clearly not a rarity in Britain.

Conclusion

The variations in reported prevalence rates within and across national boundaries may be due to any combination of differences in definition, sampling, and methodology (Painter, 1986; Peters, Wyatt, & Finkelhor, 1986; Wyatt and Peters, 1986a, 1986b).

Among the differences in the definition of child sexual abuse in various studies are the upper age limit adopted for victims of such abuse, the inclusion or exclusion of abuse that does not involve physical contact such as encounters with exhibitionists or sexual solicitations, and the criteria for defining a sexual encounter as abusive such as the extent to which it is unwanted or coercive and the required age discrepancy between victim and offender.

Differences in the characteristics of the subject samples in various studies may contribute to variations in the prevalence rates that are reported. Relevant sample characteristics might include the age range of the subjects and their educational level, socio-economic status, ethnic membership, and geographical location.

Finally, variations in prevalence rates may be influenced by differences in the methodology utilized in various studies. These differences might involve the techniques used to draw the subject samples, the response rates obtained for participation in the study, the type and number of questions about sexual abuse, or the format in which these questions are administered such as in a questionnaire to be completed by the subject or by means of a face-to-face interview or telephone inquiry.

Despite the variations in reported prevalence rates for any of the reasons just outlined it is evident that child sexual abuse is common among females in the general populations of several countries. The upshot of this for clinicians is that they are virtually certain to encounter women who have had such experiences among their clients. There is support for this in the rather sparse evidence, mainly from North America, which indicates that sexual abuse is prevalent in several different client groups as exemplified in Table 1.2. These data are presented only to indicate the likelihood of any clinician having clients who have been previously sexually abused. It is not intended to show that such abuse is more prevalent in these clinical groups than in the general population or that it is a major cause of the problems concerned, although either or both of these inferences are sometimes valid. Certainly, as discussed in later chapters, past sexual abuse may well contribute to current problems and therefore needs to be addressed in therapeutic attempts to resolve these problems.

Finally, in order to address problems that may be associated with child sexual abuse and its surrounding circumstances it is necessary for clinicians to identify any such experiences in the histories of their clients. This has already been done for those clients who are referred to special facilities for previously sexually abused women such as the U. of M. program but in other mental health facilities these women will need to be identified from among those presenting with a range of complaints. In view of the commonness of child sexual abuse in both general and clinical populations it seems quite appropriate to ask all clients if they have had such an experience. After a reassuring statement that many women do have unpleasant or distressing sexual experiences during childhood a client can be asked if anything of this nature happened to her. Such an inquiry is seldom if ever regarded as intrusive or offensive by clients and some welcome the opportunity to disclose their abuse. The fact that the clinician raises the matter specifically signals that he or she is comfortable in dealing with sexual abuse, is knowledgeable about it, and regards it as a very relevant issue in therapy. If such an inquiry is not made routinely with all clients then clinicians may be alerted to the need to do so more particularly with those clients who present with problems and histories that are known to be common among previously sexually abused women. These problems include mood disturbances, substance abuse, self-injurious or suicidal behaviour, dissocia-

Table 1.2. *Prevalence of Child Sexual Abuse Among Women in Clinical Samples*

Source	Country	Description of sample	Size of sample (N)	Proportion abused (%)
Herman (1986)	USA	Psychiatric outpatients	105	13
Friedman & Harrison (1984)	USA	Schizophrenic inpatients	20	60
Briere (1984)	Canada	'Walk-ins' for counseling	153	43
Bliss (1984)	USA	Multiple personality disorder	70	90
Coons & Milstein (1986)	USA	Multiple personality disorder	17	82
Benward & Densen-Gerber (1975)	USA	Drug abuse	118	44
Baisden & Baisden (1979)	USA	Sexual dysfunction	240	90
Oppenheimer *et al* (1985)	UK	Anorexia/bulima	78	51
Gross *et al* (1980)	USA	Psychogenic pelvic pain	25	36

tive phenomena, marital conflict, and sexual dysfunctions (Parts 2, 3, 4). Among the relevant historical features are absence of natural father/presence of step-father, poor or disrupted relationship with mother, discord between parents, and parentification of the child (Chap. 3).

CHAPTER 2

Nature of Child Sexual Abuse

In this chapter the nature of the sexual abuse experienced by female victims is described in terms of their ages at the time of the abuse, its duration and frequency, the sexual acts involved, the relationship between victim and offender, the methods used to induce victims to participate in the abuse, their reactions to it at the time, and the issues of secrecy and disclosure.

Data from the U. of M. program are introduced for the first time in this chapter, therefore this is a convenient place to summarize some demographic information about the 51 women in this series (Jehu, McCallum, Klassen, & Gazan, 1987). The selection criteria required all victims to have attained 18 years of age when they commenced treatment in the program and 46 (90%) were aged between 20 and 39 years. Twenty-four (47%) of them were married or living as married. Some form of technical, vocational, or university education at tertiary level had been received by 26 (51%) of the women and the same proportion were in the professional or student occupational groups. The ethnic background was Caucasian for 39 (76%) of the women and another 10 (19%) were Metis, native Indian, or Inuit. Twenty-three (45%) were protestant and another 13 (25%) were catholic.

Age of Victims

There is some variation across non-clinical samples concerning the ages at which victims most commonly begin to be sexually abused but a review and analysis of this evidence by Finkelhor and Baron (1986) indicates that girls are most vulnerable at ages 10 to 13 years inclusive. In the U. of M. clinical series the abuse tended to commence earlier, in 23 (45%) cases before 6 years, in 44 (86%) before 10 years, and in all 51 (100%) before 15 years. Whether an earlier commencement of abuse is associated with a more adverse adjustment in adulthood is still a controversial and undecided issue, some investigators have reported that younger, pre-pubertal victims tended to make poorer adjustments while other investigators have not found such an association (Browne & Finkelhor, 1986a, 1986b).

Duration and Frequency of Abuse

While not unanimous the evidence from non-clinical samples is strongly suggestive of a positive association between the duration of the abuse (which is highly correlated with its frequency) and an adverse adjustment in later life (Browne & Finkelhor, 1986a, 1986b).

As shown in Table 2.1, in the U. of M. series the abuse lasted over 1 year for 92% of the victims and over 3 years for 78%. The selection criteria for the program required victims to have been abused on more than one occasion and for 34 (66%) of the 51 victims this had happened on more than 100 occasions. The ages of the victims when the abuse terminated are shown in Table 2.2; this was between 14 and 17 years in over half the cases.

Sexual Acts

While not entirely consistent the available evidence appears to indicate that any form of abuse that involves bodily penetration of the victim including

Table 2.1.   *Duration of Abuse Prior to Age 17 Years (N = 51)*

	Victims	
Years	n	%
Less than 1 year	4	7.8
1–3	7	13.7
4–6	10	19.6
7–9	16	31.4
10–12	7	13.7
13 or more	6	11.8
Missing data	1	2.0

Table 2.2.   *Age of Victim at Termination of Abuse (N = 51)*

	Victims	
Years	n	%
5–8	9	17.7
9–13	15	29.4
14–17	26	50.9
20	1	2.0

Note The abuse referred to here was by any offender who had abused the victim before she attained the age of 17 years. Some victims were victimized at later ages by assailants who had not abused them prior to age 17 years and these assaults are not included.

Table 2.3. *Sexual Activities During Abuse (N = 51)*

Activity	Victims	
	n	%
Erotic fondling of victim's body by offender	44	86.3
Manual stimulation of victim's genitals by offender	43	84.3
Exhibitionistic display of offender's genitals to victim	34	66.7
Penile penetration of victim's vagina by offender	32	62.7
Manual stimulation of offender's genitals by victim	32	62.7
Simulated/'dry' intercourse	31	60.8
Erotic kissing	30	58.8
Erotic fondling of offender's body by victim	29	56.9
Oral stimulation of victim's genitals by offender	24	47.1
Oral stimulation of offender's genitals by victim	23	45.1
Victim observes offender masturbating	23	45.1
Voyeuristic observation of victim by offender	13	45.1
Digital penetration of victim's anus by offender	13	25.5
Offender observes victim masturbating	12	23.5
Penile penetration of victim's anus by offender	4	7.8

fellatio, cunnilingus, and anal or vaginal intercourse is associated with greater trauma and more adverse adjustment in later life; fondling may be less traumatic and damaging (Browne & Finkelhor 1986a, 1986b; Russell, 1986).

The selection criteria for the U. of M. program required that the abuse must have included manual or oral stimulation of the victim's and/or the offender's genitals or penile penetration of the victim's vagina. Thus, some form of genital contact was experienced by all victims and the prevalence of these and other sexual activities is shown in Table 2.3. It is noteworthy that penile–vaginal intercourse is reported by almost two-thirds of victims.

Relationship with Offender

The selection criteria for the U. of M. series required that the victim must have been abused by at least one offender who was known to her prior to the abuse and who met the age discrepancy criteria described in the note to Table 2.4, which shows the relationships between the victims and their offenders.

Overwhelmingly the offenders are male (n = 103, 94%). This is consistent with many other studies (Finkelhor & Russell, 1984; Russell & Finkelhor, 1984) and raises important questions about why this gender gap occurs; these are addressed in Chapter 8.

The age discrepancy criteria ensured that all offenders were substantially older than their victims and this has been found to be associated with enhanced trauma in several studies (Browne & Finkelhor, 1986a, 1986b).

A substantial proportion of the victims were abused by more than one offender and this is another factor that has been shown to increase the traumatic effect of the abuse (Browne & Finkelhor, 1986a, 1986b).

The relationships are what is usually defined as incestuous or intrafamilial (fathers, brothers, sisters, grandfathers) in 64% of cases, and offenders are related to the victim in some degree in 75% of cases. The largest category of offenders consists of father figures. The available evidence is not clear on whether intrafamilial abuse generally is more damaging but there is strong support for abuse by natural fathers or step-fathers being especially traumatic (Browne & Finkelhor, 1986a, 1986b; Russell, 1986).

Methods of Inducement

The methods used by offenders to induce the victims in the U. of M. series to participate in the abuse are shown in Table 2.5, the three most common methods being the exercise of authority and the use of threats or physical force. The available evidence generally offers strong support for an association between the use of force or coercion in the abuse and poorer subsequent adjustment by victims (Browne & Finkelhor, 1986a, 1986b).

Victim's Reactions

The reactions of the victims in the U. of M. series when they were being abused are shown in Table 2.6. These reactions were predominantly negative, more than two-thirds of the victims reported each of the reactions of guilt, fear, helplessness, compliance, anger, avoidance, denial, and dissociation.

The negative nature of these reactions, not only at the time of the abuse but also on the victim's longer term adjustment, is discussed at length in other parts of this book. For example, guilt may persist into adult mood disturbances, fear into later phobias, and while reactions such as avoidance, denial, and dissociation can serve as coping strategies at the time of the abuse, often the only ones then available to a child, they may also persist as inappropriate ways of handling other life stresses.

Some reactions that may appear less negative at the time of the abuse are additional sources of adverse psychosocial adjustment at later stages. For example, the reactions of using the abuse to obtain attention, affection, favors, or rewards, of experiencing physical or emotional pleasure, and of cooperating actively, may all later evoke considerable self-blame and guilt. Similarly, reacting with feelings of love, protectiveness, or compassion towards the offender may entail adverse consequences for the victim's future relationships with others, and leaving home may lead her into a self-destructive lifestyle perhaps involving prostitution and/or substance abuse.

Another piece of evidence is the highly significant positive correlation

Table 2.4. *Relationship of Offender (N = 106) to Victim (N = 51)*

Relationship		Offenders	
		n	%
Father:	natural	15	14.3
	others	*16*	*15.2*
	total	*31*	*29.5*
Brother:	natural	21	20.0
	step	7	6.7
	adoptive	*1*	*0.9*
	total	29	27.6
Male acquaintance		26	24.8
Uncle/great uncle		7	6.7
Grandfather		5	4.8
Male cousin		4	3.8
Sister		3	2.8
Brother-in-law		1	0.9

Note Many victims were abused by more than one offender. In accordance with the selection criteria for the U. of M. program to be included in this table: (a) an offender must have been at least 5 years older than a victim aged 12 years or under; (b) an offender must have been at least 10 years older than a victim aged 13 to 16 years; and (c) an offender must have been known to the victim prior to the abuse.

Table 2.5. *Methods of Inducing Victims (N = 51)*

Method	Victims	
	n	%
Exercise of adult authority	40	78.4
Threats	34	66.7
Physical force	30	58.8
Misrepresenting activities as a game, fun, 'something special' or 'fooling around'	30	58.8
Opportunity for attention and affection	28	54.8
Bribery	26	50.9
Promise of sexual gratification	17	33.3
Misrepresenting activities as sex education	14	27.4
Proclamation of romantic love	12	23.5

between the degree of trauma at the time of the abuse and subsequent negative life experiences such as rape, out of wedlock pregnancy, spouse abuse, and separation or divorce, that is reported by Russell (1986).

Table 2.6. *Victims' Reactions to Abuse (N = 51)*

	Victims	
Reaction	n	%
Guilt/shame/disgust	44	86.3
Fear	43	84.3
Feelings of helplessness	42	82.4
Passive compliance	41	80.4
Anger/resentment/hostility	39	76.5
Avoidance of offender	36	70.6
Denial of/dissociation from abuse	36	70.6
Used abuse to obtain attention/affection	33	64.7
Physical pleasure	30	58.8
Verbal resistance	29	56.9
Loving/protective/compassionate feelings towards offender	25	49.0
Shock/surprise	24	47.1
Physical resistance	22	43.1
Left home	22	43.1
Emotional pleasure	22	43.1
Used abuse to obtain material fovors/rewards	21	41.2
Actively sought protection from others	20	39.2
Active cooperation	19	37.2

Secrecy and Disclosure

Forty-nine (96%) of the 51 victims in the U. of M. series kept the abuse secret for some period of time as a result of certain factors listed in Table 2.7, particularly fear of disbelief, blame, or anger. Twenty-seven (52%) of the victims did eventually disclose the abuse before they attained the age of 17 years and the reactions of the significant others to whom the disclosures were made are shown in Table 2.8. These reactions were overwhelmingly negative towards the victim, only the two least common reactions attach any blame to the confidant or the offender.

The pressures on the victims to maintain secrecy and the negative reactions of others to disclosure are very consistent with the literature on these topics (e.g. Herman, 1981; Sgroi, 1982; Summit, 1983). It is quite possible, however, that the reactions from others experienced by the victims in the U. of M. program were unusually consistent in their negativity, for Myer (1984/5) and Russell (1986) have reported much wider variability, including more positive reactions among the responses of mothers to the disclosure of their daughters' victimization.

Doubtless because of many confounding factors such as the reactions of others, the limited evidence available does not permit any firm conclusion on the validity of the common assumption that secrecy is damaging and disclosure is helpful to the victim's adjustment, but there is greater empirical support for

Table 2.7. *Factors Contributing to Secrecy by Victims (N = 49)*

	Victims	
Factor	n	%
Fear of disbelief, blame, or anger by third party, e.g. mother	40	81.6
Fear of physical violence from offender	25	51.1
Loyalty to offender	25	51.1
Attention/affection	22	44.9
Actual physical violence from offender	20	40.8
Enhanced self-esteem	17	34.7
Sexual pleasure	15	30.6
Favors/rewards	14	28.6
Fear of offender harming someone else	11	22.4
Fear of being taken away from home	9	18.4
Fear of offender being jailed	7	14.3
Fear of offender harming himself/herself	3	6.1

Table 2.8. *Reactions of Significant Others to Disclosure Prior to Age 17 Years*

	Victims (N = 27)	
Reaction	n	%
Shock/horror	18	66.6
Denial of victimization	17	63.0
Conflict of loyalties between victim and offender	17	63.0
Anger/hostility towards victim	14	59.2
Denial of impact on victim	14	51.8
Withdrawal from crisis of disclosure	14	51.8
Disbelief of victim	13	48.1
Anxiety concerning disruption of family	13	48.1
Self-interest/self-defence	13	48.1
Blaming victim	12	44.4
Pressure on victim to suppress allegations	12	44.4
Attempts to undermine victim's credibility	10	37.0
Guilt over failure to protect victim	8	29.6
Anger/hostility towards offender	7	25.9

the hypothesis that negative parental reactions to disclosure are associated with an adverse outcome for the victim (Browne & Finkelhor, 1986a, 1986b).

Conclusion

The nature of the sexual abuse that was generally experienced by the victims in the U. of M. series includes several features that are believed to be especially traumatic and pathogenic. These are: (a) abuse over a lengthy period; (b) bodily penetration including intercourse; (c) offenders who were substantially older than their victims; (d) more than one offender; (e) abuse by father figures; (f) coercion or force by offenders; (g) negative reactions to abuse by victims; and (h) negative reactions by others to disclosure. In the light of the number and combination of these pathogenic features it is understandable that these victims experienced psychosocial problems in adult life for which they sought treatment.

To complement this review of the nature of the sexual abuse experienced by the U. of M. series of victims some case illustrations of the abuse experienced by individual victims are included in Chapters 10 (Alison), 14 (Dawn), 18 (Sara), and 21 (Elaine).

CHAPTER 3

Families of Sexually Abused Children

In this chapter the families of origin of sexually abused children are described in terms of the relationship between the parents, the roles and characteristics of the father and mother figures, and their effectiveness as parents to the victims.

During their initial assessments the victims in the U. of M. series were asked if certain commonly reported features in the families of sexually abused children had occurred in their own families of origin. The prevalence of these features is shown in Table 3.1. Additionally, the victims were asked which of 24 psychosocial problems had been exhibited by each of their parental figures. The eleven most frequently reported problems among father and mother figures respectively are shown in Tables 3.2 and 3.3.

Parental Relationship

There is substantial evidence of parental discord in the victims' families of origin. The parents of 21 (41%) of the 51 victims were known to be divorced or separated, 33 (64%) had a father figure in addition to the natural father, 44 (86%) had a mother figure in addition to the natural mother. Marital conflict and/or disruption was reported by 72% of the victims, and 68% lived in a milieu

Table 3.1. *Features of Victims' Families of Origin*

Feature	Victims reporting (N = 51)	
	n	%
Marital conflict/disruption	37	72.5
Milieu of abandonment	35	68.6
Poor supervision	35	68.6
Male supremacy	30	58.8
Role confusion	29	56.9
Oversexualization	23	45.1
Social isolation	22	43.1

16

Table 3.2. *Problems Exhibited by Father Figures*

	Victims reporting (N = 51)	
Problem	n	%
Ineffective/non-nurturing parent	40	78.4
Limited social skills	38	74.6
'Psychological absence' from family	34	66.7
Anger/hostility/violence	28	54.9
Physically abusive towards spouse	28	54.9
Interpersonal isolation/alienation	25	49.0
Physical absence from family	23	45.1
Promiscuity	23	45.1
Alcohol abuse	23	45.1
Physically abusive to children	22	43.1
Sexual dysfunction/dissatisfaction	22	43.1

Table 3.3. *Problems Exhibited by Mother Figure*

	Victims reporting (N = 51)	
Problem	n	%
Limited social skills	39	76.5
Overdependent on others	35	68.6
Ineffective/non-nurturing parent	35	68.6
Oppressed by others	33	64.7
Interpersonal isolation/alienation	31	60.8
Depression	27	53.0
Anger/hostility/violence	27	53.0
'Psychological absence' from family	20	39.2
Low self-esteem	18	35.3
Sexual dysfunction/dissatisfaction	18	35.3
Poor physical health	18	35.3

of abandonment in which they constantly feared that they would be deserted by significant others and/or there were frequent changes among those living in the home (Table 3.1). Physical abuse of the mother and promiscuity were problems exhibited by around half the father figures, while limited social skills such as poor communication were reported in about three-quarters of both father and mother figures, and over one-third of each category was known to have experienced sexual dysfunction and/or dissatisfaction (Tables 3.2, 3.3).

Such discord between the parents has been shown to enhance the risk of a child being sexually abused (Finkelhor & Baron, 1986). In general it is readily understandable that the children of discordant parents may lack adequate attention, support, affection, and love, and that this may render them vulnerable to sexual exploitation by any adult who seems to meet these needs. More specifically, there is evidence indicating that having a step-father is associated with a markedly increased risk of a child being sexually abused (Finkelhor & Baron, 1986; Russell, 1986). There are several possible reasons for this. Even before the step relationship is established a child may be in jeopardy from sexually exploitive men who are being dated by her mother. Predatory males may also have access to the home by virtue of their friendship or relationship with the step-father and they may be less restrained with a step-daughter rather than a daughter of their friend or relative. Lastly, step-fathers are more likely to abuse their step-daughters than are fathers their natural daughters. This may be because a step-father has not been involved in the child's nurturing from an early age (Parker & Parker, 1986), as well as being less constrained by the normative taboo against incest.

Role and Characteristics of Father Figures

Male supremacy was featured in the families of origin of 58% of victims (Table 3.1), and around half the father figures exhibited the problems of anger/hostility/violence, physical abuse of spouse, and physical abuse of children (Table 3.2). Several other authors have noted the prevalence of what are variously described as tyrannical, imperious, autocratic, patriarchal, or dictatorial father figures in the families of sexually abused children (e.g. Finkelhor, 1984; Herman, 1981; Russell, 1983, 1984; Summit & Kryso, 1978).

Such father figures exercise absolute authority and control, often maintained by the use of intimidation, threat, and force. They view women and children as the property of the male head of the household, and this includes the right of sexual access. Commonly, these men believe very strongly in the subordination of women and the obedience of children who are often indoctrinated to comply with the demands of any older man even if the child feels that these are wrong or distressing. This patriarchal structure entails a power imbalance that also increases a daughter's vulnerability to sexual abuse because no family member has the power or authority to challenge the father in order to protect her.

Role and Characteristics of Mother Figures

Many of the problems exhibited by the victims' mother figures are the obverse of those displayed by supremacist father figures. The mothers tended to be overdependent (68%), oppressed (64%), and depressed (53%), with limited social skills, including unassertiveness (76%), low self-esteem (35%), and poor physical health (35%) (Table 3.3). This general picture of a subservient, oppressed, and incapacitated mother figure is consistent with the reports of other authors (e.g. Finkelhor & Baron, 1986; Herman, 1981; Russell, 1984; Sgroi, 1982).

One consequence of these characteristics is that the mother is unable to protect, supervise, and guide her daughters, who are consequently more vulnerable to victimization. Another consequence is that the mother does not model or transmit self-protective and assertive skills to the daughters. Oppressed and demoralized wives who are victims themselves are in a poor position to instruct and equip their daughters to avoid these hazards.

Parent Effectiveness

There are many indications of inadequate parenting in the victims' families of origin. Poor supervision (Table 3.1) and ineffective and/or non-nurturing parenting by both father and mother figures were reported by over two-thirds of the victims, 43% had a father figure who was physically abusive towards the children, 45% of the father figures were physically absent, and 66% of the father figures and 39% of the mother figures were described as being 'psychologically absent' in that they were emotionally distant, unaffectionate, or often ill, so that the victims lacked a close, confiding relationship with them (Tables 3.2, 3.3). Such physical or psychological absence by father or mother figures has been shown to increase the risk of sexual abuse in several studies (Finkelhor & Baron, 1986). Finally, 45% of the victims reported that oversexualization was a feature of their families of origin in that they were inappropriately exposed to sexual behavior and talk by their own parent figures (Table 3.1).

Children who receive such inadequate parenting are likely to seek care and affection elsewhere with consequent risks from offenders who are often very perceptive of such needs and ineffective or absent parents may well fail to warn and protect their daughters against this exploitation.

Social isolation was reported as a feature in 43% of families of origin (Table 3.1) while 49% of father figures and 60% of mother figures were isolated and/or alienated in their interpersonal relationships (Tables 3.2, 3.3). A number of writers have described the isolation and reclusiveness that is typical of many incestuous families (e.g. Finkelhor, 1984; Finkelhor & Baron, 1986; Herman, 1981; Sgroi, 1982). The outside world is viewed as hostile and only family members are to be trusted. All social needs are to be met within the family circle; outside friends and activities are strongly discouraged. Father figures enforce the seclusion of their daughters by virtually confining them to the house and exercising absolute control over their social contacts, thus preventing the development of normal peer friendships. Any attempt by the girl to reverse this process often arouses intense jealousy in the father. This isolated and reclusive style of family functioning is said to facilitate intrafamilial sexual abuse in that it both limits sexual opportunity outside the family and encourages dependence on family members for all needs, while also preventing scrutiny and interference from the external community.

Role confusion or role reversal was reported to be a feature of their families of origin by 56% of victims (Table 3.1), and this is alleged to be typical of incestuous families (e.g. Herman, 1981; Sgroi, 1982; Summit & Kryso, 1978). The oppression and incapacity of mothers in many such families is discussed above. Consequently, these women tend to turn to a daughter for assistance in their family tasks. Gelinas (1983) terms this process 'parentification' in that the daughter takes on what are normally the parental responsibilities for domestic tasks, child care, family finances, and meeting the emotional demands of family members including the sexual desires of the father figure. The child is taught and expected to subordinate her own needs to those of other family members which come to assume priority for her.

Conclusion

The quantitative data in this chapter are illustrated by case reports on the families of origin of some individual clients in Chapters 10 (Alison), 14 (Dawn), and 18 (Sara). These data and these reports indicate the prevalence of parental discord, of supremacist and dominating father figures, of mother figures who were oppressed and incapacitated, and of parenting that was generally inadequate. The possible contribution of these factors to the later psychosocial problems of the victims is discussed in the next chapter.

CHAPTER 4

Therapy with Women who were Sexually Abused

In Parts 2, 3, and 4 of this book very high prevalence rates for various mood disturbances, interpersonal problems, and sexual dysfunctions are reported for the previously sexually abused women in the U. of M. series and other clinical samples.

Clearly, such women who enter therapy are selectively biased towards pathology and their prevalence rates cannot be generalized to other victims who have not sought treatment. At present there is very little satisfactory evidence concerning the proportion of sexual abuse victims who experience psychosocial problems in adult life (Kilpatrick, 1987). The survey of the British general population conducted by Baker and Duncan (1985) and described in Chapter 1 is one of the most informative sources to date. Among 119 female victims there were 61 (51%) who considered their abuse to have been un-pleasant and harmful at the time but to have had no long-lasting effects, 16 (13%) considered it to have been permanently damaging with long-term effects, 40 (34%) considered it to have had no effects at all, and 2 (2%) considered it to have improved the quality of their lives. Perceived permanent damage appeared to be associated particularly with intrafamilial abuse of a repeated nature, which commenced before the age of 10 years. Similarly, Russell (1986) has reported on 187 experiences of intrafamilial sexual abuse that were described by 152 victims drawn from her random sample of the population in San Francisco. Of these experiences, 33% were described as extremely upsetting, 20% as very upsetting, 27% as somewhat upsetting, 12% as not very upsetting, and 9% as not at all upsetting. Again, of these experiences, 25% were described as having had great long-term effects 26% to have had some effect, 27% to have had little effect, and 22% to have had no long-term effect. Thus, the sexual abuse was considered to have been per-manently damaging by 13% of the victims in the Baker and Duncan study, and 25% of the experiences in the Russell study were described as having had great long-term effects. Clearly, more rigorously established prevalence rates for

21

more precisely defined problems are needed from representative samples of previously sexually abused women.

The U. of M. project is primarily a study of the treatment rather than the epidemiology of problems associated with child sexual abuse. Consequently, the project did not include comparison groups of women who had not been abused and who were either (a) in therapy, or (b) in the general population. Thus, it is not possible to be certain how the prevalence rates for various psychosocial problems among the victims in the U. of M. series compare to those for non-abused women in other clinical or non-clinical groups. Such comparisons between abused and non-abused samples have been made in some other investigations which are cited in Parts 2, 3, and 4, and they are a necessary basis for ascertaining the extent to which sexual abuse is a pathogenic influence over and above other events in the lives of victims.

Even when sexual abuse does appear to be associated with increased pathology in adulthood it is difficult to distinguish the extent to which this is attributable to the sexual acts *per se* or to other circumstances surrounding the abuse such as the negative parental reactions to disclosure discussed in Chapter 2, and the adverse family backgrounds discussed in Chapter 3 (Rieker & Carmen, 1986).

In summary, very high prevalence rates for a range of psychosocial problems are reported in the U. of M. study, but these rates cannot be generalized to victims who have not entered therapy, and it is not certain how they compare to the rates for similar problems among non-abused women. Furthermore, if these problems are more common in groups of sexually abused women it is not clear to what extent this is due to the sexual acts involved or to other circumstances surrounding the abuse. Despite these limitations the fact remains that the women in the U. of M. series were experiencing many problems and the components and process of the intervention program aimed at their alleviation are introduced in the remainder of this chapter.

Components of Treatment

The components of treatment can be conceptualized as: (a) certain general conditions of a therapeutic nature, such as the therapist–client relationship; and (b) more specific treatment procedures for particular types of problems, for example, cognitive restructuring, assertiveness training, and sexual assignments. The relatively specific treatment procedures are discussed in Parts 2, 3, and 4. The general therapeutic conditions are outlined below, and they are regarded as closely related and often overlapping conditions which are a necessary basis for the deployment of specific procedures and the attainment of beneficial change in clients. By themselves, the general conditions may not be sufficient for such change to occur; this often requires the addition of appropriate specific procedures.

Therapeutic Relationship

It is generally held that a good therapeutic relationship is characterized by mutual feelings of liking, respect, and trust between client and therapist (Goldstein, 1980). Some particular ways in which such a relationship may contribute to the treatment of previously sexually abused women are outlined below.

Prognostic Expectancy

A second general therapeutic condition is that clients have some expectation of receiving effective help, which has long been recognized as a significant influence on the progress and outcome of treatment. Many previously sexually abused women have feelings of hopelessness when they present for therapy, and it is important to communicate to them that while the effects of abuse can be long term and very distressing this does not mean necessarily that they are irremediable and permanent. It has been suggested (Torrey, 1972) that a client's prognostic expectations are determined by several factors: (a) the degree to which the therapist's ability to name the problem and to identify its causes agrees with the views of the client; (b) the degree to which the therapeutic techniques employed are considered by the client to be of value in helping him or her; and (c) the degree to which the therapist's personal qualities match the client's expectations of what a therapist should be like; including his or her expertness, status, and credibility, as perceived by the client.

Exploration and Disclosure

On the bases of a therapeutic relationship and the prospect of effective help victims are likely to enter the painful process of exploring and disclosing their experiences, feelings and problems, often including self-blame for the abuse, self-injurious impulses, anger and revenge towards the offender, and feelings of hostility, hurt, and betrayal towards abusive or non-protective parents. These negative feelings are commonly mixed with more positive feelings towards the same individuals, which further increases the victim's distress and confusion. More specifically, for some previously sexually abused women this is the first time that they have shared the secret of the abuse with anyone, while the attempted revelations of other victims had been met with disbelief (Chap. 2). Consequently, it can be an enormous relief for a victim to unburden herself of the secret and to know that the therapist accepts the truth of her disclosure.

Acceptance and Support

The victim's disclosure of her abuse and related problems is often accompanied by intense feelings of shame, and perhaps by fear that the therapist will not be willing or able to deal with these issues. It is therefore very important that she is accepted and supported by the therapist. Acceptance involves a deep respect for the victim's worth as a person, without judging what she says, thinks, or feels, as either good or bad (although some limits must be set on her actions). Thus, a therapist who is respectful, non-judgmental, and immune to shock or embarrassment offers a non-threatening, safe, and trusting relationship in which the victim is free to explore her experiences without restraint or restriction and that enhances her self-esteem. Associated with such acceptance is the therapist's genuine concern for the victim's welfare and deep commitment to helping her. This can be very supportive to the victim who now has a source of aid and is no longer alone in attempting to cope with her problems. She is, moreover, seeing a therapist who views her problems as not unusual and as potentially amenable to treatment.

Empathic Understanding

The quality of a therapeutic relationship and the outcome of treatment are both strongly influenced by the level of empathic understanding exhibited by the therapist and perceived by the client (Goldstein, 1980). Such understanding involves the ability to comprehend both the experiences and feelings of a client, together with their meaning and significance for her. The therapist is able to see the client's world from her subjective viewpoint. It is essential also that this understanding is communicated to the client so that she feels deeply understood by the therapist. One example of an area in which therapists need to demonstrate empathic understanding with victims is their feelings of responsibility and guilt over having been abused. Another example is the incest victim's feelings of loyalty and love, as well as anger, towards both her father and mother. An empathic therapist can validate such inappropriate or ambivalent feelings as understandable from the victim's viewpoint which is reassuring to her and facilitates further self-exploration and disclosure, as well as strengthening the therapeutic relationship.

Causal Explanation

A related general condition is some shared understanding between the therapist and client about the causation of her problem. Victims often experience difficulties that seem inexplicable, strange, and bizarre. They may, for example, experience flashbacks, dissociative reactions, and sexual aversion, with a partner whom they trust and love (Part 4). It can be very reassuring for victims to have a plausible explanation for such difficulties, as an alternative to their common belief that they are 'going crazy'. The fact that the therapist appears to understand their problems also tends to reduce anxiety and to engender hope for successful treatment. Finally, a shared understanding of the problems by client and therapist constitutes a rationale for the procedures to be used in treatment.

Repeated Exposure

It is well substantiated that repeated or prolonged exposure to traumatic events, either symbolically or in real life, and without adverse consequences, is accompanied by a reduction in the anxiety evoked by these events (Marks, 1981). Thus, repeated discussion of disturbing problems in a safe therapeutic environment tends to reduce their stressfulness for the client.

Therapist Influence

A therapeutic relationship of mutual liking, respect, and trust, is likely to decrease a client's defensiveness and to increase her openness to influence from the therapist. Ethically, this influence is directed towards the successful accomplishment of the therapeutic tasks and goals that have been negotiated between the therapist and client, and to which the latter has given an informed consent. The following are among the many ways in which a therapist's influence can be transmitted to the client: (a) suggestions and advice; (b) permission giving and sanctioning; (c) support and encouragement; (d) therapist modeling; (e) therapist self-disclosure; and (f) praise and other forms of social reinforcement.

Replication

A client's maladaptive interpersonal relationship patterns may be replicated in her interactions with the therapist, whose response can constitute new learning experiences for the client through which she may acquire more appropriate ways of relating to others. Instances of this process are commonly encountered during therapy with previously sexually abused women; for example, a victim may be seeking constantly for a substitute for the ideal father or mother she never had, and she can learn that it is unrealistic to expect the therapist or other people to fill either of these roles for her. A victim's profound mistrust of people can be mitigated in a corrective relationship with a therapist who does not dominate or exploit her as the offender did, or neglect or abandon her like a non-protective parent. A tendency to oversexualize all relationships (Chap. 11) can be countered by a therapeutic experience that demonstrates that the victim is valued and cared for without any expectation of sexual payoff.

Instigation

Clients often avoid certain situations because they fear some unpleasant or harmful consequences. A therapist may encourage and support a client to confront such situations and to try out new patterns of behavior in real life. If these therapist-instigated tasks are not accompanied by adverse consequences—and every attempt is made to ensure that they are not—then the new more appropriate ways of behaving may replace the former avoidance reactions.

Networking

A related general therapeutic condition is the facilitation of a client's use of other community resources whenever this is appropriate. Examples of such resources include: (a) detoxification centres for clients in alcoholic crises; (b) psychiatric emergency services for suicidal clients; (c) eating disorder clinics for anorexic or bulimic clients; (d) residential homes for those requiring accommodation of a supportive nature, such as battered wives; (e) self-help groups, like Alcoholics Anonymous; and (f) parent effectiveness training programs.

Process of Intervention

Of the 51 women in the U. of M. program, 20 (39%) were self-referred, 15 (29%) were referred by social agencies, and smaller proportions were referred by physicians, psychologists, and other sources.

The number of years that elapsed between termination of the child sexual abuse and entry into the U. of M. program is shown in Table 4.1. For 39% of victims this interval was 10 years or fewer, and for 35% it was between 16 and 25 years.

Over half the victims had previously received some form of treatment as adults (Table 4.2), although the extent to which this had included attention to issues associated with the child sexual abuse is not known.

Table 4.1. *Interval Between Termination of Abuse and Entry Into U. of M. Program (N = 51)*

	Victims	
Years	n	%
Less than 5	9	17.6
6–10	11	21.6
11–15	6	11.8
16–20	10	19.6
21–25	8	15.7
26–30	5	9.8
More than 30	2	3.9

Table 4.2.   *Previous Treatment of Victims (N = 51)*

	Victims	
Treatment	n	%
Individual psychotherapy	27	53.0
Psychotropic medication	15	29.4
Professionally led group therapy	12	23.6
Inpatient psychiatric treatment	6	11.8
Marital therapy	4	7.8
Family therapy	3	5.9
Self-help group	2	3.9
Sex therapy	1	2.0

Next, the various stages in the intervention process are outlined. These stages often overlap, they may be recycled in the light of new problems or blocks to progress in treatment, and the amount of time devoted to each stage is likely to be different across clients.

Preliminary Interviews

One or more preliminary interviews are conducted, preferably by the therapist who will be treating the victim if this is appropriate. Among the purposes of these interviews are to ascertain whether the victim can receive the treatment she needs in the program being offered, to provide the victim with the information she needs to enable her to give an informed consent to her participation in the program, and if she is not going to participate, to advise her of any alternative facilities she may wish to pursue. With victims who are to be treated in the program the preliminary interview serves the additional purposes of beginning to establish a therapeutic relationship and associated general therapeutic conditions as discussed above, structuring the respective roles of therapist and victim, and enhancing the victim's motivation for change. These last two purposes are discussed below.

The victim's partner may or may not participate in a preliminary interview, and this is probably best decided according to whether an individual or joint interview is more acceptable and comfortable for the victim. When a partner does participate, the purposes mentioned above also apply to him where appropriate (throughout this book the partner will be referred to as male, this being the commonest case, but the same considerations apply when the victim is in a lesbian relationship and the partner is female).

Most clients enter treatment with limited and often inaccurate conceptions about the respective roles of client and therapist. For instance, clients often believe that they will be passive recipients of therapy—that the therapist will cure them without their having to do anything themselves—an expectation generalized from the traditional physician–patient relationship. It is important therefore, that therapists help clients to understand that they will be responsible for participating actively in therapy, through such tasks as providing information, negotiating the goals of treatment, and carrying out homework assignments. The therapist's role is that of a professional helper who will assist the client to achieve goals that are acceptable to both parties and which yield maximum benefit for the client.

It is often assumed erroneously that entering treatment is prima facie evidence of a desire to change. In fact, clients commonly have considerable resistance to changing, for reasons which include conflict over giving up the *status quo*, fear of the unknown, presenting for treatment under pressure from a partner or some other person or agency, or presenting for treatment only to get confirmation that their problems are incurable and caused by factors beyond their control, thus providing professional absolvement from any responsibility for disturbing or deviant behavior. Some ways of enhancing a victim's motivation to change are discussed in a later section on deficient motivation as an obstacle in treatment.

Initial Assessment Interviews

When a victim can be treated suitably in the program and gives her informed consent to this, then the next step is to conduct several initial assessment interviews, usually numbering between four and six, each lasting 60 to 90 minutes. Some of these interviews may be with the victim and partner together, providing that the victim is comfortable with this, but it is usually desirable to see each person separately at some stage in the initial assessment process in case there are matters that either would prefer to discuss privately.

The 'Protocol for Initial Assessment Interviews' (Appendix A) sets out a suggested content for these interviews. The information in the 'Demographic Data' and 'Client's Family of Origin' sections is collected first. Next, it is sometimes useful to give some form of relaxation training (Chap. 23)—often breath control relaxation is sufficient—in order to help the victim to cope with the stress of discussing the circumstances of her victimization. Quite commonly, when the information in 'The Victimization' section of the protocol is being gathered the victim will be unable to recall or unready to disclose certain aspects of the abuse. In such circumstances it is usually better if the therapist does not press the victim for this information, which is often remembered and revealed later as she becomes increasingly at ease with her victimization and in the therapeutic situation (Cole & Barney, in press). A related issue is that in contrast with many therapeutic approaches to victimized women, in the U. of M. program it was not found either necessary or beneficial to require the victim to describe the sexual acts involved in great detail and on numerous occasions.

In our experience it is the psychological meaning of the abuse to the victim that needs to be explored more thoroughly than the physical acts. The final section of the protocol covers information on the 'Psychosocial Adjustment' of the victim, both in the past and at the present time.

Many of the items in the protocol contain examples of the topic being explored that can be used as checklists to ascertain whether the event or reaction occurred with the particular victim being assessed. It may be thought that asking about these numerous and possibly disturbing examples would be stressful and annoying for the victim. In fact, for many it is reassuring and normalizing to know that these checklists were compiled on the basis of experience with other previously abused women so that the victim is not alone in experiencing the events or reactions concerned.

Negotiating Treatment Objectives

The goals of treatment are chosen mainly by the client in accordance with her own wishes and values, although in consultation with the therapist. The major contribution of professional treatment *per se* is to provide effective ways of achieving these goals only after they have been selected on personal, social, and ethical grounds. The aim is to negotiate a therapeutic contract in which mutually agreeable goals are specified. This is not always a simple task however, for the client's goals may not be acceptable to the therapist in the light of his or her own values or professional knowledge. In these circumstances, the therapist will explain his or her reasons for not being able to accept the goals proposed by the client. Whenever possible the therapist will suggest alternative goals, but if these cannot be satisfactorily negotiated and agreed, then it is not possible for the therapist to offer treatment, and he or she may well offer to refer the client to another therapist. Apart from the ethical imperative of clients agreeing to the goals of treatment, it should be noted that there is evidence from a number of sources that clients are more likely to work towards change when they feel that they have some say in the goals of change (e.g. Kanfer, 1980). This is likely to maximize collaboration and minimize resistance during treatment.

Quite commonly, the assessment reveals that a victim has a number of problems, and this raises the issue of which to treat in what order of priority. Some guidelines for this selection process include the following:

(a) The values and preferences of the victim; for example, she may not want to work on maintaining or improving an unsatisfactory marriage.
(b) The values and preferences of the therapist; for example, he or she may not be willing to help a client to function sexually in an extra-marital affair.
(c) The degree of danger, distress, or incapacity that the problem entails for the victim and others; for example, high risk of suicide would necessitate urgent therapeutic attention.

(d) The potential benefits that the resolution of the problem entails for the victim and others; for example, resolution of a sexual dysfunction may sustain and improve a marital relationship.

(e) Some problems are so closely related to each other that their concurrent treatment is indicated; for example, guilt and low self-esteem associated with sexual victimization in childhood.

(f) It is preferable to concentrate on a small number of problems at any one time. This focusses the treatment efforts of client and therapist, and it is likely to expedite demonstrable benefits to the client which will serve to promote motivation in treatment.

(g) The resolution of certain problems is sometimes a necessary pre-condition for the successful treatment of other problems; for example mood disturbances and any serious discord in the current partnership both usually need to be alleviated before specific treatment for sexual dysfunction is implemented.

In practice, the mood disturbances associated with sexual victimization in childhood are the problems that are most often selected to be treated first, but other high priority problems may require concurrent or even prior attention, especially when they are sources of acute distress or danger.

Finally, although goals are initially selected at this stage in the intervention process, it will often be necessary to revise them during the course of further assessment and treatment, either because the therapist has reconceptualized the problem in a different way, or because the victim has presented the therapist with new problems.

Assessment and Formulation of Target Problems

Next, the problem(s) selected for the initial intervention are further assessed and specified as discussed in Parts 2, 3, and 4.

The information gathered during the assessment stage provides the basis for a clinical formulation of the client's problems that includes: (a) a precise specification of the nature of the problems; (b) some hypotheses about the current events that evoke and maintain these problems; (c) any historical or developmental factors that have predisposed the client to react in these problematic ways; and (d) an appraisal of the resources available for treatment from the client, significant others, or the therapist. This formulation is not regarded as definitive or final, it is open to modification in the light of the feedback that is actively solicited from the client and is subject to constant revision as treatment proceeds. The formulation is shared with the client in terms and language that she can understand. Additionally, it is personalized to the particular client's problems rather than being presented as a routinized and didactic description of the therapist's preferred theoretical model. The formulation is likely to be much more credible to the client if the therapist demonstrates how theory casts light on the client's own problems, rather than seeming to force the client into some abstract theoretical system. A causal explanation that makes sense of problems that previously seemed inexplicable and strange may be very reassuring for a client. Finally, the shared formulation provides a necessary basis for planning of treatment and evaluation.

When the therapist and client agree that sufficient progress has been made in resolving a particular problem, the processes of selecting and assessing target problems are repeated with the remaining problems.

Planning Treatment and Evaluation

The next stage in the intervention process is to draw up a treatment and evaluation plan that reflects the clinical formulation and selection of objectives. This plan requires decisions concerning the therapist(s), the client(s), the timing of treatment, the specific treatment procedures to be employed, the sequencing of these procedures, and how the client's progress and outcome is to be monitored and evaluated.

Therapist(s). If any choice is available, the selection of the therapist(s) may involve factors such as gender, age, ethnicity, qualifications, experience, and whether a single therapist or a male–female co-therapy team should be provided.

In the U. of M. program, the treatment was in almost all cases conducted by a woman, so no empirical data are available on the important issue of whether the process and outcome of treatment are influenced significantly by the gender of the therapist. Similarly, as treatment was delivered by a single therapist, no data are available on the related issue of the influence of this format compared to a male–female co-therapy team. The psychotherapy literature, generally, provides no unequivocal conclusions on the influence of the gender of the therapist and no clear guidelines as to optimal client–therapist matching on the basis of this variable (e.g. Mogul, 1982).

As far as the treatment of previously sexually abused women specifically is concerned, some suggestions have been made concerning the potential advantages and disadvantages of male and female therapists (e.g. Herman, 1981). It may be easier for victims to talk to a woman, at least initially, and a female therapist may provide good empathic understanding and modeling opportunities. On the other hand, a female therapist may tend to overidentify with the victim and to feel so threatened and distressed that in some degree she avoids the topic of the abuse, and/or is so angry towards the offender that she does not recognize and accept the victim's more ambivalent feelings towards him.

As far as male therapists are concerned, if problems such as mistrust of men or the oversexualization of relationships are replicated in the treatment situation, then a male therapist can provide appropriate corrective experiences (Chap. 14). A male therapist would be disadvantageous however:

(a) if he became sexually involved with a victim, thus compounding her sexual exploitation;
(b) if he found it difficult to accept a victim's anger towards the offender, whose abusive behavior he tended to rationalize or blame on the victim;
(c) if he colluded with a common tendency among victims to disparage women (Chap. 16);
(d) if he became defensive in response to charges of accepting those aspects of male roles—such as patriarchy and dominance—that are believed to contribute to sexual abuse.

An additional point is that a co-therapy team may provide role modeling of male–female relationships that are egalitarian and warm without being sexual (Gottlieb & Dean, 1981).

All these suggestions and other unresolved issues concerning the influence of the gender of the therapist with female victims remain to be systematically investigated. Until this is done some useful working hypotheses in selecting therapists are:

(a) In addition to general professional competence the essential qualities for undertaking therapy with victims include sensitivity to, knowledge of, and experience with their particular problems. These qualities can be exhibited by both male and female therapists.
(b) Any preference by the victim regarding the gender of her therapist should be very important consideration.
(c) On balance, a female therapist probably has advantages over a male in most cases, particularly in the early stages of treatment when it may be less stressful for a victim to disclose her abuse to a woman.
(d) Whenever relationships with men are a problem for a victim it is desirable to involve a male therapist at a suitable stage in treatment.
(e) The potentialities of male–female co-therapy teams with victims are worth exploring thoroughly, perhaps especially if the partner is also involved in treatment.

Clients. The victim might be treated individually, or in a couple format with her partner if she has one, and/or in group therapy. In the U. of M. program it was usual for partners to attend most sessions conjointly with the victims, although she was likely to have some sessions on her own, and because the conjoint sessions were focussed on her treatment needs the partner was also seen individually at regular intervals so that his concerns could be given specific attention. Additionally, some partners attended a group designed to address their needs specifically (Chap. 13). As well as receiving individual or couple therapy some victims in the U. of M. program participated in an assertiveness training group, and those who did so evaluated this experience very highly (Chaps. 14, 19).

This and other forms of groups therapy might be provided as an adjunct to individual or couple therapy or as the major treatment format, and the relative effectiveness of these two interventions has not yet been systematically investigated although some clinicians advocate an adjunctive role for group treatment (e.g. Herman & Schatzow, 1984). Several writers have described professionally led or self-help groups for previously sexually abused women (e.g. Blake, White & Kline, 1985; Cole & Barney, 1987; Courtois & Leehan, 1982; Fowler, Burns & Roehl, 1983; Goodman & Nowak-Scibelli, 1985; Gordy, 1983; Herman, 1981; Herman & Schatzow, 1984; Leehan & Wilson, 1985; Tsai & Wagner, 1978; Wachtel & Lawton-Speert, 1983; Wooley & Vigilanti, 1984). The following are among the reported merits of such groups in alleviating some of the problems being experienced by the participants:

(a) Their feelings of difference, alienation, isolation, loneliness, and boredom are likely to be mitigated.
(b) In the understanding and supportive environment of the group the members can extend their sharing of the abuse experience and related problems beyond their individual therapist.
(c) Through the shared experiences of other participants a victim may gain a better understanding of her own reactions to the abuse and of its subsequent consequences.
(d) There is an opportunity to develop trust in other participants as a possible basis for trusting people on a wider basis.
(e) Their respect for other women may be enhanced.
(f) Their ability to help others in the group may increase their self-respect and self-confidence in social relationships.
(g) Effective methods of coping with interpersonal problems may be disseminated between members.
(h) The group may provide a springboard for social action concerning, for example, public education about sexual abuse or the provision of therapeutic resources for victims.

Timing. This aspect of treatment planning involves matters such as the number, length, and spacing of therapeutic sessions, as well as the overall duration of treatment. Thus, in the U. of M. program the victims were usually seen for about an hour and a half, at weekly intervals with some breaks, typically over a period of between one and two years. As indicated above, partners also attended most of these sessions, and additionally they were seen on their own at four-weekly intervals.

Procedures. The specific procedures that are available for the treatment of particular problems are discussed in Parts 2, 3, and 4. These procedures are drawn upon to constitute individualized treatment programs for particular clients. They may present with similar problems, and perhaps with similar objectives, but their personal characteristics and life situations differ in many ways, and these differences necessitate unique treatment programs that are individually tailored to suit each client.

Sequencing. Having selected the procedures to be implemented, it is necessary to plan the sequence in which they are to be delivered for particular problems. Often, an important aspect of this is the arrangement of a series of intermediate steps to the ultimate treatment goal. For example, situations that evoke anxiety may be introduced into treatment in a graded manner from the least to the most disturbing, so that the client is not overwhelmed or precipitated into escape or avoidance reactions. Similarly, while an ultimate goal is beyond a client's current capacity, then the achievement of a series of intermediate goals will minimize his or her experience of failure and optimize success.

Evaluation. This requires the systematic monitoring of the progress and outcome of therapy on a continuous basis throughout the assessment, treatment, and follow-up stages. Such evaluation serves several useful functions for clinical practitioners. It provides feedback to the client on her progress, it tends to enhance motivation and to confirm positive therapeutic expectations, and it reveals any necessity for the revision of her treatment. Additionally, this has been called the 'age of accountability'. Increasingly, administrators and funding sources are demanding evidence that practitioners are effective in helping clients. The results of systematic evaluations can serve to demonstrate this. These functions are integral and essential parts of responsible professional. practice and evaluation needs to be undertaken by all practitioners rather than being a task that only researchers perform. Extensive discussion of clinical evaluation is beyond the scope of this book but two excellent sources are Barlow, Hayes, and Nelson (1984) and Bloom and Fischer (1982).

Interviews, questionnaires, client records, and other assessment and evaluation methods are discussed in Parts 2, 3, and 4 as appropriate for particular categories of psychosocial problems. A suitable selection of these measures is administered repeatedly at appropriate intervals throughout the assessment, treatment, and follow-up periods. It is a good idea to start administering these measures very early in one's contact with a client, subject to having established sufficient rapport and trust. In this way, a quite substantial picture of the state of the problem can be established before treatment is commenced. Those measures that are likely to be sensitive to shorter term changes are then applied repeatedly—perhaps at weekly intervals before, during and after treatment, while other measures that are not likely to be sensitive to shorter term changes can be administered at longer intervals—perhaps before treatment, and on termination and follow-up.

As repeated measures are collected throughout the assessment, treatment, and follow-up periods it becomes necessary to record, synthesize, and interpret the data, and to share them with the client. A convenient way to do this for quantitative data is in the form of line graphs which show: (a) *time* from assessment through treatment and follow-up—indexed on the horizontal axis; (b) *scores*—indexed on the vertical axis; and (c) *events* that might account for variability in scores—these would include the assessment, treatment, and follow-up periods, as well as any life events. There are examples of such graphs in Figures 15.1, 19.1, 19.2, and 19.3.

The simplest and the most feasible evaluative design for practitioners to use with individual clients is the AB design, which comprises first establishing a baseline (A phase) and then implementing the treatment (B phase) during which repeated measurement of the target problems is continued.

The baseline establishes the level, stability, and trend of the client's function-ing prior to any specific treatment, and thus provides a standard against which any changes accompanying treatment can be evaluated. Usually, a baseline is established while the client is being assessed. There are, however, some circumstances in which this is contraindicated, particularly in situations of crisis or danger when an immediate intervention is essential, for example, with a potentially suicidal client. In such circumstances one would proceed directly with treatment and repeatedly measure the client's progress during it (B design). This at least yields information on whether the client is improving and whether treatment needs to be revised.

It is generally held that the *length* of a baseline should cover at least three measurement points, though more are desirable. Three points are probably an essential minimum to establish the level, stability, and trend of the client's pre-treatment functioning. A baseline need only be *stable* enough to permit any later therapeutic effects to be clearly seen. For example, if total reduction of a problem is anticipated, then extreme variability in the baseline would be acceptable. Conversely, if baseline variability could not allow any treatment effect to be seen, then it would be less desirable to proceed with treatment immediately. A final consideration is the *trend* of a baseline. When treatment is expected to produce increases in the data, a falling or flat baseline is desirable. When deceleration is expected, rising or flat trends are beneficial. These are not rigid rules, however, for instance, a slowly rising baseline may be adequate if treatment is expected to increase it substantially.

After a suitable baseline is established, the treatment is commenced, and its effects are evaluated. The most usual and practicable way of evaluating the graphed data is by means of visual inspection. The argument for this is that any changes in target problems that are of sufficient clinical significance will be readily apparent. Basically, the AB design shows whether the treatment was accompanied by changes in the level, stability, or trend of the target problems. The most dramatic changes are those which are of a very large magnitude, follow closely the commencement of the treatment phase, and remain consis-tent throughout the treatment phase. Thus, one strength of the AB design is that it can provide evidence of improvement in the client, which to some extent meets the requirement for accountability to the client, the agency, and other interested parties. Another strength is that the AB design provides feedback on the progress of the client as a basis for continuing, revising, or terminating the treatment.

However, the AB design does not provide strong evidence that any change accompanying treatment is produced by that treatment, other possible causal explanations for the change such as the threats to internal validity referred to by Campbell and his co-authors (Campbell and Stanley, 1963; Cook and Campbell, 1979) are possible alternatives to the intervention as sources of change in the client, and they include:

(a) *History*: changes in clients may result from extra-therapeutic events in their lives rather than from the treatment they are receiving. Such events might include for example, getting married, a new job, receiving help from a relative or friend, or ending an unsatisfactory relationship.
(b) *Maturation*: this threat to internal validity refers to the fact that since people change in ways that are relatively independent of specific environmental experiences; such maturation might produce changes in clients, rather than their treatment being responsible. For instance some late adolescent rebellion problems in young previously sexualy abused women might be resolved through maturation rather than treatment.
(c) *Instrumentation*: a third threat to internal validity is that the measures by which client progress is being evaluated may change during treatment, and these changes may be confounded with changes in clients produced by treatment. For example, there may be a practice effect in completing a questionnaire which might influence the client's apparent progress.

If one wishes to exclude these and other alternatives to treatment as causes of client change, then it is necessary to control for their effects by the employment of designs that are more complex than the AB, such as the natural multiple baseline design across clients (e.g. see Figures 19.1, 19.2, 19.3). To implement this design one has only to collect AB designs from two or more clients with similar problems who were treated in a similar manner, but at different points in time. Furthermore, almost inevitably the baseline for these clients will be of varying lengths due to differences in scheduling and complexity across cases. These conditions in the natural multiple baseline design across clients serve to reduce the likelihood of the main alternatives to treatment as the cause of client change, and correspondingly to strengthen the plausibility of treatment as the cause of such changes:

(a) The likelihood of coincidental events in the life situations of several clients producing changes in their target problems during treatment is considerably lessened because each client commenced treatment at a different point in time, and each client commenced treatment after a baseline of different length. It is highly improbable that important life events would repeatedly coincide with commencement of treatment at different times in several clients.

(b) The likelihood of maturational processes being the cause of change during treatment in several clients is to some extent lessened by the fact that any such maturation effects do not show up during any of the baselines of varying lengths—instead change is observed only or mainly after treatment is commenced with each client—and by the fact that the clients are likely to be in different age groups.

(c) Similarly, instrument shifts are rendered less likely causes of change during treatment because any effects such shifts might have do not become apparent during any of the baselines of varying length—again, change is observed only or mainly after treatment is commenced with each client.

Thus, the natural multiple baseline design across clients is a very feasible and useful extension of the basic AB design if one wants to demonstrate not only that clients have improved but also that this improvement is the result of treatment rather than other factors.

Client change during therapy has most usually been evaluated in terms of *statistically* significant pre-/post-treatment differences in scores on appropriate measures. Statistical tests of significance indicate the level of probability that such differences could have occurred by pure chance, but they do not indicate whether the magnitude of improvement is such that it makes any real difference in practical terms to the clients concerned. In contrast, the concept of *clinical* significance does involve an evaluation of whether the magnitude of change is such that the problem is essentially ameliorated and the client's everyday functioning is enhanced.

Contract. The possible treatment and evaluation program is reviewed with the client, its rationale is explained, and some indication of the likely progress and outcome is given. As far as the progress and outcome of treatment are concerned, clients are warned that it is unlikely to follow a completely smooth course or to produce an extremely rapid improvement. Instead, obstacles and reversals in progress will probably be encountered and do not necessarily signify that treatment has failed; they can more usefully be regarded as opportunities for clients to learn about their difficulties and how they can best be overcome. At the same time, every effort is made to promote a realistic expectation of effective help from treatment, the importance of which is discussed above. This review provides the basis for the informed consent of the client to the treatment and evaluation program and constitutes a therapeutic contract between client and therapist. There is no reason why such contracts should not be of a short-term exploratory nature, with subsequent revision by agreement as treatment proceeds.

Implementation of Treatment

The implementation of specific procedures in treatment is discussed in later parts of this book and some obstacles or resistances to progress that are commonly encountered in the course of therapy are considered next. Among the many examples of these obstacles are failures to attend appointments regularly and punctually, to explore and/or disclose problems, to undertake homework assignments, to keep records, and to continue in treatment when this is still required. If such obstacles to progress are occurring, then the therapist has to take the initiative in correcting the situation. It is his or her responsibility to try to keep therapy on a goal-directed course, and how this might be done depends on the source of the obstacle. Some common sources are discussed below in the categories of deficiencies in understanding, skills, or motivation, and of stress reactions.

Deficient understanding. Clients may simply not understand what it is that they are supposed to do. For example, they may not understand how to use the record forms to identify distorted beliefs and to explore alternatives in cognitive restructuring (Chap. 7), or how to implement *in vivo* exposure assignments in stress management (Chap. 23). When such obstacles are due only to lack of understanding then repetition and clarification of the instructions by the therapist may enable therapy to proceed.

Deficient skills. Clients may lack the skills required for them to do what they are supposed to do, for example, the communication skills necessary to explore and disclose their problems in treatment sessions, or the problem-solving skills needed to resolve a marital conflict (Chap. 13). In such circumstances the obstacles to progress in treatment may be overcome by teaching the necessary skills, as indicated in the chapters cited in the examples given.

Deficient motivation. There are many related and overlapping reasons why clients may lack motivation to progress in therapy. Their expectations of improvement may be low, and it is emphasized previously in this chapter that a client's prognostic expectancy is an important influence on progress and outcome. As a result of their abuse and other experiences many victims have pervasive feelings of helplessness and hopelessness that make them very pessimistic about their ability to change. This attitude may be modified by:

(a) Cognitively restructuring dysfunctional thoughts such as 'I can't do it', or 'I'm too weak to do anything' so that they are viewed as hypotheses to be tested rather established truths (Chap. 7). One way to test such hypotheses is to explore areas in which the victim has changed in the past. These areas may be of a personal nature or they may be the acquisition of some skill such as driving a car.

(b) Emphasizing that behavior is changeable rather than a fixed characteristic of the victim's personality.
(c) Reassuring the victim that the effects of sexual abuse are not necessarily permanent, and that other women have overcome them in therapy.

Clients may also have doubts about the effectiveness of the treatment being provided. In addition to strengthening those factors that determine prognostic expectancy, as discussed previously in this chapter, such doubts may be alleviated by:

(a) The therapist having predicted the occurrence of setbacks during treatment, so that they are not unexpected catastrophes.
(b) Facilitating some speedy therapeutic changes that are recognized and reinforced by the therapist and significant others as well as the client.
(c) Prompting the client to compare his or her present level of functioning to that prevailing when therapy began. This can offset the detrimental practice of viewing therapeutic changes against the criterion of success in achieving the ultimate objective of treatment, rather than that of progress towards this goal.

Lack of motivation may also occur if treatment is not conforming to the client's perception of what should happen. There may be a discrepancy between client and therapist concerning their understanding of the objectives of treatment, and some clarification and, if necessary, renegotiation may be required. It may be desirable to repeat discussion of the clinical formulation of the client's problem, together with the associated rationale for the treatment plan. The formulation and treatment plan may need to be revised so that they are better reflections of the client's problems and needs. Further clarification of the roles of client and therapist in the treatment process may be indicated. Clients should be clear why the therapist structures a particular session in a certain way. Each session has an agenda, and each agenda bears a direct relationship to a clearly specified goal in treatment. From session to session there is continuity, coherence, progression, and predictability. Within this clear structuring there is, of course, provision for clients to raise and discuss any matters that are of current concern to them. Finally, clients sometimes complain that the requirements of treatment—such as homework assignments or record keeping—are onerous and artificial. These concerns may be counteracted and motivation maintained by emphasizing that such treatment demands are applicable only while the client is learning new patterns of behavior. Learning is effortful, deliberate, and artificial; only when new behavior is acquired does it become an easy, automatic, and spontaneous performance.

Clients may be unmotivated because there is no incentive to pursue treatment when its outcome is perceived to be not sufficiently rewarding to be worth the effort. For example, a victim may lack incentive to resolve a sexual problem if she will still be married to a physically abusive husband with whom she does not want to have a sexual relationship. Lack of incentive is particularly common among clients who enter treatment under pressure from a spouse or other person, rather than on their own volition. A cost–benefit analysis may help clients to clarify whether it is in their interests to pursue treatment. They are helped to clarify the long-term benefits of doing so, and to relate such benefits to their lifestyle and value system. This tends to mitigate the shorter term costs of changing. For example, attempting to resolve a sexual problem can be distressing for a previously sexually abused woman, but these costs may be outweighed by the benefits of preserving and improving a marital relationship that she values. It may be desirable also to renegotiate the objectives of treatment so that they are clearly of benefit to the client.

A client's motivation may also be undermined by 'psychological reactance' (Brehm, 1966), that is a tendency to actively resist being influenced by others. When a client perceives herself as having some choice, and that this choice is being restricted, threatened or eliminated by the therapist, then the client will tend to experience discomfort and to strive to restore the lost freedom. Because of their history of domination and exploitation by others, victims of sexual abuse may be especially on guard against external influence and prone to reactance during treatment. It follows, that in order to avoid or minimize reactance, clients should participate fully in decisions concerning the objectives and nature of their therapy. They should also be prompted to attribute therapeutic progress to their own efforts rather than to the therapist (Kanfer, 1980).

Finally, motivation may be deficient because a client anticipates aversive consequences if therapy proceeds. For example:

(a) A victim may fear that therapy will result in failure, with the anticipated consequences of self-blame and marital breakdown.
(b) Improvement in treatment may result in some loss of secondary gains from a client's problems, such as regular meetings with the therapist or the total support that is unquestioningly owed by a spouse to a 'sick' person in therapy.
(c) A partner may attempt to sabotage a victim's increasing self-confidence and assertiveness because he wants to preserve his current dominance in the relationship.

The upshot is that attention needs to be paid to any anticipated aversive consequences when treatment is being planned and implemented so that their detrimental effects on motivation can be mitigated.

Stress reactions. Obstacles to therapeutic progress may occur because certain aspects of treatment are stressful for the client and evoke disruptive reactions such as anxiety and avoidance (Chap. 21). For example:

(a) Victims may become so anxious when they are discussing their abuse that they are unable to continue.

(b) Quite commonly, they are so ashamed and guilty after having disclosed the abuse that they avoid future appointments.
(c) As the relationship with the therapist becomes closer this may be very threatening to a victim who fears exploitation or abandonment in all intimate relationships, and who may therefore tend to terminate therapy.
(d) Various sexual assignments may evoke anxiety or anger in some victims who therefore avoid carrying out these tasks. There are many examples of such sexual stresses and reactions in Part 4 of this book.

Stress reactions that produce obstacles in treatment may be alleviated by general therapeutic conditions such as acceptance and support or it may be necessary to use more specific stress management procedures (Chap. 23).

Termination of Treatment

Ideally, the decision to terminate treatment will be a mutual one between client and therapist, on the basis of their agreement that the client has made satisfactory progress towards the alleviation of her problems. Sometimes, however, a client will want to terminate before the therapist considers this to be appropriate. Such premature termination is sometimes suitably conceptualized and dealt with as an obstacle to therapeutic progress as discussed in the previous section. It may also be useful to check whether the client would be willing to continue in treatment with another therapist, and if so to try to arrange a transfer. If the client remains determined to terminate, rather than arguing and perhaps retaining a reluctant client, it is usually better for the therapist to accept the client's decision on the understanding that therapy can be resumed at a later point if the client so wishes.

It is not unusual for clients to balk at terminating therapy as they confront the issues of separating from the therapist whom they perceive as playing a significant role in their lives. The apprehension and distress of termination can be eased by phasing out therapeutic contact through a series of follow-up interviews, usually at gradually lengthening intervals. Some particularly vulnerable clients might need follow-up support over a prolonged period, so that the interviews might be conceptualized as a prosthetic environment for such clients. Two other benefits of follow-up interviews are that they provide opportunity for newly acquired patterns of behavior to become well practiced and reinforced, while the therapist is still available to help the client with any initial difficulties that might be encountered, and they enable evaluation of progress and outcome to be continued through the follow-up period as discussed above.

During the final stage of treatment it is important to promote the generalization and maintenance of therapeutic gains. This represents the culmination of treatment since an overall goal is to help clients to become their own therapists by extending therapeutic gains beyond the time limits of treatment and to problems that may occur after termination. Several features of the earlier stages in treatment are relevant to this task, and they may require re-emphasis prior to termination. For example:

(a) During the initial role structuring it was impressed upon the client that she is fundamentally responsible for changing her own behavior. This is true whether or not the change takes place within the context of therapy.

(b) During the assessment and formulation stages, the client learned an approach to conceptualizing her behavior that can be applied to problems that may arise in the future.

(c) During the implementation stage the client acquired some means of changing her behavior that can be used in the absence of the therapist should the client note any indications of impending difficulties. Thus, treatment can be regarded as a training in self-management, so that if an incipient relapse or a new problem does occur the client can apply the knowledge and skills she has learned to prevent it worsening.

(d) Also, during treatment it was emphasized that improvement is a function of the client's own efforts, thus enhancing the perception of effective self-control and the self-attribution of change.

(e) Finally, it is sometimes argued that therapeutic gains will be maintained by the 'natural contingencies' in the client's life situation. However, these contingencies may have been contributing to the maintenance of the problems that led the client to seek treatment in the first place. In these circumstances a good treatment program will have attempted to create new natural contingencies: either in the same environment, perhaps by altering interactional patterns with significant others, or by facilitating the transition to new environments, for example, by the client changing location, job or friends.

Conclusion

The components of treatment comprise certain general conditions of a therapeutic nature together with more specific treatment procedures that are discussed in later parts of this book. The general conditions include: (a) a therapeutic relationship; (b) a positive prognostic expectancy; (c) exploration and disclosure; (d) acceptance and support; (e) empathic understanding; (f) causal explanation; (g) repeated exposure; (h) therapist influence; (i) replication; (j) instigation; and (k) networking.

Preliminary interviews are conducted to screen and initiate clients for the program being offered. Extensive initial assessment interviews are then undertaken with those clients who enter the program. On the basis of these interviews the objectives of treatment are negotiated with each client. The problem(s) selected for the initial intervention is then further assessed and clinically formulated. On the basis of the negotiated objectives and clinical formulation a treatment and evaluation plan is drawn up which includes decisions concerning the therapist(s), the client(s), the timing and sequencing of treatment, and the specific procedures to be employed. This plan is embodied in a therapeutic contract with the client(s).

When the treatment and evaluation plan is implemented certain obstacles or resistances are likely to be encountered and to require therapeutic resolution. When sufficient progress has been made in resolving a particular problem then the further assessment and clinical formulation process is re-applied in turn to the remaining problems. The termination of treatment is negotiated between therapist and client(s) and contact is progressively reduced during a follow-up period.

In the next three parts of this book the general components of treatment and process of intervention discussed in this chapter are applied, together with more specific procedures, to the mood disturbances, interpersonal problems, and sexual dysfunctions that are very prevalent among the previously sexually abused women in the U. of M. series.

PART 2

Mood Disturbances

CHAPTER 5

Introduction

During the initial assessment of the 51 victims in the U. of M. program is was found that 47 (92%) reported low self-esteem, 45 (88%) feelings of guilt, 36 (70%) depressive episodes, and 47 (92%) at least one of these mood disturbances. At the same time there was support for these interview reports in the results from three questionnaires, each of which is discussed in Chapter 6.

(a) On the Battle Self-Esteem Inventory 24 (88%) of 27 victims scored 26 or less which is deemed to indicate intermediate, low, or very low self-esteem,
(b) Among 24 different victims, 22 (91%) scored 30 or above on the Hudson Index of Self-Esteem which is indicative of significantly low self-esteem,
(c) On the Beck Depression Inventory 29 (56%) of 51 victims scored 21 or more which is indicative of clinically significant depression.

Similar mood disturbances among previously sexually abused women are reported by many other writers (Browne & Finkelhor, 1986a, 1986b).

The related problems of attempted suicide and self-destructive substance abuse that are commonly reported among previously sexually abused women (Briere & Runtz, 1986; Browne & Finkelhor, 1986a, 1986b) are almost certainly under-represented in the U. of M. series because of a selection criterion that excluded victims who were currently in crisis situations. As far as suicide is concerned 6 (11%) of the 51 victims attempted this after being accepted into the program, and 31 (60%) had done so previously. Similarly, 6 (11%) of the victims relapsed into alcohol abuse after acceptance and 19 (37%) had a history of this problem, while 4 (7%) relapsed into drug abuse and 18 (35%) had previously engaged in this.

It is hypothesized that certain distorted beliefs associated with the victims' sexual abuse in childhood are important sources of their mood disturbances and related problems in adulthood. These beliefs are exemplified in Table 5.1, the items for which are drawn from the Belief Inventory discussed in Chapter 6. Such distorted or unrealistic beliefs are postulated to lead to distressing feelings and inappropriate actions, and to the extent that mood disturbances are a function of these beliefs then it follows that their therapeutic correction is likely

Table 5.1. *Distorted Beliefs Among Victims (N = 50)*

Belief	Responding as partly, mostly, or absolutely true	
	n	%
It is dangerous to get close to anyone because they always betray, exploit, or hurt you.	46	92.0
I am inferior to other people because I did not have normal experiences.	45	90.0
No man can be trusted.	45	90.0
No man could care for me without a sexual relationship.	43	86.0
I must have been responsible for sex when I was young because it went on so long.	43	86.0
It must be unnatural to feel any pleasure during molestation.	43	86.0
I must have permitted sex to happen because I wasn't forced into it.	42	84.0
I must be an extremely rare woman to have experienced sex with an older person when I was a child.	41	82.0
Anyone who knows what happened to me sexually will not want anything to do with me.	41	82.0
I am worthless and bad.	39	78.0
I will never be able to lead a normal life, the damage is permanent.	38	76.0
I must have been seductive and provocative when I was young.	31	62.0
It doesn't matter what happens to me in my life.	29	58.0
Only bad, worthless guys would be interested in me.	29	58.0
You can't depend on women, they are all weak and useless creatures.	28	56.0
I've already been used so it doesn't matter if other men use me.	27	54.0
I don't have the right to deny my body to any man who demands it.	24	48.0

to be accompanied by an alleviation of the disturbances. This cognitive model and the cognitive restructuring intervention discussed in this part of the book are derived from the work of Aaron Beck and his associates (Beck, 1976; Beck & Emery, 1985; Beck, Rush, Shaw, and Emery, 1979).

The role assigned to distorted beliefs associated with child sexual abuse in the etiology of mood disturbances among victims does not exclude other possible contributory factors to these disturbances such as organic causes of depression, adverse experiences in the victims' families of origin, self-destructive lifestyles, or discordant marriages. These and any other contributory factors are addressed by other components in the U. of M. program such as those discussed in Chapter 4 and Parts 3 and 4, or by referral to other treatment facilities.

CHAPTER 6

Assessment and Evaluation Procedures

A variety of procedures and instruments is available to identify and monitor distorted beliefs and mood disturbances in victims. This assessment
process includes helping the victim to become more aware of her own
beliefs. Often these are of an automatic and habitual nature so that certain
thoughts influence her mood without her being aware or scrutinizing their
validity.

Interviews

Relevant beliefs and feelings are often revealed to the therapist and victim
during their ongoing discussions of the victim's history and problems, for
example, during the initial assessment interviews described in Chapter 4. With
victims who may be depressed at a clinically significant level or who may be
high suicide risks it is necessary to assess these possibilities in greater depth and
the following are some useful reference sources for such interviews:

(a) Suggestions on the conduct of assessment interviews for depression are
contained in Beck *et al.* (1979, pp. 87–103).
(b) The assessment of suicide risk is discussed in Beck *et al.* (1979, pp.
209–243) and in Burns (1980, pp. 337–356).
(c) Beck *et al.* (1979, pp. 354–384) and Burns (1980, pp. 375–398) discuss the
very important differential diagnosis of: (i) depression which may be
secondary to an organic condition and therefore requires referral for
medical investigation; and (ii) depression for which antidepressant
medication may be indicated and which therefore requires referral for
psychiatric evaluation.

Instant Replay

If a victim becomes distressed but cannot pinpoint the thoughts and beliefs that
preceded these feelings, she then immediately reviews the sequence during
which the distressing feelings occurred in an attempt to identify the relevant

50

cognitions on the second occasion. One instance of this technique occurred when a victim was shown the film *Incest: The family secret* (Millican, 1979). About 10 minutes into the film, the victim began to cry, to complain of a 'vicious headache', to feel nauseous and confused, and to be unable to concentrate on the film. The showing was discontinued and a review of the film events was undertaken. The victim reported that the adverse reactions began to occur when one of the women in the film stated that the sexual abuse she had experienced had robbed her of a childhood. With support the victim traced the source of her reactions to the thought that her mother did not protect her so she ended up as damaged goods.

Remote Recall

When a victim recalls an occasion in the past when distressing feelings were experienced but she cannot recall what her thoughts and beliefs were at the time, she then reviews the past events in slow motion in an attempt to revive the relevant cognitions. One example occurred when a victim reported that she felt very angry when the initial assessment covered descriptions of her mother and family functioning. She then reviewed her mother's frequent unprovoked physically and emotionally abusive behaviour toward herself and was puzzled that she wanted to convince the therapist that the consequences to her (the victim) were minimal. The following week, the victim reported that she had thought carefully about the contradiction between recognizing that she had been significantly abused by her mother and yet felt deep loyalty towards her. She stated that it was with some surprise that she began to recognize that the reasons for loyalty to the mother were the thoughts that:

(a) she (the victim) wanted to protect the mother from knowing what her spouse was 'really like' in that he had another woman—the victim—with whom he was having a sexual relationship;
(b) she wanted to help her mother to preserve her myth that the spouse was a 'wonderful man'.

Another victim started to cry during her initial assessment when asked if she knew any reasons that could explain why she had run away from home as a teenager. Up to that point, she had been recounting the incident in a factual manner without a great deal of affect. The feelings that had been triggered by the questioning came out in quiet tears of anguish. She vented her sorrow for several minutes and then was gently asked if she could recount what cognitions had passed through her mind just prior to the time when she had started to cry. Unable to recall her thoughts directly, the victim was again asked to recount, slowly, her running experience as a teenager. By reviewing the same material, the victim was able to pinpoint her feelings first, and then the beliefs she had held, which were 'I was terribly unhappy and in fact I was trying to put this across to my parents' and 'Nobody seemed to care about me'.

Role play

A recent or past event that evoked distress can be re-enacted in a role play, perhaps with the therapist assuming the role of the other person in the interaction, so that the thoughts that evoked the distress are repeated and can be identified. For example, a victim reported that she had telephoned her mother to confront her with the fact that she had been sexually victimized by the offender/father. The victim was unable to recall what was said but felt very confused and suicidal following the conversation. The therapist assumed the role of the mother in an imaginary telephone call. In the process, the victim recalled that the mother had stated that she (the mother) had been as abused as the victim and that she 'had turned out all right', that the victim was 'just feeling sorry for herself', and that the victim 'should smarten up and stop acting crazy'. The victim was then able to identify the thoughts which she had when her mother berated her, namely: (a) 'I'm just crazy'; (b) 'I shouldn't make such a big thing out of being sexually abused'; (c) 'Maybe I just imagined all of this'; and (d) 'I guess I'm just feeling sorry for myself'.

   Another victim had experienced distress when she had been in a check-out line in a grocery store and the man in front of her, and another male behind her had stood too close to her. In order to bring out the exact feelings that this woman had felt and to role play a successful management of this incident, the (female) therapist re-enacted the situation with the victim. Her thoughts of being boxed-in, of the men being physically dirty and smelling, that she didn't want to be touched by them, and her feelings of not being able to do anything about this were extracted from the re-enactment of the situation.

Induced Imagery

The victim is asked to relax, to close her eyes, and to imagine vividly and clearly an event during which distressing feelings were experienced, so that the thoughts that evoked these feelings can be recaptured. This technique was used with a victim who became very distressed when she began to describe five specific episodes of sexual victimization by the offender. She was requested to relax, close her eyes and review one or all of the events she had just described and that had caused her distress. She was then able to recall the following thoughts: (a) 'I've failed to teach him [the offender] that what he is doing is morally wrong'; (b) 'I should not be angry with his behavior because he comes from a minority group and an abusive family'; and (c) 'my parents have taught me to be very kind to him because he has had such a bad life'.

Confrontation

The victim is asked to confront a situation which is known to be distressing to her so that she can identify her thoughts in that situation. One example of this occurs when victims are exposed to audio-visual and bibliographical material on sexual abuse during therapy. Exposure to such material is very distressing for many victims and these confrontations can help to identify the distorted beliefs that contribute to these feelings. There is an instance of this in the section on instant replay above.

Recording by Victim

Very commonly victims are asked to record their thoughts and the feelings that accompany them. Initially this is often best done with the therapist in the office situation, but as the victim becomes competent and confident enough to undertake the task on her own then she does so as a regular home assignment. Ideally, records are written as soon as possible after distressing feelings occur so that the preceding thoughts are not lost. If this is not always possible then the recording should be done at a specified time on each day during which the victim is asked to replay the situation and the thoughts and feelings associated with it. It is important that the victim actually writes down her thoughts rather than simply trying to recall them which does not seem to be nearly as effective as the written record. The recording may cover all occurrences of distressing feelings or it might be restricted to specific situations that have already been identified as disturbing for the victim. There are many formats in which the recording may be done including notes, letters, diary entries, essays, and double or triple column forms or the slightly more detailed Daily Record of Dysfunctional Thoughts (Beck *et al.*, 1979, pp. 164–165, 286–287, 403; Burns, 1980, pp. 58–74).

Belief Inventory (BI)

This inventory was developed in the U. of M. program as a measure of some common distorted beliefs associated with child sexual abuse (Jehu, Klassen, & Gazan, 1985/6, 1986). In the program the inventory was used in its original form consisting of the first 17 questions as shown in Appendix B. Our experience of using the inventory indicates that it could usefully be extended to include items reflecting certain categories of self-blaming and self-denigratory beliefs that are reviewed in Chapters 8 and 9. The numbers of the additional items in the revised version of the inventory together with the categories of self-blaming and self-denigratory beliefs that they are intended to elicit are: (a) 18. sexual curiosity; (b) 19. 'sickness'; (c) 20. emotional pleasure; (d) 21. alcohol; (e) 22. material benefits; (f) 23. sexual frustration; (g) 24. sex education; (h) 25. relationship enhancement; and (i) 26. the child's gratification.

At present psychometric data are available only on the original 17-item version of the inventory. Its test-retest reliability was obtained from the responses of 25 previously sexually abused women over an interval of one week during their initial assessment. The Pearson correlation was .93, $p < .001$, a very high level of reliability. The inventory has face validity and because of the alleged association between the distorted beliefs and mood disturbances one might expect it to have reasonable concurrent validity with the Beck Depression Inventory (see below). This was supported by a Pearson correlation of .55, $p < .01$, between the scores of 25 previously sexually abused women on the two instruments.

A total score for the Belief Inventory is derived by adding the scores for each item. A total score of 15 or above is considered to indicate a clinically significant level of distorted beliefs on the original 17-item version. In addition to this quantitative estimate of distorted beliefs the inventory can be used to identify particular beliefs as therapeutic targets as indicated in Chapters 8, 9, and 10.

In the U. of M. program the Belief Inventory was normally completed at weekly intervals during initial assessment and the treatment of mood disturbances, and again at follow-up sessions.

Beck Depression Inventory (BDI)

This very well-established instrument was developed by Aaron Beck (Beck, 1978) and it covers all the major symptoms in the depressive syndrome, including low self-esteem, guilt, and dysphoria (sadness, 'blues', feeling 'down', despondent, pessimistic, or hopeless). Thus, it is a very useful comprehensive measure of mood disturbances in victims.

In many studies the Beck Depression Inventory has been shown to have good levels of reliability and validity (e.g. Rehm, 1981). A total score for the instrument is obtained by adding the victim's scores on each item. A score of 21 or above is recommended as the cut-off point indicating a clinically significant level of depression (Beck & Beamesderfer, 1974). The interpretation of the victim's responses to the inventory is discussed by Burns (1980, pp. 19–27). In addition to providing a quantitative estimate of the severity of depression the BDI is a useful indicator of particular symptoms that require therapeutic attention (Beck *et al.*, 1979, pp. 89, 168).

In the U. of M. program the BDI was administered to all victims during initial assessment, at termination of treatment for mood disturbances, and on follow-up. It was administered more frequently with particular victims whose mood states required closer monitoring.

Battle Culture-Free Self-Esteem Inventory (SEI)

This measure of self-esteem was developed by Battle (1981) and it includes items on general, social, and personal self-esteem, together with other items to test the subject's tendency to lie in answering the questionnaire. The reliability and validity of the inventory are at acceptable levels and the scoring system is described together with some normative data, although these norms are derived from college students which is not an entirely comparable population to victim groups.

The SEI was administered to the early victims in the U. of M. program but it did not appear to be sufficiently sensitive to therapeutic change, was not very easy to score, and lacked clinical norms, consequently it was replaced by the Hudson Index of Self-Esteem which proved more satisfactory, and this is described next. In the U. of M. program either the SEI or the Hudson ISE was administered to each victim during initial assessment, at termination of treatment for mood disturbances, and on follow-up. Additional administrations were conducted with particular victims as clinically indicated.

Hudson Index of Self-Esteem (ISE)

The ISE was developed by Hudson (1982) who reports high levels of reliability and validity. He also describes the scoring system for the instrument and recommends a cut-off point of 30 or above an indicative of significantly low self-esteem. In addition to this quantitative estimate of self-esteem the subject's responses to individual items in the ISE can indicate particular therapeutic targets.

Conclusion

Having reviewed some major assessment and evaluation methods separately, it is important to note that it is usual to combine more than one of them in a multi-modal assessment and evaluation program and this was done in the U. of M. study. One reason for this is that all methods have certain strengths and weaknesses, therefore if a problem or therapeutic change can be demonstrated on several measures then one can have more confidence in the nature of the problem or the effectiveness of treatment. Another reason is that the target problems in therapy are usually multi-faceted, and no one measure is likely to encompass all aspects of a problem. A third reason for advocating multi-modal assessment and evaluation is that it facilitates a more comprehensive monitoring of progress and outcome. One may be interested in change not only in the target problems specifically, but also in other important aspects of the client's functioning; for example, whether improvements in mood disturbances are accompanied by a reduction in marital discord. Again, no one measure will tap all such variables, but a suitably constituted multi-modal assessment and evaluation program is more likely to pick up both the direct and side effects of treatment.

Finally, it is desirable to gather information from more than one person whenever practicable. One reason for advocating this is that it is likely to increase the accuracy of the information if each person knows it is being substantiated from another source. Another reason is that one can have more confidence in the effectiveness of treatment if relevant changes are reported by more than one informant.

CHAPTER 7

Treatment Procedures

Cognitive restructuring is based on the premise that beliefs have a significant influence on feelings and actions. If the beliefs are distorted or unrealistic then feelings and actions are likely to be distressing and inappropriate. In this way distorted beliefs may contribute to many emotional and behavioral problems. It follows that the correction of distorted beliefs is likely to be accompanied by the alleviation of such problems. In order to correct distorted beliefs it is necessary for clients: (a) to become aware of their beliefs; (b) to recognize any distortions they contain; and (c) to substitute more accurate alternative beliefs.

These aims are pursued by means of a variety of procedures but common to many of them is a Socratic style of questioning (Beck *et al.*, 1979). The therapist does not in a didactic manner tell the victim what her beliefs really are or what she should be thinking. Instead, the therapist asks appropriate and well-timed questions to induce the victim to discover this information for herself. For example, the therapist might ask questions along the lines of: (a) 'what is the evidence . . . ?' for a certain statement the victim has made; (b) 'what other possible explanations could there be . . . ?' for a certain event; or (c) 'what would be the worst thing that could happen?' In short, the style of the therapist is to ask questions rather than to give answers. Next, some procedures are outlined in the framework of certain stages in cognitive restructuring although it is important to recognize that in practice these stages often overlap with each other.

Explaining Rationale

The process starts with the therapist explaining the rationale for cognitive restructuring along the lines indicated in Chapter 5 and in language that the victim can understand. Some everyday examples of the influence of beliefs on feelings and actions are given. For instance, if the victim's telephone call was not returned she might interpret this as a rejection with corresponding loss of self-esteem and an avoidance of calling again. In contrast, if she believed that her message had not been passed on, then her self-esteem would remain unimpaired and she would try to reach the other person again. It is often useful to supplement the therapist's verbal explanation of the rationale by asking the victim to read Chapter 3 in Burns (1980).

Identifying Beliefs

The next step in therapy is to help the victim to become aware of any of her beliefs that may be contributing to her mood disturbances. This is done by means of a suitable combination of the assessment procedures described in Chapter 6.

Recognizing Distortions

The third step in cognitive restructuring is to help the victim to recognize any distortions in her beliefs. It is beneficial, though not essential, for her to familiarize herself with a range of common distortions in thinking and to use these to examine her own beliefs for the presence of these distortions. A very useful reference for victims on this topic is Burns (1980) in which the following distortions are discussed in Chapter 3.

All or Nothing Thinking

This distortion is also called dichotomous thinking and it refers to a tendency for a victim to evaluate herself in an extreme category; for example, as totally ugly or absolutely beautiful, or as a complete failure or a brilliant success. Such black or white categorizations are unrealistic because most people are likely to be somewhere in between in the grey area.

One consequence of this form of distortion is vulnerability to low self-esteem because even a slight or imagined imperfection leads a victim to place herself in the totally negative category. For example, a victim says 'I am weak for making such a big thing out of the abuse, especially when I know that many women have been abused in degrees far more severe than me'. Her alternative to this belief is 'like everyone else I am not completely weak or completely strong'.

Overgeneralization

This distortion involves drawing a general rule or conclusion on the basis of isolated events and applying the rule to a wide range of situations. An example is a victim's belief that 'I can't trust my [male] therapist not to be sexual with me'. Her alternative belief is 'not every man will take advantage of me sexually as happened in the past'. Similarly, a victim believes that 'All that men are interested in, in a relationship, is sex'. Her alternative belief is 'my husband has had largely a sexless marriage with myself, yet, he has stayed in the marriage for 17 years. There are obviously other factors than sex that keeps him in our relationship.' Another example of overgeneralization is a victim's statement that 'because everyone touched my body so early it was defiled, I was dirty inside and could never be clean again, I could not be special to any man'.

Mislabeling

An extreme form of overgeneralization is mislabeling in which a victim creates a completely negative image of herself on the basis of a single deficiency. This is irrational because no person can be equated with any one action or characteristic. For example, the fact that a victim has difficulty in coping with the consequences of her abuse does not mean that she is a wholly weak and inadequate person, she may have many strengths and positive characteristics. Thus, one victim says 'I'm a weakling, I'm afraid to change'. Her alternative belief is 'I've shown courage and strength coming for counseling and if I didn't want to change I wouldn't have come'.

Mental Filtering

Another term for this distortion is selective abstraction and it refers to a tendency to pick out a negative detail in any situation and to dwell on it exclusively. Thus, the whole situation is perceived as negative and anything positive is filtered out. Thus, a victim may filter out the many areas of her life in which she functions satisfactorily and focus only on a problem she is having as a result of her abuse. For example, a victim says 'I've made a mess of my life, I've failed in my marriage, I'm an alcoholic and have been through the mill—I'm a loser'. Her alternative belief is 'I've done many worthwhile things including bringing up my children on my own. I've been sober for five years and am really determined to overcome this problem, and I'm going to return to school to upgrade my skills.'

Disqualifying the Positive

One way of filtering out positive experiences is to discount them for some reason, consequently they are transformed into negative experiences. In this way distorted beliefs can be sustained despite evidence to the contrary. An example is a victim's belief that 'when a man pays me a compliment all he wants is to get inside my pants for his own gratification'. Similarly, a victim stated that a man in her office paid her attention because he could tell how hard up she was for male companionship. Another victim said 'Anybody who gives me a compliment, I wonder how am I going to pay them back—it means that I owe them. Safer to think that they don't mean it and then I don't owe.'

Jumping to Conclusions

This type of distortion is also referred to as arbitrary inference and it involves drawing a negative conclusion that is not necessarily justified by the facts of the situation. For example, a victim believes that 'my [male] therapist will be insulted if he knows I don't trust him'. Her alternative belief is that 'he will not be surprised that I am hesitant to trust him because he knows that my trust was betrayed in the past'. Another victim thought that 'my friends will shun me if they know that I've been sexually abused'. This person's alternative belief was 'if my friends are truly my friends they will not blame me for the abuse. If they are the empathetic people I think they are they'll be supportive. If they are not, then they aren't the kind of people I want to associate with.'

Magnification and Minimization

Magnification occurs when a victim looks at her mistakes or deficiencies and exaggerates their importance. This has also been called catastrophizing because things are blown completely out of proportion. For example, many previously sexually abused women hold the belief that 'I will never be able to lead a normal life, the damage is permanent' (Table 5.1). In contrast, minimization involves the victim in playing down or shrinking her good points. There is an example of this distortion in the section below on assigned activities. Both the magnification of imperfections and the minimization of good points are liable to be very damaging to self-esteem.

Emotional Reasoning

This kind of reasoning occurs when a victim takes her feelings as evidence that something is true or real. It can be very misleading because her feelings may reflect her thoughts and if these are distorted then the accompanying feelings will be invalid evidence of truth or reality. For instance, the fact that many previously sexually abused women *feel* guilty about the abuse does not mean that they *are* guilty. Similarly, a victim expressed the alternative belief that 'The fact that I feel helpless does not mean that I am helpless. I have got myself into therapy and am working on coping better with the abuse.'

'Should' Statements

A client may believe that she or another person should behave in accordance with expectations that are unrealistic. If these 'should' statements are applied to herself, then any failure to live up to the unrealistic expectations will be accompanied by guilt and low self-esteem. If 'should' statements are applied to another person who falls short of the unrealistic expectations, then the client is likely to feel frustrated, resentful, and angry. The following are some examples of 'should' statements by victims:

(a) 'I should be able to handle the effects of my abuse better and not let them interfere with the lives of myself and others.' The victim's alternative belief is that 'It is not very realistic or productive to expect better coping from myself. I'm only human and many women have difficulty in coping with the long-term effects of sexual abuse.'

(b) 'I should have been able to teach the offender that what he was doing was morally wrong.' The alternative belief is 'Teaching the offender what is morally right or wrong is not my responsibility then or now'.

(c) 'I should have known better than to have gone into his room with [the offender]. I knew what he was going to do.' This victim's alternative belief is 'I had no options other than to go with him. I had no one to tell who might have protected me. I did not believe that had I told, anyone would have believed me. I was so little (5 years old) and he was a grown man.'

(d) 'I shouldn't have put on a skirt when he asked me to, and then gone into the barn.' The victim's alternative belief is that 'I was raised to follow my elder's instructions. I was afraid of this boy and I did what he said. I was putting on a skirt, but that wasn't the same thing as giving the boy permission to have sexual contact with me. I didn't even know what sex was. . . .'

Personalization

This distortion is also called misattribution and it involves a victim assuming responsibility for an event that was not her fault. Understandably, this is a very common source of guilt among previously sexually abused women who often assume responsibility for their abuse. This is exemplified by a victim's quite typical belief that 'I must have been responsible for sex when I was a child because I wasn't forced into it and it went on so long'. Her alternative belief is that 'In a sense I was forced into it and could not stop it because: (a) the offender kept persuading me by saying "what's the matter, don't you want to help an old man?" I had been indoctrinated with the belief that nice little girls were supposed to help and please people, especially older people, and did not want to hurt him by not continuing to participate; (b) I desperately wanted attention from someone outside my family and he gave me this; (c) I could not refuse to take his lunch out to the field where the abuse often happened, because I would have to explain to his wife why I was refusing; (d) I did not want to upset her; (e) I feared that if I told my mother she would do nothing to protect me; (g) I could not consider telling my father because I hated him, I feared that he would blame or punish me or not do anything.'

Similarly, another victim felt responsible because she accepted gifts and money in exchange for sex. Her alternative beliefs were: (a) she had resigned herself to the fact that the abuse would not stop and that the offender should 'pay' for her 'cooperation'; (b) the family from when she was aged 14 years on expected that she earn her own money for clothes and spending money; (c) she was already a 'prostitute' so that payment was appropriate; and (d) previous disclosure of the abuse to her parents did not prevent further abuse by offender.

Exploring Alternatives

The final stage in cognitive restructuring consists of the therapist exploring with the victim some more accurate and realistic beliefs as alternatives to the distorted beliefs that were identified previously. The following are some of the procedures used to elicit alternative beliefs.

Provision of Information

Although a Socratic style of questioning is emphasized and typical in cognitive restructuring there is still an educative role for the therapist in providing factual data to correct any inaccurate information that may be contributing to a victim's distorted beliefs. For example, information about the prevalence of sexual abuse often serves to reduce her feelings of difference and alienation from others. As well as disseminating information verbally, it is very useful for the therapist to prescribe appropriate reading materials for clients. Gil (1984) is a useful general reference on the emotional problems of previously sexually abused women that was written especially for reading by these victims. Some more specific materials on particular topics are cited in Chapters 8, 9, and 10.

Logical Analysis

The victim's logic is reviewed to determine whether the evidence necessarily entails the conclusion that she has drawn and what alternative conclusions there might be. There are many instances of this process in the previous section on recognizing distortions. Another example is the previously sexually abused woman who concludes that 'I must have been to blame, because I was removed from home'. Clearly, another possible conclusion is that she was removed from home for her own protection.

Decatastrophizing

We saw above that a victim may magnify certain events so that she predicts the direst consequences for herself. In such circumstances the therapist may be able to decatastrophize the situation by widening the client's perspective so that she takes all the relevant information into account when she makes her predictions. Thus, a victim who believes that her sexual abuse has damaged her permanently so that she will never be able to lead a normal life, may benefit from knowing that many previously sexually abused women do achieve a satisfactory adjustment.

Distancing

This term refers to the process of a victim shifting from a subjective to an objective perception of her own beliefs, so that they are no longer regarded as self-evident truths but rather as hypotheses that may or may not be valid. As Beck (1976) puts it 'Distancing involves being able to make a distinction between "I believe" (an opinion that is subject to validation) and "I know" (an irrefutable fact)' (p. 243). Let us take as an example a woman who 'knows' that she was responsible for her previous sexual abuse. If she is exposed vicariously to the abuse experiences of other women then she may strongly deny that they were to blame for being abused and consequently begin to shift to a more objective view of her own responsibility for what happened to herself. Such vicarious exposure might be arranged through participation in group therapy with other previously abused women, or by reading their personal accounts of sexual abuse (e.g. Allen, 1980; Armstrong, 1979; Brady, 1979), or by viewing equivalent audio-visual presentations (e.g. Krause & Hirsh, 1983; Millican, 1979; Sharp & Yantzi, 1983).

Reattribution

This procedure is designed to correct a victim's tendency to assume total responsibility for her abuse and not to take into account factors that were beyond her control. The therapist and victim review the circumstances of the abuse to arrive at a more appropriate assignment of responsibility by showing that the facts do not support the victim's complete acceptance of blame (see examples under 'Personalization' in previous section on recognizing distortions). The more appropriate assignment of responsibility may involve: (a) showing that the facts of the situation do not support the victim's self-blame; (b) demonstrating that the victim is applying a double standard to her own behavior compared to that of others; or (c) challenging the victim's belief that she is 100% responsible for what happened.

Assigned Activities

Another way of changing beliefs is by means of activities that are specifically assigned to disconfirm distorted beliefs and/or confirm more accurate alternatives. This is a kind of behavioral experiment in which the client tests certain hypotheses or beliefs about herself. This procedure was used with a woman who believed that her father sexually abused her out of pity because she was so ugly as an 8-year-old child, and that she was still ugly at the age of 24 years. In fact, she is a very attractive young woman. She and the therapist agreed on some criteria for attractiveness in women, and the victim predicted that at least 50% of women would meet these criteria. She and her partner then visited a supermarket where he counted 102 women coming through a turnstile, while she identified 16 (15%) of these as being attractive. This discrepancy between her predicted incidence (50%) of attractiveness and the actual incidence (15%) formed an empirical basis for restructuring the victim's beliefs that 'the whole world is cute, but me'.

Such assignments should be negotiated between the victim and the therapist in a collaborative manner, for example:

(a) The therapist will provide a rationale for the assignment so that it makes sense to the victim.

(b) The therapist also helps the victim to express any objections or obstacles to carrying out the assignment so that these can be circumvented or resolved.

(c) The therapist and victim should also agree to the criteria by which the results of the assignments are to be evaluated. In this respect it is particularly useful for the victim to write down any predicted dire consequences of the assignment before she undertakes it, so that the hopefully less catastrophic actual outcome can be used to undermine the certainty of the victim's belief in these and similar dire predictions.

Conclusion

Like any other treatment approach, cognitive restructuring is likely to encounter certain resistances from victims. Among such resistances are some countertherapeutic beliefs that are discussed by Beck *et al.* (1979). One of these is 'I know I look at things in a distorted way but I can't change the kind of person I am'. First, the therapist might inquire why the victim believes she cannot change; for example, she may believe that her abuse experiences make this impossible. Once the basis for the belief is discovered, then it can be cognitively restructured as discussed earlier. This might include: (a) exploring the alternative belief that the victim does not have to change her whole personality, only certain habitual ways of thinking; (b) the victim might be asked whether she has ever changed any of her beliefs in the past—perhaps things that she has been told by parents, teacher, or friends—in order to provide evidence that she is capable of change; or (c) demonstrating to the victim that other women have overcome abuse and other adverse experiences.

Another common countertherapeutic belief is 'I believe what you are saying intellectually, but not emotionally'. This reflects a confusion between 'thinking' and 'feeling'. The victim cannot believe anything emotionally. She is really talking about the degree of belief—that she does not have 'a gut feeling' that what the therapist is saying is correct. From this point the usual cognitive restructuring procedures can be used to examine and test the validity of the beliefs that are in issue.

A third common countertherapeutic belief is 'I can't think of alternatives to my distorted beliefs when I'm emotionally upset'. The therapist can explain that this problem occurs because the victim is in a state that makes reasoning difficult. The answer is often for the victim to wait until she is less upset before attempting to think of alternative beliefs—it is unrealistic to expect rational alternatives when she is distressed.

CHAPTER 8

Self-Blaming Beliefs

Many victims hold certain mistaken beliefs indicating that they are themselves responsible for the sexual abuse they experienced in childhood. Such distorted beliefs are likely to give rise particularly to feelings of guilt as well as to low self-esteem and depressive episodes. Some of these distorted beliefs are discussed below together with more accurate alternatives to them that can be explored by means of the treatment procedures described in the previous chapter. Both the distorted beliefs and the alternatives are, of course, individualized for each victim. Throughout this discussion it is important to bear in mind that 45% of the victims were aged under 6 years, and 86% were under 10 years, when the abuse commenced (Chap. 2).

Victim Responsibility

Compliance

Eighty percent of victims in the U. of M. series reported that they reacted with passive compliance when they were being abused (Table 2.6).

Distorted beliefs. Such compliance connoted self-blame to many victims. For example, item 5 on the Belief Inventory which reads 'I must have permitted sex to happen because I wasn't forced into it' was endorsed as partly, mostly, or absolutely true by 84% of victims during their initial assessment (Table 5.1). Some further examples of expressed beliefs indicating self-blame associated with compliance are: (a) 'I did not physically resist, therefore I must have wanted to have sex'; (b) 'I put on a skirt when the offender asked me to, therefore, I was going along with him'; and (c) 'I did not resist when the offender's mother asked me to go into her son's room, I knew what was going to happen, I shouldn't have walked up those stairs'.

Alternative beliefs. The power differential between a child and an adult makes it very difficult indeed for a child to say 'no' to an adult's sexual advances. Thus,

78% of offenders exercised adult authority, 66% made threats, and 58% used physical force, to induce victims to engage in sexual activities (Table 2.5), and 82% of victims reported feelings of helplessness when they were being abused (Table 2.6). It is customary for children to be taught to obey their elders who thereby acquire psychological authority over victims, and this is particularly relevant if the offender is a father figure or close relative of the victim as almost two-thirds of offenders were in the U. of M. series (Table 2.4). The doctrine of obedience is especially strongly transmitted and enforced by supremacist father figures with whom many victims have been raised (Chap. 3).

Secrecy

Ninety-six percent of victims kept their abuse a secret for some period of time (Chap. 2).

Distorted beliefs. For some victims this silence contributed to the belief that they were responsible for their own victimization. One possible indication of this is that during their initial assessments 86% of victims endorsed as partly, mostly, or absolutely true item 12 on the Belief Inventory which reads 'I must have been responsible for the sex when I was young because it went on for so long' (Table 5.1). Other examples of similar beliefs include: (a) 'I didn't tell others about the sex because I must have really enjoyed it and wanted it to continue'; (b) 'I had a chance to tell somebody but I didn't, so I must have wanted to continue'; and (c) 'I didn't tell anyone because I didn't leave the room when [the offender] was in it, therefore I was asking for the sex'.

Alternative beliefs. Over 80% of victims kept the abuse secret because of fear of some adverse consequence such as disbelief, blame, anger, or physical violence, and over 40% suffered actual physical violence to prevent disclosure (Table 2.7). These and similar apprehensions were not ill-founded for if the abuse was eventually disclosed this led overwhelmingly to negative reactions by significant others (Table 2.8). Summit (1983) provides very useful prescribed reading for victims on the topics of secrecy and disclosure in relation to the child's responsibility for the abuse.

Seductiveness

It is not unusual for members of the general public to attribute sexual abuse to seductive behavior by the child and this argument is often advanced in defence of offenders (e.g. de Young, 1986; Herman, 1981; Meiselman, 1978; Sgroi, 1982).

Distorted beliefs. Some victims share this distorted belief. For example, item 8

on the Belief Inventory which reads 'I must have been seductive and provocative when I was young' was endorsed as partly, mostly, or absolutely true by
62% of victims during their initial assessments (Table 5.1). Two more examples
are: (a) 'I was sexually provocative when I was a child, I initiated the sexual
contact. I went into my brother's tent and I knew what he wanted'; and (b) 'I
wanted my Dad to hold and touch me, I liked the closeness, it felt good. It was
my fault, I didn't scream or push him out of my bed when he came in.'

Alternative beliefs. Behavior, which if performed by an adult would be considered seductive, does not properly merit this label when it is enacted by a child
who does not understand its sexual connotations and possible consequences. It
is the responsibility of the adult concerned to set appropriate limits on the
child's behavior rather than to exploit it for his own gratification.

Sexual Curiosity

Distorted beliefs. Closely related to the issue of seductiveness is the belief held
by some victims that they initiated and were responsible for the abuse because
they asked the offender about sexual matters. For example, a victim who was
sexually abused by a much older brother was gradually introduced to a variety
of sexual practices by this offender who encouraged her to ask questions about
sexual matters.

Alternative beliefs. When a child asks an adult about sex this does not mean that
the child wants to see the adult's genitals or to have a demonstration of sexual
activities. Again, it is the responsibility of the adult to answer the child's
questions without using these as an excuse for sexual exploitation.

Physical Pleasure

Fifty-eight percent of victims reported that they experienced physical pleasure
when they were being sexually abused (Table 2.6), and this is often a particularly potent and intractable source of guilt among victims.

Distorted beliefs. One indication of this is that 86% of victims endorsed as
partly, mostly, or absolutely true item 15 on the Belief Inventory which reads
'It must be unnatural to feel any pleasure during molestation'.

Alternative beliefs. In fact, the opposite is true, for sexual arousal is a very
'natural' response to sexual stimulation even if the victim is also experiencing
negative feelings and knows that what is being done to her is wrong. Sexual
arousal is an automatic, reflex response and it is useful to discuss with victims
some similar responses so that their automatic nature and naturalness can be

understood. One such example is the erotic sensations that some women experience when they are breast feeding an infant. Another example is the laughing and wriggling reactions to tickling even if the person does not want to respond in these ways. It may be useful also to discuss with victims the need that most people have for physical touching and closeness with another person and that the satisfaction of this need rather than sexual gratification might have been the source of their physical pleasure during the abuse.

Emotional Pleasure

Sixty-four percent of victims reported that they used the abusive sexual encounters to obtain attention and/or affection from the offender, and 43% experienced emotional pleasure associated with the abuse (Table 2.6). Moreover, the opportunity for attention and affection was used as an inducement to participate in sexual activities by offenders with 54% of victims, and proclamations of romantic love were made to 23% of them for the same purpose (Table 2.5).

Distorted beliefs. The fact that they obtained certain emotional benefits from the abuse is perceived as blameworthy by some victims.

Alternative beliefs. They may however have sought and obtained an emotional relationship with the offender without in any way intending this to be accompanied by a sexual relationship, and probably without understanding that the two aspects are often linked in intimate relationships between adults. Whatever the child's intentions and understanding may be it is the adult's responsibility to set and observe appropriate limits in relationships with children. Some children so desperately need affection from someone that they will pay any price—however unpleasant—in order to get this. To have to pay for affection by acquiescing in sexual activities is an improper imposition by an adult on a child.

For example, when she was eight years old one victim was told by her step-father that she was 'so skinny and ugly that no one else would ever pay her any attention', and that he was 'doing her a favour by showing her attention' in this manner. 'She'd never get it anywhere else.' Cognitively restructuring the above beliefs which the victim had assimilated entailed a realistic reappraisal of the victim's level of attractiveness. It also included evaluating what kind of a favor her step-father had been doing her when the sexual abuse: (a) undermined her self-esteem; (b) severely distorted her views of male–female relationships; (c) limited her ability to trust intimate relationships; (d) affected her sexual relationship and her views about sexual activity; and (e) left her feeling guilt ridden and responsible for the sexual abuse. The victim also had to wrestle extensively with the idealized relationship she fantasized and the real relationship she actually had with her step-father. The compassionate, caring man she had wanted to father her, had in fact been a self-centred, manipulative, abusive parent.

Material Benefits

Forty-one percent of victims reported that they used their sexual abuse to obtain material favors and rewards (Table 2.6) and 28% kept the abuse secret at least in part in order to retain these benefits (Table 2.7). Bribery was used by offenders with 50% of victims as an inducement to participate in sexual activities (Table 2.5).

Distorted beliefs. Because they obtained such material benefits some victims believe that they were to blame for the abuse.

Alternative beliefs. As in the case of emotional benefits it is the adult's responsibility not to utilize the resources he controls in order to exploit a child sexually.

Informed Consent

The essence of many of the distorted beliefs reviewed above is that the victim perceives herself as having consented to the abuse and therefore holds herself responsible for what happened. Finkelhor (1979a; 1984, Chap. 2) very usefully integrates several of the alternative beliefs into the argument that a child is incapable of giving an informed consent to sex, and this is valuable prescribed reading for victims on the issue of self-blame. An informed consent requires that the child understands what she is consenting to and that she has the freedom to say yes or no. Apart from their limited understanding of the basic facts of sex, children are relatively ignorant of what is considered appropriate sexually in their particular culture, and they will certainly be unaware of the potential damage to their own development and adjustment that may result if they engage in sex with an adult. In the light of these and other gaps in their knowledge children are incapable of an 'informed' consent to sex. They are incapable also of meeting the second requirement for such consent, that is the freedom to say yes or no. This is precluded by the unequal distribution of power between children and adults that is discussed under 'compliance' and several other headings above. In the absence of informed consent it is always unacceptable for a child to engage in sexual activities with an adult even if the child acts in ways in which she and others might construe as willingness to do so.

Offender Exoneration

Typically, victims hold a number of beliefs indicating the existence of certain circumstances that mitigate or exonerate the offender's responsibility for the sexual abuse. Someone must be held responsible for what happened and to the extent that the victim exculpates the offender then she is likely to inculpate herself.

Sex Education

Twenty-seven percent of victims were induced to engage in sexual activities by offenders misrepresenting this as sex education (Table 2.5).

Distorted beliefs. A victim might have been indoctrinated with the belief that the offender engaged her in sexual activities because he believed that this would make her a better sexual partner when she became an adult. For example, a victim was told by her offender/father that his sexual 'teaching' would prevent her from becoming frigid like her mother and that she would be fulfilling the proper role of a woman—'to satisfy a man's every sexual need'.

Alternative beliefs. If the offender really believes in the positive value of sex between himself and the child why does he conceal this 'sex education' from other adults? He might argue that he does so not because he believes sex is wrong between adults and children but because it is considered unacceptable and illegal in society at the present time and that this disapproval may well be lifted in the future. The victim, however, is not living at some such time in the future, she is living now and is subject to current social and legal realities. Secondly, it is the responsibility of adults to appreciate the consequences of any decisions that they may make regarding children and to avoid any actions that may result in distress or harm to them. Clearly, the adult adjustment of some victims is adversely affected by their sexual abuse and it is the offender's responsibility to avoid this risk.

Child's Gratification

The offenders of 33% of victims used the promise of sexual gratification to induce them to participate in sexual activities (Table 2.5), and 58% of victims did experience physical pleasure during the abuse (Table 2.6).

Distorted beliefs. In these circumstances some victims may argue that the offender engaged them in sexual activities in order to give them pleasurable sensations. For example, a victim reported that the offender would not discontinue sexual activity until she experienced or feigned orgasm to prevent her from developing 'frigidity'.

Alternative beliefs. Even if some victims do experience physical pleasure this is typically accompanied by other distressing reactions to the abuse (Table 2.6).

Furthermore, it is noted above that experiencing physical pleasure during the abuse is a major source of guilt among victims in adulthood. Again, it is the responsibility of the adult not to expose a child to such distress and harm despite any immediate gratification for her, just as adults control any potentially dangerous play activities or unsuitable eating habits in order to prevent any adverse consequences for the child.

Relationship Enhancement

Forty-nine percent of victims reported loving/protective/compassionate feelings towards the offender as reactions to the abuse and emotional pleasure was reported by 43% (Table 2.6).

Distorted beliefs. In such circumstances, as in the case of sexual gratification, some victims may believe an offender's rationalization that he engaged them in sexual activities in order to enhance the relationship between them.

Alternative beliefs. These are similar to those for sexual gratification. Any positive reactions to the abuse are typically accompanied by other distressing reactions and may be followed by longer term adverse effects, therefore it is incumbent on the adult not to expose the child to these risks.

Sexual Frustration

Forty-three percent of victims reported that their father figures had experienced sexual dysfunction and/or dissatisfaction in their marriages (Table 3.2). It is noted in Chapter 3 that role confusion is a feature of the families of origin of many victims and that they often tend to be 'parentified' into assuming the responsibilities of a mother and wife, sometimes including acting as a surrogate sexual partner to a father figure who complains of sexual frustration in the marital relationship.

Distorted beliefs. Victims may believe that it was their duty to alleviate the offender's alleged sexual frustration, and that their own needs and rights were subordinate to those of the offender. Additionally, the victim may have accepted this duty in order to protect her mother from further oppression and to prevent the break-up of the family. This was especially clear in the case of a victim who as the eldest daughter had cared for a mother who was always sick or pregnant or both, as well as all the victim's siblings. This victim had been trained by her father from babyhood to meet all his sexual demands because 'she [the victim] was pure and virginal' whereas the mother was not at the time of marriage, having had a child out of wedlock.

Alternative beliefs. The majority of offenders are able to demand and obtain conjugal intercourse concurrently with their sexual abuse of a child. This abuse is in addition to rather than instead of sex with their wives (Russell, 1984). Even if a man is frustrated in his marital sexual relationship and wants some other source of satisfaction there are many alternatives to his daughter or another child. More fundamentally, the needs and rights of a child are not subordinate to those of an adult, and it is always his responsibility to ensure that she is not exposed to distress or harm as discussed above.

Alcohol

Many studies have shown that offenders had often been drinking at the time of the sexual abuse (Araji & Finkelhor, 1985, 1986; Russell, 1984).

Distorted beliefs. Some victims may excuse the offender for abusing them because he was under the influence of alcohol at the time.

Alternative beliefs. Alcohol may well have a disinhibiting effect on sexual restraint but it is the adult's responsibility to control his drinking so that he does not distress or harm others, particularly children. Similarly, a person is still held morally and legally responsible for injury or damage caused while driving in an impaired state.

'Sickness'

Distorted beliefs. Some victims exonerate their offenders because they were 'sick' and therefore not responsible for their actions. For example, one father/offender who was later diagnosed and hospitalized as a schizophrenic had sexually victimized his daughter from babyhood until age 11 years. Because of his eventual hospitalization, it was not difficult for her to believe that the father's behavior during the entire period was 'sick' behavior. Another victim felt protective towards the offender because 'he's mentally slow, and didn't really mean to hurt me'.

Alternative beliefs. In fact, only a very small proportion of offenders are mentally retarded, senile, or psychotic (Araji & Finkelhor, 1985, 1986; Russell, 1984). The vast majority do know that they are sexually abusing a child and that this is morally and legally unacceptable in the society in which they live.

Conclusion

A constant theme in treating victims is why men sexually abuse children and the beliefs reviewed in this section imply that this may be: (a) to teach the child about sex and how to be a good sexual partner; (b) to give the child sexual gratification; (c) to enhance the relationship between the child and the offender; and (d) because the offender is sexually frustrated, under the influence of alcohol, or 'sick'. It may help to correct these distorted beliefs if victims are exposed to an alternative more accurate, balanced, and comprehensive explanation of why men abuse children. Finkelhor (1984, Chaps. 4, 5) has proposed such an explanatory model consisting of four factors, all of which must be present if abuse is to be satisfactorily explained. This reference is suitable prescribed reading for many victims.

The first of these factors addresses the question of why an adult is interested in having sexual contact with a child and Finkelhor suggests that it may be because: (a) this meets the offender's emotional needs; or (b) it is sexually arousing for him; or (c) equally satisfying sources of sexual gratification are blocked for some reason. Not all these conditions need be present for an adult to be motivated towards sexual abuse, any one or more of them are sufficient.

There are several possible reasons why a sexual relationship with a child may meet the offender's emotional needs, including the following:

(a) His own immaturity may lead him to wish to relate to children whose psychological development is at a similar stage to his own.
(b) His low self-esteem and sense of inadequacy may be lessened in relationships in which he is dominant and powerful.
(c) He may attempt to master the trauma of having been abused himself as a child by in turn becoming an abuser who is in control rather than a powerless victim.
(d) Finally, male socialization may place such value on being dominant and powerful in sexual relationships that some men prefer to relate to partners who are smaller and weaker than themselves.

Next, some adults are motivated to abuse a child because this is sexually arousing for them. The types of experience, and perhaps biological factors, that result in an adult being sexually aroused by children are currently unknown, but Finkelhor reviews several possible explanations that have been proposed in the literature.

Finally, adults may be motivated towards sexual abuse because there is a blockage in their sexual relationships with other adults. The blockage may arise from: (a) the individual's inadequate heterosocial skills; (b) sexual dysfunction with adult partners; (c) sexual frustration in the marital relationship; or (d) repressive sexual standards that preclude masturbation or extra-marital sex as alternative outlets.

The second necessary pre-condition for sexual abuse to occur is that the offender must overcome any internal inhibitions he may have to engaging in sex with a child. Among the factors that may contribute to such disinhibition are: (a) the use of alcohol; (b) senility, psychosis, retardation, or lack of impulse control; (c) personal stresses on the offender; (d) family conditions, such as step-relationships, that negate the incest avoidance mechanism (Parker & Parker, 1986); and (e) social and legal attitudes and values that condone or facilitate the sexual exploitation of children.

An adult may be motivated and have overcome his internal inhibitions but certain external factors may still restrain him from abusing a child. Such factors constitute the third pre-condition for abuse. Their preventive function may be overcome however, if: (a) the child is poorly supervised; (b) the mother is incapacitated, oppressed, or absent; (c) the family is socially isolated; (d) the offender has ample opportunity to be alone with the child; or (e) the sleeping arrangements render her vulnerable.

The fourth and final necessary pre-condition for abuse is that the child's resistance be reduced or overcome. This may occur if she is: (a) deprived of attention or affection, insecure, and unsupported by caring adults; (b) lacking in understanding of what is happening in the abuse situation; (c) in a relationship of trust with the offender; or (d) coerced into submitting to the sexual exploitation.

Finkelhor points out that the four necessary pre-conditions for sexual abuse come into play in logical sequence:

> Only some individuals have a strong motivation to become sexually involved with children. Of those who do, only some overcome their internal inhibitions to act on these motives. Of those who overcome their internal inhibitions, only some overcome external inhibitions— the surveillance of other family members or lack of opportunity—and act on the motives.
>
> At this point, three things can happen. (1) Any particular child may resist either directly or indirectly, for example by running away or having a confident, assertive, or invulnerable demeanor, and in such a way avoid the abuse . . . (2) Any particular child may fail to resist and be abused . . . (3) Any particular child may resist but have his or her resistance overcome through coercion . . .
>
> All four pre-conditions have to be fulfilled for the abuse to occur. The presence of only one condition such as lack of protection by a mother or social isolation or emotional deprivation is not enough in itself to explain abuse. To explain abuse requires the presence of all four prior conditions . . .
>
> The four pre-conditions model of sexual abuse puts the issue of responsibility into somewhat better perspective . . . the problem of a mother's failing to protect her child or a child's failing to resist victimization are taken seriously as contributing elements. However, it is clear that these factors are not germane to the situation until after the potential offender has already taken some giant strides on the

road toward committing the offence. The matter of victim's and mother's behavior are relevant only because the offender is already embarked on an antisocial train of events, better showing where responsibility lies (1984, pp. 61–64).

CHAPTER 9

Self-Denigratory Beliefs

In the previous chapter we discussed some beliefs concerning responsibility for the abuse that contribute particularly to feelings of guilt in victims. Some additional but closely related beliefs are of a self-denigratory nature and give rise especially to low self-esteem as well as to guilt and depressive episodes.

Worthlessness and Badness

Distorted beliefs. Seventy-eight percent of victims reported on the Belief Inventory that they considered the statement 'I am worthless and bad' to be partly, mostly, or absolutely true (Table 5.1).

Alternative beliefs. To the extent that thoughts of worthlessness and badness arise from self-blame for the abuse then the reattribution of responsibility to the offender as discussed above will tend to correct the self-denigratory beliefs and enhance the victim's self-esteem.

Difference from Others

During their initial assessments 88% of victims complained of feelings of difference from others.

Distorted beliefs. One source of such feelings of differences may be the belief that 'I must be an extremely rare woman to have experienced sex with an older person when I was a child' which was endorsed as partly, mostly, or absolutely true by 82% of victims on the Belief Inventory (Table 5.1).

Alternative beliefs. This particular source of feelings of difference may be corrected and self-esteem enhanced by providing victims with information on the prevalence of sexual abuse as discussed in Chapter 1. Exposing victims vicariously to the abuse experiences of other women as discussed under the heading of 'Distancing' in Chapter 7 may also be particularly helpful.

77

Stigmatization

Victims may feel stigmatized by having been abused and this might be reflected in the insecurity in relationships reported by 82% and the isolation/alienation reported by 64% of victims at initial assessment.

Distorted beliefs. Item 7 on the Belief Inventory reads 'Anyone who knows what happened to me sexually will not want anything to do with me' and 82% of victims endorsed this statement as partly, mostly, or absolutely true. Similar endorsements of item 14 on the same inventory which reads 'Only bad, worthless guys would be interested in me' were made by 58% of victims (Table 5.1).

Alternative beliefs. A victim's sense of stigmatization may have arisen from factors such as her self-blame for the abuse, the offender's pressure to keep it secret, and the negative reactions of others to its disclosure. To the extent that distorted beliefs associated with such factors are corrected as discussed above then there may be a corresponding reduction in the victim's perception of being stigmatized by others.

Dysfunctional attitude (Beck *et al.*, 1979, Chap. 12; Burns, 1980, Pt. 4). A victim may be particularly prone to feelings of stigmatization because she holds the dysfunctional attitude that the approval of other people is the appropriate measure of her worth as a person, therefore if she feels stigmatized by others because of her abuse then this seriously undermines her self-esteem. Some victims may believe that it would be a catastrophe if anyone disapproved of them, because if one person disapproves of them it means that everyone would disapprove of them, and this would mean that there is something wrong with them and they feel badly about this. But note that it is the victim's belief that there is something wrong with her that influences her mood state, what other people say or think about her cannot influence her emotions directly.

Being extremely dependent on the approval of others means that approval has to be sought constantly which leaves victims vulnerable to manipulation and exploitation. There are several general arguments against such over-dependence on approval:

(a) Disapproval often reflects another person's irrational beliefs, for example, that victims are to blame for their abuse.
(b) Victims may misconstrue disapproval of a specific action on their part as disapproval of them as people, that is, they mislabel themselves. One might also inquire whether when a victim disapproved of someone else's action she meant to judge that person as worthless. If not, why assume that others are judging her in this way?
(c) Disapproval *feels* bad and approval *feels* good, but this is emotional reasoning and not a valid measure of self-worth.

(d) Approval does not necessarily imply worth, for example, offenders are often highly regarded members of their churches and pillars of society.

Within the general approach in cognitive restructuring there are some specific techniques that may be useful in challenging the dysfunctional attitude of basing self-esteem on the approval of others. The first technique is to list the advantages and disadvantages of each assumption on the Dysfunctional Attitudes Scale (Burns, 1980, pp. 241–255) or derived from other sources that indicates the victim's belief that being disapproved of makes her less worth while. A second technique is to rewrite any assumption that is more disadvantageous than advantageous. In rewritten form the assumption will be more realistic and self-enhancing. For instance, Burns (1980, p. 262) gives the example of a woman whose dysfunctional assumption was 'I must always do what people expect of me'. This overdependence on the approval of others led her to subordinate totally her own needs and desires. The dysfunctional assumption was rewritten along the lines of 'It can be enjoyable to have someone approve of me, but I don't need approval to be a worthwhile person or to respect myself'. A third technique is for the victim to write a brief essay on 'Why it is irrational and unnecessary to live in fear of disapproval or criticism'. Victims would include reasons that are convincing and helpful to them why disapproval is unpleasant but not catastrophic. Burns (1980, pp. 264–265) lists a number of such reasons as examples: (a) irrational thinking may underlie another person's disapproval of you; (b) if criticism is valid you can pinpoint and correct your error, you can learn from mistakes rather than being ashamed of them; and (c) if you have made an error, this does not mean that you are an inadequate person, you have done many things right and you can correct errors. In addition to learning to *think* differently about disapproval, it is useful for victims to learn how to *behave* differently towards those who express disapproval. Such training to be appropriately assertive in the face of criticism is discussed in Chapter 19.

Inadequacy and Inferiority

Distorted beliefs. There are several items on the Belief Inventory that may contribute to a sense of personal inadequacy and inferiority in victims. Item 16 which reads 'I am inferior to other people because I did not have normal experiences' was endorsed as partly, mostly, or absolutely true by 90% of victims. Similar endorsements of item 13 which reads 'I will never be able to lead a normal life, the damage is permanent' were made by 76% of victims. Many victims include themselves in the statement that 'You can't depend on women they are all weak and useless creatures' (item 3) which was endorsed as partly, mostly, or absolutely true by 56% of victims (Table 5.1).

Alternative beliefs. Sexual abuse is not all that rare or unusual, many victims do overcome its effects, and it is not accurate to label all women as incompetent in all aspects of their lives.

Dysfunctional attitude (Beck *et al.*, 1979, Chap. 12; Burns, 1980, Pt. 4). Some victims base their self-esteem on the dysfunctional attitude that 'My worth as a human being is proportional to what I have achieved in my life'. It follows that if such a victim believes herself to be inadequate or inferior to others in her competence and accomplishments this will be seriously damaging to her self-esteem.

A useful initial technique in modifying this dysfunctional attitude is for victims to do a cost–benefit analysis of its advantages and disadvantages for them. An advantage might be that success makes the victim feel good and motivates her to achieve more. On the other hand some disadvantages of overemphasizing achievement might be:

(a) That in focussing on achievement the victim might lose out on other satisfactions in life.
(b) If for any reason—such as illness, unemployment, or retirement—a victim can no longer meet her own standards of achievement then she will feel inadequate and depressed.
(c) An overachieving victim's family may also feel neglected and resentful.

If victims decide that it is disadvantageous for them to base their self-esteem and satisfaction on achievement, then they can use the double column technique to list their achievement-oriented thoughts and to argue back against these. Some common arguments against achievement-oriented thoughts include:

(a) Success does not guarantee happiness—victims could be chasing a mirage, and this often leads to disillusionment in middle and later years.
(b) Also success is not the only road to happiness—most people are not superachievers and yet most are happy.
(c) Everyone who achieves is not worth while—Hitler, for instance.
(d) Everyone who is worth while is not an achiever—for example, an infant.
(e) A person may be better than most in some particular quality or achievement but this does not necessarily make him or her a better person.

Thus, victims can be helped to recognize that achievement and success can be satisfying and enjoyable, but they are neither necessary nor sufficient for self-esteem and satisfaction in life.

Subordination of Rights

Distorted beliefs. Several items on the Belief Inventory indicate the tendency of many victims to subordinate their own rights to those of others (Table 5.1). Item 9 which reads 'It doesn't matter what happens to me in my life' was endorsed as partly, mostly, or absolutely true by 58% of victims. 'I've already been used so it doesn't matter if other men use me' (item 17) was similarly endorsed by 54% of victims. Some variations on this belief are 'I've slept with so many guys that it doesn't matter who I sleep with anymore' and 'No man could ever want me because I'm used trash'. 'I don't have the right to deny my body to any man who demands it' (item 6) was considered to be partly, mostly, or absolutely true by 48% of victims. Similar beliefs include 'A woman is supposed to please a man sexually', 'I have no right to deny my husband sex', and 'Sex is a duty'. Item 10 which reads 'No man could care for me without a sexual relationship' was endorsed as partly, mostly, or absolutely true by 86% of victims. A common variation is 'I can't refuse my partner sex because he'd go looking for it elsewhere'.

Alternative beliefs. Distorted beliefs such as those above are often the result of the 'parentification' process discussed in Chapter 3 in which the child is socialized into believing that it is her duty to subordinate her own rights to those of other family members, and to the extent that her belief in the duty of subordination is cognitively restructured then she may acquire greater respect for her own rights. (Gelinas, 1983, is suitable prescribed reading for many victims on this topic.)

The victim's subordination of her own rights applies not only to her relations with her family of origin but also in her relations with a partner (Chap. 15). Low self-esteem arising from this may be alleviated by cognitively restructuring the 'traditional' distribution of rights and power in such relationships to more equitable and reciprocal role expectations which are then negotiated and implemented by the couple.

Conclusion

We reviewed some self-denigratory beliefs associated with childhood sexual abuse that contribute to low self-esteem and other mood disturbances in victims, together with some alternative beliefs that can be explored by cognitive restructuring.

Some victims may be particularly vulnerable to some of these beliefs undermining their self-esteem because they base this on certain dysfunctional attitudes. The only genuine basis for self-esteem is the victim's *internal* sense of worth rather than some *external* criterion such as the approval of others or what she achieves in her life. In order to develop an internal sense of worth victims need to examine and correct the dysfunctional attitudes that underlie their low self-esteem. The victim needs to turn off self-criticism based on these attitudes and instead to develop a more realistic internal self-evaluation system.

CHAPTER 10

Process and Outcome of Treatment

In this chapter two illustrative case studies are presented, followed by an analysis of outcome for a series of 36 victims.

Case Study: Alison and Michael

Demographic Characteristics

Alison (31) was referred to the program by a psychologist who had been treating her for marital problems and mood disturbances. She had been married to Michael (36) for nine years and they have two children (5 and 3). Both clients were educated to university level, are in the professional occupational group, are Caucasian and protestant.

Family of Origin

Alison's father is a retired business manager, and she described him as a bear of a man, arrogant, egotistical, tyrannical, and very controlling. He was physically violent towards his wife and children and not at all affectionate. He was very unpredictable in his moods and behavior, and had periods of withdrawal, melancholy, and depression, when he would not speak or go out. Alison hated and feared him, she wished he would go away and tried to persuade her mother to leave him. She cannot remember any sexual abuse by her father but said that she had a feeling that there might have been some sexual involvement with him early in her life.

Alison's mother had originally obtained a professional qualification but she had been a homemaker throughout her marriage. She was described as a kind and nice person who was completely passive and let her husband dominate her. As a child Alison felt close to her mother and never doubted that she was loved by her although she did not attend to her welfare or protect her from known risks of sexual abuse.

Victimization Experience

The major victimization was by a great-uncle when Alison was aged 11 to 15 years and he was in his sixties. There were more than 100 incidents consisting of mutual manual stimulation of the genitals and attempts by the offender to make Alison perform oral sex on him which she refused to do.

He induced her to participate in these activities largely by saying 'what's the matter, don't you want to help an old man'. She complied because she had been taught that little girls were supposed to please and help people, especially old people, and because she desperately wanted attention from someone outside her own home and her great-uncle gave her this.

Alison felt very guilty about the sexual encounters, that they were wrong, and that she should not be participating in them. She coped with the abuse by dissociating during it.

Alison did not disclose the abuse to her mother whom she perceived as being completely ineffective in the family, and she did not consider telling her father because she hated him and feared that he would blame or punish her.

Description of Mood Disturbances

The following description of Alison's mood disturbances is based on her initial assessment report.

Guilt. The victim felt guilty at the time of the abuse and feels guilty now because she does not believe that she is coping with the effects of her abuse as well as other women are coping with effects from much more severe abuse. On the Beck Depression Inventory she endorsed: (a) 'I feel guilty all the time'; (b) 'I feel I may be punished'; and (c) 'I am critical of myself for my weaknesses or mistakes'. On the Battle Self-Esteem Inventory she reported that she often feels ashamed of herself. The items checked partly, mostly, or absolutely true on the Belief Inventory were: (a) 'I must have permitted sex to happen because I wasn't forced into it'; (b) 'I must have been responsible for the sex when I was young because it went on so long'; (c) 'It must be unnatural to feel any pleasure during molestation'; and (d) 'I must have been seductive and provocative when I was young'.

Low self-esteem. The victim often thinks that people are evaluating her adversely. She cannot believe that she is worth anyone's care and concern without there being some payoff for them, or that anyone could accept her if her past is known to the person concerned. She feels that she is unjustifiably imposing on others if she makes any demands on them, however reasonable, and disqualifies positive things concerning herself, for example, that she must have got an A on a paper because the professor was an easy marker who took pity on her as an older student. On the Beck Depression Inventory she endorsed 'I am disappointed in myself', and the items checked partly, mostly, or absolutely true on the Belief Inventory were: (a) 'I am worthless and bad'; (b) 'Anyone who knows what happened to me sexually will not want anything more to do with me'; (c) 'It doesn't matter what happens to me in life'; (d) 'No man could care for me without a sexual relationship'; (e) 'I will never be able to lead a normal life, the damage is permanent'; and (f) 'I am inferior to other people because I did not have normal experiences'.

Depression. The victim has experienced periods of low mood since her teenage years. These episodes were usually precipitated by some adverse event. During periods of depression she is prone to 'crying jags', feels ugly and angry with herself, and wants to be cared for in an unconditional way. Shortly before starting current therapy the victim was very withdrawn for a period. She kept the drapes closed, delayed making telephone calls, did not answer the telephone, avoided people and shopping, dropped out of organizations, and drank sherry alone at home. On the Beck Depression Inventory she scored 21 which is just into the clinically significant range. The victim heard once that her father had been diagnosed manic-depressive but he refused to continue in psychiatric treatment, and her sister has a history of depression.

Attempted suicide. In grade 6, the victim swallowed mixtures of poppy seeds and aspirins to get someone to care for her in hospital, but she did not want to kill herself. In grades 7 and 8 she would cut her wrists. At the beginning of the current therapy she experienced a revival of feelings of wanting to do something self-destructive.

Process of Treatment for Mood Disturbances

The first 4 weeks of therapy were devoted to the initial assessment. This was followed by 16 weeks during which the major therapeutic focus was on the cognitive restructuring of beliefs associated with mood disturbances, although many other problems also required some therapeutic attention. From the termination of this phase of treatment to the final follow-up a period of 135 weeks elapsed.

As part of the whole cognitive restructuring process the victim and her partner viewed the videotape *Incest: The family secret* (Millican, 1979) which she found quite distressing although it made it obvious that the child is the victim rather than being responsible for the abuse. The victim and her partner also read the following prescribed materials:

(a) Burns (1980, Chap. 3) on the rationale for cognitive restructuring which they found excellent.
(b) Geiser (1979, pp. 105–111) on the prevalence of child sexual abuse. This was helpful to them. The victim realized that sexual abuse is not rare and is

damaging. She was comforted that she is not on her own and not so weird. Reading had however triggered off guilt because she was making too big a deal when her abuse was less severe than that endured by other women who are coping better with its effects.

(c) Sgroi (1982, Chap. 3) for the general background on sexual abuse, particularly family roles and functioning. She found it easy to read but somewhat disturbing because it caused her to think back to her own family. Her uncle was the abuser but it was her father who was the perpetrator in a lot of senses and her mother did not protect her.

(d) Gelinas (1983), Herman (1981, Chap. 6), Jehu, Gazan, and Klassen (1984/5, 1985), and Meiselman (1978, Chap. 6) on the long-term effects of sexual abuse. The victim had always wanted to understand the sources of her problems and this material was very helpful in this respect.

(e) Summit (1983) on secrecy and disclosure issues.

Self-blaming beliefs. Several such beliefs that were cognitively restructured are shown in Table 10.1. Another was item 15 on the Belief Inventory which reads 'It must be unnatural to feel any pleasure during molestation'. The alternative beliefs explored were along the lines of the body responding automatically even though the person concerned disapproves of her responses, for example: (a) erotic sensations during breast feeding; (b) pleasurable sensations derived from smoking, alcohol abuse, or overeating despite guilty feelings associated with them. The victim did not find it easy to accept such alternative beliefs and continued to maintain that she personally had not felt anything during the abuse. This may well have been true as she dissociated during the encounters.

Self-denigratory beliefs. Some of these beliefs are shown in Table 10.2, and among the victim's general comments on these topics were:

(a) that she had always felt different from other people and believed that they would see her as different;
(b) that she had always been preoccupied with how others are evaluating her;
(c) that she has grown up being the nice compliant girl in her family of origin but she does not feel nice any more because she is no longer complying with the family's demands.

Between weeks 21 and 123 in treatment the major focus shifted from mood disturbances to interpersonal and sexual problems, but some attention also needed to be given to the victim's low self-esteem, depression, and attempted suicide, as described below.

Low self-esteem. The victim described herself as: (a) mean; (b) not nice; (c) not a happy person; (d) not likeable to others; (e) selfish; and (f) not trying to please others any more, and said that people do not like people like her, they like happy, rewarding people. She is not a nice person because: (a) she snaps

Table 10.1. *Cognitive Restructuring of Self-Blaming Beliefs: Alison*

Distorted beliefs	Alternative beliefs
I feel guilty about drawing attention to myself about the abuse (1. emotional reasoning, 2. 'should' statement).	1. The fact that I *feel* guilty does not mean that I *am* guilty of something. Drawing attention to myself in order to get the help I need is a constructive thing to do for me and my family. 2. Why should I not draw attention to myself when doing so will benefit myself and others.
I must have permitted sex to happen because I wasn't forced into it (jumping to conclusions personalization).	In a sense I was forced into it because [the offender] knew and exploited my emotional weak spots: (a) I had been indoctrinated with the belief that nice little girls were supposed to help and please people, especially old people. He persuaded me by saying 'what's the matter, don't you want to help an old man'. I did not want to hurt him by refusing to participate; (b) I desperately wanted attention from someone outside my family and [the offender] gave me this.
I must have been responsible for sex when I was a child because it went on so long (jumping to conclusions, personalization.	As a child I could not stop the abuse because: (a) the offender persuaded me to continue 'helping' him, and I had been taught to do this; (b) I feared that if I told my mother she would not do anything to protect me; (c) I could not consider telling my father because I hated him, I feared that he would blame or punish me, and the family situation was chaotic; (d) I had been taught that drawing attention to myself in any way was unacceptable in my family; (e) I could not refuse to take [the offender's] lunch out to the fields where the abuse often occurred because I would have to explain to [his wife] why I was refusing; (f) I did not want to upset her.
Victim bears some responsibility for the abuse (jumping to conclusions, personalization).	The child is not to blame, the offender is entirely responsible for the abuse.

and loses her temper a lot at home; (b) she is not a wife because there is no sexual relationship; (c) she is self-destructive and purges with suppositories; and (d) she wallows in the past and self-pity. The partner said that he is tired of this low self-concept that the victim has; he doesn't see her this way, and she is very much liked by other people.

Table 10.2. *Cognitive Restructuring of Self-Denigratory Beliefs: Alison*

Distorted beliefs	Alternative beliefs
I must be an extremely rare woman to have experienced sex with an older person when I was a child (disqualifying the positive, jumping to conclusions).	The evidence is that it is not rare for a woman to have such experiences, many women have them and I am not isolated, alone, or weird.
I am weak for making such a big thing out of the abuse, especially when I know that many women have been abused in degrees far more severe than me (1. all or nothing thinking, 2. overgeneralization, 3. mental filtering, 4. disqualifying the positive, 5. mislabeling, 6. minimization).	1. Like everyone else I am not completely strong. 2. The fact that I have difficulty coping with the abuse does not mean that I have difficulty in coping with everything. 3. There are many areas of my life in which I function quite satisfactorily. The problem I have with the abuse is only one part of my life. 4. In many aspects of my life I am not weak. 5. Having difficulty in coping with the abuse does not mean I am a weak person. 6. It is difficult to say what makes some abuse experiences more severe than others, or where the experience I had would rank in this range of severity.
I should be able to handle the abuse better and not let it interfere with my life, and other's, in the manner that it is (1. emotional reasoning, 2. 'should' statement).	1. The fact that I *feel* helpless does not mean that I *am* helpless. I have got myself into therapy and am working on coping better with the abuse. 2. It is not very realistic or productive to expect better coping from myself. I'm only human and many women have difficulty in coping with the long-term effects of sexual abuse.

The interventions used included: (a) referral to Burns (1980, Chap. 4) on the basis for self-esteem; (b) emphasizing that she is doing all she can in therapy to remedy her perceived deficiencies; (c) cognitively restructuring the expectation that *everyone* should see her as a nice person (including family of origin); and (d) cognitively restructuring the belief that *any* demands made upon her by others (including family of origin) are reasonable and should be met.

Low self-esteem was a persistent and pervasive problem, which now seemed to relate more to current functioning rather than past abuse. Later there were several reports of some improvement including the victim: (a) feeling stronger all the time; (b) being more assertive; and (c) realizing the need to live by her own standards rather than other people's expectations of her, to be her own person. There were also some less prominent reports of self-hate, and lack of strong sense of self-identity.

Depression and attempted suicide. Just after the phase of treatment focussed upon mood disturbances ended the victim had an episode of depression. There was no obvious precipitant and recovery was apparently spontaneous following some reassurance and support from the therapist and partner. During the episode the victim reported that she: (a) felt empty rather than sad; (b) had difficulty in concentrating; (c) was having to expend a lot of energy to cope with problems; (d) blamed herself for her problems; (e) doesn't care enough about herself; and (f) doesn't feel deeply about her children. Everything seemed black and negative, and she felt she ought to give up treatment because she was not sure she wanted to change and was not ready to grow up.

The victim was still able to derive enjoyment from her studies and other things; her sleep appeared to be essentially undisturbed but it was difficult to judge her eating pattern because of her anorexia/bulimia. There is a history of similar depressed moods, with episodes irregular, often several years between them, apparently of short duration and self-limiting, sometimes with no obvious precipitants in the victim's life situation. No elevated moods were reported. The victim was concerned about the possible inherited nature of her depression in view of the diagnoses of her father as manic-depressive and sister as depressive. She was reassured that her episodes did not appear to be of an endogenomorphic or major type.

During the depressive episode the victim reported that she sometimes thinks of suicide but she feels in control of herself and would call someone. Also the thought of her children stops her from doing it. A little later she called the therapist about her binge eating. He had difficulty in hearing her on a bad line and changed to another telephone. She interpreted this difficulty as rejection and anger from the therapist because she should not have called him at home—despite having been encouraged to do so when necessary. The victim then took 15–25 analgesics, called a crisis line, and on their advice went into a general hospital for the remainder of the day. The partner responded very well to this incident and did not blame or get angry with the victim. He was quite shocked and in a subsequent therapeutic session said that the victim's presence to bring up the children and her studies were much more important than his sexual gratification, if the latter was putting her under pressure in treatment. The therapist emphasized some positive things about the incident: (a) she handled it well in using the crisis line and the hospital; (b) she was able to discuss her reactions to the telephone call with the therapist afterwards; and (c) she could learn from it to look for possible alternatives to rejection and anger from others, and if others do evoke these feelings in her then they—including the therapist—may be partly responsible for this.

Over the next six months there were three episodes of dysphoria each terminating within a couple of days which was much shorter than previously. The most severe of these episodes is described by the victim as follows:

At times, probably the greater percentage of the time I just don't care what happens to me. Though I recognize that to 'get better' I really have to want to change, I'm troubled by a deep inner sense of really wanting to hurt myself. I'm becoming more and more preoccupied with these thoughts and because I know I'm capable of acting on them in a stupid moment when I have little self-control I want to talk about them, now. What's distressing about them is that I can look around me and say there's absolutely no reason for me to feel badly—and I don't feel badly, I might be a little bit sad but I'm not depressed and my life situation is such that I shouldn't have such intense thoughts. I feel an awful lot of tension and pressure but I understand the reason for the tension and generally see it as being a temporary state related to the changes I'm undergoing and the issues I'm facing. It's very hard because I'm trying to change when I sense my marriage will withstand little rocking . . .

I find myself thinking I'm either going to kill myself or I'm going to leave [my marriage] which is it going to be? The thoughts never seem to go away. They are always there in varying degrees of intensity. Yet I really don't want to do either and all the while [Michael] and I are moving ahead. But I feel very empty yet also more at peace. Today I went for a walk and as I was walking I felt I have found the answer to my life and that is that there is nothing—nothing means anything. There doesn't seem to be any purpose for me. It all seems empty—I feel like I am just existing, vegetating, wasting. I'm functioning but almost like a robot. I could just as easily have laid down in the snow and been quite content and peaceful. I'm only disturbed by the thoughts because I feel I shouldn't have them and I'm afraid I may act on them. I don't understand them and no matter how I challenge them the challenge always seems artificial.

I know I would be sorry if I acted on them. I recognize I'm surrounded by everything that should make me happy and make me feel like a very fulfilled woman. I always seem to be driven to do things that do hurt or have the potential of hurting me.

Outcome of Treatment for Mood Disturbances

Distorted beliefs. The victim's total scores on the original 17-item Belief Inventory during initial assessment ranged from 20 to 28. From week 13 in therapy through to the final follow-up at week 155 her total scores were all at clinically non-significant levels of 14 or lower.

Her scores on the self-blaming items in the inventory (5, 8, 12, 15) had all declined to zero at final follow-up, and this was also the case for all self-denigratory items (2, 6, 7, 9, 10, 14, 16, 17) except 13 that reads 'I will never be able to lead a normal life, the damage is permanent' which the victim scored as 2. *partly true, partly untrue.* She commented 'Sexually I believe I have come as far as I am likely to and that whatever disability remains is likely to be permanent and something for my husband and I to adjust to and work around'.

Guilt. The interview data, double column forms, and victim self-recordings indicated substantial alleviation of guilt associated with the sexual abuse which was sustained through to final follow-up. For instance, in the following notes the victim discussed the respective responsibilities of those involved in the abuse situation and indicated that she no longer blames herself for what happened:

> Who was responsible for me when I was a child?
> My parents and whoever my parents entrusted with my care. My parents are ultimately responsible for their decisions. My aunt and uncle [the offender] accepted responsibility for me when I was with them. They shared this responsibility equally.
> What does it mean to be responsible for a child?
> It means that you will accept the job of ensuring that the child under your care will come to no harm either physically or mentally. You must provide and maintain a safe environment, be sensitive to the child's needs, and place the child ahead of yourself at all times.
> Did my uncle fulfill his responsibility?
> He did until I matured for until then he made me feel so special but then he destroyed it all by placing himself ahead of me—by using me and expecting me to do things that were wrong. By putting me in a position from which I had no recourse. During these times he showed me that he became all important, he had all the feelings and I became merely a thing, an object used by him. I wasn't to feel, I was only to do. His satisfaction was the only thing that mattered and I was only a means to an end.
> Was my Aunt in any way responsible for what happened?
> Yes. She must have known but she let it go on. She must have known her husband's character. It seems many others did, but she continued to leave me with him. She continued to send me out with the lunch. She never spoke to me. She never warned me. She never gave me any sign that maybe I didn't have to do what I did. Now he's dead and we're all still pretending—even my other aunts could have said something. But I was good at covering up and keeping people from focussing on me.

Low self-esteem. The interview data, double column forms, and victim self-recording indicated improvement in the victim's self-esteem although some identity confusion and ambivalence towards herself still remained.

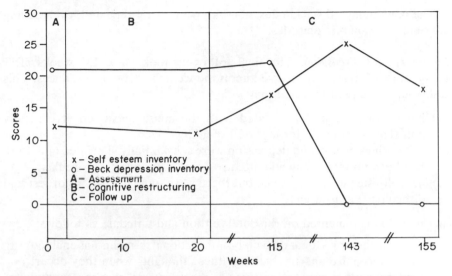

Figure 10.1. Scores on Battle Self-Esteem Inventory and Beck Depression Inventory: Alison

Figure 10.1 shows that the victim's score on the Battle Self-Esteem Inventory at initial assessment was 12, which placed her in the 6th percentile according to the college student norms for the instrument. At the termination of cognitive restructuring her score remained essentially unchanged at 11 and was still in the 6th percentile. There was a slight rise to a score of 15 (8th percentile) at first follow-up, and a further increase to 26 (73rd percentile) at second follow-up, followed by a decline to 18 (22nd percentile) at final follow-up. This decline is not altogether consistent with other evidence on the victim's self-esteem from the self-denigratory items on the Belief Inventory, interview reports, self-recordings, and Beck Depression Inventory, although as noted above some residual difficulties with self-esteem are indicated among these sources.

Depression and attempted suicide. Interview data indicated that depressive episodes became less frequent and of shorter duration during the course of treatment. The victim seemed to be coping with them much better.

Figure 10.1 shows that her scores on the Beck Depression Inventory remained at the same just clinically significant level of 21 from assessment to termination, probably because of the serious interpersonal and sexual problems that remained to be treated after the specific treatment of mood disturbances. These other problems remained unresolved at the first follow-up and the BDI score rose slightly to 22. By the time of the second follow-up there was considerable improvement in the interpersonal and to a lesser extent in the sexual problems and the BDI score had declined to zero, where it remained at the final follow-up.

The one attempted suicide described above was not repeated, even during subsequent dysphoric episodes.

Summary and discussion. The final follow-up took place 135 weeks after termination of treatment focussed upon the victim's mood disturbances. This follow-up evaluation revealed that:

(a) her distorted beliefs associated with the abuse had been at clinically non-significant levels for a period of 122 weeks;
(b) her feelings of guilt and depression were substantially alleviated and there had been no further suicide attempts over a period of 111 weeks;
(c) her self-esteem had improved but there were some indications of residual difficulties in this area.

The victim commented on this intervention and outcome as follows:

> . . . the therapy's focus on beliefs and irrational thoughts has enabled me to recognize and to challenge these thoughts when they occur. Consequently, I now feel my moods are within my own control and this is terrifically liberating. To summarize this point, the therapy has taught me to be my own therapist. The therapy has provided me with not only the theoretical but a practical means by which to monitor my moods, and has enabled me to take a rich repertoire of information and adapt it to meet my own needs and personality. In a sense I feel I have become a person of my own making instead of a person for the making of someone else.

As indicated previously the victim was followed up for 135 weeks after the termination of the phase of treatment which was focussed upon her mood disturbances. It is important to note that during the first 123 weeks of this period she was receiving further phases of treatment focussed upon her interpersonal and sexual problems respectively, although with undoubted influence on her mood state. Only during the final 12 weeks of the follow-up period was she receiving no treatment at all. Therefore, the improvement in mood disturbances cannot necessarily be attributed entirely to the phase of treatment that was focussed upon these disturbances specifically, later phases almost certainly also contributed.

Case Study: Ruth and Doug

Description of Mood Disturbances

This description is based on the initial assessment report:

Guilt. The victim felt guilty at time of abuse, and she feels guilty now because she 'erotically fondled' a younger brother (aged 5 years) when she was aged 14 years. On the Beck Depression Inventory she endorsed: (a) 'I feel guilty a good part of the time'; (b) 'I expect to be punished'; and (c) 'I am critical of myself for my weaknesses or mistakes'. On the Battle Self-Esteem Inventory she reported that she often feels ashamed of herself, and the items checked partly, mostly, or absolutely true on the Belief Inventory were: (a) 'I must have permitted sex to happen because I wasn't forced into it'; (b) 'I must have been responsible for the sex because it went on for so long'; and (c) 'It must be unnatural to feel any pleasure during molestation'.

Low self-esteem. The victim feels that she is 'damaged goods' and different from others because of her history of sexual victimization. She does not feel that others will find her acceptable, that is as rich, smart, or well educated. On the Beck Depression Inventory she endorsed 'I am disappointed in myself', and the items checked partly, mostly, or absolutely true on the Belief Inventory were: (a) 'I am worthless and bad'; (b) 'I don't have the right to deny my body to any man who demands it'; (c) 'Anyone who knows what happened to me sexually will not want anything more to do with me'; (d) 'It doesn't matter what happens to me in my life'; (e) 'No man could care for me without a sexual relationship'; (f) 'I will never be able to lead a normal life the damage is permanent'; (g) 'Only bad, worthless guys would be interested in me'; (h) 'I am inferior to other people because I did not have normal experiences'; and (i) 'I've already been used so it doesn't matter if other men use me'.

Depression. The victim stated that she has always been depressed, and that she usually loses appetite, is unable to sleep and has nightmares when she is feeling sad. She used drugs and alcohol to counteract sad feelings when she was younger. At initial assessment she scored 39 on the Beck Depression Inventory which indicates severe depression.

Attempted suicide. The victim reported that she had never attempted suicide but lived a lifestyle that placed her in dangerous situations especially when procuring drugs and alcohol from people she did not know. At the beginning of the current therapy she reported that she had thoughts of killing herself but would not carry them out.

Process of Treatment for Mood Disturbances

The initial assessment consisted of 6 sessions conducted over a period of 13 weeks including a break due to the partner's hospitalization. Treatment focussed on mood disturbances consisted of 15 sessions over 34 weeks including a break to accommodate the birth of the victim's second child. From the termination of this treatment to final follow-up a period of 51 weeks elapsed.

To facilitate the cognitive restructuring process in this phase of treatment the following audio-visual and reading materials were used to address various problematic issues which the victim faced:

(a) Videotape *Incest: The family secret* (Millican, 1979). The victim found that she was very sympathetic with the offender in the film, that is she felt that he did not really mean to hurt the victim. Further exploration of the victim's sympathy for the offender revealed that when she was aged 14 years she had 'sexually victimized' a brother 9 years younger than herself. Thus she felt that if she were angry with the offender in the film or the offenders in her own life then she would have to be angry with herself and therefore not deserving help with the negative consequences of having been abused herself. She was, however, very angry with the mother in the film for not protecting her daughter. In short, the victim's perception of herself was that of an offender not a victim.

(b) Burns (1980, Chap. 3) on the rationale for cognitive restructuring.

(c) Geiser (1979, pp. 105–111) on the prevalence of sexual abuse.

(d) Finkelhor (1979b, pp. 89–91) and Forward and Buck (1981, p. 85) on sibling incest, to assist victim in understanding the differences between her sexual victimization by her much older brothers and her own 'sexual victimization' of the younger brother.

(e) Gelinas (1983) was used to highlight the parentification of the victim.

(f) Herman (1981, Chap. 6) was used to help the victim to understand some of the long-term effects of sexual abuse, many of which had up to this point made her think that she was 'crazy' rather than being seen as ways of coping with the abusive circumstances.

(g) Summit (1983) was useful in assisting victim to understand the process of entrapment she experienced and mislabeled as being a consenting participant in her own sexual abuse.

Self-blaming beliefs. The victim's belief that she had sexually victimized her younger brother prevented her from perceiving herself as a victim. Cognitive restructuring of this belief that her sexual abuse of her younger brother was as traumatizing and exploitive as the sexual abuse experienced by her from much older brothers is shown in Table 10.3.

Several other sources of guilt were cognitively restructured as shown in Table 10.4. Initially, the victim denied feeling any sexual feelings during the abuse. However, when she was successful in changing her perception of herself as an offender with her younger sibling, she was able to discuss how she used dissociation or detachment ('tuning out') as soon as she felt any sexual feelings. She stated that she often felt very angry that her body 'betrayed' her when she did not want to respond in any way.

The victim commented on her experience of being abused and the incidents with her younger brother as follows:

I was abused by 3 of my half brothers. It started when I was about 4 years old and ended when I was about 20 or 21.

I felt very responsible for my abuse, thinking that it was my fault and that it was something that I asked for. My shame of feeling responsible kept me from telling anyone. Another reason I didn't tell was that I was afraid of the consequences, i.e. my mother flipping out, I thought I would get my brothers in trouble. Also, I was told not to tell anyone about what we were doing by one of my brothers. My mother has had cancer a couple of times and I thought that if I told her that I was sexually abused, she would definitely get it again. I was concerned about it causing anxiety for her because one of the offenders always goes out to the farm [where she lives]. I took on responsibility for her feelings. I was afraid also, that she would blame me for the abuse . . .

I felt that I had to take responsibility for my sexual victimization because I thought that I had sexually victimized my younger brother. Through therapy, I learned that what I did was not the same as what was done to me. It didn't even compare. But still, it had to do with sex because of the way I perceived it. It did not necessarily mean the same thing to my brother. I know that it was wrong but I was taught and conditioned to think of sex as something with a younger sibling. The only difference is I did not carry out what was done to me to my younger brother. I have decided that I will mention it to him and if he does remember it, I will tell him that it was me and not him who was responsible and that I am sorry. By the way, I should tell what was done to me by my offending brother and what I did to my brother. I had my undergarments removed and there was direct contact of my (older) brother's penis to my vagina. Blood came out one time. It went on for years and he knew I did not want to do it. Also one of them would feel up my breasts when I was sleeping.

All I did was have close body contact with my (younger) brother. We had all our clothes on and to him it was probably like a hug, but to me it was more than that.

Through therapy I came to see that what was done to me was not my fault. It was not my duty to keep it a secret, to protect the offenders. It was something *they* did to me, so why should I take on the responsibility to protect them from their consequences. I had to stop worrying about other people's reactions because they could handle them themselves and start having some concern for myself and my feelings. I finally told my family about the abuse and I feel very relieved and good about it.

Table 10.3.   *Cognitive Restructuring of Victim As An Offender: Ruth*

Distorted belief	Alternative beliefs
I feel that I have to take responsibility for my sexual victimization because of my sexually victimizing my brother (jumping to conclusions).	I am assuming that I sexually abused him when I really didn't. I didn't kiss him, there were *no* clothes removed or even any skin contact at all. All I did was rub my body against his 5 or 6 times. There was no force used. It was like the only way I really knew how to show affection. I didn't exploit him like my brothers did to me.

Table 10.4.   *Cognitive Restructuring of Self Blaming Beliefs: Ruth*

Distorted beliefs	Alternative beliefs
I must have permitted sex to happen because I wasn't forced into it (personalization).	I couldn't have stopped what was happening because I was just a child.
I feel as though I was the one who did it (emotional reasoning).	Just because I feel as though I did it, it doesn't mean that I did it. I didn't do anything. I was the victim.
I kept it a secret all this time so it seems like and feels as though I am responsible (1. personalization, 2. emotional reasoning).	1. I kept it a secret because I was told to when I was a child. It automatically made me feel responsible. But I am not responsible I was just a kid. 2. Just because I *feel* responsible doesn't mean that I *am*. I was also very scared and didn't understand what was happening. I can see from the films about victims that I saw that they kept the secret for the same reasons I did.
I feel responsible for the sexual abuse because I got some pleasure (i.e. attention) by participating and could have stopped it if I wanted to (personalization).	Any kid should have attention and in my family that's the only way I got it, and from the readings that's a common way for offenders to get victims.

Self-denigratory beliefs. The cognitive restructuring of some of these beliefs is shown in Table 10.5.

Depression. The victim was severely depressed when she first presented for therapy. Cognitive restructuring of her self-blaming and self-denigratory beliefs appeared to alleviate this mood disturbance and restructuring was ex-

Table 10.5. *Cognitive Restructuring of Self-Denigratory Beliefs: Ruth*

Distorted beliefs	Alternative beliefs
I feel there is no hope for me in the future (jumping to conclusions, disqualifying the positive, catastrophizing).	I am going for therapy. There is already some improvement. The reason why it has been terrible is being dealt with now, it wasn't before.
I feel defeated sometimes or most times (emotional reasoning).	Just because I *feel* defeated, it doesn't mean I *am* defeated. That's unrealistic, I am getting help!
I always feel screwed up (emotional reasoning).	Just because I feel discouraged on a bad day, does not mean that things are bad and that they aren't going to be better. I do have good days. We *all* have our bad days. That's part of life.

Table 10.6. *Cognitive Restructuring of Depressogenic Thoughts: Ruth*

Distorted belief	Alternative beliefs
I feel unhappy and it seems like I'll never be happy (mental filtering, overgeneralization, magnification).	I am happy a lot of times. It seems like I don't notice the good. I just notice the bad times. I don't really feel unhappy, a lot of times I just feel bored or dead to the world. I just have to start doing things and getting involved with other people. The other night we went out with another couple and I really had a lot of fun – I was happy so it's up to me to do things to make me happy. I just can't sit around and wait to get happy.

tended as exemplified in Table 10.6. She commented on her depression as follows:

Before therapy, I became super depressed. Doing housework and making meals became too much for me and I ended up not doing anything. I felt so helpless and hopeless. I saw no way out of what I was feeling. Everything looked black to me. I felt there was no hope for the future. My sex life was getting worse than ever and I would try super hard to make it better, but I just couldn't. I was convinced that things would never get better. The only time I enjoyed sex was when I was either drunk or stoned. . . . I haven't been depressed for months now. Doing housework is not such a hard task to me today. I am excited about life and I even feel happy usually. I didn't know how sick or depressed I was until I got better. As far as my sex life goes, it has improved 100%. I do enjoy having sex with my husband, I do. I had to remember that I am making love with my husband and not think about the abuse. Through therapy, I am able to see that I was the victim, it was done to me and I did not ask for it or do it. Knowing and feeling this has done wonders for my sex life. The guilt is what hindered me and now it is gone.

Outcome of Treatment for Mood Disturbances

Distorted beliefs. The victim's total scores on the original 17-item Belief Inventory during initial assessment ranged from 40 to 62. From week 39 in therapy through to the final follow-up at week 97 her total scores were all at clinically non-significant levels of 14 or lower.

Her scores on the self-blaming items on the inventory (5, 8, 12, 15) had all declined to zero at final follow-up, and this was the case also for all self-denigratory items (2, 6, 7, 9, 14, 16, 17) except items 10 and 13 that were scored as 1, *mostly untrue.*

Guilt. The interview data, the double column forms, and the victim's self-recordings indicated substantial alleviation of guilt feelings associated with the sexual abuse.

Low self-esteem. The interview data, double column forms, and the victim's self-recordings indicated improvement in the victim's self-esteem. Her total score and percentile rank on the Battle Self-Esteem Inventory during initial assessment were 9 and 4% respectively. At final follow-up her total score and percentile rank were 25 and 64% respectively, indicating a significant increase in her level of self-esteem.

Depression. The interview data and the victim's notes quoted above indicated that her degree of depression decreased significantly during the course of treatment. Her scores on the Beck Depression Inventory decreased from 39 at assessment indicating severe depression to 2 at the final follow-up indicating that she would not be considered to be depressed.

Summary and discussion. The results presented above show that cognitive restructuring was accompanied by a reduction in the victim's distorted beliefs and an alleviation of her mood disturbances that were sustained through to final follow-up 51 weeks later. She commented on her treatment as follows:

I feel that this therapy is the best, although I haven't had any other therapy. The cognitive restructuring has helped me immensely. My therapist was very 'easy going' in that she dealt with me as an individual with no set order of doing things. She dealt with what seemed to be important to deal with at that time with *me*. All I know is that this therapy worked very well for me. It has changed my life so much and I am very grateful for it.

Series Analysis

Among the 51 clients in the series: (a) 1 did not receive treatment focussed upon mood disturbances because this was provided in a previous pilot program; (b) 10 did not complete this phase of treatment; and (c) 4 were not available for follow-up. The reasons for non-completion of treatment were: (a) relocation—3; (b) transport difficulties—1; and (c) other problems/circumstances necessitating a change of treatment—6. Non-availability for follow-up was due to: (a) distance—1; (b) hospitalization—1; and (c) judged therapeutically inappropriate—2. Thus, except where otherwise indicated this section is based on 36 victims in the U. of M. program who completed treatment focussed on mood disturbances and who were available for follow-up.

In the following summary of the chronology of the intervention the duration of assessment, therapy, and follow-up is expressed in terms of weeks rather than therapeutic sessions, and while clients were seen normally on a once a week basis during assessment and therapy there were some weeks in which sessions were not conducted due to missed appointments, illness, holidays, and other exigencies. Thus, the number of sessions was often less than the number of weeks during assessment and therapy.

The initial assessments of almost two-thirds of the clients were completed in under 6 weeks and 91% were completed in under 11 weeks. The range of duration for the assessments was 2–25 weeks.

The mean duration of therapy focussed upon mood disturbances was 21.2 weeks with a range of 3–47 weeks, and 75% of clients were treated for between 11 and 30 weeks.

The mean duration of follow-up after termination of treatment focussed upon mood disturbances was 57.6 weeks with a range of 8–135 weeks.

Distorted Beliefs

Clinically significant change. The highest score on the original 17-item Belief Inventory during initial assessment was at a clinically significant level of 15 or more for 94% of victims. This proportion was reduced to 13% at termination of therapy focussed upon mood disturbances, and to 5% at the final follow-up.

Among the 34 victims who scored at clinically significant levels of distorted beliefs at assessment, 5 and 2 still did so at termination and follow-up respectively. There were no victims whose scores changed in a negative direction from satisfactory to clinically significant levels of beliefs across the assessment, termination, and follow-up periods.

Statistically significant change. A one-way repeated measures analysis of variance was applied to the average scores on the Belief Inventory at assessment, termination, and follow-up. This revealed that the therapeutic change across these occasions was very highly significant (F = 186.77, df = 2,70, $p < .00001$).

Post hoc comparisons using Tukey's (1947) multiple range comparison technique indicated that these mean scores improved significantly from assessment to termination (Q = 22.93, df = 3,105, p at least $<.01$) but there was no significant change from termination to follow-up (Q = 1.57, df = 3,105, p, $>.05$). Thus, there was significant improvement to termination which was maintained at follow-up.

Mood Disturbances

Beck Depression Inventory. At initial assessment 58% of victims scored at clinically significant levels of 21 or above on this inventory. This proportion was reduced to 8% at termination of therapy focussed upon mood disturbances, and to 5% at the final follow-up.

Among 21 victims who were clinically depressed at assessment, only 3 remained so at termination, and only 1 at follow-up. One other victim who was not clinically depressed at initial assessment or termination did score at this level on follow-up.

A one-way repeated measures analysis of variance was applied to the average scores on the Beck Depression Inventory at assessment, termination, and follow-up. This showed that the therapeutic change across these occasions was very highly significant (F = 58.56, df = 2,70, p, $<.00001$).

Post hoc comparisons using Tukey's (1947) multiple range comparison technique indicated significant change from assessment to termination (Q = 12.92, df = 3,105, $p1 <.01$) with no further significant change from termination to follow-up (Q = 0.64, df = 3,105, $p >.05$). Thus, there was a significant improvement to termination that was maintained at follow-up.

Hudson Index of Self-Esteem. Because of the apparent limitations of the Battle Self-Esteem Inventory (Chap. 6) the scores of 21 victims to whom this instrument was administered are not analyzed. On the Hudson Index of Self-Esteem 86% of the remaining 15 victims scored at clinically significant levels of 30 or above during their initial assessments. This proportion was reduced to 53% at termination of treatment focussed upon mood disturbances, and to 40% at final follow-up.

Among the 13 victims whose scores indicated low self-esteem at assessment, there were 8 who scored at this level at termination and 6 who did so at follow up. No victims changed scores from satisfactory to low self-esteem levels across the assessment, termination, and follow-up periods.

A one-way repeated measures analysis of variance was applied to the mean scores on the Hudson Index of Self-Esteem at assessment, termination, and follow-up. This showed that the therapeutic change across these occasions was very highly significant (F = 23.78, df = 2,28, p <.0001).

Post hoc comparisons using Tukey's (1947) multiple range comparison technique indicated that these scores improved significantly from assessment to termination (Q = 6.74, df = 3,42, p at least <.01) but there was no significant change from termination to follow-up (Q = 2.73, df = 3,42, p >.05). Thus there was significant improvement to termination which was maintained at follow-up.

Side Effects

There are indications that treatment focussed upon mood disturbances had beneficial side effects on the marital relationships and/or sexual functioning of some victims. It should be noted, however, that this treatment might have included some attention to these other problems although no specific treatment was provided for them.

This part of the analysis is not restricted to the 36 victims in the series reported above. Nineteen victims who completed treatment for mood disturbances were ascertained to have marital problems. In 6 (31%) of these 19 cases the marital problems were resolved during the treatment of mood disturbances to an extent that further marital therapy was unnecessary. Similarly, 38 victims who completed treatment for mood disturbances were sexually dysfunctional. In 20 (52%) of these 38 cases the sexual dysfunctions were resolved during the treatment of mood disturbances to an extent that further sex therapy was not needed.

Client Satisfaction

There were 31 victims who completed treatment for mood disturbances and who did not receive any further treatment focussed upon interpersonal problems and/or sexual dysfunctions. The responses of these victims on the Client Satisfaction Questionnaire (Larson, Attkinson, Hargreaves, and Nguyen, 1979) are shown in Table 10.7. Overwhelmingly, they fall into the two positive response categories for every question, the lowest proportion in these two categories being 87% for question 3, with the corresponding proportions for all the other questions being not less than 93%.

Table 10.7. *Responses on Client Satisfaction Questionnaire From Women Who Received Only Treatment Focussed Upon Mood Disturbance (N = 31)*

	n	%
1. How would you rate the quality of service received?		
Excellent	26	83.9
Good	3	9.7
Fair	2	6.4
Poor	0	0.0
2. Did you get the kind or service you wanted?		
Yes definitely	18	58.0
Yes generally	12	38.7
No not really	1	3.2
No definitely not	0	0.0
3. To what extent has our program met your needs?		
Almost all my needs have been met	14	45.2
Most of my needs have been met	13	41.9
Only a few of my needs have been met	4	12.9
None of my needs have been met	0	0.0
4. If a friend needed similar help would you recommend our program to him/her?		
Yes definitely	28	90.3
Yes I think so	2	6.4
No I don't think so	1	3.2
No definitely not	0	0.0
5. How satisfied are you with the amount of help you received?		
Very satisfied	24	77.4
Mostly satisfied	5	16.1
Indifferent or mildly dissatisfied	0	0.0
Quite dissatisfied	2	6.4
6. Have the services you have received helped you to deal more effectively with your problems?		
Yes they have helped a great deal	26	83.9
Yes they have helped somewhat	4	12.9
No they really didn't help	0	0.0
No they seemed to make things worse	1	3.2
7. In an overall, general sense how satisfied are you with the service you received?		
Very satisfied	22	71.0
Mostly satisfied	8	25.8
Indifferent or mildly dissatisfied	0	0.0
Quite dissatisfied	1	3.2
8. If you were to seek our help again would you come back to our program?		
Yes definitely	24	77.4
Yes I think so	6	19.3
No I don't think so	1	3.2
No definitely not	0	0.0

Summary and Discussion

On the Belief Inventory the scores of 32 (94%) of 34 victims improved from clinically significant levels at assessment to satisfactory levels at follow-up, and statistically significant improvement occurred in the whole series of 36 victims.

On the Beck Depression Inventory the scores of 20 (95%) of 21 victims improved from clinically significant levels at assessment to satisfactory levels at follow-up, and statistically significant improvement occurred in the whole series of 36 victims.

On the Hudson Index of Self-Esteem the scores of 7 (53%) of 13 victims improved from clinically significant levels at assessment to satisfactory levels at follow-up, and statistically significant improvement occurred in the whole series of 15 victims.

Treatment focussed upon mood disturbances was accompanied by beneficial side effects on the marital relationships of 31% of victims and on the sexual functioning of 52% of victims. Responses on the Client Satisfaction Questionnaire indicated very positive consumer evaluation of this part of the program.

Thus, the cognitive restructuring intervention was accompanied by clinically and statistically significant improvements in the victims' distorted beliefs as measured on the Belief Inventory, which in turn were accompanied by similar improvements in the victims' mood disturbances as shown by the results from the Beck Depression Inventory and to a lesser extent the Hudson Index of Self-Esteem.

The findings that these improvements on all instruments occurred mainly from assessment to termination, rather than from termination to follow-up, is one indication that the improvements are attributable to the cognitive restructuring intervention rather than any subsequent treatment or life events, although such treatment and/or events might have contributed to the maintenance of the improvements after termination. Another reason for attributing the improvements to the cognitive restructuring intervention is that they occurred in substantial numbers of victims all of whom are unlikely to have experienced life events concurrently with the intervention that might have constituted possible alternative explanations for the improvements that occurred.

The active ingredients in the restructuring package that were effective in producing the improvements in belief and mood are unknown at this stage (Persons & Burns, 1985). In particular, at present it is not possible to distinguish the relative contributions of the specific cognitive restructuring procedures and of the general therapeutic conditions such as the therapeutic relationship and a positive prognostic expectancy that are discussed in Chapter 4. There can be little doubt that such general conditions are necessary for the effective alleviation of mood disturbances in victims but whether these conditions are sufficient for this task without the addition of more specific specific procedures is an issue for further controlled research. Unless and until this shows the specific cognitive restructuring procedures to be unnecessary it may be wise to include them in treatment. Incidently, reading about cognitive restructuring may give the impression that it is an emotionaly cold and purely intellectual process. Quite the contrary is true, the detailed disclosure and discussion of extremely distressing topics, often for the first time, is an intensely emotional experience for both victim and therapist, and general therapeutic conditions such as the therapeutic relationship, a positive prognostic expectancy, acceptance and support, and empathic understanding are vital to enable the victim to continue the painful process.

Some fundamental questions that remain to be resolved by further research concern the relationships between belief systems and mood states and the mechanisms underlying changes in them during therapy. As indicated and referenced previously, Beck and his co-workers claim that mood is a function of beliefs, and that it is the correction of distorted beliefs that produces improvements in mood disturbances. Theoretical and empirical appraisals of these hypotheses are available in several sources (e.g. Beidel & Turner, 1986; Coyne & Gottlieb, 1983; Dush, Hirt, & Schroeder, 1983; Fennell, 1983; Hollon & Kiss, 1984; Kuiper & MacDonald, 1983; Schwartz, 1982). Despite these remaining questions it is perhaps of some clinical value to know that the cognitive restructuring intervention does appear to be accompanied by beneficial changes in both belief systems and mood states whatever the theoretical basis for this may be.

PART 3

Interpersonal Problems

CHAPTER 11

Introduction

Table 11.1 shows that at the time of their initial assessment all the victims in the U. of M. series had some problem in their interpersonal relationships, that 90% had such a problem with men and 49% with women, while among those who were married or living as married 100% of victims reported discord, oppression, or physical abuse in that relationship.

There appear to be the common themes of isolation, insecurity, discord, and inadequacy permeating many of these interpersonal problems and these themes are reviewed next.

Isolation

Some indications of isolation in interpersonal relationships were revealed during the initial assessment of victims. For example, 88% reported feelings of difference from others and 62% felt isolated and/or alienated (Table 11.1). The item on the Belief Inventory which reads 'Anyone who knows what happened to me sexually will not want anything to do with me' was endorsed as partly, mostly, or absolutely true by 82% of victims (Table 5.1). These findings are consistent with those of Briere (1984) who reported that among a series of women who were seeking counseling the symptom of feelings of isolation was significantly more frequent in those who had been sexually abused (64%) compared to those who had not been abused (48%).

Herman (1981) attributes the feelings of difference and isolation experienced by so many victims to the self-blame and self-denigration arising from their participation in the sexual abuse. She writes:

> The most common complaint was a feeling of being set apart from other people. Many of the women described themselves as 'different' or stated that they knew they could never be 'normal' . . . The sense of being an outsider, cut off from ordinary human intercourse, often reached extreme proportions . . . Many women made an explicit connection between their feelings of isolation and the incest secret.

107

Although they had been helpless as children to prevent the incest, they nevertheless felt they had committed an unpardonable sin which left them permanently stigmatized . . . what set them apart from others was their own evilness. With depressing regularity, these women referred to themselves as bitches, witches, and whores . . . (pp. 96–97). (Reproduced from Herman, 1981 by permission of Harvard University Press.)

Table 11.1. *Victims Presenting With Interpersonal Problems*

	Victims	
Problem	n	%
General social relationships (N = 51)		
Feelings of difference from others	45	88.2
Insecurity in relationships	42	82.4
Limited social skills	42	82.4
Mistrust of others	40	78.4
Isolation/alienation from others	32	62.7
At least one of these problems	51	100.0
Relationships with men (N = 51)		
Fear of men	35	68.6
Anger/hostility towards men	28	59.4
Overvaluation of men	26	50.9
Avoidance of long-term relations with men	23	45.1
Dissonant relations with men	17	33.3
Oversexualized relations with men	15	29.4
Transient/casual/promiscuous relations with men	9	17.6
At least one of these problems	46	90.2
Relationship with partner (N = 24)		
Partner discord	24	100.0
Oppressed by partner	22	91.6
Physically abused by partner	8	33.3
At least one of these problems	24	100.0
Relationships with women (N = 51)		
Disparagement of women	25	49.0
Anger/hostility towards women	20	39.2
At least one of these problems	25	49.0

Insecurity

During initial assessment 82% of victims reported insecurity in relationships and 78% mistrusted others (Table 11.1). At the same time on the Belief Inventory the statement 'It is dangerous to get close to anyone because they always betray, exploit, or hurt you' was endorsed as partly, mostly, or absolutely true by 92% of victims (Table 5.1).

The interpersonal insecurity felt by many victims is commonly accompanied by a strong need to retain control in relationships, rather than trusting others to share this without exploiting the victim. The insecurity and need to control experienced by victims may well stem from the betrayal and powerlessness involved in their abuse (e.g. Finkelhor & Browne, 1985, 1986). This involved betrayal in that an offender whom the victim trusted and loved exploited her for his own gratification, and/or that someone else on whom she was dependent failed to protect her from distress and harm. A victim experiences powerlessness in the abuse situation in that her own wishes and sense of mastery over what happens to her are persistently overridden by the offender, and any attempts she makes to obtain support from others to counter his control over her are found to be ineffective. In the light of such breaches of trust and lack of control it is understandable that victims grow up feeling insecure and vulnerable in their relationships with others and with a strong need to retain personal control in their social interactions.

Discord

Instances of this theme in interpersonal relationships at the initial assessment of those 24 victims who were married or living as married included partner discord in 100% of cases. Furthermore, 54% of the 51 victims reported anger/hostility towards men, while such reactions were reported towards women by 39% of these victims (Table 11.1).

The many sources of discord and anger in the relationships of victims with men, partners, women, offspring, and families of origin, are considered in the chapters on each of these specific groups.

Inadequacy

At initial assessment 82% of victims complained of limited social skills in areas such as communication, problem solving, assertiveness, and coping with stressful encounters (Table 11.1).

While the isolation, insecurity, and discord that pervade the relationships of many victims often originate in their sexual abuse experiences it is also true that limited social skills can maintain and exacerbate these problems. For example, isolation may be maintained by communication difficulties, insecurity may persist because the victim is unable to handle stress or to be assertive, and discord may continue because the necessary problem-solving skills are lacking. These and other limitations in social skills may be due at least in part to the sexual abuse situations experienced by victims.

Conclusion

In Chapters 14 to 18 the general themes of isolation, insecurity, discord, and inadequacy, are considered in the more specific contexts of the relations between victims and men, partners, women, offspring, and families of origin respectively.

CHAPTER 12

Assessment and Evaluation Procedures

The interpersonal problems of victims and partners can be assessed and evaluated by means of interviews, questionnaires, reconstructive techniques, confrontation, and recording by these clients. The reconstructive techniques of instant replay, remote recall, induced imagery, and role play, together with confrontation and client recording, are discussed in Chapter 6 and they can be used to identify interpersonal situations that the client finds difficult together with the distressing thoughts and feelings evoked by these situations. Discussion of assessment and evaluation procedures that are specific to the problem of assertiveness is deferred until Chapter 19. The remaining procedures for interpersonal problems are reviewed below.

Interviews

These problems often become apparent during ongoing assessment and treatment interviews, for example, during the initial assessment interviews described in Chapter 6. More detailed information about a couple's marital relationship can be obtained by following the 'Protocol for the Assessment of Discordant Relationships Between Victim and Partner' that is attached as Appendix C. Some background reading for using this protocol is available in Jacobson and Margolin (1979, pp. 51–105) and Stuart (1980, pp. 76–88).

Belief Inventory (BI)

This inventory is attached as Appendix B and discussed in Chapter 6. The following items on the inventory can provide useful indications of possible therapeutic targets in a victim's interpersonal functioning: 3, 4, 6, 7, 10, 11, 14, and 17. This information is usefully obtained during the assessment of interpersonal problems and the entire questionnaire or particular items may be re-administered during treatment and follow-up to evaluate progress and outcome.

Hudson Index of Self-Esteem (ISE)

This instrument is discussed in Chapter 6, and the following items can indicate possible therapeutic targets in a victim's interpersonal functioning: (a) 'I feel that people would not like me if they really knew me well'; (b) 'When I am with other people I feel they are glad I am with them'; (c) 'I feel that people really like to talk to me'; (d) 'I think I make a good impression on others'; (e) 'When I am with strangers I feel very nervous'; (f) 'I feel I bore people'; (g) 'I think my friends find me interesting'; (h) 'I feel very self-conscious when I am with strangers'; (i) 'I feel that other people have a good time when they are with me'; (j) 'I feel like a wallflower when I go out'; (k) 'I feel that I get pushed around more than others'; (l) 'I feel that people really like me very much'; (m) 'I am afraid that I will appear foolish to others'; and (n) 'My friends think very highly of me'. This information is usefully obtained during the assessment of inter-personal problems and the entire questionnaire or particular items may be administered during treatment and follow-up to evaluate progress and out-come.

Dyadic Adjustment Scale (DAS)

This scale was developed by Spanier (1976) to assess the quality of a marriage and similar partnerships. The 32 items can be subdivided into four component subscales assessing dyadic satisfaction, dyadic cohesion, dyadic consensus, and affectional expression. These four components have been substantiated by factor analysis (Spanier, 1976; Spanier & Thompson, 1982). A sample of married, divorced, and recently separated persons was used to determine the scale's psychometric properties. Evidence is reported supporting its construct, criterion, and content validity (Spanier, 1976). Reliabilities of the subscales range from .73 to .94. Overall reliability is .96 (married and divorced sample) and .91 (recently separated sample) (Spanier, 1976; Spanier & Thompson, 1982). The total and subscale scores of the clients can be compared to those for married and divorced samples, and the clients' responses to particular sub-scales or items may also serve to indicate possible therapeutic targets. In the U. of M. program this instrument was administered to victim and partner during the assessment of their relationship, at the termination of treatment focussed on problems in this relationship, and again on follow-up.

Marital Relationship Questionnaire (MRQ)

The male (M) and female (F) versions of the MRQ were designed by Jemail and LoPiccolo (1982) to assess a couple's tendency to respond in a socially desirable manner to questions about their marital relationship. Psychometric data indicate that the questionnaire has good reliability (.90) it is also reported to have adequate construct validity. Finally, comparison of the questionnaire with other measures of social desirability (e.g. the Marlowe Crowne Social Desirability Scale) indicates that it provides a more accurate measure of social desirability response tendencies regarding marital relations. Thus the MRQ provides a useful indication of the degrees of defensiveness and social desirability response set manifested by a victim and her partner when responding to the Dyadic Adjustment Scale and similar inquiries. In the U. of M. program the MRQ was administered to victim and partner at the same times as the DAS.

Target Complaint Scales (TCS)

As soon as interpersonal problems are identified and negotiated with clients as therapeutic targets each problem can be noted on one or more Target Complaint Scales (Mintz & Keisler, 1982) and administered at weekly or more frequent intervals throughout the remainder of the assessment and treatment periods, and again at follow-up sessions. The format of these scales used in the U. of M. program is shown as Appendix D.

The data available on the reliability and validity of the Target Complaint Scale are not yet adequate but it is important to bear in mind that estimates of these psychometric qualities are usually based on the scores of groups of subjects and do not necessarily provide information about the reliability or validity of a measure with any individual client—the scores for a group may be consistent across administrations or across methods of measurement, while those for an individual may be very inconsistent. Thus, the classical psychometric criteria of reliability and validity based on group data are not entirely appropriate when one is interested in evaluating change in individual clients and it may be more useful to pose questions such as: (a) if no intervention occurs, and assuming that this individual client and his or her environment remain stable, will the method produce consistent results (test–retest reliability)? and (b) will the use of the method reveal information about this individual client that is consistent with that gathered by another method (concurrent validity)?

Conclusion

For the reasons discussed in the conclusion to Chapter 6 a suitable selection of the procedures reviewed above is combined into a multi-modal and multi-informant assessment and evaluation program for each client or couple.

CHAPTER 13

Treatment Procedures

Several of the general therapeutic conditions reviewed in Chapter 4 have particular relevance in the treatment of interpersonal problems.

The acceptance and support by the therapist following the victim's disclosure in treatment of her abuse and related problems can help to alleviate her feelings of rejection and isolation from other people.

The loyalty and idealization that often feature in a victim's relationships with her family of origin are noted in Chapter 18 and it is vital that the therapist conveys empathic understanding and validation of these positive attitudes if treatment is to proceed satisfactorily. If they are ignored or challenged then the victim is likely to refuse to consider the roles of family members in her abuse or to terminate treatment. The therapist needs to demonstrate to the victim that he or she recognizes and appreciates the good qualities of family members before exploring the issue of their abusive or non-protective behavior.

A victim's profound mistrust of other people may be replicated in her relationship with the therapist who does not dominate, exploit, or neglect her and thereby increases the victim's capacity to trust others. She may be helped to recognize that her generalized mistrust is inappropriate, that it stems from her abuse, and that it is more realistic to discriminate between trustworthy individuals like her therapist and those who are untrustworthy such as her offender or non-protective parent.

The therapist may instigate, encourage, and assist victims to confront interpersonal situations that they perceive as threatening and distressing. For example, we have noted that many victims are socially isolated and reclusive. While they would like to have friends and to engage in social activities they are afraid to do so. In order to reduce these feelings of loneliness, alienation, and lack of gratification experienced by many victims their therapists may strongly support and facilitate the development of social relationships and leisure activities.

The therapist facilitation of the use of community resources by victims is indicated in Chapter 4 and such networking may be of particular value in alleviating certain interpersonal problems. The difficulties in child management that are experienced by some victims are discussed in Chapter 17 and referral for parent effectiveness training may be helpful in such cases. The physical abuse of victims by their partners is mentioned in Chapter 15 and when this occurs it is sometimes essential for the safety of the victim that she be admitted to a suitable residential facility. Additionally, or alternatively, it may be desirable for both the victim and partner to participate in separate programs for abused and abusive spouses respectively. Treatment programs for previously sexually abused women may provide conjoint sessions for the victim and partner with the aim of reducing discord so that their relationship can survive. This aim is not always achieved however, in which case either or both clients may profit from referral to a program of separation or divorce counseling on an individual basis. Finally, victims who are treated mainly in individual or conjoint sessions may benefit from participation in a group for victims as an adjunct to their primary therapy as discussed in Chapter 4.

In addition to these general therapeutic conditions the interpersonal problems of previously sexually abused women may be treated by a range of more specific procedures, several of which are discussed elsewhere in this book. Distorted beliefs such as those listed under the heading of Belief Inventory in the previous chapter may be contributing to a victim's interpersonal problems in which case it may be appropriate to deploy the cognitive restructuring procedures described in Part 2. Victims who are insufficiently assertive in their relationships with others may benefit from a course of assertiveness training such as that described in Chapter 19. When certain interpersonal situations evoke stress reactions such as anxiety and avoidance then stress management as described in Chapter 23 may be an appropriate form of intervention. Finally, a situation/transition group for the partners of victims is described in Chapter 15. In the present chapter the additional procedures of communication training, problem solving, and anger control are discussed.

Communication Training

The basic communication skills comprise listening, speaking, and certain non-verbal components (Jacobson & Margolin, 1979, pp. 189–211). Victims and partners can be trained in any aspects of these skills in which they are assessed to have deficiencies and that they would like to improve.

Listening Skills

Effective listening requires the recipient to demonstrate to the speaker that what he or she has said has been heard and understood. In addition to listening attentively this task involves the skills and summarizing, reflecting, and validating.

Direct feedback that the message has been heard and understood may be given to the speaker by the listener summarizing its content. This active response also enables the speaker to clarify or correct any miscommunication that has occurred.

It is desirable that the listener reflects the emotional connotations of the speaker's message as well as summarizing its content. For example, a partner might say 'It is difficult for me to fit your therapy in with my hectic work schedule'. The client could simply summarize this by saying 'You're very busy at work'. It might be more desirable, however, for her to capture the feeling behind the message by saying 'You're feeling pretty overwhelmed at work and therapy is an additional and quite upsetting demand on your time'. Such demonstrations of empathic understanding indicate attention and sensitivity to the speaker's feelings and express concern and caring for him or her.

Closely related to reflection and empathy is the concept of validation, meaning that what the speaker says or does is seemed to be a valid and understandable response, even though the listener may not necessarily agree with it. For example, the listener might respond 'I can understand how you feel, it must be awful to feel so sad and hopeless'. Such validating responses are often very appropriate when the speaker is emotionally upset. It gives him or her permission to be distressed while knowing that he or she is still cared for and loved.

Speaking Skills

The bases of effective speaking are being direct and expressing feelings appropriately. Being direct means that the person speaks for him or herself, for example: (a) 'I would like . . . ' or (b) 'I feel . . . '. Such direct statements contrast with other alternatives, for example: (a) speaking for others—'we should . . . '; (b) invoking the support of others—'other people do . . . '; or (c) referring to abstract principles—'married couples ought to . . . '.

Many victims and partners tend to express anger in inappropriate ways; for example: (a) by not stating clearly the reason for their anger; and (b) by augmenting their expression of anger with threats, demands, and criticisms. Consequently, the recipient may not be clear what he or she has to do to avoid annoying the complainant in future and he or she has to attend to a threat, demand or criticism toward him or herself instead of focussing on the complainant's distress. As an alternative to such inappropriate expressions of anger, victims and partners can be trained to express the cause for their complaint and the feelings it arouses in them. For example, an inappropriate expression of anger might be: 'If it happens again, I'm going to leave you'. This excludes the cause of the anger and is accompanied by a threat. A more appropriate expression might be: 'When you call me a "bitch", it makes me feel very angry and upset'. The reason for the anger is clear and delimited, the recipient does not have an attack upon himself to attend to, and he is more likely to recognize and accept his wife's distress and anger.

Some victims and partners fail to express affection and caring or to give praise and compliments, so that the other person feels neglected and unappreciated. There are several possible reasons for these deficiencies including embarrassment, a dearth of ways of expressing positive feelings, and an assumption that the other person knows that he or she is loved and appreciated so that there is no need to say so. Through the training procedures discussed below a couple can explore the positive expressions that they would like to receive from each other, and any impediments such as those listed in the previous paragraph can be remediated.

Non-Verbal Skills

In addition to the verbal components of listening and speaking in effective communication, there are also certain non-verbal components in which some clients or partners may need specific training. Eye contact should be maintained intermittently, interspersed by gazing in the direction of the other person. Both constant eye contact (staring) and the absence of eye contact are generally inappropriate. Voice volume should approximate to normative conversational level, neither too loud nor too low. Voice intonation should not be monotonic, but should employ inflections to communicate emphasis and affect. The response latency to a message from another person should generally be short. Physical gestures such as head nods, hand movements for emphasis, and leaning forward, all add to the qualitative impact of the individual. Smiles, frowns, and other facial expressions should be displayed in appropriate conjunction with verbal content. Posture should be relaxed rather than wooden.

Training Procedures

The following are the three major procedures used to train victims and partners in verbal and non-verbal communication skills:

(a) Feedback, in which trainees are provided with information about their current, maladaptive, communication patterns.
(b) Coaching and modeling, in which the therapist provides alternative, more desirable, communication patterns.
(c) Behavior rehearsal, when trainees practice the communication patterns provided by the therapist.

These procedures form a circular model, since behavior rehearsal is followed by further feedback and coaching and modeling. The same training procedures are used to impart the problem-solving skills discussed in the next section.

Problem Solving

Problem solving is also referred to as conflict resolution or decision making. More extensive discussion of it is available in Jacobson and Margolin (1979, pp. 211–261), which includes an excellent manual for clients on which this outline is based. Problems, conflicts, and disputes are probably inevitable at times in all longer term relationships. One of the characteristics of successful relationships is the ability to resolve such problems smoothly and in a way that is satisfactory to the individuals involved. Those in seriously discordant relationships often lack the capacity to resolve problems in this way and may benefit from specific training in the necessary skills. While the basic communication skills discussed in the previous section can lead to an *understanding* of relationship problems, these skills alone do not necessarily produce *solutions*.

Training in problem solving involves the skills of: (a) defining the problem; (b) generating possible solutions; (c) evaluating these solutions; and (d) negotiating an agreed solution. These skills should be deployed in two distinct, non-overlapping phases; a problem definition phase, and a problem solution phase. During the definition phase, a clear statement of the problem is produced, which is understood by both parties. No attempt to reach a solution is made at this stage. During the solution phase, discussion is focussed upon find a way to resolve the problem. Once this phase has begun, the parties should avoid returning to the definition of the problem. There are two main reasons for stressing the distinction between these phases. It focusses the discussion in each phase, which tends to be more efficient. Problem definition tends to be negative and backward looking, while problem solving should be positive and forward looking. Collaboration and constructive change are likely to be impaired by the intrusion of past misdeeds.

Problem Definition

The way a problem is first stated sets the tone for the entire discussion. If a complainant is going to say something critical about someone else, it should be said in a way that will not make the other person angry and defensive, and more inclined to argue and counterattack than to collaborate in resolving the problem. One way of doing this is to begin the statement of the problem with a positive remark, such as an expression of appreciation; for example, 'I love you, even though you sometimes make me so mad. The thing that I'm angry about now is . . . '. The positive remark reminds the other person that he or she is appreciated and cared for although some aspect of his or her behavior is distressing and unacceptable. Such limited complaints are much easier to accept than criticism that may be interpreted as more comprehensive than it was intended to be.

The complainant should describe exactly what it is that the other person does or says that is distressing. Vague complaints may leave the recipient unclear about what the problem is. One way of being vague in defining a problem is for the complainant to use derogatory labels as substitutes for descriptions of distressing behavior; for example, 'You are inconsiderate'. This does not enable the recipient to know what he or she has done to warrant this label, and it is also provocative and likely to evoke anger, argument, and defensiveness, rather than collaboration in resolving the problem. A better statement of the problem might be 'I know you really care about me, but I do find it difficult when you harass me to have sex when I'm tired or not in the mood'.

Another common way of being vague is to use overgeneralizations like 'always' or 'never'. In response to an overgeneralized complaint, the recipient is likely to dispute the overgeneralization rather than to discuss the substance of the problem.

Finally, the complainant should simply describe the distressing behaviour rather than attempting to infer the other person's intentions; for example, 'I feel very upset when you tell me I'm crazy, you are trying to hurt me'. Thus the complainant is accusing the recipient of bad intentions, when she has no way of knowing what his or her motives were. The recipient is then obliged to defend his or her intentions and the dispute is diverted into an unproductive area; for example, 'No I wasn't trying to hurt you, I was only joking'. The real issue is the recipient's behavior, which is upsetting to the complainant regardless of the intentions behind it. An exception to this general principle occurs when more accurate alternative beliefs about these intentions are being explored in the context of cognitive restructuring (Chap. 7).

As well as pinpointing the problem it is important for the complainant to express the feelings it evokes in him or her. This avoids the uncertainty involved in the recipient trying to guess how the complainant feels.

Both parties should admit their contributions to the problem. Typically in disputes, each party tries to blame the other. In problem solving, both parties should be prepared to accept some responsibility rather than casting blame entirely on the other person. Almost always some responsibility can be shared for any given problem.

The problem definition phase should be as brief as possible so that the focus can quickly shift towards the future and a resolution of the problem. Getting bogged down in the definition phase involves an unproductive focus on the past and increases the possibility of argument over what happened then. Some common reasons for excessive time being spent on problem definition include: (a) discussing more than one problem at a time. Many people find it difficult to talk about a particular problem in their relationship, which makes the task overwhelming; (b) mentioning as many instances of the problem as can be remembered, and then arguing over the details of each occurrence; (c) analyz- ing the problem in an attempt to discover its cause. The task in problem definition is to define *what* happens not *why* it happens.

Defining a problem along the lines discussed should yield: (a) a description of the behavior that is the subject of the complaint; (b) a specification of the situations in which it occurs; and (c) a statement of its consequences for the complainant who is distressed by it.

Problem Solution

The parties concerned should generate as many possible solutions to the problem as they can think of. No regard should be paid to the quality of the solutions at this stage, indeed some absurd solutions should be encouraged, so that nothing is censored because it seems unacceptable, silly, or unworkable, although it might in fact contain some merit. Each proposed solution should be written down.

The next step is to go through the list of solutions that have been generated and to evaluate each one. Some may be eliminated immediately as ridiculous or absurd. The remaining list of reasonable solutions is discussed at greater length. One important criterion in evaluating solutions is the degree to which they involve some change in behavior by both parties. There are several reasons for this: (a) one party is likely to be more willing to change if the other party is changing also; (b) one party can often help the other to change by providing feedback, encouragement, and assistance; and (c) the behavior of one party may be contributing to the undesirable behavior of the other party, so that both need to change if the problem is to be solved. Another criterion in evaluating a solution is the extent to which it involves compromise between the parties. People in dispute often act as if they want their own ideal solution immediately, or they do not want a solution at all. They also frequently demand major changes that seem so overwhelming to the other person that he or she simply refuses these demands. An alternative is to start with something less than the ideal, but something that seems possible to the other person.

The proposed solution that is selected for implementation is embodied in a final agreement. To avoid future disputes over what was agreed, the terms should be clearly stated and should include a description of the specific changes in behavior to be made by each party, and when these changes are to occur. Such structured agreements may seem mechanical and artificial to the parties, but they are often necessary when fundamental changes in a relationship are being initiated. Later, changes may be made more naturally. It is sometimes useful to record final agreements in writing. This has several advantages: (a) it avoids reliance on memory, which may be selective or distorted in favour of the party concerned; (b) writing agreements makes the parties more precise and tends to eliminate any ambiguities; and (c) the agreement can be posted as a reminder for compliance.

Maintenance and Generalization

The *sine qua non* of successful training in problem solving is the parties' abilities to use the skills independently of the therapist. To the extent that their improved problem solving does not generalize beyond the presence of the therapist then the task has not been completed. This highlights the importance of the parties practicing the skills during the behavior rehearsal stage of training. With feedback, coaching, and modeling, from the therapist the parties actually resolve a problem in a therapeutic session. This experience of mastery probably lays a foundation of confidence in their own abilities to resolve problems after therapy is terminated. It is primarily because of the importance of such mastery experiences that the therapist must not solve the problem for the parties. When a solution is imposed by the therapist, the nature of the treatment becomes essentially crisis intervention, where the therapist expeditiously intervenes to ease current tensions, but the parties are not in any way prepared to handle future problems independently of the therapist. Thus, problem solving is a process approach: clients and partners learn the skills needed to solve their own problems whenever these are encountered in future.

Anger Control

Anger is a particular reaction to stress as this is defined in Chapter 21. It involves physiological components such as muscle tension, rapid respiration, and increased blood pressure. Because of the provocative circumstances in which this heightened state of physiological arousal occurs it is cognitively labeled 'anger', or a similar term such as 'annoyed', 'irritated', or 'enraged'. It is often assumed that anger always leads to aggressive behavior. In fact, while anger does facilitate aggression, such behavior is not an inevitable accompaniment of anger. When anger is accompanied by aggression, this tends to heighten the level of anger. Other behavioral accompaniments of anger include coping responses such as assertiveness, problem solving, or leaving the situation. These alternatives to aggressive behavior tend to lower the level of anger, which has obvious implications for therapy. Thus, to summarize, anger is conceptualized as a reaction to stress that consists of a combination of physiological arousal and cognitive labeling, and it may be accompanied by aggression or other behavioral responses.

The stressful situations that evoke anger reactions are perceived by the individual concerned as frustrations, annoyances, insults, or assaults. It is important to emphasize that it is the perception or appraisal of such events as provocative, rather than the events themselves, that evoke anger. For example, if an injury is believed to be the result of an intentional act by another person, then this act is likely to be perceived as provocative and will evoke anger. In contrast, if the injury is believed to be the result of an accidental act, then the act will probably not be perceived as provocative and anger will not be evoked. It follows that if a person's beliefs about an event are distorted, then anger may be evoked in appropriate circumstances.

The interventions discussed below are not intended to suppress anger, rather their aims are to *prevent* anger from occurring when it is inappropriate, or to enable the client to *regulate* the level of anger when provocation occurs and to *manage* the provocative experience. Some of these interventions are discussed elsewhere in this book. Competence in verbal and non-verbal communication is essential for the control of anger during provocative exchanges: For example: (a) empathic understanding of another person's behavior may reduce the anger it arouses even if the client does not agree with the behavior; (b) requests for changes in another person's behavior are less provocative then demands; (c) appropriate expression of negative feelings reduces hostility; (d) appropriate eye contact, posture, and gestures, together with a modulated tone of voice, are less provocative than staring, a threatening posture or gesture, and a harsh tone. Similarly, effective problem solving can serve to reduce provocative conflicts between people, to regulate the level of anger evoked by such conflicts, and to provide an alternative to aggression as a means of managing conflict situations. Finally, assertiveness training, which provides clients with socially effective alternatives to hostile responses in provocative situations, is discussed in Chapter 19. The remainder of this section is devoted to the application of cognitive restructuring and stress management procedures in the particular task of anger control.

Prevention

One major approach to the prevention of inappropriate anger responses is cognitive restructuring, and its application to problems of anger specifically is reviewed by Burns (1980, pp. 135–177). As stated above, it is the beliefs that a person holds about an event that determine whether it is perceived as provocative. If these beliefs are distorted, then the perception of the event as provocative may be inaccurate and anger will be evoked in inappropriate circumstances. It follows that if distorted beliefs are corrected, then there will be less likelihood of inaccurate perceptions and inappropriate anger. This is the aim of cognitive restructuring.

As a first step, a client's motivation to control anger may be enhanced by asking him or her to list the advantages and disadvantages of anger for himself or herself. Both the short-term and long-term consequences should be included. The expression of anger is often advocated so that it will be 'drained away' or 'purged'. The available evidence supports the contrary view, that such ventilation tends to increase anger and to facilitate aggressive behavior. Consequently, interpersonal conflicts are likely to escalate, often to the disadvantage of the client. Similarly, when clients believe themselves to have been wronged they often feel revengeful and want to retaliate, but again such anger and aggression can escalate conflicts to the detriment of the clients. Adverse consequences of anger and aggression for clients are especially likely if these are inappropriate responses to events that the client incorrectly interprets as being provocative. Even if anger is fully justified it may still be disadvantageous in that the pain and suffering it entails for the client may far exceed the original provocation. There are some circumstances in which anger can be advantageous to the client, and perhaps other people. For instance, he or she may control the level and expression of the anger, and it may be used to motivate the remediation of some wrong or inequity. Thus, a woman's anger at her own abuse may motivate her to initiate or participate in self-help programs for other victimized women. In certain circumstances, therefore, anger can be adaptive and positive in its effects.

If the cost–benefit analysis motivates a client to improve his or her anger control then therapy can move on to the identification of distorted beliefs that may be evoking anger inappropriately and to the exploration of alternatives to these beliefs. The following are some common distortions in thinking that often contribute to inappropriate anger reactions. A person may incorrectly infer the motive for a perceived provocation (jumping to conclusions). For example, the partner of a previously sexually abused woman may attribute her avoidance of intercourse to her lack of love for him, whereas it is really due to an aversive reaction to sex arising from the earlier abuse. The importance of a provocative event may be grossly exaggerated, so that the intensity of the anger it evokes is out of all proportion (magnification). A provocative act may be overgeneralized so that the perpetrator is labeled as a totally negative person (labeling). The focus is on his or her defects (mental filter) and any good points are ignored or discounted (disqualifying the positive). Consequently, anger is evoked by what the person 'is' rather than what he or she 'does'. For example, a previously sexually abused woman may say that her mother is a bad, weak, or inadequate person because she did not protect the client from abuse when she was a child. This disparaging label of the mother may also be overgeneralized to all women. Such labeling is unrealistic because in reality everyone is a mixture of good and bad qualities.

When someone does something that a client percieves as provocative, he or she may believe that the other person 'should' have behaved differently ('should' statement). This may be unrealistic because: (a) other people may not agree with the client's view of how they should behave, there is no unanimously accepted view of what is the right, fair, or just way to act; (b) human beings are not perfect, they do make mistakes or act wrongly; and (c) the client is not 'entitled' to get what he or she wants, no one has an entitlement to instant and complete gratification. When a client is experiencing inappropriate anger as a result of unrealistic 'should' statements it may be helpful for him or her to rewrite his or her personal rules for human relationships. For example, a previously sexually abused woman for whom sex is aversive may believe that her husband should accept a celibate marriage if he loves her as a person and not just as a sex object. It might be more realistic for the woman to rewrite this expectation in terms of the need for mutual communication, negotiation, and compromise in order to cope with and resolve the sexual problem and its implication for the relationship generally.

Regulation and Management

As stated above anger is conceptualized as a particular reaction to stress, accordingly coping skills are used to regulate the level of anger and to manage provocative experiences. First, clients are given a rationale for the coping skills approach to anger which includes: (a) the physiological and cognitive components of anger, together with its behavioral accompaniments; (b) the determinants of their anger, including their cognitions; (c) the discrimination between adaptive and maladaptive anger; and (d) the coping skills they can use to handle provocative experiences that are mentioned below and discussed more extensively in Chapter 23.

People who have anger problems are usually quick to respond to provocative events. They need to be taught to pause between impulse and action. During this pause they should think of alternative interpretations of the perceived provocation and the likely consequences of any behavior they may engage in. These tasks during the delay are more constructive than simply counting to 10 which may only postpone an outburst. Thus, anger becomes a cue for a task-oriented response set that prevents the escalation of arousal and lowers the likelihood of aggressive reactions.

During or soon after an impulse delay clients may also usefully commence breath control or muscle relaxation. These procedures can reduce physiological arousal, and provide a sense of mastery and self-control so that the client is more confident of being able to cope with the provocation which is correspondingly less stressful.

Thought and image-stopping procedures can be used to control any thoughts or images of provocative or violent events that are triggering, enhancing, or maintaining a client's anger and aggression.

Drawing upon the skills of impulse delay, relaxation, and thought and image stopping that have been taught to the client, he or she works out with the therapist a coping plan for the client to use in provocative situations as exemplified in Table 13.1.

Some common coping statements for guided self-dialogue in preparing for, confronting, coping with, and reflecting on provocative situations are listed in Table 13.2.

For imagery rehearsal purposes the therapist constructs with the client a hierarchy of provocative situations that he or she is likely to encounter. The client is then relaxed, asked to imagine himself or herself applying the newly

Table 13.1. *Specimen Coping Plan for Provocative Situations*

If you believe that you are being frustrated, annoyed, insulted, or attacked, and begin to feel angry:

1. Don't respond immediately.
2. Take several short deep breaths to fill your chest and relax as you breathe out.
3. Think of other possible explanations for what is making you angry.
4. Think of the consequences of reacting in different ways.
5. Start to respond in some way that will control your anger and is an alternative to aggression.

Table 13.2. *Common Coping Statements For Provocative Situations*

Preparing for a provocation
 This could be a rough situation, but I know how to deal with it.
 I have worked out a plan to handle this. Easy does it.
 Remember, stick to the issues and don't take it personally.
 There won't be any need for an argument. I know what to do.

Contronting a provocation
 As long as I keep my cool, *I'm* in control of the situation.
 You don't need to prove yourself. Don't make more out of this than you have to.
 There is no point in getting mad. Think of what you have to do.
 Look for positives and don't jump to conclusions.

Coping with arousal
 My muscles are getting tight. Relax and slow things down.
 Time to take a deep breath. Let's take the issue point by point.
 My anger is a signal of what I need to do. Time for problem solving.
 He probably wants me to get angry, but I'm going to deal with it constructively.

Subsequent reflection
 Conflict unresolved
 Forget about the aggravation. Thinking about it only makes you upset.
 Remember relaxation. It's a lot better than anger.
 Don't take it personally. It's probably not so serious.

 Conflict resolved
 I handled that one pretty well. That's doing a good job.
 I could have been more upset than it was worth.
 My pride can get me into trouble, but I'm doing better at this all the time.
 I actually got through that without getting angry.

Note Adapted by permission from R.W. Novaco (1979). The cognitive regulation of anger and stress, in P.C. Kendall & S.D. Hollon (Eds.) *Cognitive-Behavioural Interventions: Theory, research, and procedure* (p. 269), Academic Press, New York. Copyright 1979 by Academic Press.

learned skills to cope with the least provocative situation. This procedure is applied progressively to each item in the hierarchy.

It may be feasible to practice the application of coping skills to a hierarchy of provocative situations in role plays with the therapist or others in therapeutic sessions. This procedure may be employed either after some prior preparation through imagery rehearsal, or without this when it seems that the client can proceed directly to role plays.

Similarly, either with or without prior preparation through imagery rehearsal and/or role plays, a client may undertake a graded series of assignments in real life in which he or she confronts and copes with a hierarchy of provocative situations.

As in the case of other situations, those of a provocative nature that are likely to arise after therapy has ended should be specifically guarded against by warning the client of their probable occurrence and ensuring that he or she is equipped to respond with appropriate coping skills.

Conclusion

Although the prevention of anger and its regulation and management are discussed in that order in this section, in practice the first intervention is often training in the coping skills used to regulate the level of anger and to manage the provocative situation. The reason for this is that it usualy takes time to prevent anger by cognitively restructuring the distorted beliefs that contribute to it, consequently clients are provided initially with skills that they can use to cope directly with immediate provocative situations.

The interpersonal problems and assessment, evaluation, and treatment procedures discussed so far in this part of the book are applied and illustrated in the following five chapters devoted respectively to relations between victims and men, partners, women, offspring, and families of origins.

CHAPTER 14

Relations With Men

In this chapter the relations or previously sexually abused women with men generally are considered, while their relations with partners and father figures specifically are discussed in Chapters 15 and 18 respectively. At initial assessment, 90% of the women in the U. of M. series reported at least one of the problems with men that are reviewed below (Table 11.1).

Insecurity

Sixty-eight percent of these women reported that they feared men (Table 11.1) and this problem was significantly more common among the abused compared to the non-abused women (47% v. 15%) in Briere's (1984) series of women seeking counseling. On the Belief Inventory, 'No man can be trusted' was endorsed as partly, mostly, or absolutely true by 90% of the U. of M. series (Table 5.1), and 45% of the women reported that they avoided long-term relationships with men (Table 11.1). One reason for such avoidance may be that the more intimate a relationship becomes the more likely it seems to the victim that it will recapitulate the earlier traumatic experiences with an offender who was emotionally close to her. Thus, fear, mistrust, and the avoidance of long-term commitments appear to characterize the relations of many victims with men. These problems are exemplified in the following case illustrations.

Ruth

At the termination of her treatment this victim described one aspect of her problems and progress as follows:

> I lived in constant fear of men. I was afraid to walk to a bus stop alone during the day. I lived a very confined life and only went places when I was with my husband or in a car. There was a time where I didn't even want to go in the car alone. I was afraid to even be at home alone

126

thinking that someone would break in and rape and kill me. The doors would always be locked . . . this therapy has worked very well for me . . . My fears have decreased. I don't dwell so much on not being able to trust men. I know that *some* men can't be trusted in some situations. But I also know that some men can be trusted.

Alison

With her male therapist in the U. of M. program this victim experienced certain thoughts during relaxation training that were cognitively restructured as shown in Table 14.1.

The victim was referred to the program by a male psychologist with whom she has been in individual therapy for about one year. This therapy did not address her sexual abuse. In the early stages of her current therapy the victim regularly met with her previous male therapist for a short coffee break once a week. This arrangement was made with the agreement of the current therapist to avoid a sudden withdrawal of the previous therapist's support to the client and to extend the victim's contact with this older man which appeared to be a corrective relationship for her. This contact gave rise to a number of distorted thoughts that were cognitively restructured as shown in Table 14.2. The victim also wrote the following:

[My previous male therapist's] physique brought a rush of feelings in regards to my avoidance of men in that I had to face the issue if I was going to receive the therapy I sought. His coloring, his posture, his mannerisms in so many ways were similar to [the offender's] though even yet I am not sure how much of what I saw in him was really there. The whole experience was very anxiety producing, though probably very therapeutic; marked by approach/avoidance responses throughout. The whole experience became an intellectual exercise of my mind challenging my feelings, somewhat aided by other students' evaluations that this was a man who was sincere and genuine and could be trusted.

Another way in which the victim's mistrust of men was addressed was by cognitively restructuring the Belief Inventory item 'No man can be trusted' as shown in Table 14.3. Additionally, it is likely that her contact with her previous and current therapists who were both older men also contributed to the mitigation of her mistrust. Further specific therapeutic attention to this problem was not necessary and the victim commented that she recognizes its origin in her victimization and realizes that many men can be trusted. Any that are untrustworthy she can now cope with, whereas this was not feasible when she was a little girl. It is preferable to trust men, until they prove untrustworthy, otherwise she may miss out on helpful and rewarding relationships.

Table 14.1. *Cognitive Restructuring of Beliefs Concerning Current (Male) Therapist:*
Alison

Distorted beliefs	Alternative beliefs
During relaxation training I cannot trust the therapist (a) not to be sexual with me (b) not to have sexual thoughts about me (1. jumping to conclusions, 2. overgeneralization).	1. The therapist has not said or done anything that might indicate that he is interested in me sexually. 2. Not every man will take advantage of me sexually, as happened in the past.
The therapist will be insulted if he knows I don't trust him (jumping to conclusions).	The therapist will not be surprised that I am hesitant to trust him completely because he knows that my trust was abused in the past.

Table 14.2. *Cognitive Restructuring of Beliefs Concerning Previous (Male) Therapist:*
Alison

Distorted beliefs	Alternative beliefs
Previous therapist doesn't really care about me (jumping to conclusions, disqualifying the positive).	He has shown his willingness to keep in touch with me when he didn't need to do so.
Like all men my previous therapist will expect something in return for anything he does for me (1. overgeneralization, 2. jumping to conclusions, 3. disqualifying the positive.	1. There are men who can care for me without exploiting me as my uncle [offender] did. 2. He hasn't done or said anything to indicate that he expects something in return. 3. He really is concerned about me without any payback.
Previous therapist and other men who know about my past will think that I am trying to seduce them (Jumping to conclusions).	I have not done or said anything of a seductive nature and previous therapist has not shown any sign that he regards me as seductive.
Previous therapist might be afraid of me and can't like me because he knows about my past (Jumping to conclusions, disqualifying the positive).	He saw me for a year during therapy. He voluntarily continued to see me after I stopped having therapy with him. He has never done or said anything to indicate that he was afraid of me, or that he didn't like me.
If previous therapist knew that I still cannot trust him completely after all this time in therapy he would say that our relationship is getting nowhere and terminate it (Jumping to conclusions).	He would not be surprised that I cannot trust him completely after all those years of having my trust abused as I grew up. He would understand why I find it difficult to trust any older man.

Table 14.3. *Cognitive Restructuring of Belief Concerning Mistrust of Men: Alison*

Distorted belief	Alternative beliefs
No man can be trusted (jumping to conclusions, overgeneralization).	I tend to feel that when I am alone with a man he automatically sees me as a sexual object and should I let my defences down it will be proven that I truly am at his disposal. The older or more authoritarian the man, the less control I feel. I realize this feeling developed when I was younger and there was enough evidence to teach me that this was the way it was with men. I now realize this is not necessarily so with all men. It is me who has the 'screwy' thoughts, not the man.
	Just because some men can't be trusted I assume all men can't be trusted.
	I certainly don't believe the converse to be true so the truth must lie somewhere in between. The point seems to be that a woman invariably controls her environment, and if she finds that a particular man can't be trusted she can deal with it at that point, that it's no big deal and that she need not be coerced into a situation in which she does not feel comfortable. So rather than no man can be trusted, a truer statement would be some men can be trusted — the trick is finding which ones.
	Perhaps it is time to risk checking this out in the present, but I find that I feel sufficiently awkward around men that I really don't know how to act or what to say, because I never really know what they're thinking or how they're perceiving me.

Subordination

Many victims tend to subordinate themselves to men whom they idealize inappropriately and value excessively. Thus, at initial assessment, 51% of victims reported that they overvalued men (Table 11.1). The low self-esteem of victims obviously contributes to their subordination of themselves to men, but such overdependence on 'strong' males may also represent an attempt to redress the lack of protection and nurturance that victims have often experienced in childhood. The issue of subordination to men is exemplified in the following case illustration.

Demographic Characteristics

Dawn (35) was referred to the program by a psychologist who had been treating the client, her partner (intermittently), and their child. The client had been involved with her partner (44) for 9 years and they had had one child (7) together. The client had been married prior to her current relationship. Her partner, Jim, had been married for 24 years, had two children by this union, and lived with his legal wife.

Dawn had completed all of her high school education, and Jim most of it. Both were employed in white collar positions. They are Caucasian and adhere to no particular religion.

Family of Origin

The client's natural father died when she was two years of age. She has vague recollections of the man and believes that she witnessed his accidental death in the parental home. She has strong feelings of abandonment associated with his death; feelings that she has never been able to express to anyone.

Dawn's mother remarried when the client was seven years old. The client's step-father exhibited multiple behavioral problems. He was an alcoholic (reformed six years ago) who physically abused his wife, verbally abused the children, and specifically sexually abused the client. He has limited social and communication skills, has few friends, has been promiscuous and has complained about his marital sexual relationship. He is poorly educated, has had a poor employment history, a criminal history (crimes against property and drunken driving) and has poor health.

The client's mother is a woman dominated by her husband, who is isolated socially, drinks alcohol excessively, and is physically abusive towards her spouse. She has been physically and sexually abused by her husband. This woman was sexually promiscuous, and his discontinued the sexual relationship with her husband for many years. The client views her mother as an ineffective, non-nurturing parent who is poorly educated, depressed, and very lonely.

Victimization Experience

The client was victimized by her step-father between the ages of 13 and 16 over 100 times, and at the age of 8 on one occasion by a friend of her step-father.

Dawn's victimization involved manual stimulation of her genitals and numerous occasions when she witnessed explicit sexual activity between various family members and their parents.

The client complied with the sexual advances made to her because she had been taught to listen to her male elders without question, and it was one of the few times when any attention or affection was directed her way. As for the sexual activity she witnessed, it was so all pervasive (she can remeber seeing such activity at least from the ages of 4 through 15) that she thought that it was part of most familial life.

The client felt fear, physical pain, helplessness, shame, disgust, guilt, dissociation, and some emotional pleasure from her sexual abuse. Her pleasure derived from the attention that was paid to a very lonely child by a group of human beings (men) whom she had been taught to consider her superiors.

The client attempted to tell numerous people about her abuse. As a child, she tried to tell her mother about her step-father's friend abusing her. Her mother sent the crying child to bed without any response. Her mother also had personally witnessed her child being abused by her husband; but, just like the sexual activity she viewed between adult females and her husband, between their adult friends, the children, and her own personal involvement in exhibitionistic sexual activity, she did nothing to stop it. As Dawn grew older she saw no point in telling any non-familial adult about her sexual abuse because her whole family had laid the precedent that disclosure brought no response.

As an adult, Dawn had been a rape victim on numerous occasions, had been involved in the sexual victimization of her child and had been made to perform deviant sexual practices by her partner. On entry to the U. of M. program she was embroiled in a court case whereby she and her partner were accused of sexually abusing their child. They were subsequently found guilty and sentenced to jail terms.

Relations With Men

This victim's relationships with men had always been characterized by an attitude of servility. She had been raised to believe that women should defer to a man's will in all things. Dawn's belief in a total subservience to men had led her to consider herself a second class citizen. She did not question a male's opinions, even when she considered them grossly inaccurate. It was inconceivable to her that she had a right to oppose their opinions or that she could express displeasure at demeaning and/or degrading requests or remarks. Dawn invariably would find fault in her own thinking before she questioned that of a man's. She believed that she could not control a situation in which a male played a prominent role, and she held a paradoxical belief that women were responsible for men's actions but that women had no control over those actions. An example of this double-edged belief was 'I had to give my ex-husband my paycheck, and if he overspent and we didn't have any money then it was my fault'.

Thus, Dawn believed that she was subordinate to men, and this belief, nurtured in her family of origin and exacerbated by her own sexual abuse, had far reaching implications for her adult relationships with males. It caused Dawn to defer to men at work even though her opinion and/or performance was more satisfactory than theirs, to allow service personnel to treat her uncivilly, to allow male family members to mistreat her any way they pleased because she felt that she had 'to take it' because she 'couldn't be rude', and to defer her own opinions and desires with male partners to the point of participating in deviant

Table 14.4.   *Cognitive Restructuring of Beliefs Concerning Male/Female Responsibilities:*
Dawn

Distorted beliefs	Alternative beliefs
Men are not responsible for anything, women are.	In an adult relationship, I can be only 50% responsible for what goes on.
I am responsible to set sexual limits.	All my life I was told that the woman had to please a man in bed, that it was her job. I was also told that I was a slut for having sex with a married man. No matter what I did, I was wrong. Well, my error was trying to please too much.
	The limits in sex are not just my responsibility. If that were true then I'd also be in control, and I'm not in control of Jim (partner). He's always been in control of himself and of me. Or at least I thought he was. Also, if I can't control him, I'm not responsible for him. If I can't control his sexual urges, then I can't set all the limits. He's at least 50% responsible for those urges.
I am responsible for not managing the money I gave to my ex-husband.	I was told by my ex-husband to give my paycheck to him. He gave me an allowance. I had no access to the rest of the money I could not control the budget because I had no way of getting to the money. My husband was responsible for his own spending.
I was responsible for my former partner molesting our daughter.	I was only 50% responsible for the molestation of our daughter. I was unable to protect her; but, I did not initiate the action, Jim (partner) did. I feel badly about the effects this abuse has had and might have on my little girl; but, as bad as I feel, I did not abuse her myself — but neither did I have the emotional strength to stand up to Jim at that time to stop him. I do now, and would stop him if he ever tried it again.

sexual activity and the sexual abuse of her daughter with her former partner (Jim).

Upon cognitively restructuring the distorted beliefs that had allowed Dawn to maintain a subordinate role for herself as exemplified in Table 14.4 her attitude and behavior towards herself and others greatly changed. For example, Dawn began to voice her opinions more openly at work and actually opposed a male with a differing opinion. She acted more assertively in social situations; for example, at a dance she refused to buy a man's drink where formerly she would have meekly done so. She completely terminated contact with her former partner and set effective limits with her family of origin. For example, upon learning that her parents were continuing to allow her former partner to visit them, Dawn curtailed all contact with her parents in their home. This she did to protect her daughter from possible running into her father unexpectedly at her grandparents and to voice her disapproval that they would remain friends with their granddaughter's victimizer. Dawn now possessed a firm belief that her opinions, morals and principles are accurate and sound, and that it is acceptable to listen to these internal indicators ahead of a man's. The final say can and does come from Dawn.

Promiscuity and Oversexualization

Several writers have noted the associated problems of promiscuity and over-sexualized relationships among victims (e.g. deYoung, 1982; Gordy, 1983; Herman, 1981; Meiselman, 1978). In this context the term 'promiscuity' is used to refer to a series of transient, casual, and superficial relationships that the victim seems to pursue compulsively and from a sense of obligation rather than desire. Many victims appear to have a promiscuous stage at some time in their lives and 60% of those in the U. of M. series reported having been promiscuous in the past, although this continued to the time of initial assessment for only 17% of these victims. Fromuth (1986) has added a note of caution to findings such as these. In her college student sample she found that previously sexually abused women were more likely to describe themselves as promiscuous than non-abused women, although the two groups did not differ in the actual number of sexual partners. Thus, the reported promiscuity of victims may to some extent reflect their negative self-labeling rather than their actual behavior.

Oversexualization implies that a relationship must include a sexual component however inappropriate it may be, or that it is perceived to have such a component when none exists. For example, a victim said that she is not comfortable in her relationships with men in case the man sees her as 'easy'. She *knows* that relationships need not be sexual but *feels* that they might be. She recognizes that she is overgeneralizing from her experience with the offender and this adverse experience has not been corrected because she has avoided subsequent exposure to men, especially older men. Another aspect of this oversexualization is that the victim believes that men may think that she is trying to seduce them. She recognizes that there is no real basis for this and is now checking her automatic thoughts. They may originate from her father's reactions, such as calling her a 'floozie', whenever she wore makeup or showed any interest in boys. Additional examples of oversexualization are shown in Tables 14.1, 14.2, 14.3, and 14.4.

Among the U. of M. victims 51% reported that they had oversexualized their relationships with men in the past, while only 29% were doing so at initial assessment. On the Belief Inventory the following items were endorsed as partly, mostly, or absolutely true by the proportions of victims shown: (a) 'No man could care for me without a sexual relationship' by 86%; (b) 'I've already been used so it doesn't matter if other men use me' by 54%; and (c) 'I don't have the right to deny my body to any man who demands it' by 48% (Table 5.1).

There are several possible reasons for this oversexualization of relationships. The victims may not be able to distinguish sex and affection because of the confusion of parental love and sexuality in childhood (Meiselman, 1978). They may have learned to use sex as an effective means of getting rewards (Herman, 1981), and some may have a compulsive need for sex as proof of being loved and of being an adequate woman (Courtois, 1979). Whatever the reason, the result is often a constant series of brief, unsatisfying, hurtful, and damaging relationships, which only serve to increase the victim's distrust and resentment of men.

Rape

In the U. of M. series 41% of the women had been raped in addition to their sexual abuse in childhood. An increased-vulnerability to rape among previously sexually abused women is reported by several investigators. For example, in her random sample drawn from the San Francisco population, Russell (1986) found that 65% of women who experienced serious incestuous abuse prior to age 14, and 61% of women who had suffered severe extrafamilial sexual abuse before that age, were revictimized by rape or attempted rape after that age. The corresponding proportion for women who were never sexually abused before age 14 was 35%. Similarly, in her college student sample, Fromuth (1986) found a significant positive correlation between having been sexually abused before age 13 and having non-consensual sexual experiences involving force or threat after age 12 years.

The increased risk of rape for child sexual abuse victims may be due to the danger of being on the streets after running away from the abuse situation (McCormack, Janus, & Burgess, 1986), and/or to low self-esteem and unassertiveness which renders them vulnerable to sexual exploitation by predatory males.

Prostitution

In the U. of M. series, 15% of the women had engaged in prostitution in the past and 1% was still doing so at initial assessment. Other investigators have reported high rates of sexual abuse among prostitutes (James & Meyerding, 1977; Silbert, 1984; Vitaliano, James, & Boyer, 1981). For example, among 200 street prostitutes there were 60% who had been sexually abused prior to age 16 by an average of two offenders each over an average period of 20 months. The mean age at commencement of the abuse was 10 years; for 67% of victims the offender was a father figure, and in 82% of cases some sort of force was used. Seventy percent of women reported that the sexual exploitation affected their entry into prostitution (Silbert & Pines, 1981, 1983).

It is possible that sexual abuse lessens a victim's resistance to viewing herself as a saleable commodity. For example, the prostitutes interviewed in the Silbert and Pines study made remarks such as 'My brother could do it; why not everybody else? Might as well make them pay for it.' and 'My father bought me, so who cares who else does' (1981, p. 410). Herman (1981, p. 4) makes a similar point when she writes 'The father, in effect, forces the daughter to pay with her body for affection and care which should be freely given. In so doing, he . . . initiates his daughter into prostitution.'

In addition, the factors of running away, low self-esteem, and unassertiveness, that were mentioned above as possible facilitators of rape, may also contribute to the involvement of victims in prostitution.

Anger

Finally, some previously sexually abused women feel angry and hostile towards men generally. The proportion of such women in the U. of M. series was 54% (Table 11.1).

Conclusion

In summary, the relations of many victims with men generally appear to be characterized by the features of: (a) fear; (b) mistrust; (c) avoidance of long-term commitment; (d) subordination of the victim; (e) promiscuity and oversexualization; and (f) anger and hostility. Additionally, it appears that child sexual abuse increases the risks of rape and involvement in prostitution.

CHAPTER 15

Relations With Partners

The relationships of many previously sexually abused women with their partner tend to be characterized by discord, often arising from the exploitation of the victim by the partner, the overdependence of the partner on the victim, and the dissatisfaction and distress of the partner concerning certain aspects of the relationship.

Discord

Discord is a major and pervasive feature of the relationships between many victims and partners. At the initial assessment of the 24 victims in the U. of M. series who were married or living as married, all of them were experiencing discord in these relationships, 91% were oppressed by the partner, and 33% were physically abused by him (Table 11.1). Furthermore, among the 19 of these 24 victims who did not terminate therapy prematurely, there were 5 (26%) whose marital relationships had broken up during or after treatment. In each case the therapist considered this to be advantageous to the victim because of the oppression and exploitation she had been experiencing from her partner (e.g. Sharon and Dick below).

Such problems have been reported by other investigators. For example, Briere (1984) found that among women seeking counseling, 49% of those who had been sexually abused complained of battering by a partner compared to 18% of those who had not been sexually abused. Similarly, in Russell's (1986) random sample of San Francisco women, 27% of the victims intrafamilial sexual abuse had suffered physical violence from a husband compared to 12% of non-victims. Moreover, Russell found a significant positive correlation between the reported degree of trauma associated with the abuse and later separation or divorce. These marital disruptions occurred in 37% of those who were extremely traumatized, 31% of those who were considerably trauma-tized, 22% of those who reported some trauma, and 7% of those who reported no trauma.

Many victims seem to have a tendency to establish relationships with apparently unsuitable partners who often misuse the women, and in some cases such ill-matched and punishing relationships are repeated in the lives of the victims. For example, on the basis of their experience in running therapy groups for women who were sexually molested as children, Tsai and Wagner (1978) noted the seeming compulsion of some of these victims to get involved with unworthy men, who not infrequently resemble the molester.

Exploitive Partners

Some partners show a complete lack of respect for the victim and will dominate and exploit her, sometimes to the extent of physical abuse. The reactions of some victims to such exploitation has been described by their therapists as 'masochistic', in that 'their willingness to tolerate mistreatment allowed them to endure relationships that a more mature, assertive woman would have ended or never begun at all. In most of these cases, there were no definite indications that the woman gained pleasure from the abuse itself, but the therapist used the term "masochistic" to describe the patient's inability to avoid or terminate such relationships. Informally, therapists used such terms as "doormat", "punching bag", and "dish rag" to describe the passive, depending woman who would suffer almost anything to be attached to a man' (Meiselman, 1978, p. 215).

This leads to the question of why victims tend to get involved and to remain in relationships with exploitive partners. One reason may be that the victim's self-esteem is often so low that she selects and retains such partners because they do not embody high standards which she feels she could not live up to. There is some support for this point in our finding that 58% of victims endorsed as partly, mostly, or absolutely true the Belief Inventory item 'Only bad, worthless guys would be interested in me' (Table 5.1). Other possible reasons are that the victim may never have learned the skills required to protect herself and assert her rights in a relationship, and she may have acquired only very limited or inaccurate expectations of what she might reasonably demand from a partner. Any such deficiencies in skills or expectations could stem from the victim's modeling of her mother's passivity and misuse with a dominant father-figure, a situation that is typical of the families of origin of many victims (Chap. 3). Finally, Herman (1981) has suggested that some victims feel obliged to their partner for marrying them at all knowing that they had already been used by the offender, and that furthermore this knowledge gave the partner power to put down and shame the victim.

Overdependent Partners

The overdependence of the partner on the victim is another common source of discord in such relationships. Gelinas (1983) ascribes these problems in part to the extension into adulthood of the parentification of the victim in childhood (Chap. 3). As an adult she continues to be a caring person who is ever ready to meet the demands of others regardless of her own needs and preferences. Consequently, there tends to be a mutual attraction between parentified victims and men who are immature and overdependent. Their relationships may be satisfactory until they have children who require the victim's care so that the attention she is able to give to her husband is reduced. At the same time she may be seeking help and support from him in respect of her increased child care and domestic tasks. These increased demands and reduced attention may evoke feelings of anger and abandonment in an overdependent man, and the victim may be feeling exhausted and resentful, consequently their relationship becomes markedly discordant.

Partners' Dissatisfaction and Distress

Discord in marital relationships may arise also from the dissatisfaction and distress being experienced by the partners as well as the victims. For example, in the account of the situation/transition group for partners that is described below it is reported that they tend to complain of feelings of deprivation, confusion and loss of control in their marital relationships, including the sexual and communication aspects of these relationships.

Before this report two case studies are presented to illustrate the relationship problems experienced by some victims and partners and the interventions that were implemented with the aim of resolving these problems.

Case Study: Alison and Michael

Alison (31) and Michael (36) had been married for nine years and had two children aged 5 and 3 years (see case study in Chap. 10). For the first 21 weeks the focus of treatment was on the victim's mood disturbances (see Chap. 10). The major focus then shifted to their marital relationship in weeks 22 to 44, after which it shifted again to their sexual relationship (see Chap. 23). During this last period, however, it became evident that problems in the non-sexual aspects of their relationship were impeding the treatment of sexual dysfunction, therefore a second phase of marital therapy was implemented. The main areas of difficulty in the relationship between Alison and Michael are outlined next.

Commitment to the Marriage

When Alison first sought therapy with the psychologist who subsequently referred her to the U. of M. program her main presenting complaint was a wish to separate from her husband. When she entered the program her major point of identification and reference group was her family of origin. They were the primary influence and top priority for her—she was more concerned to be a compliant, dutiful, approved of daughter than an adequate wife (see Chap. 18). These priorities began to be reversed, and this shift of priorities pushed Alison to work things out in her marriage. She no longer felt that it was doomed to failure and was committed to making it work. Michael was also strongly committed to the marriage, but he had some doubts about its long-term viability if the victim's problems were not significantly improved over the next decade. He was experiencing some ambivalence because something strange had happened during therapy. He liked Alison becoming more independent and assertive, but was confused about their relationship and whether her problems would ever be resolved. He had never realized the impact of her childhood experiences and felt overwhelmed.

The issue of commitment to the marriage was a constant theme in therapy. Early on, the victim concluded that she wanted to stay in the marriage and to resolve their problems. The partner repeatedly expressed uncertainty and fear about the outcome of treatment and the future of the marriage. If there was not a successful outcome and resolution of their problems then he envisaged them living as friends rather than spouses until the children grew up and then probably separating. To prepare himself for this outcome he was to some extent distancing himself and withdrawing from the victim. Her reactions to this and related issues are described in her notes as follows:

> I'm really questioning whether [Michael] and I love each other or whether we're not trying to hang in there as more of an intellectual exercise. Looking at the facts and all that [Michael] represents, I easily can say I'd be a fool not to love him but the truth is that any feeling I believe love should evoke eludes me. I'm preoccupied with feelings of what I would imagine life on my own would provide yet at the same time am overwhelmed by fear of the reality of the issues that that situation would entail. I depend on [Michael], I don't know that I love him. All I know is that at one point in my life I loved him and cared for him very very deeply. Now I am only overwhelmed with guilt at what I am doing to him, to us, and to my family. I know I manipulated [Michael] into marrying me because I couldn't bear the possibility of being rejected by him. Now I fear I'm paying the penance of that manipulation which is manifesting itself as a sexual aversion. We are at such odds and I don't know whether it's sexual aversion related to the abuse or sexual aversion because I doubt my love for [Michael].

As therapy progressed the couple were dealing with their relationship by giving each other room for individual growth, with less dependency on each other, and as friends rather than spouses. This situation is described by the victim as follows:

> [Michael] and I are both very worn, which in some ways concerns me because I feel our resistance and immunity to each other is down at a time when I feel our hardest work, our work together, is just to begin. But contradicting these feelings of fear and over-sensitivity to each other is a sense of personal strength and determination for each of us to survive and grow as individuals. I don't think either of us has any illusions as to what the relationship means to us and why we are still in it.
>
> We both know what the relationship means to us, why we want it to be continued, what our limits as individuals are and what we feel our potential for growth as a couple is. We have a long-lasting friendship and neither wants to tread on the other's potential, but we also have a sense that our individual growth is most likely to be achieved within the relationship. In other words we need each other but what has been stripped away is the dependency factor in the relationship. Each of us knows we can survive outside the relationship, what we want is to learn how to survive within it. Neither of us has had strong role models for the development of husband–wife or parenting skills but what we do have is a sense of what it is to be a friend and some education and common sense to help us with parenting.
>
> So for the time being we'll think of ourselves as being friends trying to help each other with a problem and see what develops. I think we have a common goal of wanting to see ourselves blend and develop into a fuller relationship of being husband and wife but for the time being thinking of ourselves in that context seems to create problems.

During the second phase of marital therapy the couple's commitment to their marriage was stronger and provided a sound basis for collaboration in communication training and problem solving. At that time the victim summarized the remaining problems in the marriage and her current attitude towards it in the following notes:

> I feel the marriage is salvageable—can be worked on. According to my perception our two main problem areas are communication and problem solving. Improvements in these two areas would yield vast improvements in the marriage. I feel we are compatible but a lot of respect between us is gone and needs to be restored . . .
>
> Right now it seems easier to find fault with the marriage and identifying strengths seems difficult. I think [Michael] and I are both hurting—possibly from misunderstandings and a very negative way of

communicating with each other and I think these hurts are interfering with our ability to get close.

When we do discuss issues we can usually arrive at a mutually satisfying resolution. Problem solving together does give us a sense of working together and compromising for a common purpose. We both have a commitment to the children and have a strong desire to work out our personal problems so that we can provide a healthier emotional environment for them to grow up in. Separation and divorce would have a very negative effect on all concerned and I feel the negative consequences of separating would be far greater than any benefits. Really, I am the only person who would gain in any way from separation and that gain would be minimal given that [Michael] and I can resolve our problem.

The partner summarized the situation from his point of view as follows:

I would probably feel somewhat better if I felt that my efforts in a general sense were, or appeared to be a little more appreciated than what I think they have been for quite some time. There has been, and still is, a danger of my becoming discouraged should my role be one of bill payer and fixer of broken items, etc., etc. I do believe that I have gone out of my way on many, many occasions to make circumstances easier, and more pleasant for my spouse. At one time I felt that it was recognized as such. However, I do not have the same sense of appreciation. . . . I consider that I am pretty easy to get along with and am not a demanding individual. Naturally, I have deep regrets that the sexual abuse took place and has resulted in our damaged sexual relationship. I most certainly want her to change that immediately if it could be so willed. But I do accept that it cannot be willed. Therefore I must patiently wait for the final outcome of therapy. I would, of course, be a little more satisfied if my spouse could more fully appreciate what it might be like for the husband who has had to adjust to the altered conditions and expectations of the relationship. I do believe that much of the concern, empathy, and understanding has been quite one-sided. However, it has been a long time and I feel I can deal with these concerns should they remain unchanged.

The main objective is to restore and maintain the marriage on a solid, healthy track. I do not believe that there are too many areas that are in great need of overhaul. It is my belief that there are more positives than negatives to carrying on with the relationship. I am not comfortable with the concepts of separation and divorce. I believe myself to be a pretty decent husband and I believe the equal of my wife. I think it would be a tragedy not to resolve this road block, particularly when I believe that much of the problem and damage was not created by either myself or my wife. I would not wish to dissolve the relationship because of the evils of an old dead uncle [offender].

Roles in Marriage

As therapy progressed, Alison was very concerned that she should have the rights to be herself, to express herself, and to set limits (e.g. on unwanted sexual approaches from partner) without being labeled a victim or abnormal. Her mood state, self-esteem, and assertiveness had increased markedly, and she wanted to move from a fairly traditional role in the marriage to a more equal relationship with greater sharing of responsibilities.

These personal developments in the victim and the consequent need to make changes in the marriage relationship were difficult for the partner to accept and he was resentful and defensive towards any need for him to change. For example, he said 'I now have a different person in my marriage—more liberated—that's fine, but I have to adjust to it—the new you, doing your own thing is fine for you but not for me, I have to deal with it'. The partner was very concerned about having to change himself, he saw this as something his wife should do because she is the one with the problems. He wanted to remain as he is and any suggestion that he need change was perceived as a threat and criticism that made him feel as if he had failed and was responsible for their problem. He emphasized that he had been a consistently good husband, a good provider, and not alcoholic or abusive like many men, therefore it is the victim who needs to adjust to him rather than both of them needing to make changes. In summary, the partner was experiencing considerable distress arising *inter alia* from: (a) the victim stating that she no longer felt totally dependent on him (although she *wanted* to remain with him); (b) the need for him to change if he wanted to preserve the marriage; and (c) his perception that this implied that he was an inadequate husband and in some way to blame for the current problems.

With a view to alleviating this distress the therapist suggested that the partner might have a few individual treatment sessions focussed directly on his concerns and that as this therapist was identified as being concerned primarily with the victim's problems it might be wise for the partner to see another therapist for individual sessions while still continuing to attend couple therapy with the original therapist. Initially, the partner was very resistant and defensive towards this suggestion. He strongly denied that he had any difficulties for which he might benefit from entering the client role himself rather than attending joint sessions 'to help his wife's therapy'. Subsequently, largely due to his wife's encouragement, the partner did agree to enter individual therapy with the female co-therapist from the partners' group he had attended previously (see below) and both he and his wife reported that he found these sessions extremely helpful.

Mutual Understanding and Acceptance

Examples of difficulties in this area include:

(a) The partner's belief that the victim should be able to dispel her problems by an act of will, to forget them, and to get on with her life.

(b) The partner did not really listen to, empathize with and validate the victim's problems and feelings. In particular, he did not accept her thoughts and feelings as valid even if he does not agree with them—instead of accepting their genuineness from her point of view and negotiating any differences between them the partner just put her down.

(c) The victim and partner guessed at the intentions behind the other's behavior. For example, the victim alleged that her partner 'makes nasty remarks because he wants to hurt me', and he said 'if she doesn't have sex with me, it is because she doesn't love me'. Similarly, when Alison is upset Michael wants to hold and kiss her. At these times she does not want this and pushes him away which he perceives as a sign that she does not love him.

(d) The victim complained that her partner continued to touch her in ways that she does not like, and that he did not accept her attempts to set limits, for example, she has tried to stop his unacceptable remarks and touching for three years without success.

(e) The partner responded that the victim is not explicit enough in expressing herself, that she only reveals her real views and feelings in treatment sessions when she will not lie to the therapist, and that she misperceives the partner's remarks as intended to hurt when they are really only teasing.

With the aim of alleviating such problems the couple received systematic training in communication and problem solving, on which they worked assiduously and with some success as reported below.

Expressing Hurt and Anger

The victim had difficulty in expressing such feelings to her partner, and when she did so it tended to be in an aggressive rather than an assertive manner. These feelings are especially likely to be triggered off by hurtful remarks from her partner—sometimes flippant, sometimes not—which indicate an inability to change on her part, for example, 'you really are crazy', 'you'll never get better', and 'we'll hang in for the sake of the kids'. The partner was also resentful and critical towards the victim. He understood her difficulties rationally, but then told her that she is 'nuts'. Her reaction was 'how can I be expected to have a sexual relationship with a man who thinks I'm nuts?' He also opened a separate bank account in contrast to their usual joint financial arrangements—in case they split up—and stopped wearing his wedding ring.

These developments undermined the victim's trust in her partner and made her angry.

The interventions deployed for these problems included anger control, attendance at an assertiveness training group for the victim (Chap. 19), and at a situation/transition group for the partner (see below). This experience, together with seeing *Incest: The victim's perspective* (Sharp & Yantzi, 1983), helped him particularly to accept the normality of his feelings of anger, incomprehension, and confusion arising from his wife's victimization and its effects on their marriage, and to express his feelings generally.

Outcome of Marital Therapy

At the beginning of the first phase of marital therapy the victim's total score on the Dyadic Adjustment Scale was near the mean for divorced couples, and her partner's score was near that for married couples. At week 42 in treatment her score was unchanged and his had fallen to within the range for divorced couples. Both their scores remained at those levels until follow-up when they rose and were maintained about the mean for married couples, as well as being less discrepant between the spouses than on any previous administration (Figure 15.1).

Both spouses completed Target Complaint Scales for 'demonstrating understanding and acceptance of each other' and 'expressing hurt and anger to each other'. During marital therapy the highest rating on each scale was 13 (couldn't be worse) from the victim, and 6 (just below *pretty much* of a problem) from her partner. During the follow-up period the highest ratings on each TCS from both spouses was 2 (just above *not at all* a problem).

Throughout marital therapy and follow-up the scores of both spouses on the Marriage Relationship Questionnaires indicated either zero or low defensiveness.

These favorable questionnaire results were consistent with the couple's interview reports of considerable improvement in the non-sexual aspects of their relationship, there was greater understanding between them and conflicts were fewer and more easily resolved. The victim commented in writing as follows:

> The involvement of my husband has been vital to the identification and resolution of many issues critical to our relationship. Though my husband's presence made therapy very encompassing and at times painful, I entered therapy determined to do all I could to work through what difficulties I had and that my husband would simply have to rise to the occasion, or our relationship would dissolve. It has been important for me to have my husband know me and understand me as I really am, and to have our relationship based on that

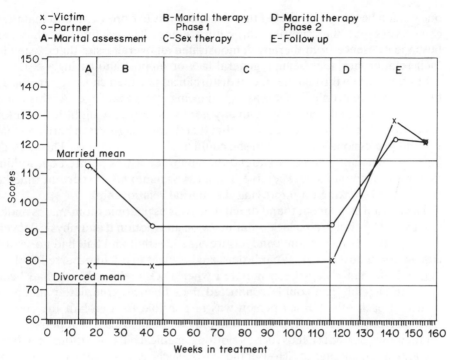

Figure 15.1. Total scores on the Dyadic Adjustment Scale: Alison and Michael

knowledge and understanding. My husband's presence throughout therapy enabled our strengths and limitations to be exposed to the other, and we have been able to work out our own way of integrating these into our relationship. Rather than shielding ourself from the other I feel we are more comfortable with declaring and exposing ourselves to the other.

It is noteworthy that this improvement in the non-sexual aspects of the relationship was achieved despite some residual sexual difficulties (Chap. 23), and it must be recognized that the improvement in the non-sexual aspects might to some extent be due to the treatment focussed upon sexual dysfunction, the victim's assertiveness training group, and the partner's situation/transition group, rather than to the marital therapy alone.

Case Study: Sharon and Dick

Sharon initially entered the U. of M. program for treatment of mood disturbances associated with her childhood sexual abuse. She had wanted her husband to accompany her throughout the therapeutic process but he had declined after one session because of his belief that the abuse was her problem, and that they could work out their marital difficulties alone. The victim felt that her husband's absence from therapy demonstrated an overall issue that existed in their relationship, that being a general lack of support and caring.

Sharon worked through her mood disturbances and then chose to refocus on the relationship problems she was experiencing in her marriage. At this point Sharon again asked Dick to accompany her to therapy leaving little room for dissension. She strongly voiced her belief that the marriage was in peril and that without professional intervention she could not see it continuing. The victim's husband reluctantly agreed to attend therapy when it was pointed out to him that in the six months between the initial assessment and the current time he had avoided working on improving the marital relationship.

The marital assessment found the clients living as platonic room-mates under one roof. They both felt a lack of intimacy on an emotional and physical level. They spent little recreational and leisure time together and had had no sexual contact for almost a year. What little sexual contact that had occurred in their married life had always been initiated when Dick and/or Sharon had been drinking alcohol. The couple conducted their finances completely independently of each other. Each person was responsible for one-half the cost of mortgage payments, food, utility bills, and other expenses. Each person paid for their own personal needs such as clothing, medical bills, vacations, personal car and its maintenance. Household costs, such as new furniture, interior decorating and so forth were considered to be Sharon's financial responsibility. If she wanted a new sofa, for example, it was up to her to save for it out of her own income. Dick did not see any need to contribute financially to articles he considered 'extravagances'. Likewise, funds for vacation trips were considered, by Dick, to be each individual's responsibility. If Sharon could not save enough money to accompany him on a trip, then he went alone. The financial demands put on each person in the marriage did not reflect their individual incomes. Expenses and savings were not split fifty-fifty. Dick managed his financial dealings with Sharon as if she were a boarder with whom he split living expenses. They did not conduct themselves as a marital unit.

This 'room-mates only' attitude seemed to pervade the relationship on every level. Day-to-day contacts were pleasant enough between Sharon and Dick but lacked anything but surface cordiality. Sharon considered the relationship superficial and was greatly distressed by the lack of intimacy. Dick presented as someone who would have been happy to continue on in this manner, refraining from investing himself in the relationship, because he found 'his business more rewarding' and in fact his 'number one priority'. Dick had experienced a strict, fundamentalist upbringing, characterized by parents who had traditional roles in their marriage and who refrained from emotional or physical expressions of caring. He considered that making a lot of money and remaining married were his primary methods of demonstrating his love for Sharon.

Sharon had held a distorted view of family life stemming from her sexual abuse by her step-father and the alcoholism evident in her mother, maternal grandmother and step-father. She had always believed that affection was conveyed through sexual activity and by the presents that were given. This view of caring had begun to alter when the victim gained sobriety in her third year of marriage. Without alcohol, the victim began to realize that sex was aversive to her, that her husband did not support her on an emotional level and that, in fact, she found him to possess qualities that she did not admire in a human being.

Personality traits such as an inability to show respect, an intolerant nature, an incapacity for demonstrating affection, and a lack of nurturing qualities were apparent in Sharon's husband. Prior to the victim gaining sufficient self-esteem during her individual therapy in the U. of M. program, she had not felt deserving of a man who possessed more positive qualities.

Sharon had begun to gain insight into her husband's character prior to entering treatment. In the early years of their courtship she had some misgivings concerning the appropriateness of the relationship. The victim had considered her partner 'a narrow-minded red-neck whom I didn't respect'. In fact, Sharon even broke up with Dick at that time but later married him because of a fear of being alone and that 'nobody else would ever want me'. Both partners drank heavily throughout their courtship and early marriage. Sharon realized, several years into the union, that she was an alcoholic and that she might lose Dick because of her excessive drinking. She joined Alcoholics Anonymous and overcame her addiction. Dick continued to drink and refused to accompany Sharon to her meetings or to read any literature she brought home dealing with alcoholism. He did not consider her addiction his problem and was insensitive towards how his continued drinking (socially and at home) could have any emotional impact on the victim. Sharon also quit cigarette smoking shortly after having gained sobriety. Dick, himself a chain-smoker, around this period likewise attempted to stop smoking for approximately one week but found his tobacco addiction just too difficult to overcome. His own inability to stop smoking did not, however, sensitize him to the great effort it took Sharon to give up her smoking and drinking habits. This lack of understanding, empathy and/or interest on Dick's part towards Sharon left her hungry for attention. She continuously brought up their lack of involvement in conversation which left Dick with the impression that Sharon 'was a nag'. He quite bluntly admitted that he received more pleasure from his work which led him to spend more and more time away from home. At the time the couple came to therapy, Sharon was almost desperate to elicit some type of emotional response from Dick, while he attempted to maintain control in the relationship by remaining aloof and by not 'giving in' to Sharon's insecurities. In summary, there were significant difficulties in the marriage including a lack of intimacy and expressed affection, insufficient trust and security, and an inability to

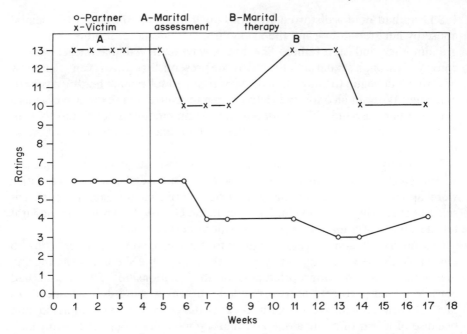

Figure 15.2.   Ratings on Target Complaint Scale for lack of communication: Sharon and Dick

communicate. Interestingly, Dick did not see these problems as important enough to determine any individual targets for himself on the Target Complaint Scale, and only rated the 'lack of communication' target when directly indicated to do so by the therapist.

The couple's questionnaire results during the marital assessment were consistent with the interview data. On the Dyadic Adjustment Scale the total, dyadic consensus, dyadic satisfaction, dyadic cohesion, and affectional expression scores for each spouse were all within the ranges for divorced couples. Their Marriage Relationship Questionnaire scores indicated zero defensiveness. On a Target Complaint Scale for 'lack of communication' Sharon's ratings were 13 (*couldn't be worse*) and Dick's were 6 (*pretty much* of a problem) (Figure 15.2).

Course of Treatment

The couple chose to work firstly on their inability to communicate. This inability to convey their opinions largely focussed on certain 'difficult topics' such as handling finances, having children, and discussing their sexual difficulties. These problematic areas, in turn, were underscored by a power struggle in the marriage and a lack of intimacy associated with a real lack of time spent together.

Sharon and Dick did not know how to enjoy each other's company and both felt that their relationship was all work. In order to attempt to foster an atmosphere whereby both partners would feel more amenable to improving their situation, it was suggested to them that they spend leisure time together by a certain number of times a week engaging in a mutually satisfying activity. The particulars of this homework exercise had to be worked out in session, because Dick refused to participate in planning this activity with Sharon at home. He did not make excuses for his behavior, but rather ignored it by continuing to pour all his energies into his business

One particular reason for Dick's stubborn refusal to participate in homework exercises was his belief that 'nobody could tell him what to do'. This attitude did not permit his wife to act as an equal partner because any suggestions that she made were labeled by him as 'being told what to do'. In therapy, he openly admitted this belief by stating that the therapist could not make him 'do anything' because this just 'made him dig in his heels'. He in turn felt that he had 'never made his wife do anything against her will' because he had never verbally demanded anything of her. He was oblivious to how his behavior, through given and withheld attention to Sharon, had worked just as effectively in controlling their relationship.

During the eleven sessions that the couple attended treatment, there was a continuous battle for control between them. This was evidenced in their sessions when Sharon would attempt to gain equal footing with Dick by bringing out her concerns while maintaining eye contact with the therapist for moral support. She felt unable to talk with Dick at home because 'he uses big words to confuse me and I feel stupid'. Dick in turn would maintain the *status quo* by responding to her emotional pleas with coolly detached intellectualizations. This *modus operandi* was brought to their attention with both partners acknowledging this as each person's mode of communication. This two-level method of communication—emotional v. intellectual—understandably left each person feeling frustrated. They were not conveying and receiving messages in language that each person understood.

As part of communication training Sharon asked Dick how she could show caring and support in a manner that he found acceptable. He responded by saying that 'not talking' and leaving him alone for an hour after work was a considerate demonstration. He needed time alone, he said, to unwind at the end of each day and then he would be ready for interaction. Sharon, in turn, told Dick that holding hands, going for a walk, his sitting down to have a cup of coffee with her instead of drinking a beer showed her that he was considerate of her feelings. The couple systematically talked with each other about how to show affection and caring towards each other at home, at work, and when in a social situation. They talked about their different styles of emotional expression which stemmed from their very different upbringing. They also explored how they could accommodate each other's perspectives of 'acceptable emotional input'.

For a time, Dick was encouraged by Sharon's change of behavior. He viewed it as 'she nags a lot less'. Unfortunately, Sharon did not perceive a similar improvement in Dick's behavior. He continued to pour his energy into his work and found it practically impossible to schedule any free time for mutual leisure time. After eleven sessions, over a period of four months, a break in therapy was contracted. The treatment focussed on improving their communication was not being beneficial as can be seen on the Target Complaint Scale in Figure 15.2. Dick was still putting up resistance to change and overt discussion did nothing to alter the situation. He took pride in his inflexibility and continued to maintain that Sharon had a 'false idea of marriage' and that she wanted him to become a 'whole new person'.

Given this stance it seemed that: (a) Dick was unwilling to change; (b) he was not likely to do it on his own since he had not done so prior to entering therapy; (c) Sharon was willing to compromise but was not allowed the reciprocal expectation from her husband; (d) Sharon now realized just how inflexible Dick was; and (e) that the viability of the marriage would be Sharon's decision alone. She either could accept what she had or else she would have to be the one to terminate the union. Dick was unwilling to work on the marriage and he was likewise unwilling to end it.

Outcome of Marital Therapy

Sharon and Dick never returned to therapy as a couple. Sharon returned for treatment to ventilate her feelings associated with the relationship and to plan emotionally and logistically for a marital separation. Two months into this line of treatment, Sharon left Dick permanently.

Since that time, Sharon and her therapist have focussed on the crisis of the actual separation, the victim's guilt at leaving her husband, and her reduced self-esteem derived from Sharon's feelings that she had somehow failed at her marriage and from her internalization of Dick's negative statements such as 'you don't deserve one-half of our assets because you've never worked in the business'.

The separation has proven to be a time of personal growth for the victim. She has come to realize that she never loved her husband and only married him out of fear that no one else would ever want her. She sees that he is a man whom she cares about, but whom she does not respect. She now has a joy and a hope in life that she never experienced in her marriage. She also realizes that she was more lonely with Dick than she is now, living alone. Sharon has also been given a chance to test out her new found assertiveness skills. She is currently in the process of asking for her rightful share of their mutual assets and she is not capitulating to Dick's opinion of what he thinks she deserves.

The victim continues to attend therapy using it as a source of emotional support and her therapist as a sounding board. She is a woman who has faced major changes in her life in the past five years—overcoming her alcoholism, her smoking, her mother's, grandmother's and aunt's deaths, has married and separated and has tackled the effects her sexual abuse has had on her life. She is emotionally strong and empathetic and is finally coming to terms with Sharon on Sharon's terms and nobody else's. She has prioritized her own growth for the first time in her life and the feeling she says is 'fantastic'.

Situation/Transition Group for Partners

A range of mood disturbances, interpersonal problems, and sexual dysfunctions are commonly reported among women who were sexually abused in childhood and who present for therapy in later life. Moreover, changes such as enhanced self-esteem and increased assertiveness as the victim progresses in therapy may cause discord unless the partner understands, accepts, and adapts to the altered relationship. Thus, the presenting problems and therapeutic changes among previously sexually abused women have important implications for the partners and yet there do not appear to be any contributions in the literature on their reactions to these problems and changes.

As an initial step in the investigation of these reactions and to explore ways of alleviating those of a distressing nature we provided a group experience for eight male partners in the U. of M. program. The goals of the group were: (a) to alleviate feelings of isolation and difference from other men; (b) to provide mutual aid and support; and (c) to assist the partner to understand, accept and adapt to the problems and changes being experienced by the victim. This last goal in particular was also being addressed in couple therapy but these conjoint sessions were inevitably weighted towards the victim with the partner largely taking the role of helping to resolve her problems. Attention was given also to problems in the relationship between victim and partner during which an attempt was made to equalize the identified client roles but many partners were reluctant to accept this shift from helper to client. Even if they did so the emphasis in therapy was on their role in the relationship rather than any individual concerns and needs that they might have. The partners' group was an attempt to fill this gap. It was viewed as supplementary and complementary to couple therapy, and as providing a forum in which the focus would be on the individual needs of the partners.

Subjects

Each of the eight partners was referred to the group by the therapist who was meeting him in conjoint sessions with the victim. The partners were all

Caucasian and ranged in age from 25 to 40 years. Their educational levels varied from partial high school to university graduate degree. Six were married and two were living as married. The duration of these relationships ranged from 3 to 17 years with a mean of 8.7 years.

Four of the original eight members dropped out of the group before its completion, at intervals of 3, 4, 7, and 12 weeks from its commencement. The first of these drop-outs was due to the member's difficulty in coping with the expressions of anger in the group and its perceived monopolization by a few individuals. The second and last drop-outs occurred because the members concerned had begun to confront the fact that they had been physically abused in childhood and were identifying themselves as victims, consequently they felt that they no longer belonged in the partners' group and sought individual therapy. The third drop-out took place when the member started a night-school course which precluded his attendance at the group. Subsequently, he disclosed that he had a sexual experience with an older woman when he was an adolescent, but he regarded this as an initiation ritual rather than a victimization. Later, he also entered individual therapy.

Procedure

The group met for approximately two hours at weekly intervals. There were 15 such sessions with a break of two weeks between the 6th and 7th sessions. After the 6th and 15th sessions each member had an individual meeting with the female therapist with the aims of increasing rapport and obtaining informal feedback and evaluation on the group experience. Three months after the group ended a follow-up inquiry was conducted by mail.

The intervention was conceptualized and conducted as a situation/transition (S/T) group. Schwartz (1975) described these as 'small discussion–education groups moderated by a trained leader . . . for mutual assistance of individuals who share some stressful life situation' (p. 744). The primary emphasis is on mutual caring and coping rather than personal insight or growth. Thus, in the partners' group it was found that verbalization and ventilation of feelings greatly reduced tension and made affect more manageable initially within the group but ultimately with life outside of the group. The members became more aware of their concerns, but that awareness appeared to offer great relief for they no longer felt singled out, painfully lonely, nor as uniquely inadequate. A sense of community developed as members felt they had found an arena where they were free to express themselves and where they could vicariously benefit from being with others who ventilated feelings and concerns they shared. The exchange of information assisted in the formulation of new coping strategies, enhanced gratification and greater self-confidence. The group provided a cognitive framework wherein an individual's feelings and reactions were made understandable and events were made meaningful, thus relieving the confusion and the unmanageability of such events and feelings. Slowly new role definitions required by changing relationships with the victims began to be formulated through the offering by fellow members of these new points of view.

During the first six sessions the members preferred to use the group time for such sharing and discussion rather than didactic or audio-visual presentations. Fairly explosive feelings of helplessness, frustration, and anger towards the offenders were expressed, and one member disclosed his own victimization. There was much caring and support for members who were distressed in each session. The individual interviews with each member at the end of this period indicated that the companionship of fellow members was a welcome addition to their lives. For some, the anger expressed at the outset of the group was still uncomfortable. They did not want the group to focus upon the anger to the detriment of other issues and needed to know that the group was a safe place. All were requesting more structure and input from the co-therapists.

Sessions 7 to 14 generally centered around the emotional and behavioral repercussions of the members' interpersonal relationships and sexual functioning with a woman who had suffered sexual abuse. Each week, all participants would share the story of their weekly events. The focus would be on the individual who had special needs on that particular evening. There was little or no struggle for the centre of attention possibly due to the special sensitivity and cohesiveness between members. As well, the co-therapists sought to provide the necessary structure to facilitate discussion among all members.

The final session comprised a social evening in a restaurant with the aim of promoting the mutual enjoyment of each other's company among the members and therapists rather than continuing discussion of problematic issues.

The group was led by two co-therapists, one male and one female. Their role in an S/T group is to facilitate and focus discussion while minimizing resistance and defensiveness. Their interventions are non-directive, supportive, clarifying, facilitative, sympathetic, and eliciting. The goal is to provide a sheltered, structured social environment where individuals who feel singled out by a stressful life event can meet with others, hear about their similar difficulties and come to understand events that would otherwise remain confusing (Schwartz, 1975).

Results

Vicarious victimization. For all the participants, the long-term effects of their partner's victimization had unexpected and overwhelming consequences that seemed to touch upon every aspect of their lives. Each man felt very much like a victim, not only in a secondary but in a primary sense. It was as if they had been the victimized individual: 'In a sense, he struck two people. He struck the wife and he struck us, too.'

Anger. Anger was experienced by all group participants and underlay much of how each thought and felt. First, there was tremendous anger against anyone who would victimize a child, thus causing damage that not only left its imprint on the victim but upon themselves and their children as well.

Secondly, a sense of outrage seemed to exist at observing the victim put aside the victim role. The participants felt left behind, no longer knowing where they fitted in, not knowing what to do within that relationship. The situation was 'I don't know what to do anymore, she has changed so much' and 'Things were more on an even keel before my wife started therapy . . . I do not know where I fit in now'. They were angry at the loss of control over their lives. They somehow felt less of a man for it.

In attempting to dissipate the anger so that the men could begin to deal with the underlying sense of victimization and loss, the co-therapists, initially, allowed expression of that anger. It was pointed out that being angry over losses was natural and contributed to their sense of victimization. Similarly, such anger may have motivated the men to seek out the S/T group and in that way facilitated self-care. Furthermore, it was stressed that each did, in fact, have control over many areas of their lives. Special attention would be needed to care for their own physical, spiritual, and emotional requirements. Their anger could be utilized to mobilize their energies toward their own self-care and perhaps the remediation of some wrong or inequity for others. In fact, one of the members who dropped out of the group subsequently established a self-help group which he entitled Abused Persons Anonymous and ran similarly to Alcoholics Anonymous, and another member who dropped out became the resource person on sexual abuse for the school division in which he is a teacher.

Negative self-concept and depression. The statement 'I start to question myself, maybe I'm a bit of a loser all around . . . ' typifies the feelings of uselessness and depression of many group participants. Each, somehow, felt responsible for the victim's difficulties. They wanted to alleviate these difficulties, yet felt inadequate in their ability to do so. Again and again expressions were heard in the group such as 'my partner still doesn't trust me'. The general mistrust of men expressed by the victim seemed to affect the partner's own self-concept. There were definite difficulties in knowing that men are usually the gender responsible for sexual victimization.

The presence of a male co-therapist assisted in the resolution of some of these concerns. As he participated in the general discussion as a compassionate and understanding individual, the men relaxed. Somehow they appeared to be reaffirmed as men.

Sexual relationship. The victim's inability to have a satisfactory sexual relationship contributed to a negative self-concept and feelings of being out of control in most partners: 'When my partner finds it difficult to have sex because of what happened in the past, deep down inside, I question whether or not she loves me' and 'she tenses up and I think I've done something he [the offender] did'.

Communication—isolation. Prior to the group, disclosure of personal feelings about themselves and their partnership in relation to the victimization was non-existent for all members. Secrecy had become as much a problem for them as the victim. They did not feel able to communicate honestly and openly with her: 'I can't say anything, because if I say anything then I'm not being a good support for my wife'. This lack of communication and sense of isolation seemed to lead to feelings that their relationship was abnormal or deviant. Typical were expressions such as 'It would be nice to have a normal argument where you could argue about something without it always going back to the abuse'.

Evaulation by members. At the termination of the group meetings and on follow-up three months later some members were asked to respond to the items shown in Table 15.1 on a 5-point scale ranging from *not helpful* to *extremely helpful*. It was judged inappropriate to ask two members who had dropped out to complete the questionnaire at termination, leaving six respondents at that stage. These six were also sent the questionnaire at follow-up when one of them did not reply. The results of these evaluations are generally positive on each occasion although there is some decrease in perceived helpfulness at follow-up. This decrease may reflect a more realistic appreciation of the limitations of the group experience in resolving all the problems being experienced by the members. Generally high ratings on both occasions are given to the components of 'Talking with other men whose wives were sexually abused', 'Hearing that other men whose wives were sexually abused were encountering similar difficulties to myself', and 'Expressing my feelings about things that trouble me', all of which are particularly consistent with the nature of an S/T group.

The following additional comments were made on the evaluation questionnaires by two members:

(a) The group atmosphere enabled me to cope with feelings of failure, of being useless when it came to dealing with my wife's situation. The weekly meetings became my 'R & R' from the tensions of my daily life. Definitely a *must*, as part of the therapy program in dealing with sexually abused women.
(b) The husbands' group was a very worthwhile experience. The experience (opportunity) is essential for understanding the problem of sexual abuse. The husbands' group does not give solutions to the many problems—but it does provide many answers and much understanding. Such groups should be a mandatory component of the social welfare system.

Table 15.1. *Members' Evaluation of Situation Transition Group*

	Termination (n = 6)			Follow up (n = 5)		
	Not/slightly helpful	Moderately helpful	Very/extremely helpful	Not/slightly helpful	Moderately helpful	Very/extremely helpful
Talking with other men whos wives were sexually abused	—	—	6	—	1	4
Hearing that other men whose wives were sexually abused were encountered similar difficulties to myself	—	1	5	—	1	4
Feeling understood by other men whose wives were sexually abused	—	1	5	2	—	3
Getting support and help from other men whose wives were sexually abused	1	—	5	2	1	2
Understanding the difficulties my wife is experiencing	1	—	5	1	—	4
Responding to the difficulties my wife is experiencing	1	1	4	1	2	2
Expressing my feelings about things that trouble me	—	—	6	—	—	5
Increasing my self-confidence	1	1	4	2	—	3
Reducing my feelings of being different from other men	—	1	4	1	1	2
Having the opportunity to support and help other men whose wives were sexually abused	—	1	5	1	—	4

Conclusion

The provision of the S/T group and the results reported are small, first steps in opening up a hitherto unexplored aspect of childhood sexual abuse. More comprehensive and rigorous investigation of the concerns experienced by the partners of victims and of the efficacy of various interventions to alleviate their distress remains to be undertaken. In the meantime, it seems that partners are prone to concerns around: (a) feelings of having been victimized vicariously; (b) deprivation, confusion, and loss of control in their relationship with the victim, including the sexual and communication aspects of this relationship; (c) anger toward the offenders; and (d) a negative self-concept accompanied by a mood of depression.

In general, the S/T group appears to be a helpful form of intervention to relieve but not eliminate such concerns for some members, and it seems a worthwhile adjunct to couple therapy in programs for previously sexually abused women and their partners. It is noteworthy that three of the four members who dropped out subsequently entered individual therapy, a decision that appeared to have been precipitated and perhaps facilitated by their participation in the group.

CHAPTER 16

Relations With Women

At initial assessment 49% of victims in the U. of M. series disparaged women and 39% reported anger towards them (Table 11.1). On the Belief Inventory the item 'You can't depend on women they are all weak and useless creatures' was endorsed as partly, mostly, or absolutely true by 56% of the victims (Table 5.1) Herman (1981) comments on such negative attitudes towards women among her series of incest victims as follows:

> Whatever anger these women did feel was most commonly directed at women rather than at men. With the exception of those who had become conscious feminists, most of the incest victims seemed to regard all women, including themselves, with contempt . . . they identified with the mothers they despised . . .
>
> The incest victims' hostility of women generally prevented the development of supportive female friendships. Women were seen as potential rivals who would betray their friends for a man, as vicious gossips, or simply as empty, inadequate people who had nothing to offer.
>
> For many of the incest victims, the overt hostility toward women masked a deeper longing for a relationship with a caring woman. This longing was rarely expressed, for most of the informants had simply despaired of having any sort of satisfactory relationship with a woman (p. 103). (Reproduced from Herman, 1981 by permission of Harvard University Press.)

The anger and disparagement towards other women described by Herman were reported by only approximately half the women in the U. of M. series, also many of the victims in this series did have close female friends and we did observe the capacity to establish supportive and caring relationships among the victims in group therapy (Chap. 19). Thus, the general tone of Herman's comments may be unduly negative, although the problems she describes undoubtedly occur in some victims, as the following example illustrates.

158

Case Illustration: Roberta and Brian

The victim presented with a belief that 'women couldn't be trusted'. She viewed females as mostly weak, ineffectual, non-nurturing, and non-protective. She based this belief largely on her relationships with her mother and her grandmother.

Roberta also held the view that women were seductive, and manipulative and 'out to get my man'. She felt that women of a comparable age category to herself would 'steal' her partner by using their physical charms to draw the man away from her 'less attractive' self.

Given that she held such beliefs, Roberta was preoccupied with the thought that her partner would be taken away from her by a better looking woman. She kept herself on the alert for any indication of this happening by constantly monitoring her current partner's behavior, for example, by watching if he looked at other women or talked a few minutes too long to any woman within ten years of his age, and so forth. She also had persistent negative cognitions that plagued many of her conscious moments such as 'he's thinking about other women' or 'he's having an affair with her'.

Roberta attributed the responsibility for a man's waywardness to factors outside of his own control. She blamed the allures of the 'other woman' for a male's indiscretions. This belief was an offshoot of another belief that she was responsible for her own victimization.

The victim's views of women had largely been molded from her relationships with the women in her family of origin. It was within this context that she had learned to believe that 'women were responsible for a man's sexual behavior', 'a man would cheat if he could get away with it', and 'a man was your meal ticket and as such he was a prized commodity for whom you had to compete with other women'. Other women were viewed as 'the enemy' because they could take 'your man' away using sexual attractiveness as leverage. Likewise the victim held a great deal of distrust towards women based on the lack of nurturing and support she had received from her mother and maternal grandmother. Inquiry into Roberta's background uncovered an absent mother who had left her to be raised by an alcoholic grandmother. Her childhood memories of rejection were the foundations for beliefs such as 'women are weak and non-supportive' and 'they will throw you to the wolves to keep their man'. More realistically, these poignant beliefs were depictions of some women but not of all women, therefore cognitive restructuring was employed to discriminate her mother's and grandmother's behavior from that of other women she had known. Examples of this are shown in Table 16.1.

The allures of other women and their manipulative use of these charms to 'get my man' was discussed at length. The false responsibility that Roberta gave to women for men's sexual behavior was a major point of distortion. Reattribution of this control to the proper source, that being an adult male who is responsible for his own sexual behavior, greatly alleviated the misgivings

Table 16.1. *Cognitive Restructuring of Lack of Trust in Women: Roberta*

Distorted beliefs	Alternative beliefs
You can't trust women.	My aunt was a very trustworthy person. She loved me, was caring and I viewed her as my real mother.
My mother and grandmother didn't protect me against the physical and sexual abuse.	My grandmother did protect me once, she didn't allow me to return from the hospital to my mother's home. I had been physically abused by my step-father and I guess this was her way of showing some concern for me.
My mother called me a 'cock-teaser' when I told her about my step-father sexually abusing me. She did not believe me against her husband.	My mother has never been able to support me against her husband. She is too needy a lady in her own right. I now know that I can get support from some good friends and my therapist. They know that I am blameless in the abuse. I can trust these people to support me, and not to waiver. They stick by me and what they say.

Table 16.2. *Cognitive Restructuring of Issues of Responsibility and Self-Esteem: Roberta*

Distorted beliefs	Alternative beliefs
Women will steal my partners. Can't trust women not to steal another's man.	A woman can't take away a guy who has a belief in fidelity to one partner. A guy who is committed to me will not 'fool around'. It is a man's responsibility, it is his behavior, if he strays. Another woman can't make him cheat. All women do not try to take somebody else's man. My partners actually haven't sexually cheated on me while they were with me. My current girlfriends have not tried to take away my husband. Actually, I am afraid that I am not attractive enough to keep a man.
Other women are prettier, thinner, and will attract my partner away from me.	I have a pretty face and dress well. I have a good sense of humor and other qualities unique to me. I can never be like a tall, thin model. There will always be women prettier than me, but beauty isn't the only quality that attracts a man. I guess I've always considered it # 1.
My husband bugged me about my weight during my last pregnancy. He compared me to a girlfriend who was much thinner during her pregnancy. I was very jealous of her.	It's not my girlfriend's fault that she carried a baby differently than me. She's not competing with me or showing me up. My husband is really the problem here. I have had four other children, and it's normal to look bigger — less muscle tone, etc. I was not overeating, I had a lot of water retention during my last pregnancy. My husband made me feel unattractive, but this wasn't my girlfriend's fault.

Roberta had towards women. The victim then focussed on the issue of lack of self-esteem which was fundamental to the belief that prettier women would steal her partner. A few examples of cognitive restructuring these beliefs are shown in Table 16.2.

Outcome of Treatment

The victim currently seems able to assess realistically the trustworthiness of most women. She still is subject to assuming negative intent from some women, but she now recognizes this tendency. Roberta has greater awareness that whenever she feels uncomfortable or threatened she will tend to attribute negative meaning to the behavior of others. She does, however, make an attempt to restructure cognitively these thoughts using observed behavior as the foundation for her reappraisals. Roberta's initial assessment response to the Belief Inventory item 'You can't depend on women, they are all weak and useless creatures' of *mostly true*, has been in the *absolutely untrue* category for over seven months subsequent to treatment aimed at this targeted area.

She also has reattributed sexual responsibility to the appropriate adult person, and no longer views women as the cause of male improprieties. She does have difficulty in giving up the notion that 'a male is a prized possession' and that the nuclear family with an intact mother–father parental system is to be preserved in the face of all wrong-doing. This ability to believe that 'a woman is *not* responsible for an adult male's sexual behavior' and that 'a man is a prized commodity' has placed the victim in a current conflict situation. A teen-aged daughter of Roberta has recently revealed that her step-father, Roberta's husband, had sexually abused her. Though taken aback by this information, Roberta did not hesitate in her belief that her daughter was telling the truth. A formal charge was laid against Roberta's husband and the situation was investigated by the police. Due to the alleged offender's complete denial of culpability and the child's eventual withdrawal of her allegations towards her step-father, the case was dropped. Roberta's daughter, however, withdrew her charges because of the emotional pressure exerted upon her by her step-father, grandmother, and grandfather. In confidence to her mother and social worker she continued to state that she had been victimized. Roberta could not draw out a confession from her husband regarding the sexual abuse and subsequently left him to live at her mother and step-father's home, although financial pressures and other circumstances eventually forced her to return to her husband.

Lesbian Relationships

The inclusion of this topic is not intended to imply that lesbian relationships are necessarily distressing or problematic; they may be just as loving and caring as heterosexual relationships. The limited evidence from the U. of M. program indicates that some previously sexually abused women are confused about their sexual orientation however, and that others who are predominantly homosexual in their orientation and lifestyle may experience similar mood disturbances, interpersonal problems, and sexual dysfunctions, as those victims who are heterosexual.

The evidence available on the prevalence of homosexuality among women who were sexually abused in childhood is inconsistent and indeed contradictory so that it is not possible to reach any reasonable conclusion on whether victims are more likely than non-victims to have a predominantly homosexual orientation in adulthood. Fromuth (1986) did find a significant positive correlation between a history of sexual abuse and having a homosexual experience after the age of 12 years, in her college student sample. In a questionnaire study of 225 homosexual and 223 heterosexual women conducted by Gundlach (1977) there were 18 subjects who had been molested or raped by a male *stranger* when the victim was aged 15 or younger. Of these victims, 55% were homosexual in adulthood. There were also 17 women who had been molested or raped by a male *relative or close friend* when the victim was aged 15 or under, and in most cases the victimization was strongly coercive. Of these victims, 94% were homosexual in adulthood. Much lower rates are reported by several other investigators. For example, in Meiselman's (1978) psychotherapy patient sample, 30% of 23 victims of father–daughter incest had either adopted a gay lifestyle or they reported significant homosexual experiences or feelings. The equivalent proportion for the control subjects is not cited, but homosexuality is said to be rare among them. Among 40 father–daughter incest victims studied by Herman (1981) only 5% were homosexual and 7.5% bisexual. Thus, no firm conclusions can be drawn on the prevalence of homosexuality among previously sexually abused women.

Although previously sexually abused women may or may not be more likely to be predominantly homosexual in adulthood compared to women who were not abused, there are certainly some abused women who become practicing lesbians and their abuse and its associated circumstances may have contributed to this sexual orientation in a number of ways. Meiselman (1978) among others has suggested that many homosexually oriented victims appear to be reacting to very negative heterosexual experiences, often involving phobic reactions to sexual activity and frequently culminating in a strong hatred of men. Quite commonly, the homosexual orientation is not manifested until after many years of heterosexual experience. Another suggestion by Meiselman is that some victims may be influenced towards a lesbian identity because difficulties in relationships with their mothers may have led to an unwillingness to assume a traditional female role in life. Similarly, Kaufman, Peck, and Taguiri (1954) speculate that the homosexuality of some victims might be motivated by their wish to be loved by an older woman to make up for the rejection they had experienced from their own mothers. Why these or other factors might lead to a predominantly homosexual orientation in some victims and not in others is at present unknown.

In the interests of homogeneity among the U. of M. research series of victims one of the selection criteria was that each victim should be predominantly heterosexually oriented. Thus, there are no predominantly lesbian women in this series. Any such women who approached the program for treatment were either helped to obtain this at another facility or they were treated by the program therapists but excluded from the research series of 51 victims.

Among these 51 victims there were 8 (14%) who had engaged in homosexual relationships in the past. Several expressed current doubts about their sexual orientation although they were not engaging in overt homosexual activity. Such doubts are not surprising in view of the difficulties, and particularly the aversion and dissatisfaction that victims often experience in their sexual relationships with men (Part 4). Both women and men who are sexually dysfunctional quite commonly wonder whether this is because they are homosexual and this concern is not restricted to those who have been sexually abused. The confusion experienced by some victims concerning their sexual orientation is exemplified in the case of Maureen presented below.

Only one victim in an established lesbian relationship was referred to the U. of M. program and she and her partner were treated by a program therapist but not counted in the program series (Klassen & Jehu, 1987). The problems exhibited by this victim were essentially similar to those observed in heterosexually oriented victims and the same treatment approach was used with apparent success. Thus, our limited experience indicates that victims who are in lesbian partnerships can be treated along the same lines as those in heterosexual partnerships.

Case Illustration: Maureen

This victim, aged 34 years, is unmarried and childless (see also Chap. 21). Her interpersonal relationships were characterized by social isolation, feelings of difference from others, and extreme mistrust of both men and women. She was also afraid of becoming a lesbian because in spite of her mistrust of women, she was still more willing to risk intimacy and closeness with them than with men. Once when this occurred she became sexually involved with the other woman.

Maureen identified the belief that 'trusting and feeling warm toward a female means I might be a lesbian'. She was afraid that she might terminate therapy with her present female therapist as she had done with her previous female therapist at the point where she began to experience warm feelings toward her. Cognitive restructuring of this belief is shown in Table 16.3, and this procedure assisted the client to recognize that she was confusing emotional

Table 16.3.   *Cognitive Restructuring of Belief Concerning Sexual Orientation: Maureen*

Distorted beliefs	Alternative beliefs

Trusting and feeling warm towards a female means I might be a lesbian.	When I feel warm or close to a female, I sometimes get a 'warm feeling' all over my body including my private parts. Just because there are warm feelings in my private parts it doesn't necessarily mean that I am sexually attracted to that person.
	  I have had this warm feeling in my private parts with men too.
	  Maybe I'm labeling my body's response as sexual just because the warm feelings also affect my private parts, and confusing this with emotional feelings of warmth and closeness.

closeness and warmth with sex, and that such closeness does not constitute lesbian tendencies. She was able to remain in therapy.

Later in therapy, Maureen joined a women's club but again avoided risking making any friendships because of her fear of becoming a lesbian. She agreed to join a professionally led group for adult women who had been sexually victimized in childhood in order to reinforce the gains she had made in resolving her mood disturbances. Maureen recognized that the group might also be helpful in modifying her belief that close, warm feelings towards women mean that the relationship will be sexual. She attended all 16 group sessions and the experience was very successful. Other group members discussed their confusion between close relationships and sex and their own fears that feelings of intimacy and closeness with women meant that they too were lesbian. Maureen made and has maintained close and satisfying relationships with several group members. None of the women in this group are interested in developing a sexually intimate relationship with each other.

Maureen continues to expand her social network of women's organizations that are focussed on her interests and she is satisfied with a friendship system based on mutual interest. In short, she is better able to experience different kinds of relationships with women such as those of an intimate, social, occupational, or superficial nature.

Conclusion

In summary, the relations of some, but not all, female victims with other women are characterized by anger, disparagement, and distrust.

It is not clear whether female victims are more likely than non-victims to be predominantly homosexually oriented in adulthood, but some victims are confused and uncertain about their sexual orientation, and some of those who are lesbian experience similar psychosocial problems to heterosexual victims.

CHAPTER 17

Relations With Offspring

It is probable that the majority of previously sexually abused women are good mothers to their children, and sometimes to other children as well. In some cases this reflects a continuance of the caretaking role acquired during parenti-fication in childhood (Chap. 3). Despite such dedication to the welfare of their children some victims fear that they will be bad mothers and impose highly unrealistic standards of maternal care upon themselves. When, inevitably, they fall short of these standards they are consumed by feelings of worthlessness and guilt (Herman, 1981). Thus, it appears likely that most victims are good mothers, although some perceive themselves to be failing by their own unrealistic standards. This leaves a proportion of victims, probably a minority, who do experience significant problems in their parenting functions.

Physical Abuse

At initial assessment 22 (70%) of 31 victims in the U. of M. series who had living children reported that they had physically abused their children in the past and 6 (19%) said that they were still doing so. The negative view of their own parenting held by many victims and the severity of the abuse experienced by those in this series need to be borne in mind when reading these prevalence rates.

Some additional evidence is provided by Goodwin, McCarthy and DiVasto (1981) who found that among 100 mothers of children who were physically or sexually abused there was 24% who reported having been incestuously abused themselves, compared to 3% of 500 women drawn from the same community whose children had not been abused so far as was known. The authors speculate that the children of the abused women are more vulnerable to being abused because their mothers tend to oversexualize any close and affectionate relationship and therefore avoid and inhibit such threatening relationships even if they are with their own children. There are likely to be many other factors contributing to any excess in the prevalence rates for physical abuse among children whose parents were sexually abused.

165

Inadequate Parenting

At initial assessment, 19 (61%) of 31 victims in the U. of M. series who had
living children reported that they had been an inadequate parent in the past,
and 11 (35%) considered themselves to be inadequate in this respect at the
current time. Again, these prevalence rates need to be considered in the light of
the tendency for some victims to adopt unrealistic parenting standards as
mentioned above, as well as the severity of the abuse situations experienced by
the victims in this series.

Perhaps because of lack of confidence and low self-esteem, some previously
sexually abused women have difficulty in setting limits and exercising reasonable discipline within a framework of love and affection. Their feelings of
helplessness and of being overwhelmed may lead them also to parentify their
daughters just as they themselves were parentified as children (Chap. 3), and
this may increase the daughters' vulnerability to sexual abuse.

Three case illustrations of victims' relations with their offspring are presented next.

Case Illustration: Dawn

This victim's family background and victimization experience are described in
Chapter 14. When she first entered treatment in the U. of M. program she and
her partner (Jim) were in the midst of being charged and brought to trial for the
sexual abuse of their daughter aged seven years. Investigation into the actual
precursors for this charge uncovered that Jim and not Dawn had been the
actual perpetrator. He had taken pornographic pictures and videos of the child
and of Dawn. He also exposed his daughter to some of his masturbatory
practices.

Dawn had been unable to extricate herself and her daughter from an ongoing
relationship with this man, and consequently, had been unable to protect her
daughter from her father's sexual exploitation. She felt completely responsible
for her daughter's abuse and openly admitted her guilt. Jim, on the other hand,
denied his involvement in the sexual abuse, blamed Dawn for instigating the
pornographic activity and laid the responsibility for having been found out on a
tattletale daughter and a prudish society.

The couple were tried separately and each person was found to be guilty of
the charges. Dawn, however, received a lesser sentence because of her open
admittance to guilt and the overwhelming evidence that her crime had been
one largely of omission rather than commission.

The abuse had come to the attention of the authorities when the little girl had
reported her own victimization to her grade school teacher after having seen
the 'Feeling Yes, Feeling No' play in her classroom. This teacher had reported
the incident to the police who in turn contacted Dawn. Dawn had immediately

admitted her part in the abuse and had willingly agreed to place her daughter with a child care agency.

The little girl had a very close and loving bond with her mother and wanted to remain living with her. Her feelings towards her father were not positive however. She saw him as a 'bad man' and did not want further contact with him. At the time of writing, this child has not seen her father in over two years.

Course of Treatment

Dawn entered the U. of M. program to help herself and her daughter. She was motivated to understand the dynamics that had led to her inability to protect her own daughter from sexual abuse and to learn alternative ways of coping so that such a situation would never occur again. In this light, all the therapy Dawn received to alter her own mood disturbances indirectly assisted in her ability to be a better parent. Further, Dawn worked in a coordinated fashion with the child care agency, her daughter's psychologist, and the therapist in the U. of M. program to give her daughter the best support possible throughout a very difficult time. Dawn's daughter was placed into care voluntarily because: (a) Dawn could not recommend any family member as an appropriate care-taker; and (b) Dawn was incarcerated in prison and her child needed shelter during this period. Assessment by the child care agency, the child's psycho-logist, and the therapist in this program found Dawn and her daughter to be a caring, close-knit unit. The child did not view her mother as having abused her; but rather placed the blame for this on her father. Dawn worked weekly with the psychologist in assisting her daughter to voice any and all feelings the child possessed surrounding her abuse and the subsequent stress of being separated from her mother and placed in temporary care. Parenting issues and the mother–daughter relationship, were dealt with within this therapeutic rela-tionship. Boundaries between agencies and therapists were delineated so that overlap would occur as little as possible, and so that a well thought out counseling package could be presented to Dawn. The child care agency dealt with the child's physical and mental wellbeing as its prime consideration, the psychologist focussed on the mother–child relationship, and the therapist in the U. of M. program focussed treatment on Dawn's own sexual abuse. All therapists kept each other abreast of their therapeutic content and progress and presented a united front with similar treatment recommendations for Dawn at her trial. (As an aside, the therapists had not supported incarceration because of the manner in which Dawn had been involved in the abuse and her very real demonstration that she was highly motivated to learn how to change.)

Dawn's own therapy in this area focussed on the guilt that she attributed to herself for the abuse of her daughter. Such beliefs as 'I am a bad parent' and 'I didn't protect my child from the abuse, I am 100% responsible' were cognitive-ly restructured. An example of this process can be seen in Table 17.1.

Table 17.1.   *Cognitive Restructuring of 'I Am a Bad Parent': Dawn*

Distorted belief	Alternative belief
I am a bad parent.	I did not protect my daughter from Jim's abuse and for that I'll always feel regret. However, I am a good parent. I play and read with my child. I listened to her needs and try to talk with her when she has a problem. I take good physical care of her. I love her and now feel better able to protect her from any further abuse. She loves me and doesn't consider me her abuser.

Outcome of Treatment

Upon Dawn's release from prison, her daughter was immediately returned into her care. All professionals involved had held a consistent view that Dawn was a caring and effective mother who, because of her own lack of self-esteem and feelings of guilt and responsibility associated with her own upbringing and sexual abuse had been unable to protect herself, and thus her daughter, from the abuse.

Dawn made excellent progress in her own treatment and her scores on the Belief Inventory, Beck Depression Inventory, and Battle Self-Esteem Inventory all showed significant improvements from the time of initial assessment to the termination of treatment. These results as well as the behavior changes in Dawn observed by herself and the therapist lend support to the belief that she now views herself more positively, feels better able to set appropriate limits for herself and her daughter, no longer feels guilt and responsibility for her own sexual abuse and is a much more effective parent. Independent observations by the child's psychologist and social worker also support these opinions.

Case Illustration: Eileen and Marc

Eileen was referred by a social agency to the U. of M. program. She had initially sought the agency's help when her daughters aged 13 and 14 years disclosed sexual victimization by the step-father one year after the couple had separated. Eileen's extreme distress during subsequent interviews was noticed by the counselor and when asked about this, Eileen revealed her own sexual victimization. The client stated that she would not be able to be of any help to her daughters unless she got help for herself.

Eileen has been married and divorced twice. Her two teenage daughters are from her first marriage. She is living as married with Marc an old family friend but they still maintain separate residences. He was recently separated and is providing maintenance support for his four children who live with his former spouse (see also case vignette in Chapter 3).

Table 17.2. *Cognitive Restructuring of 'I feel responsible for not having protected my children from being sexually abused': Eileen*

Distorted belief	Alternative beliefs
I feel responsible for not having protected my children from being victimized.	Children did not disclose the sexual victimization until now.
	It's hard to believe that the man you married is a sex offender. I'm glad I found him rotten enough to have left him before they told me about him because if I had been with him I might have believed them but might not have done anything about it.
	I wasn't willing to accept my own experiences of sexual abuse at the time. That's probably why I didn't see the 'signs'.
	My husband was the offender not me.

Table 17.3. *Cognitive Restructuring of Distorted Beliefs About Being An Inadequate Provider: Eileen*

Distorted beliefs	Alternative beliefs
I'm a bad mother because I can't give the kids the clothes and stuff they should have.	Better to be poor on my low wages than to have the wads of money we had when we lived with [daughter's offender]. Look at the price we all paid.
I feel threatened when the girls' social worker buys all those clothes for them — maybe the girls will like her better than me.	Just because the social worker buys all those nice things doesn't mean she's buying the girls off. It is possible for people to be nice without 'strings' attached.

Course of Treatment

During the cognitive restructuring of guilt about her sexual victimization, the client expressed the guilt she felt about having failed as a parent because: (a) she had failed to protect her daughters from being sexually victimized; (b) she was unable to provide adequately for them since her separation; (c) both daughters showed signs of extreme distress and emotional upset since disclosing the abuse and they required intensive treatment; and (d) she is unable to set limits on their self-destructive behavior (e.g. promiscuity, drug abuse, broken curfews) or to set limits on the angry, hostile behavior they

Table 17.4. *Cognitive Restructuring of Distorted Beliefs About Treatment for Daughters: Eileen*

Distorted belief	Alternative beliefs
I feel like I'm abandoning my daughter by agreeing to have her admitted in the [psychiatric] hospital — just like I felt abandoned when I was in the nuthouse.	Maybe my daughter will get the help she desperately needs. It's better to admit that there is a problem and work with it rather than deny it and refuse help for her.
	I care about my daughter and I'm involved in family therapy with both of them and I will be seeing her when she's in hospital — so at least she knows that I'm not abandoning her.
If I had been a better parent, they wouldn't be in such bad shape.	I was the best parent I knew how to be at the time. It sure wasn't good enough but I gave them all I had to give. I can learn to be a better parent once I can really believe that I'm a good person.

display towards her. Examples of the cognitive restructuring of these various beliefs are shown in Tables 17.2, 17.3, and 17.4.

The issue of Eileen's limit setting with her daughters was related to her lack of assertion skills generally. She subsequently attended an assertion training group during which she became increasingly abe to impose suitable limits on her daughters' behavior.

Outcome of Treatment

Eileen reported in follow-up sessions that one daughter was still experiencing serious emotional and behavioral problems, but Eileen said that she would not waste the therapist's time with self-blame and self-denigratory thoughts. Instead she stated that she 'put my energy into helping my daughter to solve her problems'. This daughter was still in treatment. During the three-month follow-up period, the same daughter was accidently found by Eileen with Marc engaging in erotic kissing at his home. She intervened immediately, left with both daughters and reported the incident to the local child welfare agency. She now sees Marc occasionally on neutral ground such as in a restaurant, but refuses to continue the relationship on the same intimate basis as before. Although saddened by this, she feels very satisfied with the fact that she is both willing and able to protect herself and her daughters if and when necessary.

The second daughter seems to have responded positively to Eileen's stability and fairness in building a good mother–daughter relationship. This daughter

Table 17.5. *Cognitive restructuring of Beliefs Concerning Abuse of Offspring: Alison*

Distorted belief	Alternative beliefs
Abused children become abusing parents, therefore I may hurt my children. I have sometimes felt that I might do so (1. overgeneralization, 2. disqualifying the positive, 3. emotional reasoning).	1. Some but not all abused children become abusive parents. 2. I have never abused my children. 3. Many parents feel that they could hurt thier children at times, but they do not do so.

expressed her concern about her sister's continuing self-destructive behavior. She made a decision that 'that's a stupid way to live' and has settled into attending to her studies and developing an age appropriate lifestyle.

Case Illustration: Alison

This victim and her partner have two children, a son aged 6 years and a daughter aged 4 years. Alison was concerned that she might abuse her children because she was abused and this belief was cognitively restructured as shown in Table 17.5.

She also expressed considerable concern about her angry feelings and outbursts towards her children. On one occasion she telephoned the therapist and described the following incident. Her son Brian had refused to give his sister Lily the only remaining paintbrush and complained about his sister using his coveralls. Alison initially attempted to reason with him to no avail, she then sent him to his bedroom and after a few minutes of 'seething' burst into the room with a pail of paint and threw it at him. Both the victim and son were terrified. She telephoned her spouse who agreed that the expression of anger was not appropriate but that 'all of us lose our temper sometimes'. Alison felt very guilty and ashamed of herself. She stated that she wished that she were her 'old self' because it was predictable and made her less like other nasty, vulnerable human beings because she always kept strong feelings in check and therefore was always in control. Now she was afraid of herself. The therapist emphasized the normality of *feeling* anger but that the inappropriate expression of anger and fear of losing control may be related to her lack of skill in coping with strong feelings. The victim was also reinforced for having told Brian that her behavior was inappropriate and unacceptable.

Alison seemed to be particularly prone to strong anger reactions in situations with her children when she feels that she is not in control, and also sometimes when the events seem to recapitulate the childhood encounters between herself and her older brother. These circumstances are implicated in the incident described above.

It was arranged that the victim would receive some anger control training and that she would participate in an assertiveness training group (Chap. 19).

Conclusion

It seems likely, though as yet unproven, that the majority of victims are adequate and caring mothers, although some perceive themselves as failures by their own unrealistic standards. Around two-thirds of the victims who had children in the U. of M. series reported that they were inadequate or physically abusive mothers at some time. These relatively high rates may reflect the particular nature of this sample of victims and/or they may be inflated by the unrealistically high standards of parenting applied by some of these victims. When inadequate parenting does occur it may include child management problems and the parentification of daughters with an enhanced risk of their being sexually abused.

CHAPTER 18

Relations With Family of Origin and Offender

Among the offenders against the victims in the U. of M. series 75% were related to the victims and the remaining 25% were acquaintances many of whom were closely integrated with the victims' families (Table 2.4). Thus, the following discussion applied to many families of origin which include offenders either as members or close acquaintances.

Exploitation of Victim

One feature of the relations between many victims and their family of origin is the expectation of family members that the victim will continue to meet their needs and demands as she did as a parentified and/or compliant child. In the eyes of family members this is a perfectly reasonable expectation which the victim should meet regardless of her own rights and wishes and of any responsibilities she has to her partner and children.

A frequent consequence of such overdependence and exploitation by the family of origin is that the victim has difficulty in undergoing the normal process of separation/individuation. As Wooley and Vigilanti describe it 'This process includes the ability to practice new ways of relating and behaving, including being able to experiment with adult behaviors rather than relying on parent/child interactions, dependency, and manipulation. In essence, it is gaining and unfolding a differentiated personality. In addition, the woman who is beginning to undergo separation/individuation appears to differentiate herself from her parents, while at the same time, moving toward more realistic expectations of them and acceptance of their limitations' (1984, p. 351).

Scapegoating of Victim

The overwhelming negative reactions by family members to the disclosure of sexual abuse by the victim in childhood are discussed in Chapter 2. Similar

173

reactions from the family of origin occur if the abuse is disclosed or discussion of it is revived by the victim when she is an adult. For example, other family members may be hostile towards her, deny the abuse, blame the victim for what happened, side with the offender, or withdraw from the crisis of disclosure or revival. In short, the victim is scapegoated rather than supported by other family members because she is 'rocking the boat' of an allegedly close family system, threatening its survival, and perhaps evoking guilt in its members for not protecting the victim.

Victim's Anger Reactions

In adulthood, many incest victims report reactions of anger and hostility towards their abusive father, and even more frequently towards their unprotective mother (e.g. Gordy, 1983; Herman, 1981). For example, Meiselman (1978) expands on these reactions in incest victims as follows:

> The daughter who continued to express hatred and contempt for her father usually had no contact with him as an adult . . . The forgiving daughters maintained contact with their fathers and usually had fixed on an explanation for the father's incestuous behavior that allowed them to think that he was 'not his normal self' at the same time of the incest. None of the daughters justified the incest as an acceptable form of behavior, but they found it understandable if they perceived that the father was drunk, psychotic, or under unusual stress at the time it occurred . . .
>
> When the daughter continued to love her mother, the relationship was usually nonconflictual, because the mother was not perceived as being responsible for the incest situation. However, when the mother was disliked the relationship with her was a serious source of stress in adult life, because in contrast with disliked fathers, very few daughters had cut off the relationship with their mother, despite high levels of anger and tension. The mothers were often seriously disturbed women who were extremely dependent on their daughters and kept them feeling sufficiently guilty to prevent an escape from the relationship . . . the mother hung like an albatross around the daughter's neck many years after the incest affair . . . (pp. 219–221).

Victim's Grief Reactions

Grief reactions have also been reported among previously sexually abused women. For example, Wooley and Vigilanti (1984) write 'the sexual-abuse victim is coming face to face with a deep sense of loss. These losses include: loss of the desired and hoped-for family and a normal childhood; loss of a healthy and appropriate parent–child relationship; loss of the role played in the family and the corresponding self-identity . . . For the clients, a psychological death occurs. There is much sadness, crying, and anguish; it is a difficult, intense time . . . This grieving process is essential to the final task of separation/ individuation. If it does not emerge, the [victim] is usually not able to relinquish her old identity' (p. 351).

Victim's Loyalty and Idealization

Alongside the negative features of exploitation, scapegoating, anger and grief, there is often considerable loyalty in the relations between victims and other family members, which perhaps arises from the previous parentification of the victim. Her feelings of loyalty are often associated with a somewhat idealized view of her family of origin. Commonly, she has been indoctrinated in childhood with the belief that her family is close, supportive, and able to meet all her needs within its ranks (Chap. 3). This inaccurate and unrealistic view may persist into her adult life.

Conclusion

The family of origin may continue its overdependence on the exploitation of the victim when she becomes an adult, regardless of her own rights and responsibilities to her own nuclear family. She may be scapegoated for disclosing her abuse or reviving this issue. Incest victims may experience strong feelings of anger towards an abusive father, and perhaps even more frequently towards a non-protective mother. Feelings of grief arising from loss of several aspects of normal childhood experience are also common. Despite these negative features the relations of victims with their family of origin are frequently characterized by considerable loyalty often associated with idealization. Case illustrations of victims' relations with family of origin are presented below.

In the U. of M. program the victims were not regularly encouraged to confront their offenders and family members on the topic of the abuse and its consequences for the victims, but during therapy some victims developed a strong desire to undertake such confrontations in which case the therapist attempted to guide and prepare the victim so that she is minimally exposed to the risk of harm and distress and most likely to benefit from the confrontation. Ideally many victims would like the offender or family members to accept responsibility for their part in the abuse and to express regret for its adverse consequences. Unfortunately, the confrontation may well instead evoke negative reactions and scapegoating of the victim as discussed above. The strong possibility of such reactions occurring makes it highly desirable to structure the confrontation and to prepare the victim for it so that the risk of damage is minimized. The following are some points to bear in mind when undertaking these tasks. First, it is usually inadvisable to attempt confrontations with offenders or family members of violent disposition who may beat or rape the victim. Before any confrontation is attempted the victim should be sufficiently advanced in therapy to have substantially rejected the self-blaming and self-denigratory beliefs associated with her role in the abuse that are discussed in Part 2. In other words she should be reasonably 'fire-proof' against similar accusations by the person she is confronting. Among the techniques used for preparing victims are role playing the confrontation, writing letters for discussion with the therapist which may or may not be sent to the offender or family member, and listing a small number of points to be made in case the victim 'goes blank' under the stress of the confrontation. More detailed discussion of preparatory structuring and guidance is offered by MacFarlane and Korbin (1983) including the following basic messages that may be helpful to victims:

> . . . expect denial and do not overreact when you get it; people need personal reasons and a sense of a secure environment to face up to this problem after so many years; the denial may be a temporary reaction.
> . . . strive for patience with the process; time can have a strong effect on the impact of initial disclosure; few people have the same internal time frames for dealing with personal reactions.
> . . . expect the intervention to bring pain and crisis to other family members; remember that you are not the cause of the pain, you have merely exposed it.
> . . . do not look to the confrontation for validation of either the abuse or yourself; do not depend on absolution from the abuser for your own feelings of guilt or self-blame; it is not essential to get those things from him and you can find them elsewhere, hopefully from within yourself (p. 234). (Reprinted with permission © 1983 Pergamon Press.)

Case Illustration: Alison

Alison's family background and sexual victimization by her uncle are described in Chapter 10, and many current sources of conflict between the victim and her family of origin were covered during therapy.

Resentment Toward Father

The victim expressed resentment toward her father because: (a) he never taught her to relate to men; (b) his upbringing really made her vulnerable to her uncle's abuse; (c) her conception was an accident and her father had always resented her; (d) he had never genuinely cared for her or anyone else; and (e) she had never had a father and had always wanted one—she feels cheated. Her feelings towards her father were expressed in the following letter she wrote to him but not with the intention of sending it.

Dear —————

Do you know that the hardest part in getting started with this letter was dear sir—It was how to greet you. Dear Dad—Why aren't you my dad.

Dear Father—Too formal, too importing of wisdom—someone that I should be able to turn to—yet I can't or won't for you are everything I want to turn against. You hurt me so badly and that pain doesn't seem to go away. I can dull it for a while but then it builds again until like today it's full blown and I want to curl up in a little ball and protect the sore or I want to burst forth and smash you. I do hate you and I feel no guilt in saying that. You were never there for me. Not even when I was small. You took from me and showed me that it didn't matter— what I gave was worthless—perhaps it was, for all I gave was me. And you hurt me you old sod. You hurt me and I hate you—I could spit in your face and feel no remorse. You chain me down but not with chains—with nothing. There's nothing you've broken me with nothing—by showing me that I don't matter—I am nothing in your life. Then why intrude into my thoughts and then affect my life. I try not to care and for a while I can dismiss you but then you sneak back and scatter my thoughts, break my ability to concentrate, wear down my faith that I'll have to succeed. Every moment every day I fight to keep on track—you don't care you don't even know—you just sit in your patriarchal throne and watch the destruction you've wrought. But you don't see, for you make no mistakes. If others struggle it must be their fault, they're the weak, they're the ones not strong enough to survive. Well I survived and now I'm weakening. I want to live, but I'm really starting to feel tired—I don't want to be a ninny, feel like a fool, disturb everyone else's lives—but I won't back up and the only way I can get that is to ask for it and I was taught never to ask for myself, I must manage on my own, never let others know I can't cope; that I'm less than in control. You and your entourage have given no support and I don't want it for you are the one who is suffering, aren't you? I'm the wicked one who is making poor old you suffer. I'm the mean one, the unforgiving one. Well I wasn't always. When I was small I'm sure I loved you like any child loves her father—I'm sure I turned to you, I'm sure I sat on your knee. You say I used to comb your hair—I can't remember those times at all—something went wrong.

You hurt me, you rejected me, so I rejected you. You weren't there for me—you never cared, you never knew. But you did know, you saw more than you let on—you're not a stupid man—just caught up in protecting your own ego at the expense of your kid. But that's OK—parenting's not easy—but the least you could do is admit you made some mistakes. Instead those years are never talked about. You want to pretend it never happened. Well I can't pretend not any longer—those years came at a crucial time for me. Consequently it's very much a part of why I'm me and the only way I can get rid of them is to get rid of me—which I don't want to do—I want to live. But to do that I need to integrate all those days into my being—to see them as they really were—to deal with the feelings at last—to allow myself to feel—to stay in situations and not to run—for you see I never did. The most I felt was confusion and inadequate and responsible. I don't know how much of my feeling towards you is related to [the offender]. In those days I just wanted to avoid you and that I could do very skillfully—with [him] I didn't.

I could have, I'm sure, but I didn't. I thought he needed me—what a fool! I was independent, I didn't *need* anyone, I only *wanted* someone and mom filled that bill when she became overwrought with you and I was a good liar or at least I thought I was though it was lying more than anything which got me into trouble.

What's interesting is that you [and the offender] lied. You wanted me to believe that you were the only men that I needed—that all other men would take my heart and hurt me but that I would be the fool for having given my heart to them in the first place—that I need only follow your advice, turn to you and all would be well—Well Mr . . . it turns out you win—you were the better liar. Here's your prize—Goodbye!

Quite early in therapy the victim's father went into a depression again. He has a long history of doing this whenever his absolute control over the family is threatened. The victim was blamed for causing his current depression by talking about her abuse and refusing to have contact with him. Her mother and sister were pressuring her to resume contact and comfort her father. Coercion included the mother's distress arising from the situation, the threat that the father might die of cancer before contact is resumed, and that their estrangement might adversely affect the disposition of his estate as far as the victim is concerned. The victim felt extremely uncomfortable in the presence of her father and she could not tolerate any contact at the present time. The therapist suggested deferring the issue of renewal of contact until the victim is coping better with the abuse experience and she can then decide what kind of contact she can tolerate. It is not unreasonable to ask her parents to give her the time she needs for this. This plan was followed throughout the remainder of this phase of therapy and the familial pressure to resume contact lessened although with some intermittent attempts at coercion.

As therapy progressed Alison reported that she was no longer troubled during contacts with her father. She dealt with him directly and expressively and this made her feel good. Later Alison's mother was diagnosed as having cancer and she died six weeks later. Initially the victim experienced some conflict over the role in relation to her widowed father as she describes in the following notes:

> My relationship with my father is being juggled and I'm not sure what I want to do. I'm so uncomfortable with him, and without my Mom as a buffer it's quite difficult. I don't want to be inhumane and ignore him, but there's really no love or respect between us. I feel very bitter towards him and I have trouble seeing his grief as being genuine. I'm feeling family pressure to ensure Dad does OK, to include him in our activities, to see that he doesn't slump, but I have no desire to play that role even for my mother's sake. Yet, I feel like a hang-man when I talk this way and that if Dad slumps into a depression it'll be my fault because I didn't care for him in a way that a loving daughter would. I know these thoughts are irrational, but nevertheless they're very real and I'm finding it difficult to strike a balance between what is expected and what is right for me. Either I'm cheating someone else or I'm cheating myself and either way I feel guilty.

In fact, the victim quite quickly established and maintained a degree of contact with her father that was within the limits of her own comfort and which she implemented of her own choice and not because she felt compelled as a dutiful daughter. No further attention needed to be given to the victim's family of origin throughout the remainder of therapy.

Ambivalence Toward Mother

Early in therapy Alison reported that she had always thought that her mother was nice and kind and that there was a close relationship between them. This positive view was now mitigated by negative feelings associated with the facts that: (a) there was no depth in the relationship, the mother always avoided anything unpleasant or threatening, and she taught the victim to cover up her feelings rather than expressing them; (b) the mother did not protect the victim from the risk of abuse by a known offender; (c) she was not supportive when the victim disclosed the abuse in adulthood; and (d) she is currently pressing the victim to make up with her father. This ambivalence towards the mother is expressed in the following letter the victim wrote, but did not send.

Dear Mom:

You know that I loved you and I love you still. I am sorry for what I'm putting you through now but it's something that I must do if I am ever going to survive. There are times when I feel so angry and so hurt and so empty and the conflict that these emotions churn up is often overwhelming. When I'm angry I want to lash out and scream at you all, when I'm hurt I just want to cry and ask, 'Why—was I that bad?' and when I feel empty I just want to curl up and be alone. There are times when I want to hold you and tell you everything will be OK, but then I think maybe they won't and I don't really care. You are a strong woman but your strength frightens me because it's like a double-edged sword with a magnetism that draws you to it and then cuts you down with its coldness and rejection. You never taught me to recognize anger and how to deal with it—you never showed anger, only hurt. You always stayed for more. You stayed beside him [victim's father] when all he did was dump on you. You never respected yourself as a woman with pride, deserving to be treated properly. And yet you always maintained a strong front, always took care of your appearance, never allowed yourself to appear beaten. You were kind and loving to your friends and to me. You enveloped me but you never saw me. You taught me to act, to protect my hurts and to feel only certain things, to feel anger as frustration even when I was ready to burst, and if I was disrespectful of him I became your brat. Boy, did you blow it. I'm not a brat. I never was. I was nice little [Alison] who did what she was told, never got into trouble, was polite to the world and had so much love to give. What a joke. You blew it and so did I. I fell apart. You never did. I'm not as strong as you. I'm sorry. I don't like the way I am now, at times I hate myself, but it seems to take less from me. I want to be nice. I want to be pleasant. I want to be loving. But I can't love people who can't feel and be open and real. Who are only concerned about maintaining pretenses. For that reason our relationship and hence our love is very superficial for though the hurt it gives is very deep a mere scratch cuts it to the quick. You are for him, you will stand beside him regardless. You will endure all sorts of ill behavior from him but not from me. For he is my father and 'thou shalt honor thy father'. Well he never honored his and as far as I'm concerned he has spat on me for the last time. I don't like him; I never have. I'm only sorry you have trouble accepting my feelings and blame me for not making his life more comfortable. I wasn't born hating him and I don't think a child decides to hate a parent just for the sake of it. So if you're concerned about blame it must lie with him. A child is taught to feel badly about herself and you and Dad taught that to four children. I can understand why you don't want to see that—it must hurt. But it also hurts to be one of those children. You provided for us but only in return for indebtedness and gratitude. And so you see Mom we've got nowhere to grow—it's finished because you refuse to see. When you used to hurt, I hurt. Now that I hurt, you refuse to help. It's my fault. How beautifully you expressed it when you said 'As far as your Dad and I are concerned we feel we are perfectly innocent for how could we do something about something [the sexual abuse] we didn't know about'. You assure me you would have done something had you known and so the responsibility for not having told you remains with me. Be that as it may—I really don't care. I just want to get on with it and get myself on track so that I can develop my own family as best as I can. You're sorry I feel the way I do and I'm sorry you feel the way you do. You choose to hide. I can't because for me to hide would be death and I've decided to live, to face it and conquer it as best as I can. I am no longer a part of your family—it's no good for me and right now I need what's good for me. You're welcome to be a part of my family but you must realize it's on my terms—I can't yield to you any longer, I just don't have the ability, the strength, the courage whatever it takes any longer. I only hope you understand that what I'm doing needs to be done so that I'll have something to give to my family. You have your family, now I have mine, and I own the responsibility for them.

Love

[Alison]

Closeness of Family of Origin

It was always stressed that the family was very close but during therapy the victim came to see this to be an illusion and myth. In fact, there is no mutual caring or support and much overt discord. All family members are completely egocentric. All are so fragile and concerned with their own self-esteem that they have nothing to give to others. All use people to meet their own needs. This is covered up by the pretence and façade of being a close family, which is ritualized by enormous emphasis on extravagant and excessive thanks, compliments, and celebrations. The victim was threatening this façade by raising the issue of her victimization.

Reactions to Disclosure

The family of origin have reacted negatively to the victim disclosing her victimization. They have not been supportive and this confirms her view that they would not have been supportive had she disclosed the abuse at the time. She feels that they do not like her now that she is no longer nice and compliant.

They will never admit that they contributed to her problems in any way. Her father has never admitted fault for anything in his life. The family see it as *her* fault, *she* cannot handle it. These family reactions are described more fully in the victim's notes after reading Summit's (1983) article:

> My family's reaction to the disclosure is nothing, no acknowledgement, no support, just a sweeping under the carpet with the unspoken message being: 'This is your problem [Alison] and if you want to let it interfere in your life that's too bad. We can't help. I only hope you get over this before it's too late and your dad dies. Otherwise you're going to feel very guilty.'
>
> The pressure to believe that I am responsible is overwhelming, makes me feel quite panicky and causes me to question—maybe I am responsible. My mother's and sister's remark 'Why didn't you say something' make it seem that had I told them at the time they surely would have done something. As a child I sensed that they would not have responded and the fear of having that proven true was enough to make me not want to risk disclosure. I see their present lack of response as being confirmation that my feelings as a child were indeed correct. By not revealing the secret as a child I kept in control of my destiny, I was responsible for myself and protected myself from what I feel to be one of the worst forms of rejection for a child to bear—the realization that their parents, whom the child is taught to love and respect, will not protect or defend the child. The pain of this realization for me at age 31 is suffocating; for a child facing this realization my heart bleeds.
>
> In my situation I see my uncle as being the perpetrator, my family (most significantly my mother and father) the collaborators and my father and oldest brother as being perpetrators of a class different from my uncle. I am angriest at my family in a way that many incest daughters are angriest at their mothers.

Individuation from Family of Origin

The victim reacted to these conflicts with her family of origin by increasingly individuating herself from them in several ways. In the face of the importance attached to celebrations in her family of origin the victim decided not to accompany her parents to her sister's home in [another city] for Christmas and New Year, and not to attend her brother's suddenly arranged wedding [in another city]. She now perceives her family more objectively and recognizes the hollowness of the façade of closeness. She is in the process of developing a new identity and role as a wife and a mother rather than a dutiful daughter; until recently pleasing her parents was much more important than her relationship with her husband. Her self-esteem was dependent on the approval of her parents but she is now moving towards becoming more confident in her own opinion of herself. These moves towards individuation, autonomy, and her own marriage were not without doubts and conflicts but the victim understood that these are to be expected during any period of transition.

To some extent her family of origin persisted in expecting to exercise primacy and control over the victim's life. She would really have liked to have their permission to individuate herself but as this was not forthcoming she had to make and trust her own decision in this respect. This led to discussion of three themes in therapy: (a) the inappropriateness of her parents expecting to retain primacy in her life rather than valuing her growing independence and establishment of her own family: (b) the need to weigh any hurt to her parents against any hurt to herself, her husband, and her children if she does not give them priority; (c) the difficulty the victim has in separating herself from her father because she has always wanted and has never had a good paternal experience, which makes her feel deprived and cheated. She knows her father can never fill this gap for her, and yet has difficulty in letting him go. Eventually, Alison no longer felt compelled to be the 'good daughter' and the family pressure on her to fill this role was alleviated.

Relationship with Offender

The offender is now dead but the victim wrote the following letter expressing how she feels about his exploitation of her trust and affection:

> Dear Uncle . . . :
>
> You know Uncle . . . I really would like to get mad at you—to scream at you, tear at you, hit you with all my might—but I can't. You make me feel only hurt, but it's a hurt so deep that it pierces my very soul, and for that I want to hate you. You see it's a hurt that never goes away, it lives with me and though I can cover it at times better than others, it's always there ready to surface. You drain me Uncle . . . , you hurt me like no one ever could. I loved you and you used me, you betrayed me, you tricked me. You never loved me. You loved only yourself, and I see now that you would use anyone to satisfy that love. I was never special to you—I was only a thing, used like a machine to do things to you and for you to do things to. How you must have laughed and been in your glory at finding another sucker. Did you ever think about what you were doing? How could you be so stupid, so selfish, so uncaring? As a child I had only one gift to give and that was my trust. You took that trust, Uncle . . . and you never gave it back.
>
> I've often thought you must have seen my pain, you must have seen how shy and timid I was. I was backward and you took advantage of

that. I needed you to be strong, direct, responsible, and caring. I wanted to believe that you were. In those days I was taught not to question an adult. But I'm beyond that now—you hurt me, Uncle . . . , and I want to know why.

Later in therapy fresh information from the extended family indicated that the offender had abused other children. This made victim feel less 'special' to the offender, whom she regarded as the only man who had cared for her as a child. This led to discussion in therapy that the offender may have loved and cared for her as well as exploiting her sexually, and that it is understandable that she may have loved the good things about him while hating the abuse. People can accept and love others while setting limits on their behavior, for example a parent with a child. It is difficult, however, for an 11-year-old to set limits on her uncle. As the victim wrote at this stage in therapy about her childhood relationship with the offender and her family:

I grappled for control and had none—I hate them all—They had no right to treat me that way for I was a good kid—I didn't hurt anyone and I didn't hurt my uncle. He hurt me so much and I can't believe why he did—I cared for him so much and he screwed it all up. Then I tried to have control but instead I just yielded. I don't know how he could care for me and do those things and yet I didn't stay away. I kept going back—I loved the farm—I loved the openness, I walked for miles across the fields through the bush—I was alone and I could dream and fantasize about what it must have been like to be a pioneer and what my grandparents on my mother's side must have been like, and why I didn't have them to love—for I always felt different, I always felt like I was on the outside looking in—I never felt a part of situations—always an observer—always alert, I always kept a safe distance from which I could see what was coming at me.

Case Illustration: Sara

Demographic Characteristics

Sara (45) was self-referred to the U. of M. program. She is the eldest of two children. Her father is alive and in good health. Her mother died 10 years ago. Sara has been married to John (44) for fifteen years and they have one son (11). Two daughters (21 and 22) from Sara's previous marriage also live with the couple. Both clients are educated to university level, employed in a professional occupational group, Caucasian, and non-denominational.

Family of Origin

Sara's father, the offender in this instance, is retired from his professional

occupational group. She described him as someone who was like two people—
'a good dad' and a 'bad dad'. The 'good dad' was charming, funloving, fond of
animals, playful and affectionate with her. The 'bad dad' was socially isolated,
unpredicatable in moods, physically violent towards his spouse, and emotionally and sexually abusive with her. The 'bad dad' was eventually hospitalized
several times for a severe psychiatric disorder and remains under psychiatric
supervision. Sara adored him as a child and prided herself in being the 'only one
in the family who could predict and handle his moods'.

Sara's mother died from cancer. The mother had originally obtained a
professional qualification but she had been a homemaker throughout her
marriage. She was described as a non-nurturing, emotionally distant person
who was domineering with her husband and children. She had a violent temper
and was frequently physically and emotionally abusive with her children. Sara
was extremely afraid of her mother and attempted to avoid upsetting her by
being a very obedient child. During the assessment process she wrote about her
mother as follows:

> I'm not sure we're working on the right parent, certainly my father
> was a swine and what he did was very wrong, but what he did hurt me
> less than what my mother did. That woman would have made Dr
> Mengele squeamish, she was the most brutal destructive, cruel,
> sadistic, and vicious person I have ever known, it goes far beyond
> being angry at her for not protecting me from my dad, I can forgive
> her [for] that easily, but I can never forgive her for the systematic
> destruction of my confidence, creativeness, and self. I shed no tears
> when she died, and I doubt I ever will for her. However, from the
> grave she rules my life very well still. I try very hard to shut her out but
> it's very hard.

Victimization Experience

The major victimization was by Sara's father from babyhood to age eleven. The
father was in his late twenties when the sexual abuse began. There were more
than 100 incidents ranging from the exhibitionistic display of his genitalia to the
victim to simulated/'dry' intercourse. One failed attempt of penile–vaginal
penetration occurred when the victim was aged ten.

The sexual victimization ceased following the father's first hospitalization,
and disclosure of the sexual victimization by the father to the treating psychiatrist. Sara believed that she was at least in part responsible for his psychiatric
breakdown and hospitalizations. The mother appeared to be aware of the
ongoing sexual abuse. For example, the father would fondle Sara's genitals in
her mother's presence. Her mother ignored this behavior. However, at these
times, Sara's father would suggest to the mother that she should be doing the
same thing with their son in order to teach him about sex. Following the father's

disclosure to the psychiatrist, Sara noted that the sexual victimization ceased and that her mother arranged for Sara to stay with maternal relatives during holidays effectively limiting the amount of time the father could spend alone with her.

Loyalty to Family of Origin

Disclosure of negative details relating to her parents, family functioning and sexual victimization precipitated feelings of intense guilt, thoughts of self-destructiveness, and a desire to terminate therapy. Sara stated that revealing these details provoked intense guilt arising from a feeling of disloyalty which in turn precipitated a strong feeling of loss of control and a desire to be self-destructive. She felt that the only solution to these intense feelings was to terminate therapy. The therapist suggested she complete a written cost–benefit analysis about therapy before she terminated. Her completed assignment is shown in Table 18.1.

Following completion and discussion of the cost–benefit analysis, the victim continued therapy and was challenged about her perception of loyalty, that is, does loyalty also mean protecting the other person when they are abusive. This assignment was completed as follows:

> I have always seen loyalty as a very idealistic condition, one is prepared to go to any lengths to protect or defend that person to whom one is being loyal. One cannot tolerate negative remarks made by others or any criticisms or attacks on that person. Ideally to be truly loyal, one should be prepared to suffer greatly even die to defend the object of one's loyalty.

Further in this narrative she questioned the validity of her definition stating 'when I see it [the definition] in black and white, it is the stuff of martyrdom . . . there is room for it within reason as long as it doesn't become self-abusive'.

Recognizing that the key factor in her definition was non-critical acceptance of the other person's behavior and non-disclosure of any negative aspects of that person, the victim agreed to explore the learning experiences which contributed to her feelings of extreme guilt and desire to be self-destructive when she engaged in behavior she felt indicated disloyalty to her parents:

> My father told me that I should not talk about the incest because other people were stupid and did not understand that he was doing the right thing, my mother also didn't understand so it was best not to talk about it with her.
>
> When my mother bloodied my eyes or left marks on my body I was told to make excuses, like I bumped into a doorknob or fell on

Table 18.1. *Cost–Benefit Analysis of Remaining in Therapy: Sara*

Possible Pros	Possible Cons
Chance to work out problems	Possibility of going really crazy
Improve sex life (do I really care at this point?)	Possiblity of wrecking marriage (very bad for [children] and [spouse])
Possiblity of fuller life, enriched relationships	Possibility of no change or worsened relationships
Gain confidence	Lose confidence

something—but I can't remember the rationale, I'm sure she can't have said people would think she was bad—I just seemed to know it would be bad to tell.

I was constantly being told that I was bad, selfish, and ungrateful and lazy, so any criticisms I might have of my parents were already answered—anything I didn't like was because I was rotten.

When my mother was beaten black and blue she never told anyone, she put her hat on and went shopping as if nothing had happened. When people asked how the family was—it was always fine, she never told anyone about the bad things. I guess I just learned by example.

It's hard to remember specific incidents where I learned not to criticize. I just never did, I never dared; to criticize or be angry meant to be screamed at or hit.

Arrangements were made for the victim to meet, in the presence of the therapist, another victim who had completed thcrapy and who also had had great difficulty with feeling disloyal to her parents when she disclosed details of her abuse by both parents. Following this Sara restructured her belief that she could not be critical of her parents. Examples of this restructuring process are shown in Table 18.2.

Sara's reactions to these and other aspects of therapy are described in the following extract from her additional comments on the Client Satisfaction Questionnaire completed at termination of treatment:

I started therapy for several reasons: (1) because I felt I was not 'normal', I wasn't like other people; (2) because I felt my husband was dissatisfied with our relationship, especially the sexual side and that he felt I was mainly to blame; (3) because I felt the need to have more control over my life.

I had heard about the program through a conference on Sexual Abuse I had attended. I was frankly skeptical, I had seen three other psychiatrists and they had all helped in very small areas, but all were

Table 18.2. *Cognitive Restructuring of Beliefs Concerning Non-Criticism of Parents:*
Sara

Distorted beliefs	Alternative beliefs
Nice people don't run down their parents, it sounds ungrateful or selfish.	Some nice people may have had very bad parents, so if they tell the truth they have to say they were bad.
I'm really not convinced they were that bad. I feel like too big a thing is made of what happened — maybe my problems are all my own and would have been there even if I'd had average parents.	Why am I so incensed by abuse of other children, why do I fight to protect my own? Why do I feel it's all right for me to have suffered but not anyone else.
	They were sometimes bad so I have to face that.
	Because I am an adult woman with valid opinions, I have the right to be honest about my past without fear of retaliation or hurt.

much too afraid, threatened, unprepared to deal with the sexual abuse problem. At the time I saw their responses as my problem in that I could not be helped—the three were all men. I had also attended a group of formerly abused women but found it to be somewhat masochistic as we tended to wallow in our pain without making any attempts to really climb out of the past.

The first positive thing about the therapy was that I liked my therapist, and I respect her intelligence and ability. It was also important that I had warned her that I might bullshit my way out of therapy—this would happen if I felt it was not working or I became bored with it, I might then begin supplying the right 'intellectual' answers and labeling them as my true emotional beliefs.

The therapist began the assessment, I had expected pain but since I have told quite a large number of people about the sexual molestation since I first disclosed in my late teens, I had not anticipated as much pain or confusion as I felt. I became very very angry about having to suffer all this pain and confusion again. I directed much of my anger at my husband, whom I saw as responsible for making me suffer the pain. If he would be satisfied with our sex life, I wouldn't have to relive the horror of my past; in a sense I began to identify him strongly with my father and realized that, in fact, I always had done. In fact, anyone who made any sexual demands on me, I immediately identified with my father and began feeling the same ambiguity towards the other person. Things would be fine while I was in the first throes of a grand passion or 'in lust' because I would usually be making all the first sexual moves or eagerly awaiting them, but anyone who would ask for sexual love, or even affection when I was not in the mood, met a zombie, I would withdraw into my own mind and leave them to pester my empty body. It was, and at times still is, a conditioned response which I have great difficulty in controlling, for me to speak once this process has begun is almost physically impossible.

As the assessment continued I became absolutely terrified by my rage and anger towards my husband and our marriage. I saw it as doomed to failure. Unable to accept the pain that I would cause him and my children I turned that rage on myself and tried to convince myself, my therapist, and my husband that I was truly mad, I seriously thought of suicide and condemned myself bitterly for not having the courage to carry it through. At this point I nearly cancelled a trip to Europe to study languages, alone, that I had planned—this was a form of self-punishment and would have been terrible since the trip was to become an integral part of my therapy.

The therapist identified the loyalty issue to my parents, particularly to my father, as being a major stumbling block and began to chip at my resistance to any serious attempt on my part at seeing my father as a real human being, and not the sweet mythical human being I had invented (who did have one or two tiny faults that were really not too important). She introduced me to another young woman who had had a serious problem breaking down the barriers of loyalty to the offender. At the time it was not a great success, I rejected the young woman and most particularly her attitude to her father and mother, I felt her a cruel and hard person, quite unforgiving and unloving. However, it did provide me with food for thought and a role model I had never had, the young lady was filed for future reference.

My equilibrium began to return to a more normal level and the therapist continued to battle with the loyalty issue until I left for my trip to Europe.

Before leaving on my trip to Europe I noticed that I had a three hour stopover on a Saturday morning at the airport of my family's city. Knowing that if the situation was reversed I would rush to see my daughter/son/brother/father, at the airport, etc. I sent a Special Delivery letter to that city to tell my family exactly when and where I would be on that Saturday.

I left for Europe with the study group, very excited and not really nervous at all. On arriving at the airport for the stopover I imagined the faces of my family—my father and my brother—I expected to see them; I waited and I looked around, I felt disappointed—I admitted to myself I felt disappointed (a very unusual thing), finally after two hours I accepted they were not coming, so I decided to phone my home to see if they were sick or had car problems—hoping there was some such excuse. I phoned, they were all at home, all well, they simply had not bothered to come up, my father talked to me for a few moments and then wandered off into the garden. Nobody ever apologized for not coming up, they had received the letter but I guess it just wasn't important to them. Well that hurt, it hurt and I was furious, all the therapist's chipping began to break into great big cracks and I began to see my family as they really were and not as I wanted to see them. . . .

When I arrived back in the UK from Europe, after a night's rest I arranged to visit my family. I named a time, but I had forgotten how far it is from the station to the house and so I was about a half hour late. As I walked up my old familiar road, I felt an enormous lump in my throat, my father was waiting at the gate—he must be waiting for me—his daughter—he obviously really loved me. As soon as I arrived he buzzed my cheek and was gone as fast as his old legs would carry him to get supper—it was not me he was waiting for it was his fish and chips.

And so great revelations are made, I watched my father that evening after he returned with his fish and chips, a poor crazy old man living in an abusive home with his son, daughter-in-law and two grandchildren, all of whom hate him, all of whom freely admit they wish he would die so that they could get all the money he has and the house. He sat there, the man who beat my mother black and blue, who sexually molested me, lost in his own thoughts; sometimes he would try to catch my eye, with the old twinkle in it that would mean 'we are co-conspirators aren't we', but I think he was afraid because he could see I wasn't a little girl anymore and I wasn't going to play his games anymore.

At the end of therapy, Sara's relationship with her family of origin was minimal. Her decision was based on the realization that neither her father nor her brother and his spouse were capable of relating to each other or to her in a genuine, caring way. She did however plan to continue her relationship with her young niece and nephew whom she liked and wanted to assure that they would not be victimized by their grandfather.

CHAPTER 19

Assertiveness Training Group

The non-assertive person is one who does not honestly and appropriately express his or her feelings, thoughts, and beliefs and who allows his or her rights to be violated by another (Lange & Jakubowski, 1976). Many women who were sexually abused in childhood tend to be passive and subservient individuals who lack communication, social, and assertive skills. This is most obvious within their general interpersonal relationships which frequently are marked by isolation, difference from others and mistrust, and their heterosocial relations which are characterized by their fear of intimacy with males, the tendency to oversexualize the relationship, and the propensity to engage in those which are dissonant (Chap. 11).

One factor in the development of this orientation is the patriarchal families in which these women commonly are socialized. The ideology of this system facilitates an atmosphere of subservience and intimidation wherein female family members are expected to be obedient and faithful to the patriarch under all circumstances and wherein these responses are modeled by the mother. Subsequently, the women do not acquire the appropriate self-protective and social skills which would enable them to exercise their rights and pursue their needs and desires within their relationships with other people (Chap. 3). In addition to this, many previously abused women have impaired self-esteem and tend to think of themselves as being somehow responsible for the victimization. These factors further exacerbate their inability to utilize assertive responses (Part 2).

With the general aim of facilitating such responses an assertiveness training group was provided in the U. of M. program for five victims who were also receiving individual or couple therapy and whose problems included non-assertiveness (Schwab, Jehu, & Gazan, 1987). The specific goals of the intervention were fourfold: (a) to provide the women with the assertive skills whereby they would be equipped to express openly their needs and desires so as to acquire and exert greater control over their own lives and environments; (b) to develop a belief system with respect to assertive behavior that would

191

improve the women's acceptance of their needs and rights; (c) to assist them in reducing the cognitions and fears which impaired their capacity to engage in assertive behavior; and (d) to provide them with the opportunity to begin resolving the difficulties experienced in heterosocial relationships.

Assessment Procedures

Prior to the implementation of the group, each of the participants was assessed by means of the Assessment Interview Protocol for Assertiveness (Appendix E) in order to identify specific difficulties related to assertiveness which required modification. These target problems were monitored by means of Target Complaint Scales (Chap. 12) which were completed by the participants on at least three occasions during the assessment period in order to establish a baseline, and then at weekly intervals throughout the group treatment, and again at follow-up. The problem was considered to be at a clinically significant level if it was rated higher than 4, *a little*.

To monitor more global changes in assertiveness the Assertion Inventory (Gambrill & Richey, 1975) was administered at assessment, termination of group treatment, and follow-up. Finally, client satisfaction was evaluated by means of a questionnaire administered at termination (Table 19.1).

The Assertion Inventory is composed of 40 items and collects information on three aspects of assertiveness: (a) response probability, a measure indicating the likelihood that an individual will behave assertively in specific situations; (b) degree of discomfort, a dimension which indicates the discomfort level experienced by the individual in these situations; and (c) the specific situations in which the person desires to be more assertive. The scale employs a five-point Likert format whereby the respondent indicates the likelihood of engaging in assertive behavior (1 = *always do it* and 5 = *never do it*) and the level of discomfort experienced (1 = *none* and 5 = *very much*). High scores on each dimension indicate a general tendency for non-assertiveness and discomfort respectively. The cutting point is 105 and above for low response probability and 96 and above for high degree of discomfort. The reliability and validity of the instrument are acceptable, but a limitation is that it was developed with a college population from which it may not be appropriately generalized to previously sexually abused women. Nevertheless it is probably the best questionnaire that is currently available for assessing and monitoring the assertiveness of victims.

Treatment Program

The assertiveness group met for 10 sessions, each lasting two hours, at weekly intervals, and there was a follow-up session six weeks after the group ended. It was conducted by a male and female therapist. The presence of the male therapist was designed to provide the women with an opportunity to relate more positively to a male within a protective and supportive environment and to assist them in resolving some of the problems such as oversexualization as well as the fear and mistrust of men which are commonly encountered in their heterosocial relations. It was hypothesized that the women's ability to differentiate between exploitive and non-exploitive situations would be enhanced as the therapist demonstrated that trusting a male is possible, that all men are not necessarily exploitive and abusive, and that some are capable of exhibiting genuine interest and caring. The content of each session is outlined below.

Content of Sessions

Session One

The assessment instruments were administered, the participants introduced themselves briefly, and the goals and rules for the group were explained. These rules included that the women were under no obligation or pressure to divulge any information concerning their sexual abuse which they did not wish to disclose. This was intended to protect their privacy and to minimize any discomfort they may have been experiencing.

Following a break to enable the participants to interact and develop friendships without the therapists (a practice that was followed in every subsequent session), a mini-lecture on the differences between assertiveness, passivity, and aggression was presented by one of the therapists, and this was supplemented by handouts (Butler, 1981, pp. 127, 130, 131; Clionsky, 1983, p. 150; Liberman, King, DeRisi, & McCann, 1975, p. 6) and by the film *Responsible Assertion* (Baxley, 1978) which depicts several models enacting the differences between assertiveness, aggression, and passiveness. The film was particularly useful because it enabled the women to observe the model's facial expressions, hand gestures, and voice tones—non-verbal behaviors which are an extremely important component of assertiveness (Lange & Jakubowski, 1976; Sank & Shaffer, 1984).

For homework assignments each participant was asked to read Bloom, Coburn and Pearlman (1975), Chaps. 1, 3, 4), and to prepare a collage depicting her real self and her ideal self. The real self referred to the way in which she felt about herself at that time whereas the ideal self represented an expression of the person she desired to be. The individuals were given the option of drawing, painting, pasting, writing or using ceramics to complete this exercise. It was intended to assist the women in becoming aware of the feelings they had regarding themselves and to share these with the other group members in the following session (Osborn & Harris, 1975).

Session Two

Following the completion of the Target Complaint Scales, a group-go-around was used to provide all participants with the opportunity to give a brief synopsis of their experiences during the previous week. This procedure promoted member participation and informed other group members of each one's current situation. It was also one method by which the therapists were able to monitor the women's progress. This component was included in every subsequent session.

Similarly during each session, a period of time was set aside to review the homework which had been assigned the previous week. In this session, the personal collage was the focal point of this component. The presentation of the collages was followed by a discussion which emphasized the way in which negative self-images often are maintained by irrational beliefs individuals have regarding various elements of their real self as well as by unreasonable expectations they have for their ideal self. The therapists underlined the importance of accepting one's real self with its strengths and weaknesses while at the same time pursuing the realistic goals and dreams identified in the ideal self.

Next, a mini-lecture which explained the concept of irrational beliefs was presented by one of the therapists. Its purpose was to describe the effect irrational beliefs have upon an individual's behavior and to demonstrate the way in which a person's thinking can be restructured (Lange & Jakubowski, 1976).

A Rational Self-Analysis structured exercise was undertaken which involves having the individuals write down a specific situation in which they desire to be more assertive but in which affective factors such as guilt or anger elicit aggressive or passive responses. Secondly, they are asked to identify and write down the negative or self-defeating thoughts that arise when they think of engaging in assertive behavior in that situation. Thirdly, they are asked to develop challenges to these thoughts (Lange & Jakubowski, 1976).

For homework assignments the participants were asked to repeat the Self-Analysis exercise on at least two occasions, to read Bloom *et al.* (1975, Chaps. 2, 5, 6), and to undertake a Like Yourself exercise (Phelps & Austin, 1975). This involved having the participants write down at least five positive statements about themselves; for example, 'I like the fact that I am endeavoring to become more assertive'. The individuals, then, were asked to stand in front of a mirror and read the list audibly while practicing good eye contact and verbally or non-verbally acknowledging each compliment they gave themselves. This procedure was structured to increase the participants' awareness of their positive traits so as to provide a basis for increased self-esteem and an improved self-concept.

Session Three

After completion of the Target Complaint Scales, the group-go-around, and a review of the previous week's homework assignments, one of the therapists presented a mini-lecture on interpersonal rights (Lange & Jakubowski, 1976). The purpose of this was to assist the group members in developing three basic beliefs which undergird a philosophy of responsible assertion: (a) the belief that assertiveness, rather than passivity, aggression or manipulation invokes self-respect as well as respect for others and, subsequently, leads to increased satisfaction within interpersonal relationships; (b) the belief that everyone has the right to act assertively and to express honestly their beliefs, opinions, and feelings; and (c) the belief that the acceptance of one's rights necessitates that the rights of others are respected as well. For example, in accepting the right to make a mistake, an individual must be prepared to accept the right of others to make mistakes.

This presentation on interpersonal rights was important because it provided the participants with a basis by which they were able to justify assertive behavior. Furthermore, the identification and acceptance of interpersonal rights functions to reduce several internal injunctions which frequently inhibit assertive behavior in individuals. Some of these are described by Lange and Jakubowski (1976) as follows: 'Don't ever inconvenience other people; Don't ever refuse to help a friend; Don't ever feel mad; Don't ever make someone else feel bad' (p. 57). Another injunction which was commonly experienced by the group participants was the fact that they were not to contradict their partners. This, however, was restructured in the following manner: 'I have the right that my feelings, opinions, and beliefs are given the same consideration as those of my spouse'. This mini-lecture was supplemented by handouts from Lange and Jakubowski (1976, pp. 56, 66–68).

Next, the participants undertook the structured exercise of Identifying Personal Rights and Accepting These in Fantasy (Lange & Jakubowski, 1976). This was introduced to increase the participants' awareness of the positive aspects of accepting the right to be assertive. It was comprised of two components. The first part of the exercise consisted of a brainstorming session in which the participants were asked to identify all the personal rights they were able to think of. Their responses were written on a chalkboard by one of the therapists. Some of the rights expressed are as folows: The right to say 'No'; the right to express one's feelings; the right to like oneself; the right to make a mistake; and the right to do nothing. Secondly, the individuals were asked to study the list and to select silently the right which was most difficult for them to accept in their individual lives. The women, then, were asked to fantasize, first of all, what life would be like if they were able to accept the right and, secondly, what life would be like without it. The fantasy was guided by instructions dictated by one of the therapists. Following the fantasy, the participants were divided into dyads and were asked to discuss the right they had selected, the feelings experienced when the right was accepted, the way in which they behaved differently when it was accepted, and any insights they had about themselves during the exercise.

For homework assignments the participants were asked to repeat the personal rights in fantasy exercise on a daily basis, to read Bloom *et al.* (1975, Chaps. 7, 8), and to complete a Satisfactions, Achievements, and Successes form (Osborn & Harris, 1975, p. 120). In this assignment the participants were given a form on which they were requested to record specific situations during the week which were successful or satisfying for them and to check the given statements which represented the positive elements of the experience. This exercise had two objectives. First of all, its emphasis on positive experiences was intended to build self-esteem and self-confidence. Secondly, it was a method by which the individual's behavior could be monitored by the therapists.

Session Four

Completion of Target Complaint Scales, the group-go-around, and discussion of homework assignments was followed by a mini-lecture on the ownership of messages (Osborn & Harris, 1975). This emphasized the importance of expressing oneself in such a way that one assumes ownership of one's messages directed at another person. Two techniques which can be used to demonstrate ownership of one's messages were described. First of all, the group members were instructed to use 'I' statements in expressing their beliefs, thoughts or feelings. This procedure assists individuals in accepting responsibility for their statements rather than projecting blame on another individual. For example, in the statement, 'I feel angry because you did not phone to say you would be late for supper', the person accepts responsibility and ownership of his or her message. Conversely, the statement, 'You are late again! You really don't care about anyone else around here', is indirect and does not represent ownership or personal responsibility for the message. The second method for 'owning' messages which was described involves paraphrasing remarks made by others into the form of questions. For example, an effective paraphrase to an angry remark made by another person would be: 'Are you feeling frustrated with me?' This procedure is important because it facilitates verbal interaction rather than impairing it.

Next, the participants engaged in a structured exercise that involved rehearsing a number of assertive statements and questions individually and in dyads (Osborn & Harris, 1975, pp. 111–113). It was intended to develop verbal assertive responses which were accompanied by appropriate non-verbal behaviors. Also, it provided the participants with the opportunity to practice 'owning' their messages by using 'I' statements and paraphrased questions. The exercise was comprised of three segments. First of all, the participants read through the list of statements and questions individually. Secondly, this procedure was repeated in dyads so as to enable the women to practice the assertive responses within a personal interaction. In this aspect of the exercise, the individuals were asked to concentrate on their non-verbal behaviors as well. Thirdly, each woman was asked to transcribe their target complaints into 'I' statements which, then, were rehearsed in dyads. This final procedure was designed to personalize the exercise in order that it would be meaningful for the group members.

For homework assignments participants were asked to read Bloom *et al.* (1975, Chaps. 9, 11), to complete the Satisfactions, Achievements, and Successes form, and to fill in data sheets regarding their assertive responses in specific situations during the week. The participants were asked to record the assertive behavior and to rate the responses they received from others as well as the degree of discomfort they experienced. This assignment enabled the women to monitor their progress and to identify situations whch were problematic for them (Osborn & Harris, 1975, p. 64).

Session Five

The Target Complaint Scales and group-go-around were completed, and during the discussion of homework a spontaneous, yet extremely important discussion emerged. It focussed on the discomfort the women were beginning to experience with respect to being assertive. Two significant themes were identified within the discourse. First of all, the women indicated that their newly acquired skills were not being positively reinforced by their significant others. Subsequently, they were feeling frustrated, disappointed, and discouraged. One group member (Kelly) remarked that her husband walked away whenever she used 'I' statements. Another individual (Alison), who had recently experienced the death of her mother was feeling particularly uncomfortable because she was 'learning to be assertive when everything out there [society] speaks against it'. She stated that her mother was a well-loved, yet non-assertive woman who constantly did things for other people. On this basis, the group member feared that she would not be loved if she became assertive.

The therapists used the discussion to identify four elements which are associated with the acquisition of assertive skills. Firstly, assertiveness is a goal individuals pursue because they are unhappy with their current situation. Secondly, assertive people are able to do things for other individuals, however, they do so because it is a choice they make rather than an expectation to which they succumb passively. Thirdly, the changes which occur in an individual's behavior as a result of the acquisition of new social skills frequently cause significant others to react negatively and, for this reason, it is important that the individual is persistent in his or her assertiveness. Fourthly, being assertive involves risks in that significant others may not necessarily respect one's rights, beliefs or feelings. For these reasons, the therapists recommended that each participant should assess the personal advantages and disadvantages of assertiveness in order to determine the significance of this behavior for her.

The second theme which emerged in this discussion focussed on power and control within interpersonal relationships. It was apparent that some of the discomfort being experienced by the women at this point in the program was associated with the fact that they were equating personal control and ownership of one's life with the licence to manipulate and exert power over other individuals. The therapists, however, stressed that assertive skills are not intended to be used in controlling or manipulating others. Antithetically, their objective is to enable a person to accept responsibility for his or her own cognitions, feelings and behaviors, and to exert control over his or her own life while, at the same time, respecting the rights of others.

Next, one of the therapists gave a mini-lecture on unreasonable requests (Baer, 1976). Its objectives, first of all, were to emphasize the importance of learning to say 'No' when one does not wish to comply with a request. Secondly, it was designed to provide the participants with specific verbal assertive skills which could be utilized in response to unreasonable demands or inconvenient requests. Pursuant to this, three suggestions were presented to the group members. These guidlines for refusing requests are as follows: (a) begin the response with the word 'No'; (b) speak in a firm voice; and (c) keep the answer short and clear.

The therapists had intended to provide the participants with two non-targeted scenarios to be role played in order to have the participants rehearse the process of refusing requests. One of the group members (Kelly), however, wanted to discuss a situation in which she did not say 'No' to a request from a friend and, subsequently, was experiencing anger, resentment, and frustration. The individual felt that she was being used and for this reason, wanted to telephone the friend in order to express her feelings. She asked the other group members for advice in responding to the situation appropriately. Following supportive and helpful input, the individual agreed to role play the situation, identifying the feelings she hoped to share with her friend.

For homework assignments participants were asked to complete the Satisfactions, Achievements, and Successes form, as well as to continue recording on the data sheets. They were also requested to read a handout on Writing Your Own DESC Scripts (Bower & Bower, 1976, pp. 123–127) in preparation for the following session.

Session Six

The Target Complaint Scales and group-go-around were completed, and during the discussion of the previous week's homework, it became apparent that the participants were no longer having such strong reservations about becoming assertive. Conversely, they stated that they were beginning to become cognizant of the benefits of the new beliefs and skills which they were acquiring.

Next, the participants engaged in a structured exercise on Using Expressive

Talk to Show Feelings (Bower & Bower, 1976). They were asked to list several feelings or emotions they had experienced during the past week in reaction to specific events or activities and, then, to write sentences identifying expressions which could be used to describe the emotions they experienced. Examples of this include the following statements: 'It was exhilarating to see the sun shining when I woke up this morning', and 'It was frustrating driving to the university this evening because the traffic was extremely slow'. When the sentences had been completed, they were rehearsed in dyads. In practicing their statements, the women were asked to concentrate on elements such as voice tone and hand gestures and to provide feedback for each other with respect to these non-verbal behaviors. The purpose of this exercise was to provide the group members with the skills which would enable them to express their feelings both overtly and honestly in specific situations. Furthermore, this form of disclosure was intended to enhance their communication skills as well as their ability to initiate and maintain friendships.

The DESC Script Writing exercise was then introduced in order to assist the participants in approaching conflicts in interpersonal relationships (Bower & Bower, 1976, pp. 123–127). DESC is an acronym whereby the letters represent the four steps constituting the script: (a) D—describe the problem to the other person; (b) E—express in a positive way the feelings experienced as a result of the other person's behavior; (c) S—specify the changes which are desired in the behavior of the other individual; and (d) C—identify the consequences which will be delivered if the other person changes his or her behavior, as well as if he or she refuses to do so.

The exercise was divided into two separate components. First of all, the non-targeted situation identified in the opening page of the handout distributed in the previous session was completed and discussed. Secondly, the individuals were asked to identify a conflict or difficulty they had been experiencing in a relationship and to write a DESC script which could be used to facilitate a resolution to the problem. When the scripts had been completed, each participant was given an opportunity to rehearse her script in dyads. During these role plays, the second individual was instructed to be initially angry and non-compliant to the message of the script so that the participants were given practice in dealing with negative responses and in being persistent in the pursuit of their goals. Following the rehearsal in dyads, one of the individuals (Alison) volunteered to discuss and role play her script in the group setting. Feedback provided by other group members as well as modeling demonstrated by one of the therapists was extremely helpful in assisting her to improve her script.

For homework assignments, in addition to completing the Satisfactions, Achievements, and Successes form and data sheets the women were asked to write a DESC script based on one of their target complaints and to utilize expressive talk to describe their feelings at least once a day during the following week.

Session Seven

The Target Complaint Scales and group-go-around were completed, and the remainder of the session was to have been used to rehearse the DESC scripts assigned as homework the previous week. The plan changed, however, because a significant portion of the session was used to respond to a problem being experienced by one of the group members.

In the previous session Alison had written and rehearsed a DESC script for a conflict she was having with her husband. When it was introduced to the *in vivo* situation for which it had been prepared, his initial response was positive. The following day, however, he was aloof and non-responsive to her and as the week progressed he made remarks such as: 'Now I'm beginning to see your real personality'. In addition to this, he pointed out that the long-term effects of her childhood sexual victimization were being experienced because she chose to experience them. Furthermore, the individual related that her husband continued to blame her for the abuse which occurred. During the discussion of these circumstances, the other participants were noticeably empathetic, supportive, and encouraging. One group member (Kerri) recommended that she should continue to be assertive with her husband, and suggested that he, perhaps, will require time and understanding as he worked through the changes he was observing in his wife. On the other hand, however, the group recognized that it might be necessary for her to terminate the relationship if her husband was unable to accommodate these changes.

For homework assignments the participants were asked to complete the Satisfactions, Achievements, and Successes form, together with the data sheets, and to read Bloom *et al.* (1975, Chaps. 12, 13, 14). They were requested also to think of a situation involving personal rights in intimate relationships—a topic that was introduced into the program at the request of the participants—for role playing in the next session.

Session Eight

After completion of the Target Complaint Scales and the group-go-around the content of this session consisted of a discussion about intimacy which was defined by the participants as being in a relationship characterized by mutual acceptance, trust, honesty, respect, caring, sensitivity, sharing of values, and vulnerability. The discourse identified three themes which had particular importance and relevance to the group members.

First of all, four of the five women (Sara, Kelly, Alison, and Kerri) indicated that they had difficulty interacting within intimate relationships. Although intimacy generally was problematic, the focus of this difficulty varied. Sara and Kelly indicated that it was easier for them to be intimate with men than with women. They stated that women tend to be more competitive and, generally, less supportive of each other. At the same time, however, each of these individuals indicated that she was experiencing or had experienced a negative relationship with her mother. Kelly associated this with the fact that her mother did not protect her from abuse whereas Sara observed that her mother had been extremely denigrating towards her. On the other hand, Alison reported that her inability to trust males made it more difficult for her to be intimate with men as opposed to women. Kerri stated that she had difficulty with intimacy generally, particularly after she had disclosed her sexual abuse to an individual. A fifth group member (Ruth) indicated that intimacy was not a difficult issue for her.

The second theme identified involved the relationship which exists between risks and rights. The women indicated that it was more difficult for them to accept their rights in intimate relationships because of the increased risk and potential for rejection which characterizes such relationships. For this reason, they reported that they have been more tolerant of subtle coercion, manipulation and emotional abuse in past, and in some cases, current relationships. The group indicated that it was necessary that people find a balance between rights and risks. They suggested that this could be achieved as individuals in a relationship make themselves accessible and available to each other while concurrently assuming personal responsibility to be intolerant and unaccepting of any form of abuse, exploitation or manipulation. This necessitates, first of all, that the individuals establish clear limits and boundaries for the relationship, and, secondly, that they express honestly their feelings and opinions, as well as their pains and frustrations.

The third issue which emerged in the group discussion emphasized the normalcy of difficulties experienced in intimate relationships by previously abused women. Subsequently, the women encouraged each other to realize that any difficulties they experienced with intimacy were associated with the fact that they had been sexually abused as children. In summarizing the problems with intimacy encountered in a past relationship, Ruth commented: 'I did the best I could and what I did was the result of past abuse and not because I was crazy'.

Session Nine

Following the completion of the Target Complaint Scales and the group-go-around the group discussed sexuality in intimate relationships—another topic that they requested be included. A number of themes were identified by the participants. First of all, they indicated that there is a basic difference in society's perception of male and female sexuality. They pointed out that male sexuality frequently is used to symbolize power and strength whereas female sexuality is equated with powerlessness. They suggested that the implication of this is the fact that female sexuality is designed to please men and, subsequently, causes many women to become 'dishmops' and to accept any 'garbage' which might be directed at them by males.

The element of control within intimate relationships was another issue underlined in this discussion. Each of the four individuals who attended this session indicated that the difficulties they experienced in this area were associated with the need for them to maintain control of their sexuality within intimate relationships. For example, the women commonly reported that it was both difficult and frightening for them to request sexual pleasure from a partner because, in their opinion, such behavior causes one to relinquish personal control to the other person. In addition to this, the participants indicated that they use different means to maintain control of their sexuality.

Alison and Kerri reported that they avoided all sexual sensations because, for them, sexual pleasure represents a loss of control and causes them to experience intense guilt. They apparently believe that their bodies betrayed them during the abusive encounters because of the involuntary pleasurable response to sex which they experienced. Furthermore, the belief that they participated in the victimization encounter willingly, causes them to feel that they were responsible for it, thereby inundating them with guilt. Subsequently, any sexual sensations which occur in their current relationships cause them to feel guilty and to fear that they will lose control. This creates difficulties for each of these women within sexual relationships. For example, Alison commented: 'Whenever I feel any sexual sensation, it tells me I'm in trouble, that I am out of control'. For this reason, she will not allow herself to get to the point at which her body will respond to something she cannot control because she feels it would increase the risk of being revictimized. This individual protects herself from this risk by allowing herself to become 'numb' during sexual experiences with her husband in order that she will not feel any pleasure. Kerri, on the other hand, stated that she protects herself from further loss of control by avoiding sexual relationships altogether.

The experiences of Sara and Ruth were somewhat different. Each of these individuals indicated that she did not experience any pleasure during the sexual abuse because she disassociated herself from the encounter as a means of maintaining a sense of control. Sara reported that she would detach herself from the situation emotionally by 'going off to the other side of the room' and, although this made her father 'damned mad', she refused to be responsive in order to maintain control and, thereby, protect herself. In addition to this, both participants stated that they have difficulty achieving orgasms in their current sexual relationships with their husbands. In view of the fact these individuals feel compelled to maintain control of the sexual relationship, they stated that they have to give themselves permission to decide cognitively whether or not they will be orgasmic in a specific situation.

A third theme which was identified centered on the importance of separating the past from the present if previously abused women are to achieve any satisfaction in their sexual relationships. Sara and Ruth, who appeared to be more adjusted in their sexuality, emphasized that the satisfaction they enjoyed in their current relationship was dependent on their ability to separate the experiences of the sexual victimization from those of the present. They indicated that an important factor in this is the recognition of choice. For example, Ruth stated that she needs to remind herself that she relates to her husband sexually because it is a choice she makes rather than a response to coercion. Also, both women pointed out that a key to accepting and experiencing their sexuality was the ability to distinguish the offender from their partner.

Session Ten

Following completion of the assessment instruments this session was devoted to a social gathering for which the participants brought food and beverages.

Follow-Up Session

This took place six weeks after the termination of the group and it was used to complete the assessment instruments and to give participants an opportunity to share experiences since they last met.

Outcome of Group Treatment

Of the various themes reflected in the target complaints of the group participants, three problems were common to, at least, four of the women: (a) the expression of opinions, feelings and beliefs; (b) saying 'No' or turning down requests; and (c) understanding and accepting personal rights.

The Expression of Feelings, Beliefs, and Opinions

During the assessment period, all the participants were identified as having clinically significant problems in expressing their feelings, beliefs, and opinions (see Figure 19.1). Their target complaints were as follows: (a) Sara—realizing that my opinion is still valid even if it is different from that of my husband or another close person and that I can choose to act in opposition to their wishes; (b) Kelly—to have confidence in my opinion with my in-laws; (c) Ruth—being able to state my point of view to people I'm close to without fear of being rejected; (d) Alison—expressing my opinions and feelings in situations; and (e) Kerri—I have difficulty expressing my emotions to others.

Results obtained by the Target Complaint Scales indicated that change had occurred in the desired direction for each of the five women. Of these changes, three (60%) reached clinically non-significant levels at the completion of the assertion training and four (80%) at the six-week follow-up (Figure 19.1).

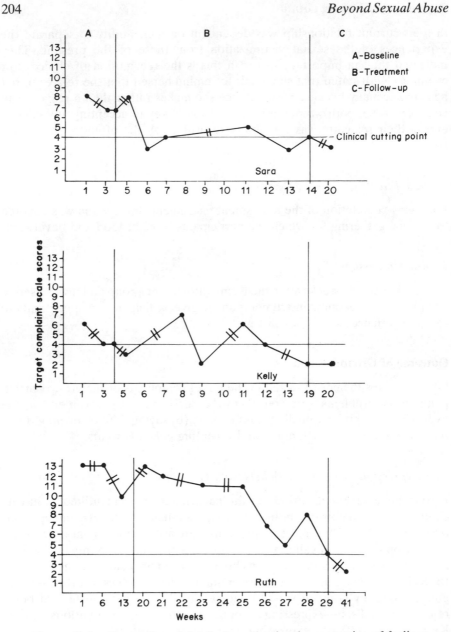

Figure 19.1.   Target Complaint Scale scores for the expression of feelings, beliefs, and opinions

Saying 'No' or Turning Down Requests

Baseline data indicated that four participants had extreme difficulty refusing

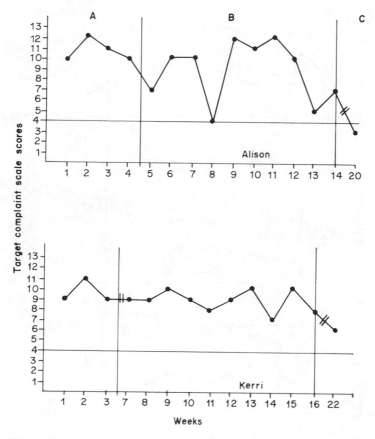

Figure 19.1. (*contd.*)

requests (see Figure 19.2). Their target complaints were as follows: (a) Sara —friends making demands on my time; (b) Kelly—being able to say 'No' without feeling guilty; (c) Ruth—turning down a request for a favor, borrowing or helping in some way; and (d) Alison—when my husband makes a sexual advance and I don't wish to respond.

Results obtained at the completion of the training program showed an improvement in the targeted behavior for each of the subjects, however, only one (25%) of the changes had reached a clinically non-significant level. At the completion of the follow-up period, clinically significant positive changes had occurred in three of these participants (Figure 19.2).

Understanding and Accepting Personal Rights

Prior to the assertiveness training, the capacity to understand and accept

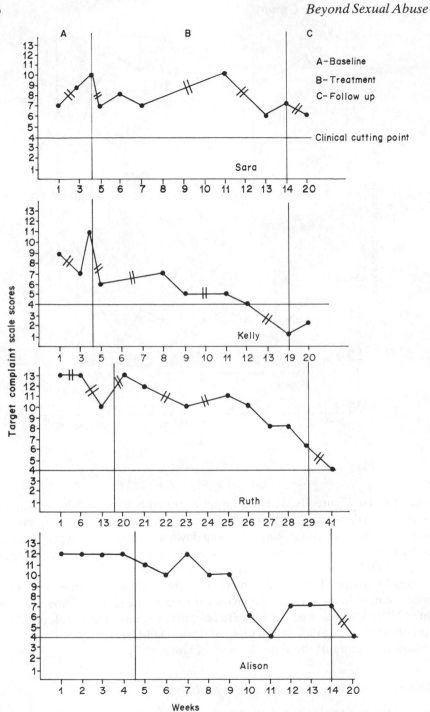

Figure 19.2.   Target Complaint Scale scores for refusing requests

personal rights was significantly problematic for four participants (see Figure 19.3). The target complaints for these individuals were as follows: (a) Sara—not knowing when I have the right to express my feelings, particularly when I know or anticipate they are directly opposed to my husband or another close person; (b) Kelly—being able to say I'm sorry without feeling inferior or guilty (this target is associated with the right to make mistakes); (c) Ruth—I would like to be able to express myself honestly with both men and women; and (d) Alison—when my husband makes a sexual advance and I don't wish to respond.

Results obtained at the termination of the program showed that clinically significant improvements occurred in two (50%) of the women whereas at the follow-up, this number increased to three (75%) (Figure 19.3).

Caretaking Syndrome

Another theme identified by the participants as being problematic for them was the 'caretaking syndrome' which refers to the compulsion they had to assume responsibility for the needs of other individuals, frequently at the expense of their own. This issue was not identified as a target during the baseline period and consequently repeated measurements are not available. Four (Sara, Kelly, Alison, and Kerri) of the group members, however, reported that the assertiveness training helped to liberate them from this responsibility. They stated that the program, firstly, enabled them to realize that they are not responsible for the needs, feelings, and behavior of all significant others. Secondly, it caused them to realize that it is their choice to determine whom they will help in specific situations and, thirdly, that they do not have to feel guilty when they decide it is inappropriate or inconvenient to assume responsibility for the needs of another.

Assertion Inventory

Degree of discomfort. At assessment the scores of the five participants exceeded the recommended cutting point, indicating that each one experienced a high degree of discomfort when confronted with assertive situations. Results obtained at the termination of the program indicated that clinically significant improvement had occurred for two (40% of the women) (Kelly and Ruth). At the follow-up, Kelly showed continued improvement whereas Ruth had deteriorated to the extent that discomfort was a significant problem once again. For a third participant (Kerri), this issue was no longer at a clinically significant level at the follow-up. Thus, clinically significant improvement occurred in two (40%) of the women at the completion of the follow-up period, and three (60%) of them continued to have difficulty on this dimension.

Response probability. The scores of all five (100%) of the participants indicated

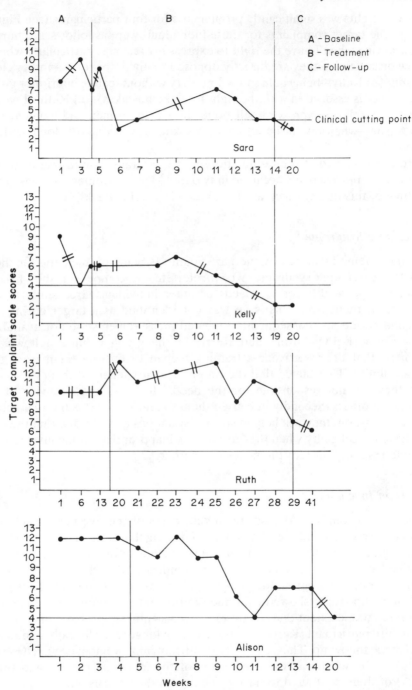

Figure 19.3.   Target Complaint Scale for understanding and accepting rights

a low response probability for assertive responses prior to the intervention. At termination, two (40%) of them had scores indicating high probability whereas four (80%) (Kelly, Ruth, Sara, and Alison) did so at the follow-up. Thus, at the completion of the follow-up period, clinically significant improvement had occurred with respect to response probability in four (80%) of the women. The score for the fifth individual (Kerri) reflected low response probability, however, her score was on the cutting point.

Evaluation Questionnaire

The results of this questionnaire are shown in Table 19.1. For evaluation purposes, they can be divided into three categories: (a) the structure and the components of the sessions (items 1 to 8); (b) the presence of the male therapist (items 9 and 10); and (c) issues related to the needs of the participants (items 11 to 16).

The structure and the components of the sessions. All the participants rated the helpfulness of the group structure (item 1) as *moderately helpful* to *very helpful*. Of the various instructional components utilized in the program, structured exercises (item 2), selected group discussions (item 5), printed handouts (item 6), and assigned readings (item 7), generally were rated as being the most useful. Behavioral rehearsals (item 4) and homework assignments (item 8), on the whole, were less helpful.

The presence of the male therapist. Results obtained on item 9 indicate that four participants considered the presence of a male therapist to be *very helpful* whereas, in the opinion of one individual, it was *slightly helpful*. In the space provided for additional comments (item 10), the group members commonly reported that the availability of a male opinion and perspective was extremely useful. Furthermore, individuals reported a male therapist assisted them in learning to differentiate trustworthy males from those who are abusive and exploitive. Examples of specific comments are provided in Table 19.1.

The needs of the participants. All five participants indicated that the assertiveness training was *moderately helpful* to *very helpful* in meeting their needs (item 11). The group experience was most helpful in that it introduced the participants to other women who had been sexually victimized in childhood (item 14). Four women reported that this was *very helpful* for them while the fifth indicated it was *moderately helpful*. Also, the program was considered to be *moderately helpful* to *very helpful* in reducing irrational beliefs about behaving assertively (item 13). Four individuals responded to item 16 by stating that more sessions were required to address the various issues adequately, whereas one individual was undecided.

Table 19.1. *Assertiveness Training Group: Evaluation Questionnaire*

Please help us to improve our program by answering some questions about the group you attend. We are interested in your honest opinions, whether they are positive or negative. Please check (√) in the column that best indicates our response to the question. We also request your additional comments and suggestions. Thank you very much for your cooperation. We appreciate your help.

A. Questions related to the components of the training program

	Not helpful	Slightly helpful	Moderately helpful	Very helpful
1. The structure of the group sessions consisted of sharing experiences of the past week, discussing homework, a mini-lecture which focused on some assertion issue, coffee break, structured exercises and discussion. Was this structure helpful?			2	3
2. To what extent were the structured exercises performed in the group sessions helpful?			2	2
3. To what extent were the mini-lectures (presented material) helpful?		1	1	2
4. To what extent were the behavioral rehearsals helpful?	1	1	1	2
5. To what extent were the group selected discussion topics of intimacy and sexuality helpful?			2	3
6. To what extent were the various handout materials helpful?			2	3
7. To what extent were the assigned readings from the book helpful?			2	3
8. To what extent were the homework exercises helpful?		3	1	1
9. To what extent was the presence of a male therapist in this kind of group helpful?		1		4

10. Could you please specify your reasons for the answer provided in Question 9. If additional space is required, please use the back of this page.

   - There is something reassuring about being able to see a so-called 'healthy' male in a communicating situation; it's hard for me to discriminate sometimes between males you can trust and ones who are on an ego trip, etc.
   - For some of us who have an image of what most men are like, it broke that image — that is, being a negative one. Because of our life experiences, most of us were mistreated by men and, therefore, feel that all men are jerks.
   - It allowed for acceptance of a male who was aware of the abuse and made me aware that some males would react differently towards a situation than my husband.
   - The male opinion was also important when you needed a balance of ideas from the male perspective.
   - I don't think a woman could have done a worse or better job; I feel this kind of therapy is based on personalities, not sex.
   - I don't think I was particularly aware of the sex of the therapists.

B. General questions

11. To what extent was the training you received helpful in meeting your needs?   4   1

12. To what extent was the training helpful in terms of increasing your self-confidence?   2   1   2

13. To what extent was the training helpful in reducing your irrational beliefs about behaving assertively?   3   2

14. To what extent was the group experience helpful by introducing you to other women who had been sexually victimized?   1   4

15. Overall, to what extent was this group experience helpful?   2   3

16. Were the number of sessions adequate? Please comment.
   - I think more sessions are necessary and it would be helpful to have a support group established after the trust in the group is established.
   - I think for a real change in my assertive behaviour, it would take a much longer, much more intensive training period.
   - Yes and No. I think if we were involved in a group for abused people we could have shared a lot of the things we shared at this group and would have been able to concentrate more on assertion training.

Additional comments and suggestions:

Conclusion

Assertive Responses

The program was effective in facilitating these responses among participants. Their scores on the response probability dimension of the Assertion Inventory were reduced below the recommended cut-off point in four (80%) of the five women. This demonstrates that there had been a significant increase in the likelihood that these individuals would behave assertively when confronted with a variety of situations.

This increase in the likelihood of assertiveness was consistent with an improvement in two targeted behaviors across participants. First of all, the difficulty surrounding the expression of feelings, beliefs, and opinions was significantly reduced in three (60%) of the women at the completion of the group sessions and in four (80%) at the follow-up. Secondly, the capacity to refuse requests was sufficiently increased in three (75%) of four women by the end of the follow-up period to minimize the disturbance this difficulty caused for each person. The results of the Assertion Inventory as well as the replication of these changes in the targeted behaviors across participants demonstrate that the assertion group had a positive impact in assisting the women to improve their assertive responses, particularly with respect to the expression of feelings, beliefs and opinions, and to refusing requests.

Understanding and Acceptance of Rights

The outcome also indicated that this program was successful in assisting the women to achieve another goal of the therapy group; to develop a belief system that would increase understanding and acceptance of their personal rights. This is evident in data obtained by the Target Complaint Scales at the follow-up session. It demonstrated that clinically significant improvements occurred in three (75%) of four women who had been assessed as having difficulty in accepting rights.

In addition to this, the women commonly indicated that the acceptance of rights had enabled them to modify the caretaking role which, previously, they had been compelled to assume. In the past, each of these women believed that they had to take care of the 'world'. This, perhaps, was associated with the parentification process which socializes childhood victims of abuse that the needs of others supersede their own needs (Chap. 3). Relinquishing this role means that they have to be able to trust that there are other individuals who are able to pick up the slack and to provide care in situations these women choose to avoid. In view of the fact that these women grew up in an environment devoid of trust, the capacity as well as the willingness to abandon this caretaking role was a big step for them.

Discomfort with Assertiveness

The results obtained on the discomfort dimension of the Assertion Inventory indicated that three (60%) of the women continued to experience a high degree of discomfort in assertive situations at both the termination and follow-up of the program. There is support for this in comments made by the participants during one of the sessions. They generally agreed that the key for them to utilize assertive responses was the capacity to understand and accept their personal rights in specific situations. In commenting on this, Sara stated that 'my biggest problem is knowing or deciding what my rights are in a situation. When I become aware of that, I can be assertive.'

There are two possible explanations for the discomfort these individuals experienced in engaging in assertive behavior. First of all, as discussed previously, the assertiveness training had been successful in assisting the participants to understand and accept their personal rights. Concurrently, however, the women indicated that they had difficulty justifying this behavior. Thus, they had become enabled to accept their rights, however, they were inundated with discomfort as they did so. Their childhood environment had socialized them to accept the misconception that they do not possess any personal rights and, subsequently, they may have been experiencing 'growth pains' as they accepted and acted upon the right to live and interact in a different manner to which they had been accustomed. It is possible that these 'pains' will be alleviated as the participants continue to behave assertively and become more confident in doing so over a longer period than the six-week follow-up.

A second possible explanation for the high degree of discomfort experienced by the majority of participants was the lack of reinforcement they received from significant others for their changed behavior. For example, Kelly stated: 'I try to express myself with "I" statements, however, it is frustrating because I don't seem convinced that screaming doesn't work better'. In the past, these women had been reinforced for non-assertive behavior, and now that this behavior was being modified, the social feedback had become aversive. This was clearly the case with Alison whose husband appeared to have extreme difficulty accepting the changes he had observed in his wife. In retrospect, it may have been helpful if the women had been more prepared at the outset of the program for the responses they could expect from significant others. This, perhaps, would have cushioned the disappointment, frustration, and discomfort they experienced. Furthermore, in subsequent programs, it might be appropriate to meet with each couple in an individual session in order to address the changes which occur in a family system when one of its members becomes more assertive.

Finally, and more generally, the participants' discomfort with assertiveness might be alleviated by the inclusion in the group program of some of the stress management procedures discussed in Part 3.

Irrational Beliefs Concerning Assertiveness

Although responses obtained on the evaluation questionnaire indicate that the group experience was *moderately helpful* to *very helpful* in reducing their irrational beliefs about behaving assertively, the women continued to have difficulty in this area. This was most evident in the negative cognitions the women have with respect to control of sexuality within intimate relationships. In discussing this issue, the women indicated that the need to control sexual relationships was a pervasive problem for them. Each of the women perceived sexuality as a weapon which had been used against them in the past and, subsequently, they were having difficulty normalizing this aspect of intimacy in their current relationships.

The basic assumption they held was the belief that they would be at risk of harm and exploitation if they relinquished or shared control of their sexuality. This was associated with their victimization experiences in which they were overwhelmed by the power differential existing between children and adults and, thereby, received the message that they must maintain control if they are to remain safe. In light of the fact that intimacy involves taking risks as well as sharing control and decision making, the need to maintain control creates a serious dilemma for these individuals. For this reason, subsequent assertiveness training programs for previously abused women should endeavour to address this issue of control more adequately. Techniques which would be helpful in doing this are cognitive restructuring of irrational beliefs and assumptions, and an emphasis upon 'I' messages which facilitate an honest expression of fears, concerns, and difficulties with their partners. In addition to this, group discussion as well as the support and affiliation it engenders can be a powerful therapeutic influence.

Heterosocial Relationships

The assertiveness training therapy group was effective in assisting the women to begin resolving the difficulties they experienced in their relations with men. In responding to the evaluation questionnaire, four (80%) of the subjects rated the presence of the male therapist as being *very helpful*. One (20%) individual indicated that it was *slightly helpful*, although this person admitted that it was much easier for her to relate to men than to women.

The women identified two primary benefits of a male therapist. Firstly, his presence made it possible for a male opinion and perspective to be provided in specific situations. Secondly, and more importantly, it enabled the women to differentiate abusive and exploitive males from those who are trustworthy. For example, one of the individuals stated that she had never equated gentleness in males with positions of power and authority because power was perceived by her as being abusive. The context of her remark clearly indicated that she was referring to the role of the male therapist. The women reported that the important ingredients in therapy with adult victims of child sexual abuse is not gender, but personality. On this basis, it seems that the key to the therapists is not so much gender as it is the capacity and willingness to understand empathetically, compassionately, and supportively the pain of these individuals.

Summary

On the basis of outcome data, it can be concluded that the group was effective in meeting three of its original objectives: the facilitation of assertive responses; increasing the understanding and acceptance of personal rights; and the mitigation of difficulties experienced in heterosocial relationships. It was not adequate, however, in eliminating discomfort with acting assertively or in reducing all unreasonable beliefs which impaired the participants' capacity to engage in assertive behavior. Also, it is necessary to emphasize that the changes achieved are not necessarily attributable to the assertiveness training alone because the women were involved in concurrent individual or couple therapy.

PART 4

Sexual Dysfunctions

CHAPTER 20

Categories and Prevalence of Sexual Dysfunctions

The whole of this part of the book is focussed on sexual dysfunction among female victims of child sexual abuse. If these victims have a regular male partner then the victim's dysfunction inevitably has implications for the couple's sexual relationship and the partner's participation and cooperation in the treatment of sexual dysfunction is highly desirable if not essential. If a male partner himself has a specific sexual dysfunction—such as an erectile or ejaculatory problem—then it will be necessary to consult other sources for additional information on the nature, assessment, and treatment of male sexual dysfunctions (e.g. Jehu, 1979; Zilbergeld, 1978).

Victims and/or their partners may consider the victim's sexual functioning to be inadequate or problematic because it is accompanied by pain, vaginal spasm or aversive feelings, or because of some impairment of sexual motivation, arousal, climax or satisfaction. This definition of sexual dysfunction involves subjective judgments of inadequacy by the victims and partners concerned. Thus, the avoidance of sexual activity because of pain, vaginal spasm or aversion may not be at all distressing to some victims or partners and there are no absolute or prescribed standards of sexual motivation, arousal, climax or satisfaction against which a victim could be judged objectively to be dysfunctional (Jehu, 1979).

At initial assessment, 78% of victims in the U. of M. series complained of at least one of the sexual dysfunctions described below, and a further eight victims were ascertained to be sexually dysfunctional during therapy, making a total prevalence rate of 94% (Table 20.1). The classification of dysfunctions used in this chapter categorizes problems not people, and more than one problem often occurred in the same victim.

Sexual Phobia/Aversion

One reason why sex may be distressing is because it evokes strong phobic or

Table 20.1.   *Victims Presenting With Sexual Dysfunctions at Initial Assessment (N = 51)*

	Victims	
Dysfunction	n	%
Phobia/aversion	30	58.8
Dissatisfaction	30	58.8
Impaired motivation	29	56.9
Impaired arousal	25	49.0
Impaired orgasm	23	45.1
Dyspareunia	14	27.4
Vaginismus	4	7.8
At least one of these dysfunctions	40	78.4

aversive reactions in the victim. Certain specific features of sexual activities, such as being touched in a particular way or coming into contact with semen, will elicit intense, irrational anxiety or other aversive feelings. In many victims these feelings of anxiety or aversion are accompanied by physiological reactions such as profuse sweating, nausea, vomiting, diarrhea, or palpitations. It is understandable that phobias/aversions also include the avoidance of eliciting events. Consequently, the woman's sexual motivation is liable to become impaired, the range of foreplay is restricted, and the frequency of intercourse is reduced. Often it is performed only under pressure from the partner, from a sense of obligation towards him, or after the victim has been drinking.

The disturbing features of sexual activity that elicit phobic/aversive reactions are often recapitulations of traumatic aspects of the sexual abuse. Among such features is the occurrence of 'flashbacks' to the victimization experience. If something happens during the current encounter that reminds the woman of the traumatic incidents, then she may have a vivid memory or image of them which is very disturbing to her. Consequently, her response is more appropriate to the past incidents than to the present activity with a partner whom she may love very much. Another common disturbing feature is any element of being coerced, used, or controlled by the current partner. This is also liable to recapitulate the earlier victimization experience and to evoke phobic/aversive reactions. For some victims, arousal is possible providing that they initiate and remain fully in control of the lovemaking. Finally, some victims experience phobic/aversive reactions to the slightest hint of pleasure arising in a sexual encounter. Possibly, any such pleasure during the earlier victimization was associated with considerable guilt and distress, so that it has become threatening to the victim. The anticipation of the anxiety evoking events may be more overwhelming than actual exposure to them, so that sexual approaches and foreplay may also become aversive. Even purely affectionate acts, such as a hug or kiss, may evoke anxiety unless the situation is such that a possible progression to sex is ruled out.

In the U. of M. series 58% of victims complained of sexual phobias or aversions at initial assessment (Table 20.1). Similarly, a fear of sex was reported by 64.3% of 28 incest victims studied by Becker, Skinner, Abel, Axelrod, and Cichon (1984).

Sexual Dissatisfaction

It is important to appreciate that some victims complain of sexual dissatisfaction despite the fact that their sexual motivation, arousal, and climax are relatively unimpaired, at least in the earlier stages of the dissatisfaction. This may arise from the frequency, timing, location, or nature of sexual activities. It may also occur if sex is perceived as dirty, disgusting, monotonous, or boring. Finally, sex may be unsatisfying if the partners are not attracted to each other, if they are insensitive to the other's sexual needs and preferences, if one feels that the other is only interested in him or her for sex, or if there is a role strain or serious conflict in their relationship.

At initial assessment, 58% of the victims in the U. of M. series complained of sexual dissatisfaction, often in conjunction with one or more other dysfunctions (Table 20.1). Further evidence on the occurrence of sexual dissatisfaction among women who were sexually abused in childhood is provided by Tsai, Feldman-Summers, and Edgar (1979) who found that a clinical group of such women currently seeking therapy for problems associated with childhood molestation reported significantly less satisfaction than either a non-clinical group of women who had been molested but had never sought therapy, or a control group of women who had never been molested.

Impaired Sexual Motivation

Some victims report that they do not experience any urge or desire for sex, they could go on indefinitely without it and abstinence is often a relief for them. This lack of motivation may extend to all sexual activities and partners. In other cases, it is more restricted, so that interest may be retained, for example, in masturbation or towards extra-marital partners.

There are a number of possible causes for such impaired motivation in victims, including depression, conflict between the partners, fear of intimacy, and the avoidance of sex because it is a painful, distressing, or unsatisfying experience for the woman (Jehu, 1979).

At initial assessment 56% of the victims in the U. of M. series complained of impaired sexual motivation (Table 20.1). Prevalence rates for this problem among previously sexually abused women are reported also by Becker *et al.* (1984) who found that 35% of 28 incest victims were suffering from desire dysfunction, and by Briere (1984) who found that among women seeking counseling, 41% of victims reported decreased sexual drive compared to 29% of non-victims.

Impaired Sexual Arousal

In some victims, either or both of the physiological and psychological components of sexual arousal are impaired. Thus, a woman does not respond to
sexual stimulation with the usual responses of vaginal lubrication and swelling,
accompanied by erotic sensations and feelings. These responses may occur
during masturbation but not with a partner.

One reason for such impaired arousal is the evocation during lovemaking of
the phobic reactions discussed above. It is well known that excessive anxiety can
disrupt arousal (Norton & Jehu, 1984; Norton, Jehu, & deLuca, 1985) and this
is also likely to be terminated by the occurrence of physiological symptoms
such as nausea, retching, and vomiting. Additionally, those aspects of lovemaking that are disturbing will be physically avoided, consequently effective
sexual stimulation may not be received. Such deficient stimulation may also
result from the cognitive avoidance, or reduced awareness, of disturbing aspects
of a sexual encounter. The woman does not perceive the stimulation she is
receiving, nor does she experience the erotic sensations and feelings usually
associated with it, consequently sexual arousal is impaired. In extreme cases,
these sensations and feelings are totally lacking even to very intense stimulation, a condition sometimes referred to as 'genital' or 'sexual anesthesia'.

At initial assessment, 49% of the victims in the U. of M. series reported
impaired sexual arousal (Table 20.1). Similarly, this problem was present in
50% of 28 incest victims studied by Becker *et al.* (1984).

Impaired Orgasm

Whether as a result of impaired arousal or for other reasons, particularly fear of
loss of control, some victims experience difficulty in reaching climax during
their current sexual encounters. Some of these victims can attain orgasm under
specific circumstances; for example, during masturbation, when they have
been drinking, with a new partner, or with a 'safe' partner who is extremely
undemanding and patient, unlike the earlier offender. In contrast, there are
other victims who can reach climax quite easily, even though they may not be
sexually motivated or aroused. The orgasm seems to come 'out of the blue'.
Often these victims can only climax during intercourse and not in response to
other stimulation by a partner (McGuire & Wagner, 1978). In some cases also,
the orgasm is not an enjoyable or satisfying experience. It is almost as if the
victim has acquired the physical response at an early age, but in traumatic
circumstances so that it has never been associated with pleasure (Tasai &
Wagner, 1978).

At initial assessment, 45% of the victims in the U. of M. series reported
impairment of orgasm (Table 20.1). The prevalence rates reported for this
problem by two other investigators are: (a) 74% of 23 father–daughter incest

victims who were in psychotherapy (Meiselman, 1978); and (b) 35% of 28 incest victims (Becker *et al.*, 1984).

Dyspareunia

Some women victims report experiencing pain during intercourse. In a proportion of cases, of course, this may be due to pelvic pathology, but it may also be caused by inadequate lubrication during the arousal process, or by the muscular contraction involved in vaginismus (Jehu, 1979).

At initial assessment, 27% of the victims in the U. of M. series complained of pain during intercourse (Table 20.1). In the Becker *et al.* (1984) series of 28 incest victims this problem was reported by 7% of victims. An interesting finding is reported by Caldirola *et al.* (1983), and by Gross (1980). They investigated 25 women complaining of chronic pelvic pain, 80% of whom were also experiencing difficulty in their sexual activities. On gynecological examination 60% of the patients were found to be normal, while 40% had only minor degrees of abnormality such as muscle spasm or pelvic relaxation. What is noteworthy is that 36% of the 25 women had a history of incest.

Vaginismus

The condition of vaginismus can be defined as a spastic contraction of the muscles at the outer third of the vagina and the perineum, which occurs as an involuntary reflex response to the threat of vaginal penetration. Consequently, intromission is either completely prevented or only possible with great difficulty and pain. The muscular spasm is often accompanied by a phobia of penetration (Jehu, 1979).

Any factor, some of which are mentioned above, that is currently causing pain during intercourse may also result in vaginismus which serves as a means of avoiding the threat of painful penetration. This involuntary avoidance reaction may also have been acquired in response to pain and distress during childhood sexual abuse so that the vaginal spasm is elicited as a reflex, automatic response to the threat of penetration in adulthood even though there is no current reason for pain or distress.

At initial assessment, 7% of the victims in the U. of M. series complained of vaginismus (Table 20.1). Among the 28 incest victims studied by Becker *et al.* (1984) the prevalence rate for this problem was 0.5%.

Conclusion

Among the victims in the U. of M. series 94% reported some form of sexual dysfunction, with negative reactions to sex such as phobias, aversions, and dissatisfaction being most prevalent. High prevalence rates are reported also in other clinical samples.

Commonly sexual dysfunctions were not manifested until some time after a sexual relationship commenced. Initially, the impairment may be masked by the novelty and limited commitment of many early sexual contacts. Once a relationship becomes more established and closer, then feelings associated with victimization by an adult who was 'related' to the child may be reactivated. Sometimes women will say that their partner has changed and has become more like the offender.

CHAPTER 21

Causes of Sexual Dysfunctions

The victimization experiences and family backgrounds of many victims of childhood sexual abuse are overwhelmingly traumatic (Chaps. 2, 3) and may well contribute to sexual dysfunctions in later life. Some processes through which these childhood experiences may result in the later dysfunctions are discussed in the section on sexual stresses below. Although sexual dysfunctions may have originated in previous experiences they are initiated and maintained by certain contemporary conditions including the organic factors, mood disturbances, interpersonal problems and sexual stresses that are outlined below and which require therapeutic attention if the dysfunction is to be alleviated.

Organic Factors

The physiological or psychological side effects of a very wide range of medical conditions, surgical procedures and drugs may contribute to various sexual dysfunctions and only a few illustrative examples can be cited here (for extensive coverage see Bancroft, 1983; Kolodny, Masters, & Johnson, 1979). Among the very many causes of dyspareunia are pelvic inflammatory disease, vaginal inflammation and infection, and tender episiotomy scarring following childbirth. Mastectomy may impair a woman's body image with repercussions on her sexual functioning that are discussed below under the heading of low self-esteem. Among the prescribed drugs oral contraceptives may cause vaginal dryness and discomfort, and they may also impair sexual motivation in some women. Among the non-prescribed drugs heroin is reported to impair sexual motivation and it has been demonstrated recently that alcohol impairs sexual arousal in women as well as men.

Mood Disturbances

The mood disturbances of guilt, low self-esteem, and depression that are very prevalent among victims (Part 2) often have adverse effects on sexual

225

functioning. The many ways in which victims tend to blame themselves for their sexual abuse are likely to result in a strong association being established between sexual activities and feelings of guilt. Clearly, a victim's sexual functioning is liable to be impaired and unsatisfying if she feels that lovemaking is wrong, dirty or evil, even when it occurs in the context of the relationship between herself and her regular partner.

If a victim has low self-esteem then this may undermine her feelings of security and comfort in sexual encounters with consequent impairment of her sexual functioning and satisfaction. In particular, a victim's body image may be important in this respect. If she perceives herself as physically unattractive perhaps because of being overweight or having breasts that are too small or too large, then she may feel uncomfortable and fear criticism or rejection by her partner.

Depression is often accompanied by some impairment of sexual motivation but arousal and orgasm are less commonly affected and occasionally there is an increase in sexual desire (e.g. Garvey, 1985; Mathew & Weinman, 1982).

Interpersonal Problems

The common themes of insecurity, discord, and inadequacy in the interpersonal relationships of victims that are discussed in Part 3 may affect adversely their sexual functioning in a variety of ways.

Insecurity

It is well established that fear or anxiety from any source is likely to have a disruptive effect on sexual functioning and satisfaction (Norton & Jehu, 1984; Norton *et al.*, 1985). The following are some common sources of fear in the interpersonal relations of victims.

Fear and mistrust of men. Effective and enjoyable sexual functioning requires that a victim feel relaxed, comfortable and secure with her partner and these conditions are clearly difficult to attain if she lacks basic trust in him and is afraid of how he might behave towards her.

Fear of loss of control. A victim's need to retain control in all aspects of her life may be so strong that she is unable to tolerate a mutual and reciprocal sexual relationship with her partner. Thus, any initiative or influence from him in their lovemaking is threatening to the victim and may impair her sexual functioning and satisfaction.

Fear of intimacy. Some victims have difficulty in functioning sexually under conditions of involvement and commitment with an established partner,

although they may be able to do so quite adequately during relatively imper-
sonal or transient sexual relationships. This is sometimes referred to as a
'splitting phenomenon' whereby the victim cannot have an affectionate and a
sexual relationship with the same person. Thus, a close, meaningful emotional
relationship renders the victim sexually dysfunctional while she may have no
such problem in a superficial, casual encounter with a partner whom she does
not love or care for. This splitting phenomenon is exemplified in the assessment
report on one victim (Alison):

> Sex and affection are split in the victim's relationships with males,
> including her partner. She finds it difficult to combine a sexual and a
> loving relationship with the same man.
>
> In her history there are many instances of her craving for caring and
> affectionate relationships which do not entail any sexual expecta-
> tions, to be loved without having to 'pay' with sex, for example:
> (a) She was disgusted by her father's sexual, but not affectionate,
> behavior towards her mother.
> (b) She always wanted a boyfriend who would care for her without
> any sexual demands.
> (c) Between ages 11 and 16 years she had many short romantic
> relationships with males older than herself in which she played
> the role of the little sister needing protection and caring. These
> males often lived at a distance from the victim and she continued
> to correspond with them which enabled her to have a boyfriend
> who was 'safe' sexually.
> (d) One of the things she found attractive about her current partner
> was that he was not at all sexually demanding during the first year
> of their relationship and she felt safe with him.
> (e) She has a strong wish to be valued as a person in her own right and
> to be loved unconditionally by her partner, rather than being seen
> as a sex object and a mother figure who may be dropped if sex is
> not improved by the time the children are grown up.
>
> This persistent and continuing craving for affection without sex
> may be strongly influenced by the sexual abuse when the victim
> desperately wanted only affection from the offender who recipro-
> cated by imposing sexual demands either instead of or in addition
> to any affection towards the victim.

Having read this part of her assessment the victim commented:

> As you have identified splitting has been highly evident in my
> relationships and obviously still is. I always wanted a male companion
> who would simply be my friend, someone who would care for me very

deeply but never 'want' me sexually, someone who would help me to understand the male perspective of life which seemed so different from my own. I always wanted a male who would see only my innocence, would value my naivety and protect me from I do not know what. I tried to present myself as being a sweet, naive innocent little girl who needed protection.

Splitting in another victim (Maureen) is described as follows:

At age 16 years, she intended to run away from home. She withdrew her savings of several hundred dollars, went to the 'red light' district of the city and was assaulted and robbed. She continued to go to this district every weekend for two years engaging in prostitution and group homosexual and heterosexual activities, as well as alcohol and drug abuse. She spontaneously aborted a fetus, alone in a back alley after being kicked in the stomach and beaten up by a 'john'.

Maureen continued this weekend lifestyle concurrently with attending school, church, etc., during the week while living at home. Her family never questioned her regular weekend disappearances. Sex was never discussed at home. Her mother was an active member in a fundamentalist religion who imposed strict standards of morality within the family.

At age 18 years, after a night of group sex and drug taking she awoke in a decrepit hovel filled with 10 or 15 men and women, filthy, broke and unable to recall the previous night's events.

She stated that she was overwhelmed with the destructiveness of this lifestyle, returned home and arranged with her family to attend a bible college in this province and remake her life over.

From that time until now she repressed all memories of her promiscuous period. She was able to disclose this part of her life now because she recognized through working through her erroneous beliefs about her victimization that her behavior patterns at the time were coping strategies to deal with her entrapment and emotional pain and not because she was inherently bad.

She is now known as a valued member in a strict religious organization. She feels guilty about her success in presenting herself as naive, virginal and very religious. This prevents her from cultivating close friendships. Group dating occurred in her 'street' network at age 15 years. She never viewed street connections as 'dating' but rather as 'scores'. She adhered to a double standard in petting—at home she would not go near a boy in case sexual touching might occur except with her offender/brother who had presented a rationale for his behavior over a long period of time. When on the 'streets' anything was allowed. She neither wanted nor sought emotional involvement. She was much more interested in seeing how many 'scores' or 'tricks' she could make on a weekend. Sexual intercourse began with the offender brother at age 9 years and continued regularly until age 14 years. She engaged in sexual intercourse 'as often as possible when on the "streets" '. Here she indiscriminately chose sexual partners and often found herself being brutalized and injured by sadistic partners.

In contrast, the victim had only one long-term relationship with a man, and she broke off this relationship when it appeared that the relationship might become sexual.

One reason for a fear of intimacy in victims is that the more intimate a relationship becomes the greater the likelihood that it will recapitulate the earlier traumatic experiences with an offender who was emotionally close to the victim. Another possible reason is a profound distrust of intimate relationships arising from having been exploited by the offender and perhaps inadequately protected by the mother. Finally, the strong desire of some victims to have a relationship with a man that is caring and affectionate but completely asexual may constitute an attempt to redress the lack of a normal, loving relationship with a father figure in childhood.

Discord

The following are among the many sources of discord between victims and partners that can have adverse effects on their sexual relationship.

Rejection of partner. If a victim perceives her partner as unattractive or if she dislikes him then his sexual approaches tend to be insufficiently stimulating or annoying rather than arousing.

Exploitation by partner. A partner who exploits, dominates or physically abuses the victim may evoke anger, hostility or resentment which is likely to disrupt her sexual response and satisfaction. Such domination by the partner may also result in a power struggle in the relationship and the victim may not respond sexually because this would represent submission to her partner.

Oversexualization. A victim who feels compelled to have a sexual relationship with a partner when she really does not want to do so is unlikely to enjoy their sexual encounters and may be unable to respond adequately.

Anger. If for any of the above or other reasons a victim feels angry, resentful or hostile towards her partner then she is likely to find it difficult to respond sexually with him. For most people anger and sex are incompatible and the emotion of anger has a similar effect to anxiety on their sexual functioning.

Role strain. To the extent that therapy produces changes such as enhanced self-esteem and increased assertiveness in a victim these are likely to entail pressure for some redistribution of roles in the marriage, otherwise role strain will occur and persist (Chaps. 15, 19). There is some evidence for an association between marital role strain and sexual dissatisfaction: 80 non-patient couples, 50 marital therapy couples, and 50 sex therapy couples completed an extensive self-report questionnaire concerning their marital relationships. Questions were included on the actual and ideal roles of each spouse in: (a) caring for the home, cooking, and shopping; (b) making major family decisions; (d) being sexually faithful; (e) having responsibility for the care of the children; (f) being sexually aggressive; (g) having interests and activities that do not include one's spouse; and (h) determining how much money is spent. The degree of discrepancy between the actual and ideal roles was taken as an index of marital role strain, and this was found to correlate positively with responses indicating sexual dissatisfaction in all three groups. The investigators comment that positive feelings about oneself are a necessary pre-condition for an intimate relationship with another person. Since one aspect of how one evaluates oneself is the degree to which one is fulfilling the roles one wants to fulfill, it is understandable that individuals who are dissatisfied with the role assignments in their marriages may also experience sexual dissatisfaction (Frank, Anderson, & Rubenstein, 1979).

Individual growth. This closely related source of discord between victims and their partners can also arise as a side effect of the victim's progress in therapy. Because of their problems and needs at the time some victims enter into unsuitable, ill-matched and perhaps punitive partnerships, often when they are quite young (Chap. 15). As the victim recovers from the effects of sexual abuse and resumes her development this partnership no longer meets her needs and frustrates the victim's individual growth. Unless these barriers are removed they are likely to lead to rejection of the partner, resentment over the restrictive nature of the partnership and power struggles between the partners, which in turn are likely to impair their sexual functioning and satisfaction.

Inadequacy

Lack of assertiveness and poor communication and problem-solving skills may have deleterious effects on sexual functioning and satisfaction. A victim who is unaware or unsure of her rights and who cannot express her preferences or set limits is very vulnerable to unstimulating or distressing sexual encounters during which she is unlikely to respond adequately or to experience satisfaction.

The importance of communication and problem-solving skills for sexual satisfaction is demonstrated in a study by Chesney *et al.* (1981) in which a group of couples who had attended a sex therapy clinic, was compared with a demographically similar group of couples who had not sought therapy. While these couples had experienced some of the same sexual problems as those who had attended for treatment, the comparison couples were able to communicate effectively and to solve these problems constructively, whereas the treatment couples could not handle their sexual problems on their own. Thus, the most important factor in determining sexual satisfaction appeared to be not the occurrence of sexual problems, but how a couple perceived and reacted to these problems.

Sexual Stresses

Stress Situations

One general definition of a stress situation is that it involves demands that are *perceived* to tax or exceed the person's coping resources. He or she perceives that the situation demands an effective response to avoid or reduce physical or psychological harm, and that no adequate response is available. Various aspects of sexual anatomy, responses, activities, thoughts, fantasies, and images may be stressful for victims (e.g. Table 21.1).

Stress Reactions

Common reactions to stress can be considered in the broad groups of emotional, cognitive, physiological, and behavioral reactions. It is important to note that there are wide individual differences in the ways people react to stress.

Emotional reactions. Some of the terms that victims often use to describe their feelings in stress situations are shown in Table 21.2.

Cognitive reactions. Some common cognitive reactions are also shown in Table 21.2. Re-experiencing traumatic events involves repetitive intrusions of the abuse experiences into the victim's thought and image processes despite her vigorous efforts to avoid or suppress these intrusions. For example, Alison described a flashback to the abuse that disrupted her current sexual relationship as follows:

> This morning the exercise began with my feeling how much easier it is for me to feel and touch all parts of my body. However, as I went on I became preoccupied with the memory that really crystallized last night and that is that I know now [the offender] tried for me to perform oral sex on him. It was in the farm house when I would be

Table 21.1. *Stressful Sexual Situations: Alison*

Victim's own body

Pubic hair (associated with offender's pubic hair and the onset of abuse).

Breasts (associated with the onset of the abuse).

Engorged clitoris (associated with male penis).

Partner-related activities

Partner caressing victim with his eyes.

Partner 'grabbing' victim during her housework.

Victim sleeping nude or in nightdress without panties (might provoke sex).

Victim rejecting partner's sexual advances.

Partner initiating sex.

Intercourse with partner.

Sexual arousal or pleasure.

Sounds of pleasure during sex.

Seeing partner nude.

Partner getting carried away in sex.

Partner kissing victim passionately.

Partner kissing victim with an exploring tongue.

Partner fondling victim's breasts.

Partner stimulating victim's breasts with his mouth or tongue.

Partner touching or kissing victim's nipples.

Partner biting victim.

Partner's pubic hair.

Victim caressing partner's genitals with her fingers.

Victim touching partner's flaccid or erect penis.

Victim stimulating partner's genitals with her mouth or tongue.

Partner taking control in sex.

Victim reaching climax (loss of control).

Sex-related thoughts, fantasies, and images

Thoughts of being valued by partner only as a sex object and not as a person.

Thoughts of sex as a payoff for financial support from partner.

Thoughts of having sex for the sake of sex with no chance of conception because of
    partner's vasectomy.

Fantasy that partner is hurting victim in some way and she wants to be hurt.

Memories, images or sensations that relate to earlier sexual abuse.

kneeling beside the couch on which he was lying. I remember him
pushing my face down into his pubic area and telling me to put it into
my mouth but I wouldn't. I remember feeling so overwhelmed and
confused by what he wanted me to do and not knowing what to do. I
know I didn't do it and when I didn't he just mashed my face all

Table 21.2. *Common Stress Reactions*

Emotional
1. Anxiety, fear, panic.
2. Vulnerable, helpless, trapped.
3. Disgust, revulsion.
4. Guilt, shame.
5. Anger, resentment.

Cognitive
1. Re-experiencing traumatic events through intrusive thoughts, ruminations, obsessions, flashbacks, images, dreams, nightmares.
2. Dissociative reactions such as amnesia, depersonalization, derealization, and multiple personality disorder.

Physiological
1. Muscle tension.
2. Sweating.
3. Rapid breathing.
4. Palpitations.
5. Dizziness, fainting.
6. Nausea, retching, vomiting.
7. Disturbances of eating, sleep, sex, and excretion.

Behavioural
1. Avoidance of stress situations.
2. Aggressive acts.

---

around in it. That's the feeling I've been fighting with [partner's] nose. It feels so much like a penis rubbing all over my face. That's why when that feeling is strong I can't help but push him away. I can't stand it—the same if he holds the back of my head while he kisses me. These associations are so strong now and right now it doesn't help for me to tell myself that it's [partner] and not [offender]. That's why we can't have much sexual contact right now.

Another victim, Jackie (age 46) reported increasing frequency of nightmares during the initial assessment process that interfered with her sleep pattern and caused her to feel chronically tired and irritable. She described one recurring nightmare of being squeezed by a man, fighting him off and throwing him out of the house and then feeling sorry for him because it is cold outside. In the nightmare these events occur in the presence of three women who appear to be in a meeting and unaware of what is going on. Jackie stated that she would wake up cold, clammy, unable to breathe and very frightened. She stated that she believed the man to be her grandfather and the squeezing tightly a recapitulation of her one vivid memory of sexual victimization. She also believed that the three women represented her mother, aunt, and an older sister all of whom dismissed her report of sexual victimization as nonsense. The nightmare continued during therapy until the fifth session when the cognitive restructuring of the erroneous beliefs that allowed her to attribute blame to herself for her sexual victimization were modified to some extent. Jackie reported that there seemed to be a direct correlation between the frequency of nightmares and degree of guilt. That is as her guilt decreased, the frequency of her nightmares also decreased. By the end of therapy for mood disturbances the client reported that her sleep pattern had returned to normal and that while she still experienced dreams, the dreams generally were not as upsetting nor thematically related to her sexual victimization. This individual case is fairly typical of the occurrence of nightmares among the victims in the U. of M. series. Many women experienced an exacerbation of nightmares during initial assessment and these usually remitted without any specific intervention as therapy progressed.

The dissociative reaction of amnesia or denial occurs in various forms. Some victims deny the whole event, particularly in the early stages of treatment. More commonly perhaps, some particularly disturbing aspects of the abuse are denied. Thus, a woman may deny that intercourse took place as well as fondling, or that she experienced pleasure during the abuse. Another form of denial is to downplay the importance, for example, 'it happened, but it didn't bother me', or 'I left it behind me a long time ago, it doesn't affect me now'.

Because children often cannot escape from sexual abuse situations physically they commonly detach themselves from the experience mentally through depersonalization and/or derealization experiences (Blake-White & Kline, 1985). For example, Alison wrote 'Though I was physically present during the abuse I remember feeling nothing other than an initial revulsion when I would first touch his penis and . . . he first touched me. In between, I felt or thought about nothing. I was gone.'

Such dissociative reactions at the time of the abuse tend to persist to stress situations in adulthood, for example, Alison wrote:

(a) About her current sexual encounters; 'If any associations to the abuse experience occur it is an immediate stop . . . I can't allow myself to think, see or feel. Sex is something that is being done to me . . . I remove myself mentally from the situation—I'm not there—I'm mentally numb—if I think, I'll freak out.'

(b) About her attempts to role play orgasm; 'I also became aware of the frequent tendency to separate from myself and to become the observer. I really had to work at sticking with myself and to feel and to know what I was doing and to say that it was alright . . . I could feel the tendency to want to get into a fantasy because it would then be the fantasy and not me . . . I became aware that my head was separate from my body—I felt it was apart

from me—immune from what was going on, sort of the overseer making sure that everything was alright but not involved.'
(c) About her genital self-stimulation assignments; 'Again I was really bothered by thoughts related to [the offender] and my family intruding and it was difficult to focus my thoughts and to concentrate on what I was doing and to remind myself that I was the one doing this to me. Everything seemed to feel like it was being done to me, even my arm seemed separate from myself and coming from the outside. So I really had to look at myself and remind myself that this was me, it wasn't [the offender]. He was dead and gone and now it's me and I'm doing this for very positive reasons.'

Another victim, Eileen, detached herself from the abuse and subsequent stressful situations by using a cognitive ritual. This consisted of naming five colors sequentially and repetitively namely: red, yellow, black, white, and green. These were the colors in the linoleum pattern in her room as a child. She generalized the use of this cognitive ritual in other high stress situations throughout her life because she found it to be an effective way of decreasing the amount of stress she might be experiencing in any given situation.

Perhaps the most extreme form of dissociative reaction is the development of a multiple personality disorder. Sexual abuse, often accompanied by physical abuse, in childhood is reported to be very common among patients exhibiting multiple personalities (Boor, 1982; Bowman, Blix, & Coons, 1985; Coons, 1986; Coons & Milstein, 1984; Kluft, 1985; Kluft, Braun, & Sachs, 1985; Saltman & Solomon, 1982; Spiegel, 1985; Wilbur, 1984). For instance, Coons and Milstein (1984) report that among 20 such patients, 75% had been sexually abused, 59% physically abused, and 85% abused in at least one of these ways. In a later paper the same authors (1986) report that these childhood experiences were significantly more common among multiple personality patients than in a matched non-dissociative disorder control group.

Bowman *et al.* (1985) offer some interesting ideas on the possible etiology and dynamics of multiple personality disorder in victims (see also Spiegel, 1985):

There is no evidence to suggest any biological cause for multiple personality . . . Multiple personality tends to have its origin in early childhood, between the ages two and one-half and eight years . . . Although other splits may occur later in an individual, the initial split, or tendency toward splitting, occurs very early in life. Therefore, it would appear that the manner of thought and typical defense mechanisms present early in life may be important predisposing factors.

Fantasy life tends to be rich in early years, and a child may fluidly switch from an animated conversation with an imaginary playmate or playmates to realistically asking his/her parent, 'what's for dinner?'

Likewise, part of 'normal' ego development may involve trying on different roles in the world of 'pretend' to the point that voice inflection, mannerisms, and actions may be altered to fit the desired role. With the richness of a child's fantasy life, the child is able to switch with ease from character to character, to talk to imaginary friends with abandon, and to switch back to 'reality' easily. This ease generally diminishes as the child 'matures' . . .

A child's ego may experience intense good/bad splitting because of a parent who cares for and nurtures a child, but who also becomes abusive. Although a father may communicate at times that he loves the child, he may then force the child into sexual acts which the child may feel are uncomfortable, painful, or wrong. Since splitting is a defense already present in early childhood, and since role playing is a natural way of maturing and coping, this kind of scenario could predispose a child to use the personalities as a defense mechanism to deal with various situations in which such anxiety may exist. During the early childhood years, because of the fluid ego of a child in role play, fantasy life, and 'reality', the child may flow with ease from one state to another. If this pattern of behavior demonstrates its effectiveness in defending against anxiety, a more definitive personality pattern may become entrenched and be associated with amnestic episodes.

These dissociations act then as a defense mechanism of the ego against painful experiences or memories . . . Personalities generally form in order to cope with specific situations or feelings, e.g. . . . one personality holds memories of the incestual activity, one is a repository for anger, and one holds memories of enjoying the incestuous relationship. Rather than attaining a solid ego structure, the personality dissociates into several parts, designated for handling specific types of experiences. (Reproduced from Bowman, E., Blix, S., and Coons, P.M. (1985). Multiple personality in adolescence: Relationship to incestual experiences, *J. Am. Acad. of Child Psychiatry*, **24**, p. 112, by permission. © Journal of the American Academy of Child Psychiatry, Baltimore, USA.)

One (2%) of the 51 victims in the U. of M. series was diagnosed as having a multiple personality disorder (Jehu, Gazan, & Klassen, 1987). This victim, Elaine, was sexually abused by her father and several other offenders. The abuse by her father began when she was a baby and continued until she was aged 12 to 13 years. It occurred on a daily basis when the offender was at home. Sexual activity consisted of exhibitionistic display of the victim's and offender's genitalia to each other, and mutual manual and oral stimulation. In addition, there was penile and digital penetration of the victim's vagina and anus. Penile penetration of the victim's vagina occurred when she was 12 years old. The offender had kidnapped her from her foster home and later that night held a knife to her throat and raped her. Her screams and cries were overheard by her mother in another room. The mother attributed the disturbance to one of the offender's routine physical beatings and did not intervene.

Elaine reacted to the sexual abuse by complying to avoid the severe physical and emotional punishment meted out by the offender if she did not cooperate. She also began using dissociative strategies at around age seven years to cope with the abuse. She would 'float away' or become 'numb all over' to the point where she had no recall of the event. Such time loss episodes would sometimes occur during the sexual abuse. At other times these time losses would last for days after the abuse and she would be unable to recall any intervening events including the sexual activity.

At the time of her initial assessment in the U. of M. program Elaine reported a variety of symptoms. She was experiencing panic attacks that were characterized by fear, palpitations, vertigo, tingling sensation in her right leg, and a feeling of unreality (derealization). The attacks would be followed by psychogenic amnesia either selective amnesia, that is an inability to complete a certain task, or localized amnesia where there was failure to recall events occurring after the panic attacks began and often lasting for several hours. She also described an uncontrollable twitching of her body and extremities lasting between 2 and 20 minutes. This was sometimes accompanied by localized amnesia. She could recall amnesic episodes since early childhood and described how at age 12 to 13 years she would experience a black cloud enveloping her starting from behind and slowly wrapping itself around her. Once totally enveloped by the cloud, she would have a memory blackout from that point on. The episode would vary from a few minutes to several hours. When consciousness was regained she occasionally noted fine tremors of the extremities. One episode occurred when Elaine was separating from her second husband and she was employed as a cab driver. It comprised (a) unidentified repetitive thoughts followed by (b) a panic attack, and (c) selective amnesia including an inability to remember how to drive, what part of the city she was in, and (d) a total memory blackout, including, for example, any awareness of how she got home. She recalls 'waking up' at home and telling her boyfriend about the events prior to her total memory blackout. Elaine manifested psychogenic amnesia, selective type, frequently throughout the therapeutic sessions. On one occasion, for example, she described the sexually abusive activities of her offender father and in the next session stated with puzzlement that she could not recall having told the therapist.

Elaine reported during the assessment that she had been aware of being several 'persons' for about four years. She described herself as hearing five or more distinct voices 'in my head' who fight and argue with one another. In addition to her original personality Elaine had named five other personalities

Table 21.3.   *Positive and Negative Consequences of Dissociative Reactions: Elaine*

Positive consequences

    Going away from things I don't want to see.

    Not looking at things.

    Not remembering my life as hell.

    Stops me from being a bad person all the time.

    Makes me different.

    Takes me out of situations I can't handle and lets someone else take over.

    Allows me control over what emotions I want to give.

    Lets me feel that things aren't really happening to me.

    I can convince myself that something is not true when I actually feel that that belief
       is true.

Negative consequences

    Neglect my kids and everything happening around me.

    Stops me from being one person.

    Stops me from giving when I want to.

---

who were the sources of the voices, and she referred to her various personalities as 'we' or 'us'. She also alluded to the fact that there were more than five entities: 'I haven't really given names to the rest of them. I'm not sure who they really are. Sometimes their (*sic*) out for short times. A few minites (*sic*), hours or days. Each one is different.' She noted that 'most of the time I don't remember what the other me does. I remember different things when I'm different people.' The personalities identified by Elaine were:

(a) Ellie—age 8–9, a little girl with glasses and braids,
(b) No name—age 12, keeps hair over her face and feels *very angry*,
(c) Pretty girl—a 'blah' about 7–9 years old,
(d) Eileen Rock–Elaine's ideal self and who she really is. She was described as super cool, looks good, feels good, enjoys herself and is well liked.
(e) Ella—the writer. She was described as the 'calm' quiet one that likes quiet times. She reads and enjoys a good book and can draw, paint, and write. She has long dark hair and a peaceful pretty face. She is the one who is most acutely aware that she has been 'away' or has 'returned', that is aware of a time loss. This person complained in her writing 'how can I get anyone to believe that I exist? She [Elaine] won't let me tell or show anyone.'
(f) Elaine—the original and presenting entity. She frequently experiences derealization and depersonalization. She is the one who prevents Ella from participating in therapy. She, Elaine, attended the therapy sessions as the client. Elaine described her self as flat, without feelings, the inadequate abusive parent, the one with the violent temper, the one who pushes away from strong positive or negative feelings as much as possible.

The victim was asked to list the positive and negative consequences of her dissociative reactions and these are shown in Table 21.3.

Physiological reactions. Some of the many physiological reactions to stress are shown in Table 21.2. Perhaps the commonest of these among previously sexually abused women are nausea, retching and vomiting evoked by sexual activity, and disturbances of sexual functioning. For example, Amanda would do anything to avoid sexual involvement because the mere thought of partici- pating in sex left her feeling nauseated, experiencing a rapid heart beat, and perspiring profusely. She went to great lengths to limit sexual contact by 'picking fights' with her husband, by getting overly involved in community activities so that she would have little free time for her mate, and if all else failed, the victim would lock herself in her bathroom to avoid going to bed at the same time as a too favorably disposed husband.

Behavioral reactions. These include the avoidance of stress situations and aggressive acts (Table 21.2). Some avoidance reactions used by Amanda are described in the previous paragraph, and among the ways that Alison avoided sexually stressful situations were experiencing a lack of desire for sex, staying out of the home for as long as possible, going to bed at different times than her partner, wearing panties and nightdress in bed, refusing sexual advances whenever possible, and when sex was inevitable, avoiding those foreplay activities that were more stressful than intercourse for her.

Victims often describe how they will push or hit a partner if he does something during sex that is provocative to the victim. For instance, Alison described the difficulty she had in controlling her aggressive impulses as follows:

> Different things were triggering flashbacks and I was too irritated and distracted by them to get any flow going between us. I asked if we could stop and try again in the morning, but [partner] wanted to know why. When I told him I was being bothered by flashbacks and couldn't get into it he got rather impatient . . . I'm sorry for having to stop, but at times it's better that I stop because if I continue I'll start to feel like I'm being pushed and pressured and I'm afraid I'll get angry and smash him. If I'm feeling pushed I have such horrible thoughts like banging my forehead against the bridge of his nose and I simply have to stop and get away.

Acquisition and Maintenance of Stress Reactions

There are probably three major theoretical models that have been advanced to explain how stress reactions might be acquired and maintained. One is

Mowrer's two-factor learning theory, consisting of classical conditioning and avoidance learning, which is discussed below. A second model, also discussed below is Beck's cognitive model in which stress reactions are attributed to distorted thinking. The third model proposes that stress reactions can be acquired vicariously or indirectly through the observation of stress reactions to certain situations by other people (Bandura, 1977), or from information about threatening or dangerous situations provided by other people, particularly parents to children (Rachman, 1977). As this model is probably less applicable to sexual stress reactions it is not discussed further here, although it should be noted that some victims have observed siblings being sexually abused and may have imitated the stress reactions of these siblings. These three models are not necessarily mutually exclusive nor do they provide a completely comprehensive or satisfactory explanation of stress reactions (e.g. Emmelkamp, 1982; Rachman, 1977). Each model may offer the best explanation that is currently available for certain types or aspects of stress reaction.

Mowrer's Two-Factor Learning Theory

The acquisition and maintenance of stress reactions associated with child sexual abuse might be explained in terms of Mowrer's two-factor learning theory with some modifications (Holmes & St Lawrence, 1983; Keane, Zimering, & Caddell, 1985; Mowrer, 1960).

Being sexually abused is commonly very disturbing for children and they respond during it with a variety of stress reactions such as intense feelings of fear and disgust (Chap. 2). In learning terms the disturbing features of the abuse are *unconditioned stimuli* and the stress reactions are *unconditioned responses*. For instance, in Table 21.4 being forced to perform oral sex is shown as an *unconditioned stimulus* that elicits feelings of disgust as an *unconditioned response*.

Any features present during the abuse are liable to become cues or triggers that elicit similar stress reactions in future. Some such cues are common among previously sexually abused women, for example, in Table 21.4, the offender's penis is shown as eliciting disgust, and the victim's feelings of sexual arousal during the abuse might also lead to such feelings eliciting disgust in non-abusive sexual situations. Other cues are idiosyncratic to a particular woman's abuse experiences, for instances, if the offender wakened her from sleep, then she may be very distressed if her partner touches her in bed, or if the offender was bald, then she may have a particular aversion to bald heads. Again, in learning terms, by a process of *classical conditioning* such features that were present during the abuse have become *conditioned stimuli* that elicit stress reactions as *conditioned responses*.

Once certain features have become established as triggers for stress reactions, then new features that are associated with the original features can also

Table 21.4. *Classical Conditioning Paradigm*

Before conditioning		
Victim forced to perform oral sex (UCS) ──────────────>	Disgust (UCR)	
During conditioning		
Forced oral sex (UCS) ──────────────> Disgust (UCR) and offender's penis (CS1)		
After conditioning		
Offender's penis (CSI) ──────────────> Disgust (CR)		
During higher order conditioning		
Offender's penis (CS1) ──────────────> Disgust (CR) and offender's pubic hair (CS2)		
After higher order conditioning		
Offender's pubic hair (CS2) ──────────────> Disgust (CR)		
Stimulus generalization		
Partner's penis		
Partner's nose		
Victim's engorged clitoris ──────────────> Disgust		
Partner's pubic hair		
Victim's pubic hair		

Note UCS = unconditioned stimulus
UCR = unconditioned response
CS = conditioned stimulus
CR = conditioned response

become triggers for such reactions, for example, in Table 21.4, once the offender's penis is established as a trigger for disgust, then his pubic hair may also become a trigger for the same feelings. This process of *higher order conditioning* is one way in which the range of stressful cues may be considerably expanded.

A second way is the process of *stimulus generalization* through which features that are similar to those present during the abuse may also elicit stress reactions. Thus, as shown in Table 21.4, the victim perceived her partner's penis and nose and her own engorged clitoris as similar to the offender's penis, and she also perceived her partner's and her own pubic hair as similar to the offender's pubic hair, so that all these stimuli became triggers for feelings of disgust.

It is important to recognize that stress reactions may be triggered off by a victim's thoughts and images as well as physical cues. For instance, she may become extremely upset when she is telling her therapist about the abuse or when she gets flashbacks to it even though there are no abuse-related physical cues present at the time.

In summary, the processes of first and higher order classical conditioning together with stimulus generalization can account for the wide range of cues

242 Beyond Sexual Abuse

that evoke fear, nausea, flashbacks, and other stress reactions in women who were sexually abused in childhood. This is the classical conditioning component in Mowrer's two-factor theory.

The second component is *avoidance learning*. Through this process the victim acquires certain ways of avoiding stress situations and these avoidance reactions are maintained because they enable her to evade these situations and to reduce the disturbing feelings they evoke, for example, a victim who loses all interest in sex and refuses advances from her partner can thereby avoid stressful sexual encounters and alleviate anxiety evoked by her anticipation of such encounters. Thus, certain avoidance reactions are very intractable and persistent among women who were sexually abused in childhood. Next, Beck's cognitive model to explain the acquisition and maintenance of stress reactions is outlined.

Beck's Cognitive Model

Very recently Beck has presented a cognitive model of anxiety that can be extrapolated to stress reactions generally (Beck & Emery, 1985). As in the case of depression, Beck's model of anxiety is based on the premise that stress reactions are mediated by some disturbance of the client's cognitive processes. More specifically, that stress reactions are precipitated by distorted thoughts and images that signal some kind of threat, and that clients are vulnerable to such thoughts and images because they hold certain dysfunctional assumptions or rules according to which they interpret their experiences and regulate their behavior. In summary, faulty thinking is said to lead to stress reactions involving unpleasant feelings and inappropriate actions.

The initial impression that the client forms of a possible stress situation is termed a *'primary appraisal'*. It provides preliminary answers to an implicit series of questions posed by the client: (a) Does the situation appear to be an immediate threat to the client's vital interests? (b) Does it involve possible physical injury? (c) Does it involve possible psychological injury? (d) Does it involve violation of rules constructed by the client to protect his or her vital interests? Successive reappraisals are made to confirm or revise the primary appraisal of the nature of the situation.

At the same time that the client is evaluating the nature of the stress situation he or she is also evaluating his or her resources for dealing with it. This process is termed *'secondary appraisal'*. The resource may be within the client's own abilities to cope with the threat, or it may comprise help from someone else.

The client's final perception of the threatening situation takes into account the amount and probabilities of damage inherent in the threat, in relation to the client's capacity to deal with it. These perceptions are not cool, conscious, deliberate computations but are generally very rapid and to a large degree automatic. If the client perceives himself or herself as subject to a threat which exceeds his or her ability to cope then he or she has a sense of *vulnerability*, which Beck describes as the core of anxiety disorders.

In clinical problems, this sense of vulnerability is magnified by certain *cognitive distortions* such as the following:

(a) Minimization—the client underestimates the coping resources available.
(b) Mental filtering or selective abstraction—the client is (i) hypersensitive to any aspects of a situation that are potentially harmful and does not perceive its benign or positive aspects, and (ii) he or she is very aware of his or her weaknesses or difficulties in handling a threatening situation but ignores his or her assets and strengths.
(c) Magnification—the client exaggerates the degrees of threat, and/or sees any limitation in his or her coping resources as an enormous gap.
(d) Catastrophizing—the client dwells on the worst possible outcome of the threatening situation.
(e) Overgeneralizing—the client feels particularly vulnerable after any difficulty in coping with a threatening situation because he or she believes that this difficulty is bound to occur again and to spread to other situations.
(f) Disqualifying the positive—successes in coping are discounted because the client believes that he or she can always fail to cope in the future, also past failures are recalled much more easily than past successes.
(g) All-or-nothing or dichotomous thinking—unless a situation is unmistakably safe, the client is likely to perceive it as extremely dangerous.

A client's sense of vulnerability may be further increased by his or her stress reactions to a traumatic situation. This compounding of vulnerability may occur:

(a) Because the stress reaction impairs the client's ability to function effectively, for example, feelings of nausea or flashbacks may impair sexual relationships.
(b) Because the stress reaction—for example, palpitations or depersonalization—is interpreted by the client as a sign of a serious disorder such as a heart condition or a mental illness.
(c) Because the stress reaction—such as a panic attack—is so disturbing that the client is afraid of it occurring again, that is he or she has a fear of fear.

Some people are particularly prone to experiencing a sense of vulnerability and consequent stress reactions because they hold certain dysfunctional *assumptions and rules* according to which they interpret their experiences and regulate their behavior. These assumptions or rules operate without the client being aware of them, in the same way that when we are speaking we apply the rules of grammar without being aware that we are doing so. This is why the term 'silent assumptions' is sometimes used. From the victim's point of view such assumptions prevent something undesirable from happening and ensure that something of value will occur. For example, a victim who assumes that she must retain control in relationships may see this as preventing her from being harmed by the partner and as ensuring that the relationship will be gratifying to her.

A client's dysfunctional assumptions often cluster around one or more of the major issues of acceptance by others, competence compared to others, and control by others or by external events. This last issue is a particularly important influence on the sexual functioning of many previously sexually abused women. They must be in control if they are to feel safe from harm. This assumption usually develops as a result of having been in a threatening situation where the victim perceives herself as having little or no control; for example: (a) with a domineering parent, such as a supremacist father; (b) with an inconsistent parent whose responses to the child are so unpredictable that she reduces the ambiguity by taking control herself; or (c) in an abuse situation where the victim is powerless and helpless.

Victims who have had such experiences tend to feel threatened in situations where they may lose control over their own functioning or to other people or events. Loss of control, over their own functioning may be threatened by, for example, anxiety reactions that the client cannot regulate, anger reactions that may escalate, fear of going crazy, an incapacitating illness, or experiencing orgasm. This last source of fear of loss of control is very common among victims and Alison describes it as follows:

> Today I also allowed myself to reach orgasm . . . The feeling is one of disappointment and disgust at myself for allowing myself to lose control, and for not being in control, for being vulnerable to something outside myself. Though I know orgasm is an internal force I feel it to be external—it's something outside and separate from me and I yield to it and feel overwhelmed and drowned. Though I didn't cry today that's the feeling I have when I have cried in the past. It's a feeling of being overcome by an outside force, a force which I wanted to feel yet to which I did not want to yield. As I'm writing I'm wondering if this feeling is not associated with the feeling of wanting to be close to [the offender] yet not wanting to yield to his control over me which is always the way it ended up—with him being the director, the one in control, the one with the power. I was so compliant I would always do what people told me to do. I had no sense of belonging to myself.

Victims may also be excessively concerned about yielding any control to other people who might attempt to dominate or direct the victim. The relevance of this for sexual functioning is described by Alison as follows:

Arousal is strongly contingent on my being in absolute control of the situation. If [partner] in any way takes the lead or if I sense or allow myself to think that he wants me sexually I will either get angry and push him away or click off and initiate intercourse and direct him to ejaculate as quickly as possible; anything to get it over and done with. Currently, arousal is strictly contingent on my directing my partner to stimulate me orally to the point of orgasm followed by immediate and direct penetration.

Thus, in summary, the basic premise in Beck's cognitive model is that stress reactions are mediated by some disturbance in the client's cognitive processes which precipitates these reactions or renders the client prone to experience them. The nature of a possible stress situation is the primary appraisal performed by the client. This is accompanied by a secondary appraisal of the resources available to the client to cope with the stress situation. If the situation is appraised as threatening and beyond the client's coping resources, then he or she experiences a sense of vulnerability. This sense of vulnerability is magnified by certain cognitive distortions, and it may be further compounded by the accompanying stress reactions. Clients may be especially prone to a sense of vulnerability in certain situations because they hold and apply certain dysfunctional assumptions or rules.

CHAPTER 22

Assessment and Evaluation Procedures

Medical Examination

In view of the possible contribution of organic factors to sexual dysfunction it is necessary to consider the advisability of appropriate medical examination and investigation to exclude or identify these factors. Such physical screening is not necessary for all victims but it is indicated in any of the following circumstances (Bancroft, 1983): (a) recent history of ill health, or physical symptoms apart from the sexual dysfunction; (b) complaint of pain or vaginal spasm during sexual activity; (c) recent onset of impaired sexual motivation with no apparent cause; (d) woman in the peri- or postmenopausal age groups; (e) history of marked menstrual irregularities or infertility; (f) history of abnormal puberty or other endocrine disorder; or (g) when the victim believes the dysfunction to be due to a physical cause, or is in some way concerned about her body (e.g. 'abnormal' labia, etc.). This last circumstance particularly indicates that appropriately conducted medical examinations can serve educational and therapeutic as well as diagnostic purposes.

Table 22.1. *Stress: Protocol for Assessment Interviews*

---

1. What is the precise nature of the victim's emotional, physiological, cognitive, and behavioral reactions to stress (see Table 21.2).
2. What current events (including thoughts and images) precede the stress reactions? These events may be the triggers for the reactions.
3. What current events follow the stress reactions? These events may be maintaining the reaction.
4. What historical and developmental factors may have contributed to the stress situations and reactions?
5. What has the victim done to circumvent or surmount the stresses and with what success? This may provide clues to effective methods of coping.
6. Are there any conditions in the victim's current life situation that impose inappropriate demands on her? Such conditions may need to be modified so that the demands are reduced.

Interviews

An assessment interview protocol for sexual dysfunction is attached as Appendix F. Relevant information is available also from previous assessment interviews at initial assessment and for mood disturbances and interpersonal problems, as well as from previous therapeutic interviews. When sexual stresses may be a significant cause of a victim's sexual dysfunction it is important to ensure that sufficient information is obtained to enable the therapist to answer the specific questions listed in the protocol shown in Table 22.1.

Questionnaires

Sexual History Form (SHF)

This 28-item questionnaire was developed by Schover *et al.* (1982) to ascertain the sexual practices and responses of males and females. In the U. of M. program it was most usually administered to the victim and partner on one occasion during the assessment of sexual dysfunction. There is no scoring system for this instrument but it can be used to categorize the client's sexual dysfunctions although this particular use is less essential in routine clinical work with victims and partners.

Index of Sexual Satisfaction (ISS)

This 25-item questionnaire was developed by Hudson and his co-workers (Hudson, 1982; Hudson, Harrison, & Crosscup, 1981) to measure the satisfaction of males and females in their sexual relationships. In the U. of M. program it was administered to victims and partners during the assessment of sexual dysfunction, at termination of treatment for this problem, and on follow-up. If desired it can be administered at weekly intervals throughout this whole process. The scoring of the instrument and its psychometric properties are described in the references above. Internal consistency is 0.91 and test–retest reliability is 0.83, with adequate discriminant, factorial, and construct validity.

Sexual Arousal Inventory (SAI)

This 28-item questionnaire was developed by Hoon, Hoon, and Wincze (1976) to assess the degree of arousal in *females only* to a range of sexual events. In the U. of M. program it was administered to victims during the assessment of sexual dysfunction, at termination of treatment for this problem, and on follow-up. The scoring system and psychometric properties for the instrument are described in the reference above. Internal consistency is 0.92 and test–

retest reliability is 0.69. The instrument was validated on a population of educated middle- and upper-middle-class North American women and according to the norms from this population 15 sexually dysfunctional women were at or below the 5th percentile.

Sexual Relationship Questionnaires (SRQ)

These questionnaires were designed by Jemail and LoPiccolo (1982) to measure the degree of defensiveness about the client's sexual relationship. Defensiveness was defined as 'the tendency to endorse socially desirable items which are unlikely to occur and deny socially undesirable items which characterize most honest responders' (p. 33). There are separate versions for males and females. In the U. of M. program these instruments were administered to the victim and partner during the assessment of sexual dysfunction, at termination of treatment for this problem, and on follow-up. The main purpose was to assess the social desirability response tendency of each client in order to help in interpreting his or her other questionnaire results. The scoring procedures and psychometric properties are described in the reference above. Internal consistency and construct validity are at adequate levels.

Reconstructive Techniques

The reconstructive techniques of instant replay, remote recall, induced imagery, and role play that are described in Chapter 6 can be used to identify the sexual situations, thoughts or images that are stressful for clients together with the accompanying stress reactions. The use of role play in this context should not of course contravene the customary privacy afforded to the sexual activities of others.

Confrontation

Also as described in Chapter 6 clients can be asked to undertake appropriate sexual assignments in order to identify stressful sexual situations, thoughts, and images and the client's reactions to these events. Several such assignments are described under the heading of *in vivo* exposure in the next chapter.

Recording by Client(s)

Clients may be asked to maintain a written record of sexual assignments and experiences and of their reactions during them. The procedure and formats for such recordings are discussed in Chapter 6.

Target Complaint Scales

These scales are discussed in Chapter 12. As soon as difficulties in sexual functioning are identified and negotiated with client as therapeutic targets then each problem can be noted on one or more target complaint scales and administered at weekly or more frequent intervals throughout the remainder of the assessment and treatment periods, and again at follow-up sessions.

Card Sort

This is another form of self-rating by clients that can be used to assess their problems and to evaluate progress and outcome. Once a problem is identified various aspects of it are recorded on separate index cards and the client is asked to sort these cards into certain categories at weekly or more frequent intervals during assessment and treatment and again at follow-up sessions. Thus, in the U. of M. program those sexual objects, events, or situations that were stressful for a victim were recorded on cards and she was asked to sort these into the categories of *not distressing at all* (0), *mildly distressing* (1), *moderately distressing* (2), *very distressing* (3), or *extremely distressing* (4). A total score is computed from the number of cards placed in each category and those cards which remain in high categories indicate residual therapeutic targets.

Conclusion

The information gathered in a multi-modal assessment (Chap. 6) process provides the basis for a formulation (Chap. 4) of the client's sexual dysfunction that is shared with the victim and partner and explained in terms of the conceptual framework discussed in the previous chapter on the causes of sexual dysfunction. This shared formulation and conceptual framework contribute to the rationale for an individualized treatment program drawing upon some of the procedures discussed in the next chapter.

CHAPTER 23

Treatment Procedures

Although a sexual dysfunction may have originated in a victim's early experiences it is the contemporary conditions that initiate and maintain the problem which require therapeutic attention. Any such organic factors may require appropriate medical or surgical interventions (Bancroft, 1983; Kolodny, Masters, and Johnson, 1979). The treatment of mood disturbances is discussed in Part 2 and although this may have been implemented at an earlier stage of therapy there may be residues or recurrences of these disturbances in the particular context of the victim's sexual functioning. Thus, the treatment approach for mood disturbances used earlier may need to be continued or reinstituted towards alleviating the sexual dysfunction. Similarly, the treatment of interpersonal problems is discussed in Part 3 but it may need to be pursued further if such problems appear to be contributing to sexual dysfunction or impeding its treatment. This leaves sexual stresses among the major causes of sexual dysfunction and it is the management of these stresses that is the focus of the discussion of treatment in this chapter.

As mentioned previously the formulation of the sexual dysfunction is shared and explained to the client(s) in terms of the conceptual framework discussed in Chapter 21 on the causes of sexual dysfunction. If the causes for the client concerned include sexual stresses then this constitutes the rationale for stress management training. Such training teaches skills that the victim can use to cope with sexual stresses, and corrects distorted thinking that contributes to these stresses. It takes time to correct the distorted beliefs and assumptions that contribute to stress reactions as described in the previous discussion of Beck's cognitive model (Chap. 21). Consequently, victims are usually trained initially in a variety of skills which help them to cope directly with immediate stresses. This coping skills training is described next and it is followed by discussion of the cognitive restructuring of distorted thoughts that contribute to stress reactions. In both these aspects of treatment it is highly desirable and perhaps necessary to have the participation, cooperation, and collaboration of the victim's partner if she is in a regular sexual relationship. At many points in the intervention both victim and partner are likely to benefit from prescribed reading in the self-help books written by Barbach (1984), Heiman, LoPiccolo, and LoPiccolo (1976), and Zilbergeld (1978).

Coping Skills Training

It is very important to select and adapt the coping skills to be taught to each victim so that they are plausible, appropriate, and effective for that particular individual. Among the procedures used in coping skills training are those discussed next.

Relaxation Training

There are several ways in which the ability to relax can help victims to cope with stress: (a) it reduces the bodily tension which is a common reaction to stress; (b) it produces a state of psychological calmness; (c) it distracts the victim's attention from her stress reactions; and (d) it enables victims to exercise some mastery and control in stress situations. The physical conditions, preparation of clients and specific procedures for relaxation training are well described by Bernstein and Borkovec (1973) and Goldfried and Davison (1976, Chap. 5) among others, and useful prescribed reading for clients on the benefits and methods of relaxation is to be found in Heiman *et al.* (1976, p. 43–50) and Zilbergeld (1978, Chap. 9).

The control of breathing with accompanying relaxation is often the first coping skill used in a stress situation. It is a rapid and effective way for the victim to gain some mastery in the situation. She is asked: (a) to fill her chest with four or five short deep breaths each lasting about one second; (b) to hold her breath for about five seconds; (c) to exhale slowly while saying the words 'relax' and 'calm' silently to herself and relaxing her whole body. This process is repeated as necessary for the victim to relax and calm herself in a stressful situation.

A more extensive procedure for achieving relaxation and calmness in stress situations involves training the victim to relax progressively the major muscle groups in the body. In respect of each of these groups the victim's attention is first focussed on the muscles concerned. The therapist then explains and demonstrates how these are to be tensed up. Next, the victim tenses the particular muscle group, and maintains the tension for about 5 to 7 seconds while the therapist directs the victim's attention to the feelings of tension being experienced. The victim is then instructed to release the tension and her attention is focussed upon the feelings of relaxation by appropriate comments from the therapist over a period of about 30 to 40 seconds. After this training phase the victim practices relaxation regularly at home, often with the aid of audiotaped instructions by the therapist. In these practice sessions the victim relaxes from the existing tension levels in the muscle groups concerned rather than deliberately tensing them as she did during the training phase. Once she has been taught and practiced relaxation the victim can use this skill to reduce tension and calm herself in stressful situations.

Thought and Image Stopping

Victims are often troubled by obsessional thoughts, fantasies, and visual images that are very stressful for them. For example, as discussed previously, it is quite common for women who were sexually abused in childhood to have 'flashbacks' to this experience, especially during current sexual encounters when an association is made between some feature of the current encounter and the earlier abuse. There are several ways in which such stressful thoughts, fantasies, and images can be disrupted and obliterated. One basic method— termed thought stopping—consists of:

(a) Asking the victim to experience the stressful thought, fantasy, or image, and to signal when she is doing so.
(b) After 30 to 45 seconds, the therapist says 'STOP' in a loud commanding voice. The victim is then asked what happened and she usually replies that the thought stopped (probably because of the increased sensory input provided by the word STOP). This process is repeated several times.
(c) The next step is to have the victim herself say 'STOP' aloud when the thought begins.
(d) The final step is for the victim to stop the thought process by verbalizing the word 'STOP' silently. In this covert, sub-vocal verbalization the victim should actually tighten her vocal cords and move her tongue as if she were speaking aloud.

Another way to disrupt disturbing thoughts is for the victim to concentrate on the immediate environment, and to attempt to describe—preferably aloud—in meticulous detail the persons and objects around her. Thus, when a previously sexually abused woman gets a flashback during sexual activity with her partner it is often helpful for her to open her eyes and to focus on the partner and their surroundings in order to discriminate the current situation from the intrusive earlier abuse experience. With practice, gaining mastery over the disturbing thoughts by such reality orientation tends to make them less stressful. Several other methods of stopping stressful thoughts, fantasies, and images are described by Beck and Emery (1985, pp. 210–231).

Coping Plans

Prior to the implementation of the next four stress management procedures it is necessary for the victim and therapist to have worked out a coping plan drawing upon the coping skills already taught for the victim to use in particular stress situations. For example, a coping plan for a previously sexually abused client to use in dealing with genital self-stimulation exercises that she found stressful is shown in Table 23.1. More extensive suggestions on coping planning are offered by Beck and Emery (1985, pp. 232–257, 323–324).

Table 23.1. *Coping Plan: Alison*

If you get unpleasant feelings and become upset during self-stimulation:
1. Stop stimulating yourself.
2. Take several short deep breaths to fill your chest and relax as you breathe out.
3. Open your eyes, look around, and remember where you are *now*.
4. Relax and calm yourself.
5. When you have calmed down either try stimulating yourself again on this occasion or try again at another time.

Guided Self-Dialogue

Handling stress situations involves preparing for them, confronting them, coping with any unpleasant feelings they evoke, and reflecting on how one coped afterwards. The victim's thoughts can influence how she feels and what she does in stressful situations. Therefore, at each of these four phases it is useful for the victim to ask herself some selected questions and to answer these to herself, and to make positive statements to herself in response to any negative thoughts she may have about handling the stress (Meichenbaum, 1985, pp. 69–74). This rationale is discussed with the victim in ways that she can understand.

Some examples of common questions and responses that the victim might use at each phase are shown in Table 23.2. It is very important, however, that the questions and responses used are appropriate to each individual victim's particular concerns and negative thoughts. The victim and therapist need to compile appropriate questions and responses together. Examples of individually appropriate statements that were used by a victim to help her cope with genital self-stimulation exercises are shown in Table 23.3 and she described their implementation and her use of other coping skills as follows:

(a) During the exercise I again worked at keeping thoughts from intruding. I tried to focus on the purpose of the exercise which is for me to feel pleasurable sensations and that it is OK for me to be doing this to myself. Other people do it and it's OK. There's nothing bad about it. It's natural to want to feel good and it's OK to feel good as a result of sexual stimulation . . . whenever I started feeling irritated or started losing sensation I would stop, do some breathing exercises and look around the room, reminding myself that this was me and that it was alright.

(b) I'm still needing to block on certain thoughts and associations that want to intrude but I'm able to stop, relax, and look around.

Sometimes all it takes is for me to open my eyes and remind myself where I am, and who I am. Throughout the exercise I reminded myself that what I was feeling felt good and that I liked the feeling. If I found myself losing sensation or starting to be a bit rough I stopped and repeated these things to myself. Then when I returned to the exercise the good feeling would return and I could tell myself that I deserved to treat myself lightly and gently.

(c) I started with my pants on and then progressed stopping to relax whenever I felt myself tensing or becoming irritated. I worked hard at keeping thoughts from intruding . . . none of them have anything whatsoever to do with my life as it is today. I also worked at reminding myself that this is me. I'm doing this to myself, I have chosen to do it, I want to do it and I can stop anytime myself. Stopping to look around our bedroom also helped for [partner] and I decorated it ourselves so there's lots to remind me about today . . . I felt pleasure and it felt good. I didn't want to stop. By stopping periodically and by consciously working at causing my body to loosen rather than tighten, I could keep the good feeling.

Imagery Rehearsal

Briefly, this procedure consists of the victim imagining situations in which she confronts stresses and copes with them (Meichenbaum, 1985, pp. 76–78). Thus, by imagining herself coping with stressful situations the victim is able to rehearse and practice coping with them in real life. Imagery rehearsal is derived from systematic desensitization (Goldfried & Davison, 1976, Chapter 6) but it contains variations on this procedure so that coping with stress rather than its elimination by counterconditioning is emphasized.

The first step in imagery rehearsal, as in systematic desensitization, is for the therapist and victim to generate a hierarchy or hierarchies of stressful situations from the least to the most disturbing. For example, the items listed under 'Partner-related activities' in Table 21.1 are in hierarchical form with the least disturbing item at the top and the most disturbing at the bottom. After the hierarchy is drawn up the victim is then relaxed and asked to imagine progressively more stressful situations from the hierarchy.

One way to conduct imagery rehearsal is for the victim to imagine a situation from the hierarchy and to signal to the therapist when this situation becomes distressing to the victim. The therapist then instructs the victim to continue imagining the stressful situation, while also visualizing herself coping with it by breath control relaxation and other coping skills.

A second method of conducting imagery rehearsal requires the victim to imagine herself initiating coping skills in response to early, low intensity cues that signal the onset of stress reactions. These cues may be in the victim's own

Table 23.2. *Common Coping Statements*

Preparing for stresses
What is your plan for coping with unpleasant feelings?
What is the likelihood of anything very bad happening?
Don't think about how bad you may feel; think about what you can do about it.

Confronting stresses
One step at a time; you can handle the situation.
Don't think about being upset, think about what you are doing to cope with the situation.
Any bad feelings are helpful cues for you to use your coping plan.
Take several short deep breaths to fill your chest — breathe out slowly — relax — you are
in control.

Coping with unpleasant feelings
When you begin to feel upset, take several short deep breaths to fill your chest and
breathe out slowly.
Focus on what is happening now, not on what might happen subsequently; what it is that
you have to do to cope.

Reflecting on stresses
You did it — you got through it, each time it will be easier.
It wasn't as bad as you expected.
You had a plan and it worked.
You are avoiding things less and less. You are making progress.
It was easier than you thought.

Table 23.3. *Individualized Coping Statements: Alison*

'*I'm* doing this, I've *chosen* to do it, I *want* to do it, and *I* can stop anytime.'
'It's OK to feel good as a result of sexual stimulation.'
'Losing control for a few seconds during climax can't harm me, I'm in a safe place.'

---

responses, for example, tension and apprehension. Alternatively, the cues may
be external, for example, a partner touching or kissing her when she fears this
may progress to intercourse which she finds stressful. Whether the cues are
internal or external, the general aim is for the victim to notice early signs of
distress or threat and react to them with coping responses rather than avoidance or panic. This is one way of building generalization into the program
because the victim's own reactions become a constant reminder to use the
coping skills she has learned.

There are two circumstances in which imagery rehearsal is particularly
useful. One is when role playing would be an inappropriate method of
rehearsing coping skills, for example, when the stress is of an explicitly sexual

nature to be confronted by the victim only in privacy. The second circumstance is when role playing and/or *in vivo* exposure is too difficult for the victim to undertake immediately in which case rehearsal in imagination may be a very useful bridge to the more difficult tasks.

Role Playing

Role playing (Meichenbaum, 1985, pp. 78–80) is presented to the victim as a way of learning and practicing coping skills that she can use subsequently when confronted with stress situations in real life. The procedure tends to reduce anxiety and other stress reactions and to increase the probability of coping skills being used when required. It is sometimes useful to role play coping with a non-targeted, less intense stress in the victim's life first, and then to move on to the targeted, more intense stresses. The victim and therapist role play interactions that are likely to be stressful for the victim (e.g. saying 'no' to unwanted sexual advances). They periodically change roles so that the therapist alternates between (a) modeling the stress reactions that the victim is likely to experience together with the implementation of coping skills to handle the stress, and (b) acting as the threatening person might while the victim practices coping with this stress.

There are two variations of this basic role-playing procedure that are useful with some victims. One is for the victim to adopt the trainer role and to instruct the therapist in coping skills. This tends to promote attitude change in the victim and ensure that she really understands how to use the coping skills involved. The second variation follows George Kelly's (1955) fixed role therapy in which the victim is encouraged to assume a role-playing attitude when trying out newly acquired coping skills in real life. The idea is for the victim to behave as a different kind of person to herself (e.g. someone who does not have to accept unwanted sexual advances) on a trial basis to see what will happen. The hopefully positive consequences will serve to reinforce the new behavior.

In Vivo Exposure

There is now general consensus that exposure to stressful situations is an important—possibly a critical—feature of the effective treatment of stress disorders (e.g. Marks, 1981). The *in vivo* exposure procedure consists of the victim progressing through a graded series of assignments in which she confronts and copes with a hierarchy of stress situations in real life (Meichenbaum, 1985, pp. 80–82; Beck & Emery, 1985, pp. 258–287). These situations are selected as being stressful for the particular victim concerned and are confronted by the victim in order of difficulty for her; from the least to the most disturbing. Thus, the individualized nature of such an *in vivo* exposure program is paramount. Graded *in vivo* exposure assignments have several functions in therapy:

(a) The stressful nature of the situations concerned is reduced for the victim as she becomes increasingly able to cope with them by using the coping skills discussed previously whenever stress is experienced during an assignment.
(b) Effective sexual stimulation and responses are promoted through appropriate assignments.
(c) Hitherto unrecognized stressful features of the situations may be revealed as the assignments are attempted, so that these stresses can then be dealt with in therapy.

For reasons of space it is possible only to present here some specimen sexual assignments in outline form and more comprehensive information on these and other assignments together with guidance on preparing clients to undertake them and on dealing with the resistances that are almost certain to be encountered is available elsewhere (e.g. see Hawton, 1985, pp. 124–146, 157–171; Jehu, 1979, pp. 135–150, 160–161).

All but the last of the assignments discussed below are in a sequence that may be appropriate for many victims although again it is emphasized that each assignment and its sequencing must be individually tailored for each victim. The last assignment of vaginal dilatation is applicable only to those victims who are suffering from vaginismus. In the U. of M. program many of these assignments were demonstrated to the clients in the film by LoPiccolo and Heiman (undated) which parallels the book by Heiman *et al.* (1976).

It is noted earlier that victims often react adversely if they feel that they are being in any way pressured or coerced during sexual activities in adulthood. Consequently, it is often desirable to negotiate with the couple for a ban on intercourse and any other threatening activities until a suitable stage in treatment is reached. Additionally, it is very important that the woman move through the stages of the program at her own pace, and without any pressure from the therapist to undertake particular assignments before she feels ready to attempt them.

Visual self-examination. Many victims have a negative body image and regard their genitals particularly as an unfamiliar, isolated, bad or dirty part of their body. This assignment may be especially helpful in helping such victims to become more aware, comfortable, and positive towards their bodies as a whole and the genitals specifically. In essence the victim is asked to examine her nude body and to appreciate its attractive features. Additionally, it is recommended that she use a handmirror to explore her genitals and to identify the various parts with the aid of a diagram. Fuller descriptions of the assignment are given in prescribed readings for clients (Barbach, 1984, pp. 62–65, 139–140; Heiman *et al.*, 1976, pp. 26–39) and therapists may wish to consult Becker and Skinner (1984, pp. 219–220).

Tactile self-exploration. The slightest sign of sexual pleasure may evoke stress reactions in some victims, and this assignment is useful in beginning the process of helping these victims to tolerate and enjoy such pleasurable feelings. The victim is asked to explore her body and genitals tactually, with the aim of locating sensitive areas that are pleasurable to touch. She is not given any expectation of sexual arousal at this stage. Prescribed readings for clients are Barbach (1984, pp. 65–70, 140–141) and Heiman *et al.* (1976, pp. 40–43).

Genital self-stimulation. The process of accepting and enjoying sexual pleasure is continued in this assignment. It is suggested that the victim should stimulate manually those sensitive areas that she located in the previous assignment. Some ways of doing this are discussed with her, including the use of a lubricant to heighten pleasure and reduce any discomfort. She may also be encouraged to explore the use of erotic materials and fantasies that are acceptable to her in order to extend and enhance her capacity for arousal. In the cases of victims who fear loss of control during orgasm, it may be helpful if they role play their conception of the orgastic response in an exaggerated manner. The simulation of anticipated reactions such as involuntary screaming or gross muscular movements may alleviate their stressfulness and sometimes results in the occurrence of a real orgasm during the role play. Again, particularly in the cases of those women who have difficulty in climaxing, a vibrator may be used instead of manual stimulation, or some combination of the two. Prescribed readings for clients are Barbach (1984, pp. 71–87, 119–157, 141–159) and Heiman *et al.* (1976, pp. 54–115). Becker and Skinner (1984, pp. 222–224) is a useful reference for therapists.

Mutual general pleasuring. Prior to assignments that involve the partner as well as the victim it is important to emphasize some general points concerning mutual sexual activities. First, because of her vulnerability to adverse reactions to any feelings of coercion or exploitation, the victim should be given control of mutual activities, including their initiation and duration. Second, if the victim experiences flashbacks to the abuse situation that adversely affect her current responses with her partner, then she should let him know that she is flashing, so that he can understand what is happening and not blame her or himself. Third, the victim may experience strong feelings of anger during current activities with her partner that he has done nothing to evoke. Again, these feelings should be recognized as arising from the past rather than the present circumstances.

Often the first mutual assignment to be prescribed is general pleasuring. Briefly this means that the clients take it in turns to explore the sensual pleasure of touching and caressing each other's bodies with tenderness and affection. At this stage the breast and genital areas are excluded, but otherwise the couple is left to discover for themselves where and how they like to be touched and to communicate these preferences to each other. Among the several reasons for this assignment is the reduction of avoidance reactions. Quite often the victim and her partner have been avoiding any physical expression of affection as well as sexual foreplay, in case these should involve or lead on to activities that are very stressful for the woman. This threat is reduced by the therapeutically negotiated limits to general pleasuring, and the associated avoidance reactions may be correspondingly alleviated. Prescribed readings for clients are Barbach (1984, pp. 160–183), Heiman *et al.* (1976, pp. 15–17, 131–156), and Zilbergeld (1978, pp. 131–149, 188–254). Sources for therapists include Hawton (1985, pp. 128–133) and Jehu (1979, pp. 138–141).

Mutual genital pleasuring. Once couples are able to respond positively to general pleasuring, then they can move on to the next step of including the breast and genital areas. It is very important to stress that this genital pleasuring is a gradual extension of general pleasuring, which is not superseded by the incorporation of the genitals. At this stage, the victim will communicate to her partner what she has learned earlier about the most effective means of stimulation for her, and it is important that he follows her guidance concerning her preferences. Prescribed readings for clients are Barbach (1984, pp. 160–183, 185–190) and Heiman *et al.* (1976, pp. 15–17, 131–156). Therapists may wish to refer to Hawton (1985, pp. 133–137, 141) and Jehu (1979, pp. 141–142).

Vaginal containment. When the victim is aroused during general and genital pleasuring and these activities are not stressful for her then the couple might move on to the next assignment of vaginal containment. The victim adopts the female superior position and inserts her partner's penis into her vagina. Initially, she simply contains the penis while experiencing the sensations and feelings this evokes. These may be enhanced by the victim contracting her vaginal muscles on the penis, and subsequently, as her arousal mounts, by moving slowly up and down and experimenting with other different movements. She is told to concentrate on her own sensations and pleasure without worrying about her partner's gratification at this stage. If he becomes too aroused, then movement can be stopped for a while, and he can either remain inside the victim or withdraw until the excitement subsides. Such withdrawal and reinsertion is often a teasing and arousing experience for the woman, and her arousal may also be maintained by clitoral stimulation while penile movement is suspended. This assignment continues for as long as the victim wishes, at which point her partner might reach climax either intravaginally or by manual or oral stimulation as long as the chosen method is not stressful for the victim. An important feature of this assignment for victims is that it provides an opportunity for them to explore and appreciate the vaginal sensations and erotic feelings evoked by the man's penis, without having to subordinate her own preferences and pleasure to those of the partner. This assignment is discussed more extensively by Hawton (1985, pp. 137–139).

Sexual intercourse. Ultimately the couple may proceed to full intercourse while either the victim or her partner concurrently stimulates her genitals either manually or with a vibrator. If the couple so desire, this concurrent stimulation can gradually be faded out by stopping it when the victim is near climax. Probably the majority of women, however, do require some more direct stimulation than that provided by penile movement alone in order to reach climax on many occasions. Prescribed reading for clients is Heiman *et al.* (1976, pp. 157–158).

Vaginal dilatation and Kegel's exercises. As stated above this assignment is designed specifically for the treatment of vaginismus (Hawton, 1985, pp. 142–145; Jehu, 1979, pp. 160–161). A sterile lubricant such as K-Y jelly is applied and the victim first inserts the tip of her own finger into the entrance of her vagina until she is able to accept this with less of a muscular spasm. This procedure is repeated with the whole of one of her fingers and then two fingers. When penetration by two of the victim's fingers can be accepted without discomfort, the whole procedure is recapitulated up to this point with the partner progressively inserting and moving his fingers under the victim's manual and then verbal guidance.

   These vaginal dilatation procedures are often combined with and facilitated by Kegel's (1952) exercises which give the victim more control over her vaginal muscles and enable her to relax them during dilatation. Prescribed readings for clients on these exercises are Barbach (1984, pp. 151–154) and Heiman *et al.* (1976, pp. 50–53). Sources for therapists include Hawton (1985, pp. 218–219) and Jehu (1979, pp. 166–167).

Cognitive Restructuring

As mentioned above, once victims are trained and competent in the skills needed to cope with immediate stresses then therapy moves on to the correction of the distorted beliefs and dysfunctional assumptions that precipitate or predispose towards stress reactions. As far as the correction of distorted beliefs is concerned this follows the cognitive restructuring process discussed in Part 2. The application of this process to stress disorders specifically is discussed by Beck and Emery (1985, pp. 190–209). The remainder of this chapter is devoted to the correction of dysfunctional assumptions or rules (Beck and Emery, 1985, pp. 288–312).

Identifying Assumptions

Induced imagery is one of several methods for identifying a victim's dysfunctional assumptions (see Part 2). The therapist asks the victim to close her eyes and to picture the earliest memory she has of a distressing experience similar to the stress she is currently facing. The victim may need time and encouragement to do this, but in most instances she will have a vivid image of some experience that is strikingly similar to the current stress. Next, she is asked to concentrate on this image and then to state in one sentence her underlying beliefs at that time. The formulation of this belief may take a while for the victim and therapist to put together in a meaningful way. The victim is asked also to describe the emotional feelings and bodily sensations associated with the recalled early experience and to compare these with her reactions to the current stress. A close fit is usually reported. One instance is a victim who recalled being molested by an uncle and experiencing disgust and loss of sensation in that situation. She believed that her uncle was taking advantage of her need for care and affection from him. In her current sexual encounters with her husband she is also experiencing aversive feelings and genital anesthesia. Her underlying assumptions seemed to be that 'you always have to pay for love', and 'that men always exploit you'.

Restructuring Assumptions

This induced imagery procedure helps the victim to see how past memories are creating problems in the present. The therapist can then suggest that the victim learned the underlying assumption at an age and level of development when she lacked sufficient ability to set some limits on the application of the assumption, so that the previous example might apply to some sexual encounters and some men but not to all encounters and all men. The therapist can also indicate how the victim was distorting her thinking on the early occasion and that the same distortion is occuring at the present time, as in the following examples:

(a) Victims often unwittingly create real situations that reconfirm their assumptions (self-fulfilling prophecy). For example, a victim is so distrustful of men that her mistrust of her husband becomes more than he can tolerate and the marriage breaks up, thus confirming the victim's distrust of men.

(b) Victims selectively take in information that reconfirms their assumptions (mental filtering). For instance, a victim may focus on material in news reports and conversations—such as abuse, rape, and violence—that supports her assumption that the world is a dangerous place in which one must retain absolute control in order to be safe.

(c) Victims often overgeneralize from particular experiences in ways that support their assumptions. Thus, abuse by one man may be overgeneralized to support the assumption that all men are to be feared.

Victims often adhere to an assumption in a rigid manner which can preclude exposure to experiences that could modify or limit the assumption. For example, a victim who assumes that 'no man can be trusted' will tend to avoid all close relationships with men. If she did risk experiencing such relationships she might modify her original assumption to 'some men cannot be trusted' which is a more flexible and adaptive assumption.

Victims are often reluctant to let go of their assumptions. They want to get rid of the stress reactions associated with an assumption but not the assumption itself. For example, a victim may want to overcome the avoidance reactions that are precluding close emotional and sexual relationships while still wanting to retain the complete control that makes her avoid any relationship that requires a sharing of control. Thus, therapists need to have realistic expectations concerning the modification of a victim's assumptions.

The therapist can help the victim to see that the benefits of these assumptions are outweighed by their costs. For example, the benefits of retaining complete control in a marriage might be outweighed by the consequent break-up of the relationship. When the benefits of an assumption are outweighed by the costs it may help the victim to make a major issue into a minor one (e.g. 'I must be accepted' to 'I would like to be accepted'), or to shift priorities (e.g. 'I have to have a partner' to 'I'm going to enjoy my life'). When a victim is not willing to modify assumptions around a major issue the therapist can point out the consequences of this choice, such as, the break-up of the marriage or sexual celibacy, and perhaps help the client to meet the conditions that follow from the assumption, for example, to follow a satisfying lifestyle without being in a close relationship. This lifestyle or other conditions may enable the victim to live comfortably with the assumption. Alternatively, if the lifestyle or conditions prove unsatisfactory then this may increase the victim's motivation to modify the assumption.

Once victims see the benefits of modifying assumptions and are motivated to make the necessary changes then any of the cognitive restructuring procedures for exploring alternatives can be implemented (Part 2). Additionally, the following strategies are useful guides to the restructuring of assumptions:

(a) Repetition—simply telling the victim a modified assumption is rarely sufficient to make her discard an existing assumption. The therapist needs to get the victim to focus repeatedly on the assumption until it is gradually chipped away.

(b) Action—it was noted previously that victims tend to act in ways that reaffirm their assumptions. They can be given assignments to act in contrary ways on repeated occasions until the assumption is undermined. For example, a woman who assumes that all men will try to exploit her sexually might be given the assignment of repeatedly being friendly towards males in an appropriate way until she comes to believe that not all of them are predatory.

(c) Lifestyle—victims can be assisted to modify their lifestyles in order to undermine their assumptions. For example, the isolated victim who assumes that others are likely to harm her and who focusses on reports of violence in the press might progressively develop a social life and start to attend to non-violent news items.

Thus, motivated victims may be helped to modify their assumptions by means of cognitive restructuring procedures and the therapeutic strategies just outlined. This will reduce the victim's vulnerability to stress reactions in sexual and other previously threatening situations. The use of coping skills training and cognitive restructuring in the treatment of sexual stresses is illustrated in the case studies that follow next.

CHAPTER 24

Case Study: Alison and Michael

Alison's victimization experiences and family background in childhood are described in Chapter 10, and the relationship between Alison and Michael is discussed in Chapter 15. The following summaries of the nature and causes of their sexual difficulties are based on the assessment that was undertaken prior to the commencement of treatment focussed upon these target problems.

Description of Sexual Dysfunctions

Impaired Motivation

Alison experienced sexual desire less than once a month. It was a relief to her not to have sex, and she could go on indefinitely without it. The decline in her motivation commenced shortly after marriage, and it had been progressive except for some temporary marked increases when Alison wanted to get pregnant and was at risk of conceiving.

Sexual Aversion

Several features of sexual activity elicited aversive reactions in Alison (see Sexual Stresses and Emotional Reactions below). These reactions had occurred since she began petting, and long before she had intercourse. They did not fluctuate with the current state of the marital relationship, even when this had been very good.

Impaired Arousal and Orgasm

Alison had some difficulty with physiological arousal, and she could only become psychologically aroused by using a fantasy (see Emotional Reactions below). She could attain orgasm on over 90% of occasions when her partner stimulated her genitals orally, but could not do so with penile movement in the vagina unless climax had already started by oral stimulation. Alison described her arousal and orgasm experiences at the time of the assessment as follows:

> Arousal is strongly contingent on my being in absolute control of the situation. If [partner] in any way takes the lead or if I sense or allow myself to think that he wants me sexually I will either get angry and push him away or click off and initiate intercourse and direct him to ejaculate as quickly as possible: anything to get it over and done with. Currently, arousal is strictly contingent on my directing oral stimulation to the point of orgasm and immediate and direct penetration. At no point do I want to feel him. It is a purely physical, mechanical act—I merely direct the oral stimulation that will bring me to orgasm—other than that I think, feel, and am aware of nothing.

> Orgasm is invariably accompanied by spontaneous crying associated with a feeling of aloneness and recognition of a sense of having yielded control over what my body was doing. Orgasm also associated with feelings of disgust towards myself, somehow though the orgasm was desired it was also something I shouldn't have done—any feelings of pleasure are quickly replaced by feelings of isolation and vulnerability.

Sexual Dissatisfaction

There were several indications of severe dissatisfaction for both Alison and Michael. On the Sexual History Form they both reported their sexual relationship as extremely unsatisfactory. On the Index of Sexual Satisfaction Alison scored 62 and Michael 84, both indicating clinically significant dissatisfaction. On the first four administrations of a Target Complaint Scale both scored 13 consistently, indicating that their sexual relationship *couldn't be worse*. This sexual dissatisfaction was the only dysfunction experienced by the male partner.

Causes of Sexual Dysfunctions

Sexual Stresses

Sexual situations that were stressful for Alison are shown in Table 21.1. She could tolerate sex as long as there was no fondling or foreplay, only oral–genital stimulation of her by Michael to a point where she is starting to climax. He could then insert immediately without her feeling his penis at all.

Emotional Reactions

During sexual encounters Alison experienced negative emotional reactions, including distress, disgust, and revulsion. She felt trapped and helpless as she did in the original abuse situation. Physical anxiety reactions were not reported but Alison was apprehensive about whether she would be able to continue the sexual encounter and if not, what Michael's reactions would be. Thoughts that the sexual encounter should not be happening were accompanied by much anger and resentment which led to self-injurious acts by the victim and sometimes aggression towards her partner. She also experienced guilt and self-disparagement because she has such negative feelings towards sex and the consequences of these for her partner. Her negative emotional reactions were accompanied by the cessation of sexual arousal.

Cognitive Reactions

Alison coped with sexual stresses by dissociating. She removed herself mentally from the sexual encounter—she was just not there—and therefore did not become aroused or participate in the lovemaking except in a purely physical sense. She also distracted herself from the ongoing sexual activity by fantasizing herself in situations in which she is in control, such as being in the role of prostitute who is driving a man crazy with sex. Alison had to rely on such fantasies to evoke and maintain any psychological sexual arousal but it distressed her to have to do this. Michael had difficulty in accepting that Alison used fantasy during their lovemaking and denied ever doing so himself. The couple were given some articles in an attempt to normalize fantasizing (Hariton, 1973; Talbot, Beech, & Vaughan, 1980; Zimmer, Borchardt, & Fischle, 1983).

Alison sometimes experienced flashbacks to her abuse and she described the reactions of herself and Michael to these as follows:

> If any associations to the abuse experience occur it is an immediate stop. For this reason I can't allow myself to think, see or feel . . . In regards to telling [partner] that I am 'flashing' it doesn't work because he can't understand or accept that after all these years it is my Uncle [the offender] that I am sensing and not him. This kind of a discourse increases rather than lessens the gap in our relationship.

Alison also had distressing thoughts of being cheapened and used during sex as if she is seen as being good for only one purpose.

Avoidance Reactions

Alison avoided the stressful features of sexual encounters by means such as experiencing a lack of desire for sex, going to bed at different times than her partner, wearing panties and nightie to bed, and not engaging in foreplay activities.

Partner Discord

The relationship between Alison and Michael is described more extensively in Chapter 15, and only its associations with their sexual functioning specifically are considered here.

Michael perceived Alison's aversion to sex as rejection and an indication that she does not love him. This view was reinforced for him by her profligate spending habits and the domestic demands she placed upon him especially during her absence at the university. He had some feeling of being exploited by the victim. This aroused in her feelings of having to pay for his financial and domestic support with sex, which recapitulated the coerciveness of the abuse. The perceived rejection and exploitation was more distressing to him than the lack of sexual gratification. He felt that it was unnatural to be in a marriage without sex, more because of the principle involved than the sexual depriva- tion, and if it continued he might want to separate.

He was unable to comprehend Alison's aversion to sex, that it originated in her sexual abuse, and she could not simply push it aside during sexual encounters with her husband. He was disturbed, however, to discover how aversive sex had been to Alison over such a long period in their marriage. He responded by saying that he could live without sex and that it was much more important for her to remain in the marriage until the children have been raised, when the couple might separate if their sexual relationship had not improved by then. Alison was very angry and accused Michael of writing off sex because he had heard some things he did not want to hear. She was not prepared to remain in the marriage simply to bring the children up until they are 18. She wanted to be valued as a person and not just a sex object and mother who can be disposed of if sex has not improved after the children have grown up. She asked 'does our relationship have something to sustain it regardless of what happens sexually?' and commented 'if you don't dish out, you don't get a relationship'. This conflict apparently recapitulated certain aspects of the sexual abuse situation: (a) whether her partner loves her unconditionally or only if he gets sex recapitulates the issue of whether the abuser really cared for her or only exploited her love and dependency on him; and (b) having to have sex to maintain her marriage recapitulates the coerciveness of the earlier abuse.

A related conflict concerns the roles of sex and affection in the victim's relationship with her husband and other males (see discussion of fear of intimacy in Chap. 21). On the one hand she thought it would be marvelous to have pleasurable sex in the context of a loving relationship with her partner, and would have liked to be able to do so. On the other hand she was still wanting a caring, companionable relationship with a male that did not entail any sexual expectations, and her continuing search for this included her partner. This splitting of sex and affection was clearly incompatible with the desire for a sexually pleasurable and loving relationship in her marriage.

Alison also explained how Michael's vasectomy had changed their sexual relationship and increased its aversiveness for her. The vasectomy had highlighted that they were having sex purely for the sake of sex, with no chance of conception which had previously given sex a purpose for her. The partner's penis no longer had a purpose, it was just part of the urinary tract, which made it less appealing and more aversive. There was also an implication that the partner was taking full control of their sexual relationship, making decisions, and denying her femininity. This was a milestone in their marriage.

Process of Treatment for Sexual Dysfunctions

Following therapy focussed upon mood disturbances and interpersonal problems, the major focus of treatment shifted to sexual dysfunctions from week 54 to week 143, with a follow-up at week 155.

1st Phase

The rationale for stress management was discussed with the couple (Chap. 23). The necessary pre-conditions for this treatment approach were negotiated with and agreed by them as follows: (a) there will be no sexual or sex-related activities at all except those that are agreed as treatment progresses; (b) all such activities will need to be initiated and controlled by Alison until it is agreed that initiation and control can be shared at a much later stage in treatment; and (c) Michael understands and accepts Alison's need to stop a sexual activity whenever it becomes stressful for her and he will accept this need to stop without discussion or disapproval.

2nd Phase

At this time the least disturbing item in the victim's hierarchy of sexual stresses (Table 21.1) was 'sleeping nude or just in a nightie'. Consequently, the first sexual assignment was for her to sleep in a nightie without pants. Her anticipated and actual negative reactions to this assignment initially included: (a) concern that it would lead to sex—she was unsure about her partner's acceptance of and compliance with the above conditions for treatment. The need to test Michael's reactions and to build up confidence and trust in his cooperation was discussed with the couple; (b) resentment that her free choice and control over what she wears in bed was being restricted. It was emphasized that she had choice whether or not to do the assignment. Over a period of about three weeks these reactions were reduced and the victim became more comfortable with the assignment.

3rd Phase

When negotiating the next assignment the victim's ambivalence about moving on through a treatment program for sexual dysfunction was increasingly apparent. In an attempt to reduce this ambivalence and to enhance motivation she was asked to write a description of her ideal intimate relationship with her partner and of its advantages for her. This she did as follows:

My ideal sexual relationship with [partner] would be characterized by freedom of choice, spontaneity of action, and naturalness of feeling. Both [partner] and I would be free to choose when and how we would respond to feelings of love and a desire to be close to each other. Actions would be tender, loving, and sensitive to the other's feelings. Feelings, both positive and negative, would be respected and accepted and there would not be undue pressure for either person to feel they must please themselves or please the other at the expense of themselves. Limitations set by either individual, must be accepted and respected for being indicative of where that individual is on that particular time, and should not be taken as a person rejection . . . To conclude, my ideal sexual relationship with [partner] would be a reciprocal exchange of loving actions that arise from a natural desire to be physically and emotionally close to the other person. What do I stand to gain from a freer, more natural sexual relationship with my husband? . . . I stand to gain fulfillment of my identity as a woman; I would accept all of me, and feel good about myself. I would relax in my body movements and posture and not be unduly preoccupied with sexual thoughts. Ability to relax with sexual contact and less preoccupation with sexual thoughts would free my mind and allow me to expend my energy in other, more constructive activities. Feeling comfortable in a sexual relationship would allow me to feel more confident, more spontaneous, and more trusting and respectful of myself than I do at present.

This description of an ideal intimate relationship was subsequently agreed with by the partner who considered it to be very normal. The victim became more willing to negotiate and attempt a further assignment.

4th Phase

Alison reported showing aversive reactions to her own secondary sexual characteristics. With the aim of reducing these reactions she was given the assignment of visual self-examination and the associated prescribed readings (Chap. 21). She was also shown the appropriate portion of the accompanying film (LoPiccolo & Heiman, undated). Her pubic hair and to a lesser extent her breasts were the parts of her body that proved most difficult for her to accept. She described her reactions to visual self-examination of her genitals as follows:

I felt ashamed that I was doing this to myself. I almost felt like I was voyeuring on myself. These are my private parts and no one is to see them including myself. I felt like the whole thing was disgusting. Yet, I was in conflict because rationally I know it's 'healthier' to be able to accept all of oneself. But, I felt repulsed and wished that it just wasn't there. It's like I could like myself better if those parts would just go away and I would look like a young girl whom people would consider sweet and innocent and young. People would know I didn't have pubic hair and consequently they would not expect me to do things. Having pubic hair changes everything—people treat you differently, they look at you differently, they expect things from you. . . .

The parts themselves have not changed for when I was young it seems I did nothing but look and try to figure it all out. I tried to remember how I felt then. I can remember cutting my labia with scissors. I can remember shaving my pubic hair . . . I always wanted to change my genitals. Even though I used to go through my mom's nursing books and knew this was the way they were supposed to be somehow they never looked right. In my mind I always liked my vagina because this was how I was going to have babies and that always impressed me. It made me very special. But it always seemed so unglamorous for something so special. Just a big hole that could open and close and I could never understand it all . . .

Now when I look at my genitals I'm astounded how prominent they are. They seem to really protrude and there seems to be an awful lot there. They look fat and the pubic hair looks masculine—it looks like a man's beard around a big mouth with lips that are far too big like some people look when they are all lip. There's too much pubic hair—I'm astounded how much there really is. I'm tempted to shave it. . . . It's my pubic hair which bothers me—it looks so gross and I just can't understand what its purpose is. It seems as human beings we should have evolved beyond the stage of having pubic hair. It serves no purpose, it's unattractive and it blatantly draws attention to something which is private. I just don't like it. I know where the feelings stem from. They stem from [the offender] who started his business as soon as he discovered I had pubic hair. Things were never the same after that. . . . The offender always found my pubic hair a source of interest and it seems he found it as soon as it appeared. He would frequently make the comment 'now you're growing into a woman' as though I was supposed to share his fascination with the idea. Around this time my cousin came and he too seemed quite struck with my pubic hair and breasts so it's easy for me to understand now how these two things became a focus for me. Then my father started calling me a floozy which implied my development was illicit and dirty and yet he became overly jealous and possessive and yet rejecting; the mixed and negative messages really took hold.

5th Phase

The next assignment undertaken by the victim involved tactile self-exploration and genital self-stimulation, together with prescribed readings and viewing of the corresponding section of the film by LoPiccolo & Heiman (undated) as described in Chapter 23. She reported her reactions to this assignment in the following notes:

(a) I am feeling much more comfortable about my pubic hair. Thinking about it in the same terms as I do my appendix has been helpful in that it put it into a context I could relate to and accept. It seemed to give it a place in the body even though it no longer has much of a purpose. Also I tried to think of pubic hair in the same context as head hair. Hair on the head adorns the face, pubic hair adorns the genitals. Both face and genitals are meant to be considered attractive. Therefore hair, both head and pubic, is supposed to draw attention to something considered attractive.

Again tonight my genital area was more sensitive to touch and I could feel some pleasurable sensation as I began to stroke my clitoris. However, as my clitoris became firm and in the mirror it had the visual and mental association to a man's penis I turned off. Thereafter touching was more painful than pleasurable and I stopped.

(b) I wondered tonight as I looked at my pubic hair and again found it rather disgusting if there's not a visual and tactile association there with [the offender]. I find pubic hair so masculine and I know I was impressed with the coarseness and wiriness of his pubic hair I wonder if I'm not confusing my hair with his and am not reacting to my own pubic hair with the same abhorrence that I know I felt in touching his. I felt sick and so pressured to do what I did. I know I didn't like it. I don't know how helpful this awareness may be because I'm still faced with the problem of not liking my pubic hair but perhaps I can accept now why and know what the association is. This is what I'm transferring to [partner] for I've never been able to look at his pubic hair and I can't stand the feel of it.

It's a similar association with the clitoris for its hood or shaft looks

so similar to a penis I'm finding it hard to stimulate myself because I'm
not really feeling anything pleasurable. My genitals feel numb.

To help Alison to manage and overcome her aversive reactions during the
sexual assignments a coping plan was worked out with her (Table 23.1),
together with some individually appropriate coping statements (Table 23.3).
The assignments were extended by intensifying genital self-stimulation and the
victim's description of her reactions and coping strategies is quoted in the
section on guided self-dialogue in Chapter 23. Generally, the assignments went
well and she was beginning to look forward to them, but she did have some
negative reactions to reaching orgasm which are quoted in the account of
Beck's cognitive model in Chapter 21.

6th Phase

With the aim particularly of reducing the victim's aversive reactions to orgasm
the next assignment focussed on this and included exaggerated role play of
orgasm (Chap. 23). She described her reactions to this assignment as follows:

> (a) Today I started with the role-playing orgasm and though I was
> quite apprehensive about doing it and have avoided it for the past
> week once I started I was glad I did because what started happening
> was quite enlightening and I feel fairly similar to what happens in a
> sexual experience with [partner]. As I began to move my body I
> became aware I was telling myself 'how disgusting' I was and this was
> followed by the haunting chant of 'who do you think you are anyway'.
> I realized that particularly the second statement disrupts me when-
> ever I'm in a situation that is somewhat stressful . . . I also became
> aware of the frequent tendency to separate from myself and to
> become the observer. I really had to work at sticking with myself and
> to feel and do what I was doing and to say that it was alright . . . I
> could feel the tendency to want to get into a fantasy because it would
> then be the fantasy and not me, but because I don't like the content of
> the fantasies and because I want to experience it first hand I didn't. I
> became aware that my head was separate from my body—I felt it was
> apart from me—immune from what was going on, sort of the overseer
> making sure that everything was alright but not involved. Perhaps
> that's where the control comes in.
>
> My mind and my feelings are separate and that is why I never really
> feel aroused because my mind hasn't given permission to feel it. I
> know it must be there because if I can experience orgasm then I must
> be physically aroused and if I'm physically aroused then it seems only
> logical that I should be able to feel it. I now easily can feel pleasure in

my genitals and I like the feeling and there is a change just before orgasm but that point seems to take a long time in coming. . . . Perhaps I'm still fighting achieving orgasm which is again an issue of feeling the need or wanting to have control over what my body does. Today I did have orgasm—I was determined not to stop the exercise until I did because I really wanted to try to get in touch with what happens to me during orgasm, what is it that I tell myself about those feelings. Again the feeling during or immediately following orgasm is an overwhelming feeling of being out of control and disappointment in myself. I feel ashamed but I don't know if it's because I wanted the feeling of orgasm or because I let myself have it. Desire and blame seem closely connected.

(b) This morning the exercise began with my feeling how much easier it is for me to feel and touch all parts of my body. However, as I went on I became preoccupied with the memory that really crystallized last night and that is that I know now [the offender] tried for me to perform oral sex on him. It was in the farm house when I would be kneeling beside the couch on which he was lying. I remember him pushing my face down into his pubic area and telling me to put it into my mouth but I wouldn't. I remember feeling so overwhelmed and confused by what he wanted me to do and not knowing what to do. I know I didn't do it and when I didn't he just mashed my face all around in it. That's the feeling I've been fighting with [partner's] nose. It feels so much like a penis rubbing all over my face. That's why when that feeling is strong I can't help but push him away. I can't stand it—the same if he holds the back of my head while he kisses me. These associations are so strong now, and right now it doesn't help for me to tell myself that it's [partner] and not [offender]. That's why we can't have much sexual contact right now and why he has to listen to me and just let me be in control. I'm sure I'll get through it and though to him it may seem like I'm getting worse rather than better because there's so many more things that bother me. But I know these things are all associated with [offender] and not [partner] and that is why I'm hopeful of working through them. At least now they're on the surface and are strong feelings rather than a lot of vague sensations.

(c) This morning I was able to do the exercise and I feel it was the most constructive session I've had to date . . . I started off feeling pleasure right away and within a short time I was very naturally lubricated probably the most to date. Sensation stayed with me for some time and I was beginning to feel actually aroused which I believe is the first time in what I would consider a natural state, i.e. without the use of fantasy. When sensation was lost and I became numb I stopped and relaxed and did some alternate stimulation. After a while sensation returned and I began saying certain things out loud to myself. I was saying how good it felt and that it was alright and I was becoming quite aroused. Then I had a flashback to [offender] in the cab of the truck. We were sitting upright side by side. My pants were off and his pants were open and his pubic hair and penis exposed. He was rubbing me sideways and this time I wasn't closing off. Instead I was opening up and was saying: 'That's OK you can do that if you want to'. With that I became very warm, my level of excitement skyrocketed and I had an orgasm and started to cry very hard. I felt totally overwhelmed by the orgasm, like my body was turning in on itself and was being pierced in a million different places. I hate the feeling of orgasm, I just can't stand it and today it was more intense than it has ever been. Then I just kind of drifted off and when I woke up I felt really alone.

I don't know what all this means if anything. It all seemed so clear this morning but now it just seems so confusing and unclear. I don't remember feeling any pleasure or getting excited in any way with [offender]. I know I liked being with him. I liked being with him a lot, but I know I didn't like what he did. But that's not the way it was this morning and that seemed so clear.

At this point Alison was asked to summarize her progress to date in the treatment of sexual dysfunction:

(a) Looking at my body is easier to do and I am more accepting of its general appearance. When I am disgusted by it I challenge those thoughts by reminding myself how those thoughts developed . . . I still have some difficulty in accepting the presence of my pubic hair but I recognize that the thoughts associated with it are futile and not very constructive. However, the aversion has lessened and it does not interfere wth me doing the exercises. It feels softer and touching it is no longer a problem—it's looking at it that creates difficulty.
(b) With genital stimulation I feel pleasure right away and have learned to manage loss of sensation with relaxation and reality orientation . . . Numbing or loss of sensation occurs far less frequently now, perhaps only 1–2 times in any given session, and I'm no longer concerned when it happens. It might be a little bit frustrating but I'm not distressed by it. I know the loss is temporary and I have control over what I can do to help it come back. Pleasurable sensations are in the comfortable range—that is they are strong enough to be easily perceived but not so strong they're irritating or painful. Natural lubrication is increasing with each session.
(c) Intruding thoughts still occur and I seem to have no control over when they occur or what they might be . . . When these thoughts

occur I stop and relax and get a handle on what's going on now. However, the frequency with which these thoughts occur is greatly diminished and I'm not as disturbed by them as much as I used to be. When these thoughts occur, I think about the issues they're concerning and I can generally resolve them by thinking in terms of separating the past from the present.

(d) Orgasm when it has occurred is very distressing and I don't like it at all.

There appeared to be several reasons for Alison's aversion to orgasm:

(a) It involved her in yielding control to 'a stronger force and feeling disgusted with herself for doing so'. These reactions were associated with the offender being in control during the abuse, when she wanted an affectionate relationship with him without having to yield to his sexual demands. She now wanted a similar asexual relationship with her partner but she realized that this is inappropriate in marriage.

(b) In the past reaching climax was perceived as wrong and was accompanied by bad feelings. These were now triggered automatically by orgasm.

(c) The victim felt powerless and angry over her failure to retain control during intense arousal and orgasm. She tried to control climaxing by experiencing this physically but not psychologically— 'splitting of body and mind'—and this prevented her from experiencing psychological arousal. She recognized that she must have been angry with the offender as a child although she does not remember this and only expressed anger towards herself and her father.

(d) Spreading her legs and overt sexual movements filled her with disgust. She could become aroused if she remained still and felt secure. She coped with aversive reactions by clicking into a fantasy of teasing partner and being in control of the encounter. Such displays and movements were associated with demands by the offender that the victim act as if she was enjoying their sexual activities and she felt that she had to comply with his wishes otherwise she would be a bad girl and be rejected and punished by the offender. This compliance made the victim feel that she was a willing participant and therefore responsible for the abuse.

7th Phase

At the end of the previous phase Alison expressed a wish and readiness to start getting closer to Michael after the lengthy period she had spent in individual assignments. Accordingly the couple were given mutual general pleasuring as an assignment with the relevant prescribed reading (Chap. 23). The victim trusted her partner not to exceed the limits of general pleasuring but she was somewhat concerned about being totally nude during it. It was arranged that she would retain some clothing if this seemed necessary for her comfort. The victim described her initial and subsequent reactions to the assignment as follows:

(a) Pleasuring exercises have gone very well. I'm finding them relaxing, pleasant, and stimulating—I'm feeling what might be described as a sensual awakening—I'm experiencing [partner] in a way that I have never experienced him before. There seems to be a good sense of respect and understanding—he is allowing me to set the pace and I'm quite comfortable in doing so. Intruding thoughts and flashbacks are occurring but I'm able to cope with them and they pass without too much difficulty. Generally it's just a matter of re-orienting myself, slowing down and talking to [partner] ensuring that limits are understood and accepted. I'm aware of the tendency to want to click into a teasing fantasy but I'm able to catch myself and focus my thoughts on the here and now and question why I might be wanting to separate. Right now I'm most comfortable with us both having underpants on but that's a whole lot further than my armored days of jogging suit and socks. I'm feeling good and it is nice to have more physical contact with [partner]. I've enjoyed the two sessions thus far; they've been positive.

(b) Exercises continue to go well and I'm very pleased. Communication is open and there is a free exchange of feelings. The prevailing attitude is that we each have ownership over our own body and that we share our body with the other because we want to. Sharing is a privilege not a right and each is free to say no. I'm now comfortable with being completely undressed. I realized that by keeping my panties on I was telling [partner] that I didn't trust him. I'm trusting him more and more and he has shown me that he will respect my limits and not push. As yet I don't want [partner] to have his underwear off. I know it sounds like a contradiction to what I've just said about trust but it's more than that—there's the visual and the feel. It just seems more threatening. I'm thinking about it and am working it through in my mind first. It will come.

(c) This week I feel the exercises have gone well, with me becoming progressively more comfortable with both of us being completely undressed. This is coming slowly however, and not without its problems which need to be worked out.

First of these problems is that it is very difficult for me to tell [partner] when something is affecting me aversively. For example, I find it quite bothersome if his penis should rub against my abdomen.

Yet, because he is likely to make it more difficult for me (by asking questions or passing comments) if I say anything, I tend to move away or change positions more subtly. However, last night this led to a discussion about his perception that I am failing to progress . . . I tried to explain to him that I feel I have made a lot of progress, that him being nude is a big step, and that we will make it if we just move slowly. Once again, I explained if there is one thing that is going to set up a reaction it is being pressured to do something I'm not comfortable with. However, all of this made me realize that [partner] is picking up from my body language what I am not expressing verbally, and by personalizing it he is misperceiving it: he is believing it is a reaction to him rather than to past experiences in which I was made to perform and to put up with all sorts of sensations that were just too much. Now I'm wanting to feel them as they are without clicking out or clicking into a fantasy, and to do that [partner] has to move slowly. I want to be comfortable with what is happening and in order to relax I need to trust that he will expect nothing from me other than that which I want to give. I know it's difficult for him and I do feel badly, but being pressured is an area where my reactions are very automatic and I know if I'm pressured or feeling overpowered (for example partner wanting to lie on top of me) I'll fight. In writing this I realize I need to plan some coping strategies that could keep me from exploding and fighting. One such coping statement that I will rehearse is: I have a right to tell [partner] what makes me feel uncomfortable and I do not need to feel badly that I have limits about what I'm comfortable with sexually. I can simply state: 'I don't feel comfortable with that'—and if he asks why not I can state: 'I don't wish to discuss it right now, but perhaps we can talk about it tomorrow when it won't interrupt the rest of the time we have together'.

I feel very badly. I'm having to assert myself in a way that infringes on the rights of [partner] that is, the right of a husband to have sex with his wife. But I'm working on it. Then again when I think about it further I'm not sure it is a husband's right to have sex with his wife. It's a convention but the right is more for each individual to give and share their body as they please.

8th Phase

The terminal illness of the victim's mother had brought the couple close to each other and they asked to move on in the treatment of sexual dysfunction while their relationship was so good. They were prescribed the assignment of gradually extending mutual general pleasuring to include mutual genital pleasuring, together with relevant reading (Chap. 23).

This proved very aversive for Alison because of the contact it involved with the male genitals and her expectation that it should culminate in intercourse. She only continued the assignments for the partner's sake and to preserve the marriage. Her heart was not in them and she really did not want to do them, she wondered if the abuse has turned her off completely?

The partner felt that his wife lacked any enthusiasm for the assignments. He wondered if the marriage could survive and whether her current sexual problems were due to the past abuse or to her present relationship with him. The probability that the problems originated in the abuse but that the current relationship was impeding their treatment was discussed with the couple.

In view of the uncertainties about the future of the marriage and the role of sex in it, the specific treatment of sexual dysfunction was suspended and the focus of therapy was shifted to the general relationship between the victim and her partner as described in Chapter 15.

9th Phase

At this point the major focus of treatment shifted back to sexual dysfunction, and the main problems remaining in this area were Alison's commitment to this treatment and her aversive reactions: (a) to reaching orgasm; (b) to the male genitals; and (c) to any initiative or control by her partner during sexual activities.

Commitment to treatment. Michael expressed very strong doubts about Alison's commitment to treatment of sexual dysfunction. He felt that she lacked enthusiasm for the assignments and avoided them as much as possible as well as being unwilling to take any 'risks' in attempting to overcome her difficulties. He doubted if she would ever be able to resolve these and wanted to know one way or the other so that they could plan appropriately for celibacy, a limited sexual relationship, or some other course. These complaints evoked the following reactions in the victim:

> I'm feeling very angry and I'm feeling very hurt but I know these feelings are irrational so I guess I'm feeling useless because no matter how I feel it always seems to be wrong. There's one way to feel and that's the way that everyone else feels and if you don't feel that way then you're wrong. I'm sorry sex doesn't feel good for me and I'm trying to turn that around but in the meantime I feel I'm being persecuted. I feel I'm being blamed for feeling the way I do and I feel I'm being punished for saying how I feel. I could and maybe I should just shut up and say and do what good little girls always do. I've done that all my life and no matter what people say it's the only way you get through life. When you try to sort out your feelings you're stuck because no one really understands and then you're alone like you

were before you opened up so what's the difference—it's better just to shut up then if you're alone you can always pretend and believe that if you opened up maybe you wouldn't be. See it keeps you in control because if you don't open up and you're lonely you've chosen it. But if you open up and reach out and then you find you're alone you're really alone and it's not because you've chosen it. You chose to reach out and the other person didn't reach back and then you're really a loser because you're not wanted. I'm feeling like such a loser and I think it's because I really am. When I try to feel any different and pretend like I've got something on the ball I'm such a phoney. I'm just one big phoney who tries to pretend that she's worth something when she's not worth shit. I hate myself so totally I can't stand it. I wish I would just drop dead.

It was agreed with the couple that treatment would continue until week 101 at which point it would be reviewed with the aim of deciding whether: (a) the problems were resolved and further treatment was unnecessary; (b) the treatment was helping and should be continued; or (c) it was not helping and should be stopped with further therapy being focussed on the implications of the sexual relationship remaining unimproved.

By week 101 both partners reported considerable progress and that the treatment was helping and should be continued. The victim was much more enthusiastic in undertaking the sexual assignments and avoided them less. The partner reported a dramatic change in his wife's attitude and willingness to involve herself in the assignments, he never thought that she would ever get to this point. Both spouses said that their relationship was better, deeper, richer, and closer. They were talking to each other during lovemaking and sex was not just a physical experience, it was more 'spiritual', a 'psychological fulfillment', 'it's whole nature has changed'.

Aversion to reaching orgasm. The victim described the aversive stimuli in the following card sort items which are not listed in order of severity: (a) experiencing feelings of arousal; (b) experiencing more intense feelings of arousal; (c) thinking about the sensations building towards orgasm; (d) thinking about experiencing orgasm; (e) thinking about the let-down feelings after orgasm; (f) experiencing orgasm; (g) feeling flooded after orgasm; and (h) the time immediately following orgasm and coping with the bad feelings. She described her climax as physiological not psychological. She tried to keep it suppressed or subdued and it was not a 'full climax'.

While Alison could not remember ever climaxing during her abuse it would not have surprised her if this had happened. If it did occur she recognized that orgasm would have been an automatic reflex response which did not necessarily signify that she wanted or enjoyed the abuse.

The major interventions with this aversion were repeated viewing of relevant film scenes, cognitive restructuring, and genital self-stimulation assignments. The film used (LoPiccolo & Heiman, undated) includes scenes of a woman reaching orgasm with her partner and the victim viewed these repeatedly as a form of symbolic exposure. She described some of her early reactions as follows:

> (a) Every time he touched her breasts or her genitals or she got aroused . . . I felt it was hurting her and I could feel the hurt as though it was happening to me. I started to cry after watching it the first time and that seemed to break the tension and watching it the second time seemed to be less hurtful though I was aware of more angry and aggressive thoughts towards him. Every time he touched her I just felt it like short little sticks of pain, like little electric shocks. I didn't feel it was yucky or disgusting, I just felt like I wish I could enjoy and find it really pleasurable.
>
> (b) I have just realized something and that is by having sex with [Michael] because I think I have to, or by doing it for him and not for both of us, I'm really reducing our sexual relationship to an abuse experience. Thus the very means I've been using to deal with sex has just been replicating the abuse experience over and over again; keeping the link between sex–abuse, sex–aggression, sex–fear forever strong. Thus as long as I continue with my thinking that sexual sensations are frightening and hurt and that someone is only using me for his own kicks, therefore I'm not supposed to feel it and don't want to, then I'm just continuing the abuse. Only this time I'm responsible for it because I know [Michael] is not abusing me and never would. I know he cares for me, and finds it insulting that I would consider having sex with him for his sake alone. I'm turning the experience of having sex with [Michael] into something that it's not through my own mental engineering. I'll have to think about that.

To counter these and other negative beliefs concerning reaching orgasm the victim undertook some cognitive restructuring as exemplified in Table 24.1. Additionally, genital self-stimulation assignments were prescribed with the major aims of (a) evoking thoughts and reactions that the victim could cognitively restructure, and (b) providing *in vivo* exposure to climaxing.

At the victim's request the partner purchased a vibrator for her and this was used in the genital self-stimulation assignments and in sexual activities with the partner. During the latter the victim climaxed in the presence of her partner who was very reassuring and supportive. Using the vibrator on her own evoked very intense feelings in the victim but she found that she could regulate her sensations more than during manual stimulation and that her arousal was more rapid so that she did not get discouraged. With the vibrator she could have multiple orgasms and thus expose herself to flooding type *in vivo* exposure experiences. The victim also reported slight urination during climax and the non-pathological and often transitory nature of this occurrence was emphasized to both spouses (Barbach, 1975, p. 107).

At the beginning of each therapy session the victim was asked to rate each of the card sort items listed above on a 5 point scale. At termination of treatment all items were rated as *not distressing at all* (0) with the exceptions of 'experiencing more intense internal feelings of arousal' and 'experiencing orgasm' which were rated *mildly distressing* (1). In interviews the victim reported that she was able to regard orgasm as a natural function that is meant to be pleasurable. She is no longer afraid of reaching climax. After doing so she was not distressed and did not cry or feel guilty or ashamed.

Aversion to male genitals. The victim described the aversive stimuli in the following card sort items which are not necessarily listed in order of severity: (a) thinking about a man being nude; (b) looking at a nude male in a magazine; (c) looking at a nude male on film; (d) looking at a nude male and female together; (e) laying on partner and feeling his penis beneath his clothes; (f) touching partner's flaccid penis; (g) being with partner and knowing that his penis is erect; (h) touching partner's erect penis; (i) touching partner's scrotum; (j) touching partner's erect penis to initiate quick intercourse without thrusting; (k) touching partner's pubic hair; (l) having partner's penis touch me accidently; (m) my face feeling partner's pubic hair; (n) partner taking my hand to direct me to touch his genitals; (o) partner's penis rubbing against my face; (p) partner rubbing his penis against me purposefully; (q) partner's hand pressing on my head to direct me to perform oral sex; and (r) partner inserting his penis into my mouth.

The major interventions used to reduce the victim's aversive reactions to these stimuli were: (a) repeated viewing of a relevant film; (b) observation of the partner's genitals in the relatively non-threatening, non-sexual situation of his taking a shower; and (c) observation of the partner's genitals during general pleasuring, proceeding to touching them during genital pleasuring. The victim had avoided looking and touching her partner's genitals during previous pleasuring assignments. The film (LoPiccolo, Friedman, & Weiler, undated) used included scenes of an impotent male patient with his penis both flaccid and erect during sexual activities with his wife. The victim described some of her reactions to this film as follows:

> I found every time he touched her breasts or thrusted I flinched. It's just so uncomfortable—scattering—for me. Looking at the erect penis became easier with repeated viewing of the film and they both seemed to just accept their bodies, not shielding or protecting them. When the woman had orgasm—she smiled. It was obviously very intense for her but pleasurable and she didn't feel ashamed. I think I see a lot of

Table 24.1.   *Cognitive Restructuring of Beliefs Concerning Orgasms: Alison*

Distorted beliefs	Alternative beliefs
He's doing something to her and he's trying to get her to respond.	She doesn't think in terms of he's trying to get her to respond and that she's giving in and being weak. She wants to experience it for herself, not because someone is trying to get her to respond. She doesn't have to keep control because she's doing it for herself not for anybody else.
She should be ashamed for showing her response in front of him.	She liked it and she's not afraid of showing it because she believes in herself and feels she's OK and is not ashamed of being her. She's not having orgasm to make him feel good, to make him feel like a man, she's doing it for herself.
It is wrong to have orgasm because it is giving in, losing, and it means you've been vulnerable or influenced by someone else.	You are no more vulnerable during orgasm than at any other time because nothing more is going to happen during that time. If you've agreed to sex with someone you should agree to the whole thing because it's meant to be a total experience and a willingness to make someone feel certain things and to accept those feelings in return . . . You agreed to be influenced because it makes you feel good and you like and want the feelings.
He's not thinking about her feelings, he's only thinking about his own. He's putting his needs ahead of her's and is not considering how she's feeling. She's lost.	There's no indication of this in the moves though at the end he's obviously thrusting and 'getting off' and at that moment he may not be able to consider her. But that's the way it is and it doesn't mean she's lost because he can't be aware of her as a separate person at that time. It's supposed to be that kind of a totally consuming experience but it doesn't mean you become lost or lose yourself or that the other person doesn't care about you as a person at the time . . . It's not an abuse experience when it's one using the other for his own kicks. It's a loving experience where two people want to share themselves with each other because they care for each other and it makes them feel special to be loved. It's a way of showing the other person you care, but as an adult in a loving relationship you can do it because you want to do it, not because you have to do it.

Table 24.1. (*contd.*)

Distorted beliefs	Alternative beliefs
If orgasm can't harm me then why to I need to protect myself from feeling intense feelings of arousal.	I don't — I only think I do to keep myself from feeling something I'm uncomfortable with. But if it can't harm me then I've no need to protect myself. I just need to remind myself it's not hurting me bacause it can't. It's only feelings — it's only sensations — it's nothing concrete — it's not an object. Also it's part of myself — it's not an external force — it's from within me — so it's natural — it's meant to be.

aggression in sex—a lot of hurt and a sense of being overpowered in thrusting. A sense of being done to rather than mutual pleasurable exchange. I'm not sure I see the need for sex. It just doesn't come naturally for me. I know that thought is going to do me in and I wish I didn't have it—I really wish it came naturally, but I have to work at every single step.

Alison described some of her reactions to the mutual pleasuring assignments as follows:

(a) Last evening we did the exercises and limited it to stroking [Michael] and looking at him without his underwear. Looking at him and thinking about it was new. I focussed on it as being [Michael] and attaching the penis to [Michael] and thinking about it as just being another part of his body made it easier. I became aware of to what degree in the past I had detached and depersonalized this part of [Michael].

(b) We have done the exercises four more times and they have all gone very well. I'm quite comfortable touching and looking at [Michael's] penis and having it rub against me and I'm beginning to trust that it will be the same every time now. I'm relaxing and am becoming aroused but not to the point of orgasm. I'm beginning to enjoy feeling the arousal and it is at a very comfortable degree of intensity. It's just very mild and very pleasant. [Michael] is very cooperative and is letting me lead and when I say it's time to stop he is able to do so without a lot of questioning. We're talking during the exercises and seem to be enjoying being with each other.

Thus, the male genitals had become less aversive for the victim, she no longer avoided looking at or touching them, and was more comfortable when

she did so. The remaining difficulties concerned the partner taking some
initiative or control during activities involving his genitals. These developments are reflected in the card sort scores for aversion to the male genitals
which at termination of treatment were zero for all items with the exception of
'Partner taking his hand to direct me to touch his genitals' which was still
moderately distressing (2), and 'Partner's hand pressing on my head to direct
me to perform oral sex' and 'Partner inserting his penis into my mouth' which
were still rated as *extremely distressing* (4). It was emphasized that neither
spouse should feel compelled to engage in particular sexual practices, such as
oral sex, that he or she does not like. The avoidance of non-preferred sexual
activities is common in the population at large and there are no prescribed
standards for what people should enjoy or do sexually, the only appropriate
standard is the couple's own satisfaction and comfort. The remaining issue of
control between the spouses was addressed therapeutically as described in the
next section.

Aversion to sharing control. For the victim the prospect of sharing control
evoked fears of trusting another person who might use, overpower, reject, or
hurt her, as described in her notes below:

> (a) Some of this links to my relationship with [uncle/offender] and
> how desperately important it was for me to keep control of myself
> when I felt so panicky and out of control and overwhelmed and
> bewildered by what was happening. I had to keep myself together
> because if I lost it I'd burst all over. Then afterwards I had to control
> myself in order to appear normal, always like I was OK—nothing was
> the matter. It was like being a criminal who has to appear super good
> in order to keep the heat off—otherwise someone might get suspicious
> and get too close.
> (b) Sexually, I still have a great need for control—it's a fear of being
> overpowered by the other person and eventually my own body
> overpowers me too and the ultimate loss of control is orgasm—the
> very real awareness of having lost it, of having let yourself go, of
> having been vulnerable to someone else, of not only having put
> yourself in a position of being with someone but of having yielded to it
> as well. Orgasm is a complete sense of being out of control of having
> let someone do things and yielding to it and then feeling ashamed and
> guilty and bad and disgusting. It's like you showed the other person
> you liked it or part of it and that made it OK.
>   Now with [Michael] I find sexual control very difficult to give up.
> I'm afraid he's not going to care for my feelings. I'm afraid he'll
> pressure me to do things I don't want to do and then take my refusal as
> indicating I'm no better. I'm finding it difficult to keep working at our
> sexual relationship—to keep policing it, to keep it within limits with

Table 24.2. *Cognitive Restructuring of Control Issues: Alison*

Distorted beliefs	Alternative beliefs
[Michael] has sexual expectations of me.	That's true he does and that's OK. Though it makes me feel pressured I need to accept the realities of our relationship — that it is to include a sexual relationship. That's OK because I want it too.
By not letting [Michael] act spontaneously during lovemaking I am controlling him and myself.	I suppose control really has no place in lovemaking because if it's safe and no one's being hurt and it's mutually agreed upon then why need there be a need to control? If I trust [Michael] and trust myself the I should be comfortable with just letting it be. I know sensations can't harm me and I know [Michael] won't harm me — then I just need to relax and let it be. If I can't be harmed then I'm not at any risk and I don't need to protect myself because there's nothing to protect myself from. There's no need for control — self-control or otherwise. I have nothing to protect myself from.

which I'm comfortable. I'm afraid of feeling so out of control or overwhelmed that I'll react and fight like I did before.

Alison cognitively restructured her distorted beliefs and assumptions concerning control as exemplified in Table 24.2. During the pleasuring assignments she was focussing on making a distinction between the current mutually desired and reciprocal interaction with her partner and the past exploitive abuse by the offender. Two extensions of these assignments were suggested to be initiated when the victim felt ready to do so: (a) a progressive sharing of control between the spouses; and (b) vaginal containment (Chap. 23).

Due to the therapist's absence overseas there was a break of 12 weeks in therapy at this point (week 143 in treatment). The couple by then had become very self-directing in therapy having thoroughly assimilated the knowledge and skills on which it is based and the therapist was gradually withdrawing into a more minor role. Consequently, the couple would continue to work on sharing control during the therapist's absence and there were no other problems that appeared to require support from another therapist at this time.

Outcome of Treatment for Sexual Dysfunctions

When the therapist returned the couple had decided that their sexual relationship had reached a level that was satisfactory to them, and that although there were residual difficulties they now knew how to cope with these on their own without needing further therapy on a regular basis although they might from time to time take advantage of the opportunity that was offered for occasional consultations as required.

Interview data at this point indicated that there were marked improvements in: (a) the relationship between the spouses including its sexual aspects; (b) the victim's aversion to reaching orgasm; and (c) her aversion to the male genitals, with the exception of activities involving initiative or control by the partner. The victim's aversion to sharing control was the major residual problem in the couple's sexual relationship.

A Target Complaint Scale headed 'Dissatisfaction with marital sexual relationship' was completed by the victim and her partner on a weekly basis through the assessment and treatment of sexual dysfunction. At assessment both clients rated their dissatisfaction as *couldn't be worse* (13). At weeks 143 and 155 in treatment they both rated their dissatisfaction as *a little* (4).

The victim's scores on the Index of Sexual Satisfaction were 62 at assessment which is highly clinically significant, and 30 and 32 at 143 and 155 weeks respectively, the latter two scores being of borderline clinical significance.

The partner's scores on this instrument ranged from the low clinically significant score of 34 at assessment, with a reduction to a satisfactory level of 18 at week 143, followed by a rise to a clinically significant score of 40 at week 155.

The victim's scores on the Sexual Arousal Inventory were 44 and 41 at assessment and week 143 respectively, but declined to 14 at week 155. At that time the victim endorsed the following items as *adversely affects arousal; unthinkable, repulsive, distracting* (-1):

1. When a loved one stimulates your genitals with mouth and tongue.
2. When a loved one fondles your breasts with his/her hands.
4. When a loved one caresses you with his/her eyes.
5. When a loved one stimulates your genitals with his/her finger.
12. When a loved one touches or kisses your nipples.
14. When you see pornographic pictures or slides.
16. When a loved one kisses you passionately.
17. When you hear sounds of pleasure during sex.
18. When a loved one kisses you with an exploring tongue.
21. When you stimulate your partner's genitals with your mouth and tongue.

These and other aversive events for the victim were being avoided or kept within tolerable limits by her retaining control of their lovemaking. She was still unable to share this with her partner, who accepted this limitation on their reciprocity.

At assessment and at weeks 143 and 155 in treatment the responses of both clients on the Sexual Relationship Questionnaire were within the normal range of defensiveness, with the exception of the partner's responses at week 155 which were moderately defensive.

This last response pattern together with the persisting clinically significant scores on the Index of Sexual Satisfaction for both clients and the victim's remaining aversive reactions on the Sexual Arousal Inventory leave some uncertainty about the satisfactoriness and stability of the couple's sexual relationship. Their ratings of dissatisfaction on the Target Complaint Scale were at low levels, however, and in interviews both clients expressed satisfaction with the current position, especially the quality of their marriage generally, and they felt confident of their ability to cope with the remaining limitations in their sexual relationship.

CHAPTER 25

Case Study: Amanda and Steve

Amanda and her husband, Steve, were both near 40 years of age at the commencement of treatment. They had been married for 17 years and had dated each other for approximately one year prior to their wedding. They had two boys, both of whom were of elementary school age, and Amanda and Steve greatly cared for their children.

The couple had their ups and downs during the years of their relationship with a particular low point occurring approximately three years prior to Amanda's treatment in the U. of M. program. At that time the couple had experienced difficulties with one of their children, with in-laws, and with the level of intimacy in their own union. Amanda and Steve had worked very diligently on trying to overcome these difficulties and at the point of entering therapy in this program, the couple had successfully managed to resolve most of their problems. What they had been unable to tackle, however, was the level of their physical intimacy. At the point of Amanda's initial assessment she stated that their relationship had been solely platonic for over two and one-half years.

Description of Sexual Dysfunctions

Impaired Motivation

Amanda presented with a complete lack of sexual motivation of a global and long-term nature. At the time of the initial assessment for mood disturbances she stated that throughout the years they had been married she and her husband had very little sexual contact. In fact she could literally count the times that they had made love in the past two decades.

The victim recounted that this lack of sexual activity had largely been due to her disinterest. She had found lovemaking tolerable only when she had wanted to have children and, infrequently, if she had had a few drinks.

Her husband, Steve, had never exerted any pressure on his wife to participate in sexual activity and he left it up to her to initiate contact. This lack of physical intimacy, however, in recent years had begun to tell on the couple's emotional closeness. They had fallen into a pattern whereby they seldom touched each other even in an affectionate way and they did not discuss the distance they both felt in their emotional relationship. They had a civil relationship with little conversation other than that directed at discussing the children, the home, finances, family matters other than their relationship, and so forth. Amanda was aware that her lack of sexual interest was somehow intertwined with her thinking processes, but she was unable to envision how she could change this state of affairs. She also knew that the lack of sexual contact with her husband denoted a general lack of intimacy in the relationship.

Impaired Arousal

Amanda disclosed that for the first couple of years of marriage she had not experienced any physiological or psychological arousal from lovemaking. She had refrained from exploring what kinds of activities might prove stimulating for her because she had always believed that it was wrong to experience sex as pleasurable. Therefore she had avoided any type of touch that might elicit erotic sensations and feelings.

Amanda recollected that her wedding night had been a disaster because she had been unprepared emotionally, physically, and knowledge-wise for physical and emotional intimacy. Her mother had told her little other than 'it was her duty to put up with whatever her husband wanted of her'.

Amanda's only premarital experience with sexual activity had been in the context of her own victimization where she had been involved in activities with her offenders that included exhibitionism and mutual erotic fondling. She had not had the opportunity in discussion or deed to experience sex as part of a mutually caring relationship. Her mother likewise did not convey a favorable picture about marital intimacy even though Amanda remembered her deceased father as a kind, affectionate man whom the victim greatly loved and admired.

Thus, Amanda had been unprepared for sexual intercourse and had found the experience very negative. However, as she settled into her marriage and grew more accustomed to her husband's gentle ways, she had found that in certain instances (for instance when she had wanted to get pregnant or had been drinking) that she could get past her lack of interest and that she could experience lubrication and some psychological arousal from sexual activity.

The victim was able to obtain orgasm whenever she was able to circumvent her lack of sexual desire and subsequently became physically aroused.

Sexual Dissatisfaction

Amanda stated that even when she participated in sexual activity that was physically appealing she found little emotional satisfaction. In fact she was aware of having feelings of disgust and of telling herself that sex was a 'gross and disgusting practice'. She often cried after participating in sexual activities that she found enjoyable and when she woke up the next morning after a night of lovemaking she had knots in her stomach and literally felt ill.

Sexual Phobia/Aversion

Initially, Amanda presented with a phobia of sexual activity in general. She would do anything to avoid sexual involvement because the mere thought of participating in sex left her feeling nauseated, experiencing a rapid heart beat, and perspiring profusely. She went to great lengths to limit sexual contact by 'picking fights' with her husband, by getting overly involved in community activities so that she would have little free time for her mate, and if all else failed, the victim would lock herself in her bathroom to avoid going to bed at the same time as a sexually interested husband. The victim was aware that she attempted to distance her husband so that he would not want anything to do with her.

Amanda also presented with aversions towards oral sex, having her genitals fondled and having the lights on during lovemaking. These were largely resolved following the cognitive restructuring treatment of the victim's mood disturbances. Many of Amanda's previous aversions seemed to dissipate completely as she worked through some of her negative beliefs.

One phobia that surfaced only after the treatment of mood disturbances was Amanda's complete aversion to her own bodily secretions, particularly vaginal lubrication and menstrual blood.

Causes of Sexual Dysfunctions

As Amanda progressed through therapy geared to dealing with her mood disturbances many of her sexual difficulties dissipated without further intervention. Her lack of sexual interest, lack of sexual arousal, and lack of sexual satisfaction hinged on a complicated interplay of negative beliefs she held towards sexual activity and an underlying phobia of her own vaginal secretions. Therapy directed at a particular sexual difficulty only occurred in the case of treatment focussed on alleviating this phobia.

The negative beliefs associated with sexual activity were cognitively restructured. Items on the Belief Inventory such as 'I must have permitted sex to happen because I wasn't forced into it', 'I must have been seductive and provocative when I was young', 'No man could care for me without a sexual relationship', and 'It must be unnatural to feel any pleasure during molestation' were fundamental underpinnings that led to Amanda's negative reactions towards lovemaking. With the realistic reappraisal of these beliefs, the victim found that her lack of self-esteem, guilt, distrustfulness towards men and more specifically, her husband, were alleviated. She found that, for instance, when the responsibility she had attributed to herself for 'somehow causing my own abuse' and for 'enjoying the molestation' was restructured using accurate information, reattribution, and so forth, she began to feel more positively towards experiencing sexual feelings.

A significant turning point for Amanda occurred when she evaluated her own relationship with her husband. Negative beliefs such as 'men are only interested in sex' and 'they will not stick to a sexless marriage' proved to be false when viewed in the light of her own relationship. Her husband had not left her because of a lack of sex in their marriage and he cared for qualities in her other than that she could be a sexual partner for him. Steve had never forced sexual activity upon her and he had remained 'faithful' to her, as best as she knew, for nearly two decades.

Another belief that Amanda had was that 'sex is a marital duty'. The victim had placed great responsibility upon herself to fulfill this wifely expectation, and she had felt guilt ridden that she was denying her husband his rightful due. Lengthy discussion realigned Amanda's reasoning to include information such as: (a) she had a right to participate or not in lovemaking; (b) her husband had never pressured her to 'fulfill her marital duties'; and (c) that her concept of sex being a duty came from her mother's teaching and her religion's doctrine rather than from her own or her husband's beliefs. A simple premise stated by the therapist that 'sex is a gift and not a duty' became a soothing message that Amanda repeated to herself to assist in the cognitive restructuring of her self-imposed guilt and responsibility. She literally clung to this thought and repeated it to herself daily because somehow it had hit a very basic chord.

One last belief that buttressed Amanda's sexual difficulties was that sexual activity and sexual abuse were one and the same thing. She had been unable to distinguish that lovemaking with a cherished husband was not the same thing as being sexually molested by an offender. Cognitive restructuring of this belief greatly alleviated Amanda's negative attitudes towards sexual activity because for the first time she realized her husband was not 'just another offender'.

Interestingly, after 22 weeks in treatment focussed upon her mood disturbances, Amanda decided to initiate sexual activity with her husband. She recounted to the therapist that her sole motivation had been to test out what her feelings now were towards sex. She had not discussed the possibility of sexual activity with either her husband or the therapist. At that time the couple had been sexualy inactive for over three years.

Surprisingly, Amanda found the lovemaking almost acceptable. She recounted that 'it had not made me physically ill' nor did the 'yucky feeling last so long' post-coitally. In fact, she made a startling discovery. It was not sex or intercourse that bothered her but rather her own secretions. Her own vaginal lubrication had made her feel 'unclean' and she had a firm impression that she associated secretions, including menstruation, with being sick. Amanda believed that this association stemmed from her recollections that her mother had called menstruation 'a sickness' and that she would baby her daughter during that 'time of the month'.

Amanda was heartened by her almost positive response to sexual activity. She was also pleased with her husband's reaction to their lovemaking. He had been kind and caring and had asked her if 'she was sure she wanted to do this'. He did not act like a man deprived of sex and he did not assume that this one interlude meant that their sex life had recommenced.

Process of Treatment for Sexual Dysfunctions

In view of the mitigation of many of Amanda's presenting sexual difficulties, it was suggested to her that further treatment might be directed at dealing with the specific phobia of vaginal secretions. She felt somewhat dubious that a phobia could be successfully treated but her faith in her progress to date motivated her to try an *in vivo* exposure approach.

The intervention began by establishing just how averse Amanda was to touching her own lubrication. The measure used was a Target Complaint Scale for the problem 'How averse I am to touching my own vaginal lubrication'. Her initial score was 11 indicating that this problem bothered her more than '*very much*'. The scale was then readministered weekly to act as a measure by which Amanda's reactions to the treatment could be monitored.

The victim with her therapist commenced treatment of her phobia by building a hierarchy of substances that would gradually in texture, colour, and so forth approximate the victim's own secretions. Amanda ranked these substances in order of difficulty for herself from the least (1) to the most (13) disturbing as shown in Table 25.1.

The victim was then asked to take the first substance on her list and rub it between her fingers, to smell it and to generally expose herself to the feel, sight, smell, and if she so chose the taste of it, for a period of about five minutes on at least two occasions each week. She was also asked to monitor her reactions to the exercise including any cognitions that might be affecting the phobia.

Within four weeks the victim had worked through steps 1 to 11 of her hierarchy, and she had found little aversion to touching these substances. In the fifth week she had progressed to touching her own genital area and vaginal secretions and found it 'not bad, surprisingly'.

Over the next six weeks the victim consolidated her gains in overcoming her phobia and regularly began to initiate sexual activity with her husband (up to three or four times a week). By the time Amanda and Steve had returned from holidays, they had established a close physical and emotional intimacy. Amanda recounted to her therapist that she 'probably had tired Steve out from their frequent lovemaking'. She happily stated that Steve had kidded her that maybe they should bought the cabin where they had vacationed because of the

Table 25.1.   *Hierarchy Used for the Treatment of an Aversion to Vaginal Secretions: Amanda*

---

1. Lard
2. Margarine
3. Vaseline
4. Noxema
5. Egg whites
6. Partially set jello
7. Whipped cream
8. Shaving cream (clear gel)
9. Moisturizing lotion
10. Hair souffle (clear and sticky)
11. K-Y gel
12. Own lubrication (non-menstrual)
13. Own lubrication (menstrual)

---

positive effect it seemed to have had on their overall relationship. Amanda expressed that 'the old tingle is back' and that she felt that she had got to know her husband all over again. The victim had also seemed to generalize the positive attitude she now held towards her lubrication from sexual arousal to include menstrual blood. She no longer felt that her menses were 'a sickness' like her mother had led her to believe and she generally just felt more at ease with her body.

The complete length of time devoted to the treatment of Amanda's phobia was 13 weeks. She overcame the brunt of her aversion in 5 weeks, consolidated her progress over the subsequent 6 weeks and expanded her sexual activity to include intercourse with her husband over the following 2 weeks.

Outcome of Treatment for Sexual Dysfunction

Follow-up of treatment 16 weeks after termination found Amanda well satisfied with herself, her marriage, and her sexual relationship with her husband. She recounted that she felt that she and her husband had improved their verbal communication and that there had been a marked decrease in their negative exchanges. Amanda stated that she could not remember having had a fight with Steve in months.

The victim's enjoyment in sexual activity had not decreased and she felt that the physical closeness that she now felt for her husband had enhanced other areas of the marriage as well. Amanda stated that Steve 'walks with a little spring in his step that reflects a general improvement in attitude that we both feel'.

The couple's sexual activity level had tapered off to a satisfactory level for both of them of one or two sessions a week. Amanda felt no pressure, internal or external, to participate in lovemaking and the freedom to choose had greatly enhanced her sexual desire.

Without the initial focus upon the victim's sexual abuse, the treatment of her sexual difficulties would, it seems, have proven futile. Four years of therapeutic intervention with two previous therapists had not ameliorated Amanda's general attitudes towards sexual activity. Only when she had explored the beliefs she held associated with her own sexual victimization which had generalized to include all sexual activity was she able to work through her presenting sexual difficulties. Her specific phobia towards her vaginal secretions completely dissipated and her termination and follow-up scores on the Target Complaint Scale were zero.

PART 5

Conclusion

CHAPTER 26

Consumer Evaluation and Future Directions

In this chapter, an evaluation of their treatment by the women in the U. of M. program is reported, and some aspects of the program that merit further investigation are reviewed including: (a) its applicability to male victims; (b) the role of partners; (c) the order of target problems; (d) group treatment; and (e) the gender of the therapist.

Consumer Evaluation

The Client Satisfaction Questionnaire (CSQ) was completed at termination of treatment by 41 of the 51 women in the series, the 10 exceptions being those victims who terminated treatment prematurely for reasons reported in Chapter 10.

The victims' responses on the CSQ were overwhelmingly favorable, over 90% of the replies to each question being in the two positive categories (Table 26.1). The responses of only one victim were generally in a negative direction. There are several possible reasons for this response pattern. When she completed the CSQ the victim was clinically depressed—possibly with an organic etiology—and this might have contributed to her negative perceptions. She had also suffered from marked mood swings and premenstrual syndrome throughout her treatment in the U. of M. program, which had prevented her from utilizing it effectively. This type of treatment was probably inappropriate for her at the time but she refused to have a medical or psychiatric evaluation until some time after she terminated in the program.

In conclusion, both the responses to the questions on the CSQ and the victims' additional comments were generally positive about the treatment they had received in the program. Among the specific beneficial aspects mentioned were:

(a) The provision of information about sexual abuse.

297

Table 26.1. *Responses on Client Satisfaction Questionnaire (N = 41)*

	n	%
1. How would you rate the quality of service you received?		
Excellent	36	87.8
Good	3	7.3
Fair	2	4.9
Poor	0	0.0
2. Did you get the kind of service you wanted?		
Yes definitely	26	63.4
Yes generally	14	34.1
No not really	1	2.4
No definitely not	0	0.0
3. To what extent has our program met your needs?		
Almost all my needs have been met	22	53.7
Most of my needs have been met	15	36.6
Only a few of my needs have been met	4	9.8
None of my needs have been met	0	0.0
4. If a friend needed similar help would you recommend our program to him/her?		
Yes definitely	37	90.2
Yes I think so	3	7.3
No I don't think so	1	2.4
No definitely not	0	0.0
5. How satisfied are you with the amount of help you received?		
Very satisfied	34	82.9
Mostly satisfied	5	12.2
Indifferent or mildly dissatisfied	0	0.0
Quite dissatisfied	2	4.0
6. Have the services you have received helped you to deal more effectively with your problems?		
Yes they have helped a great deal	35	85.4
Yes they have helped somewhat	5	12.2
No they really didn't help	0	0.0
No they seemed to make things worse	1	2.4
7. In an overall, general sense, how satisfied are you with the service you received?		
Very satisfied	32	78.0
Mostly satisfied	8	19.5
Indifferent or mildly dissatisfied	0	0.0
Quite dissatisfied	1	2.4
8. If you were to seek help again, would you come back to our program?		
Yes definitely	33	80.5
Yes I think so	7	17.1
No I don't think so	1	2.4
No definitely not	0	0.0

(b) The acquisition of skills to deal with problems—'becoming one's own therapist'.
(c) The alleviation of self-blame for the abuse, low self-esteem, and feelings of difference from others.
(d) The clarification of perceptions and feelings towards the family of origin and the offender.
(e) The participation of the partner in therapy and improvement in the marital relationship.
(f) Meeting other previously sexually abused women in the assertiveness group.
(g) The relationship with the therapist.

Some specific recommendations in the additional comments were: (a) a group opportunity to meet other victims for all those in treatment; (b) follow-up groups to maintain therapeutic progress; and (c) provision of a similar program for the adolescent age group.

Male Victims

The treatment program and empirical findings described in this book are restricted to women who were sexually abused in childhood but further investigation of their applicability to previously sexually abused men is highly desirable. Male victims of sexual abuse are relatively neglected in the professional literature and the provision of programs. One reason for this oversight may be that a major source of the current attention to child sexual abuse is the women's movement which has been especially concerned about the plight of female victims. There is also some societal reluctance to recognize abused boys as victims rather than willing participants in sex encounters. Furthermore, the boys may be held responsible for their abuse because they did not resist physically as 'a real boy would have done', or they prostituted themselves by receiving material rewards for sex, or they had identified themselves as homosexual prior to being abused (Rogers & Terry, 1984). Clearly, none of these putative reasons for blaming the victim constitutes an adequate argument for lessening or removing the responsibility from the adult offender.

Prevalence

That the sexual abuse of boys is certainly not a rarity is evident from those studies reviewed in Chapter 1 which included data on male victimization. In Lewis's (1985) sample from the entire United States, 16% of 1252 men reported having been sexually abused during childhood. The national population survey in Canada revealed that 12% of 1002 males had undergone an unwanted touching of 'a sex part' of their bodies and 10% had experienced an attempted or actual sexual assault. More than 80% of the male victims were aged under 18 years when they were first sexually abused (Sexual Offenses Against Children in Canada, 1984). Among a nationally representative sample of 970 males in Britain, 8% reported that they had been sexually abused before the age of 16 (Baker & Duncan, 1985). Thus, in terms of numbers alone there is ample justification for substantial professional attention to the problems and treatment of male victims.

Sexual Acts

In the Canadian national population survey (Sexual Offenses Against Children in Canada, 1984) the commonest sexually abusive acts against males under 16 years were: (a) fondling/touching of the genital area (12%); (b) fondling/touching of breasts, buttocks (3%); (c) oral–genital sex (2%); (d) attempted anal penetration with penis (1%); and (e) anal penetration with penis (0.6%).

Offenders

Data from the USA (Finkelhor, 1984) and Canada (Sexual Offenses Against Children in Canada, 1984) strongly indicate that sexual offenders against boys are overwhelmingly male rather than female. For example, in the Canadian national population survey only 3% of offenders against boys were female. The fact that most offenders against boys are men does not imply that these men are necessarily homosexual. Many are heterosexual and some are pedophiles with no interest in adult males (Newton, 1978).

The available evidence suggests that boys are more likely than girls to be sexually abused by non-family members, especially by someone who is known to the child such as a family friend, neighbor, teacher, or baby-sitter rather than a complete stranger (Baker & Duncan, 1985; Finkelhor, 1984).

Families of Origin

Sexually abused boys are also more likely than sexually abused girls to come from poor and single parent families, and to be victims of physical as well as sexual abuse (Finkelhor, 1984).

While the reactions of parents to the abuse of their child are generally similar for both male and female victims, on the basis of their clinical experience Rogers and Terry (1984) report two related reactions that are particularly common among the parents of abused boys. One of these reactions is to deny or minimize the victimization because of the parents' need to defend against their own feelings concerning homosexuality. The second reaction is a pronounced fear that the boy will grow up to be homosexually oriented as a result of the abuse experience.

Psychosocial Adjustment in Adulthood

The only aspects of the psychosocial adjustment in adulthood of males who were sexually abused as children that have received any attention in the literature are homosexuality, violence, and sexually abusive behavior, and these are reviewed below. Very limited experience with male victims treated outside the U. of M. program indicates that they experience many of the mood disturbances, interpersonal problems, and equivalent sexual dysfunctions that are common among female victims in treatment. Thus more comprehensive and thorough investigation of the adjustment difficulties of male victims is called for.

Homosexuality. Some evidence on an alleged association between child sexual abuse and later homosexuality in male college students is presented by Finkelhor (1984) who found that those who had been abused by older men were more than four times as likely to be currently engaged in homosexual activity than those who had not been so abused, and almost half of the abused males were currently involved in homosexual activity. The association between homosexual experience in childhood held only in respect of such experiences with much older males and not for similar experiences with peers.

Several possible reasons for an association between child sexual abuse and adult homosexuality have been suggested (Finkelhor, 1984; Rogers & Terry, 1984). Some boys might experience homosexual interest and curiosity at an early age which may render them vulnerable to exploitation by older predatory males. Boys who have been abused by an older man may label themselves as homosexual inappropriately because: (a) they were attractive partners to him; (b) they did not physically resist his advances; (c) they engaged in homosexual acts with him; and (d) they experienced erotic pleasure during the encounter. If for any of these or other reasons a boy labels himself as homosexual then he may adopt this role and lifestyle, and such self-labeling may be reinforced by parents or peers who make similar misjudgments of the boy's reactions to the abuse and his sexual orientation.

Violence. Although systematic evidence is currently lacking it may be that sexually abused boys are prone to engage in violent behavior in later life and in this respect they may differ from most female victims.

Several possible reasons have been advanced for this alleged tendency towards aggressive behavior. It may be an attempt to resolve doubts and confusion about their sexual identity through overidentification with a stereotypical machismo image which serves to reassure the male about his masculinity and to convince others of this. It may counter feelings of powerlessness that were evoked during the abuse and be a means of protection against any revictimization. It may reflect a hatred of women derived from the victim's perception of his mother as unprotective and uncaring, which may also contribute to the sexually abusive behavior that is discussed next.

Sexually abusive behavior. A number of studies have found that substantial proportions of sexual offenders against children were themselves the victims of sexual abuse in childhood. For example, 32% of 106 child molesters reported some form of early sexual trauma compared to 3% of 64 police officers (Groth & Burgess, 1979), and Langevin *et al.* (1983) found that incest offenders were five times more likely to have experienced sexual abuse as children compared to non-offender controls. Such results do not of course mean that all male sexual abuse victims become sexual abusers, and at present, it is not known what proportion of victims do so or what factors influence whether this happens (Finkelhor, 1986).

Sgroi (1982) comments as follows on adolescent males who are both current abusers and previous victims: 'We have seen adolescent males, who were themselves previous victims of sexual abuse by a male perpetrator, engaging their sisters and younger children, both male and female, in sexual behavior. Much of this sexual behavior appeared to be in the service of a need to control or dominate another person, rather than to satisfy a sexual need: Much of this type of sexual behavior was abusive in fact as well as in name; force or intimidation was used with agemates as well as with younger children and trauma to the victim would often result' (p. 31). The need to control or dominate another person mentioned in this quotation may sometimes represent an attempt by the offender to master the helplessness and hurt of his own victimization by re-enacting similar experiences with himself in the position of power, although no doubt many other factors also contribute to the sexually abusive behavior of men who were themselves abused in childhood.

Treatment

Despite the paucity and inadequacy of the evidence that is currently available it seems clear that some men experience psychosocial problems that are related to child sexual abuse and associated family experiences. There do not appear to be any intervention programs for this client group reported in the literature and this is a very significant gap, especially in view of the alleged propensity of some of these men to engage in violent or sexually abusive behavior. The effective treatment of these and other problems associated with child sexual abuse in males might prevent the victimization of other people and reduce the transmission of sexual abuse across generations.

It seems likely that some of the procedures used in the U. of M. program with previously sexually abused women might be helpful with male victims. For example, feelings of guilt and low self-esteem might be alleviated by the cognitive restructuring of distorted beliefs concerning responsibility for the abuse of sexual orientation, and violent behavior might be mitigated by procedures such as anger control and assertiveness training. Thus, it seems worth while to develop and evaluate appropriate aspects of the U. of M. program with men who were sexually abused in childhood and who present with problems associated with this earlier experience.

Partners

A number of problems relating to the victims' partners were encountered in the U. of M. program.

Discord between victim and partner occurred in all couples, often arising from: (a) the exploitation, oppression, and sometimes physical abuse of the victim by the partner; (b) the overdependence of the partner on the victim; and (c) the dissatisfaction and distress of the partner concerning certain aspects of the relationship.

This last source of discord sometimes stemmed from the implications of the victim's problems for her partner; for example, her mistrust of all men, or her difficulties in participating and responding in a sexual relationship. Partners also often found it hard to understand, accept, and adapt to certain changes in their spouse during treatment, such as enhanced self-esteem, desire for growth as an individual, reallocation of roles in the relationship, or increased assertiveness. For these and other reasons some partners felt: (a) that they were vicarious victims; (b) deprived and confused in their relationship with the victim; (c) angry and hostile toward the offender; and (d) negative about themselves and depressed in mood.

Another problematic area was the role of the partner in therapy. Some victims did not want their partner to participate, and some partners refused to do so, in either case it was difficult to deal satisfactorily with interpersonal and sexual problems that involved both spouses. Even when partners did attend sessions, typically they perceived this as helping the victim to resolve her problems—a role they had often fulfilled over many years—and were very resistant to entering the client role themselves despite the relationship and individual problems they might be experiencing. Finally, because the victim had presented as the identified client with a wide range of very distressing problems requiring prompt and intensive intervention, she had been the primary focus of therapy at least in its earlier stages. This made it difficult for the therapist to give adequate attention to the partner, who tended to think also that it would be inappropriate, unfair, and therapeutically damaging to expect the victim and therapist to yield therapeutic time to his concerns. Some useful light is cast on this issue by the comments of the female partner of a victim in a lesbian relationship who was treated with her partner in accordance with the U. of M. program but outside the research series (Klassen & Jehu, 1987):

Although dealing with my partner's victimization was harder for her than me there were times when I had thoughts and feelings which I found difficult to express and sort out. In the beginning before we started counseling I felt that perhaps there was something wrong with me because I could not help her with the problem. I thought if we worked hard enough we could sort out our sexual difficulties ourselves. And I also felt that because I couldn't, that it was a reflection on my love for her. I felt somehow inadequate.

As the counseling began for a while I felt left out of the process. Although she told me some of what she was doing it was usually only general ideas. However, I did not want to say anything because I felt it would be infringing on her privacy. This was frequently a problem throughout the counseling sessions as well because often I would only find out about what she was thinking or feeling during the sessions. I sometimes resented that because I thought she didn't trust me enough to talk about it at home.

At various times throughout counseling there were feelings of resentment because it seemed as though the total emphasis was on my partner's problem. It seemed as though my needs and wants were supposed to be suppressed. At times I wanted to scream 'what about my needs—my problems with this issue'. However, I felt that I could not say that because it might be perceived that I wasn't concerned enough about my partner.

Occasionally, when we dealt with a problem I was having during a counseling session I had some feelings of guilt because I thought it was less beneficial. I thought it was more my partner's time than mine so that it should be spent dealing with the mutual problem of our sexual difficulties . . .

The biggest problem with all these issues was not having anyone to talk with about them. I did not want to say anything to my partner because I was afraid that it would create more problems than it solved. Therefore, I spent quite a bit of time trying to sort out my thoughts and feelings without the benefit of objective insight from someone else. Some of the problems occurred before we started partner counseling. Others that occurred after we had started I still felt reluctant to discuss with my partner present because she might become discouraged.

It would be beneficial to have some format for partners of victims to talk about their feelings. A group session would be helpful in feeling you were not the only one feeling or thinking a certain way. It would also provide support plus some positive reinforcement of the partners. It would help to hear that 'you're really not a bad person', to reinforce the good things that the person is doing in the relationship to help solve the problem and also to recognize that partners of victims have just as much right to be concerned about their needs as well. It would be helpful to know how others had coped with the problems.

Also, it would be helpful to be able to discuss with someone the best way to approach the partner with the problem. This might be dealt with in an individual session with the counselor who knows the personal situation and both people involved. The counselor could help the individual to decide whether it was relevant, whether the timing was right or perhaps the right approach to deal with the particular issue.

I feel that it is important for the partners of victims to be able to work out their problems. Many of the issues directly affect the process that is going on in the counseling sessions. If the partners can work out their problems more readily it should facilitate the process that both the partners are working on together.

It was partly as a result of this partner's experiences quite early during the U. of M. program that regular individual sessions and a situation/transition group for partners were added to the other interventions with couples that are discussed in Part 4 of the manual. This range of interventions and the many other complex partner-related issues reviewed in this section call for more extensive and rigorous investigation.

Sequencing Target Problems

In the U. of M. program the most usual order of treatment for the major target problems was mood disturbances, interpersonal problems, and sexual dysfunctions, although this was subject to the guidelines listed in Chapter 4 and other high priority problems sometimes required previous or concurrent attention. There are several reasons for sequencing the target problems in this way. Prima facie, it seems appropriate to correct the self-blaming and self-denigratory beliefs that are rooted in the past sexual abuse in order to relieve the victim of this burden before she attempts to resolve her current interpersonal and/or sexual problems. There are indications also that the successful treatment of sexual dysfunction usually requires the prior alleviation of mood disturbances and marital discord (e.g. Chaps. 21, 24, 25). Finally, treatment focussed upon mood disturbances is not infrequently accompanied by the resolution of marital and/or sexual problems so that further specific marital or sex therapy is not necessary (Chap. 10). Thus, the order in which the target problems were most usually treated in the U. of M. program seems quite appropriate but more systematic exploration of the feasibility and efficacy of this and alternative sequences would be worth while, in particular in order to determine whether the duration of therapy could be reduced without detriment to its effectiveness.

Group Treatment

The primary formats in the U. of M. program were individual or couple therapy although some victims participated also in an assertiveness training group. These participants subsequently advocated the inclusion of some form of group experience in the program, and the potential advantages of this are noted in Chapter 4. Thus, it seems desirable to consider the provision of group therapy in programs for victims.

Among the many treatment planning issues that this raises is whether such therapy should be an alternative or an adjunct to the individual or couple formats. Some victims are unsuitable or unwilling to attend and participate in a group, and there may not be enough victims available to institute a group at a particular point in time, therefore it is important to keep open the options of individual or couple therapy for those who need or prefer them. There is also the question of whether some victims can obtain sufficient attention and support to meet their individual needs in a group context (e.g. Cole & Barney, in press; Herman & Schatzow, 1984). On the other hand, to the extent that group treatment can replace individual or couple therapy then this may conserve scarce professional resources. In conclusion, comprehensive and rigorous inquiries are needed into how group treatment can best be provided in programs for previously sexually abused women and their partners.

Gender of Therapist

The individual and couple therapy in the U. of M. program was in most cases conducted by a female therapist, consequently the only information available on the influence of the therapist's gender comes from the participants in the assertiveness group who found the presence of the male co-therapist to be helpful to them. Some possible advantages and disadvantages of female and male therapists respectively are reviewed in Chapter 4 and it is concluded as working hypotheses: (a) that the balance is generally in favour of females; although (b) the involvement of a male is desirable when the victim is experiencing difficulties in her relations with men; and (c) the provision of male–female co-therapy teams is worth considering, especially when the victim's partner is participating in therapy. These and related hypotheses concerning the gender of the therapist(s) merit systematic investigation, at least because the available pool of therapists is larger if it does not need to be restricted to females.

Conclusion

It seems reasonable to say that the treatment package used with mood disturbances in the U. of M. program has been shown to be feasible, acceptable, and effective for many victims, although it could usefully be replicated in other clinical settings. The packages used with interpersonal problems and sexual dysfunctions, while apparently promising, are not yet as well established and still require further development and evaluation.

Once a package is shown to be an effective treatment for specific problems in particular clients then several other clinical research issues arise including:

(a) What are the necessary and sufficient components in the package that contribute to its efficacy? Once these crucial ingredients are identified then the package can be refined by optimizing these ingredients and eliminating those that are unnecessary.

(b) What is the effect on the efficacy of the package of varying certain parameters such as its duration or the spacing of sessions? This information can be used to increase the efficiency of delivery.

(c) What is the effect on the efficacy of the package of varying the clients or therapists? The extensions to male victims or to groups of victims, and the inclusion of male therapists, that are discussed above are examples of research topics in this category.

(d) How effective is the package compared to other treatment approaches? Only when a package has been shown to be effective is it worth while mounting comparative studies that usually require considerable resources.

Thus, like all research, the U. of M. program is just one step in an ongoing process of inquiry that progressively will improve the quality of help that can be offered to the many troubled victims of child sexual abuse.

Protocol for Initial Assessment Interviews

Demographic Data

A. Client

1. Surname
2. Given names
3. Age
4. Occupation
5. Marital status and history
6. Children (names, sexes, ages)
7. Education
8. Ethnic background
9. Religion

B. Partner

1. Surname
2. Given names
3. Age
4. Occupation
5. Marital status and history
6. Children (names, sexes, ages)
7. Education
8. Ethnic background
9. Religion

Client's Family of Origin

C. Father Figure(s)

1. Relationship with client (e.g. natural/adoptive/step/foster)
2. Dead/alive
3. Age now

4. Occupation
5. Ethnic background
6. Religion
7. Client's description of father figure
8. Client's relationship with father figure
9. Problems exhibited by father figure, e.g.:
    Limited social skills
    Overdependence on others
    Oppressed by others
    Interpersonal isolation and alienation
    Anger/hostility/violence
    Physically abusive towards spouse
    Sexual dysfunction
    Promiscuity
    Prostitution
    'Psychological absence' from family
    Physical absence from family
    Ineffective/non-nurturing parent
    Excessively religious/moralistic
    Physically abusive to children
    Alcohol abuse
    Drug abuse
    Depression
    Other psychiatric disorder
    Low intelligence/poorly educated
    Poor physical health
    Poor employment history
    Criminal history
    Other problems (specify)

D. Mother Figure(s)

1. Relationship with client (e.g. natural/adoptive/step/foster)
2. Dead/alive
3. Age now
4. Occupation
5. Ethnic background
6. Religion
7. Client's description of mother figure
8. Client's relationship with mother figure
9. Problems exhibited by mother figure, e.g.:
    Limited social skills
    Overdependence on others

Oppressed by others
Interpersonal isolation and alienation
Anger/hostility/violence
Physically abusive towards spouse
Sexual dysfunction
Promiscuity
Prostitution
'Psychological absence' from family
Physical absence from family
Ineffective/non-nurturing parent
Excessively religious/moralistic
Physically abusive to children
Alcohol abuse
Drug abuse
Depression
Other psychiatric disorder
Low intelligence/poorly educated
Poor physical health
Poor employment history
Criminal history
Other problems (specify)

E. Siblings

1. Relationship with client (e.g. natural/adoptive/step/foster)
2. Name
3. Sex
4. Age now
5. Client's relationship with sibling
6. Was sibling sexually victimized?
7. Did sibling sexually victimize others?

F. Family Functioning

1. Features characterizing family functioning during client's upbringing, e.g.:
   Social isolation
   Role confusion
   Milieu of abandonment
   Marital conflict/disruption
   Oversexualization
   Poor supervision
   Male supremacy

Intergenerational sexual victimization
Others (specify)

G. *Other Domiciles*

1. Settings other than family of origin in which client lived prior to age 17 years (e.g. foster home, group home, with grandparents)

H. *The Victimization*

1. Age of client at commencement of victimization
2. Duration of victimization
3. Approximate number of occasions on which victimization occurred
4. Sexual activities that occurred between victim and any offender, e.g.
   Exhibitionistic display of offender's genitals to victim
   Voyeuristic observation of victim by offender
   Erotic kissing
   Erotic fondling of victim's body by offender
   Erotic fondling of offender's body by victim
   Victim observes offender masturbating
   Offender observes victim masturbating
   Manual stimulation of victim's genitals by offender
   Manual stimulation of offender's genitals by victim
   Oral stimulation of offender's genitals by offender
   Oral stimulation of offender's genitals by victim
   Digital penetration of victim's anus by offender
   Penile penetration of victim's anus by offender
   Simulated/'dry' intercourse
   Penile penetration of victim's vagina by offender
5. Relationship of offender(s) to victim and age of offender(s) at the time he/she began offending against the victim, e.g.:
   Male stranger
   Female stranger
   Male acquaintance
   Female acquaintance
   Father
   Step-father
   Mother
   Step-mother
   Uncle
   Aunt
   Grandfather
   Brother

    Step-brother
    Sister
    Step-sister
    Male cousin
    Female cousin
    Brother-in-law
    Sister-in-law
    Others (specify)

6. Methods used by offender(s) to induce victim to engage in sexual activities, e.g.:
    Misrepresenting activities as a game, fun, 'something special' or 'fooling around'
    Misrepresenting activities as sex education
    Opportunity for attention and affection
    Proclamation of romantic love
    Bribery
    Promise of sexual gratification
    Exercise of adult authority
    Threats
    Physical force
    Duty to replace mother
    Other methods (specify)

7. Victim's reactions to victimization at the time, e.g.:
    Fear
    Guilt/shame/disgust
    Shock/surprise
    Anger/resentment/hostility
    Feelings of helplessness
    Loving, protective, compassionate feelings towards offender
    Emotional pleasure
    Physical pleasure
    Denial of/dissociation from victimization encounters
    Used victimization to obtain attention/affection
    Used victimization to obtain material favors/rewards
    Active cooperation
    Passive compliance
    Avoidance of offender
    Left home
    Verbal resistance
    Physical resistance
    Actively sought protection from others
    Other reactions (specify)

8. Was the victimization kept secret by the victim for a period of time?

9. If so, what factors contributed to the victim's secrecy? E.g.:
    Favors/rewards
    Attention/affection
    Sexual pleasure
    Enhanced self-esteem
    Loyalty to offender
    Fear of disbelief, blame or anger by third party (e.g. mother)
    Fear of offender being jailed
    Fear of offender harming himself/herself
    Fear of offender harming someone else
    Fear of victim being taken away from home
    Fear of physical violence from offender
    Actual physical violence from offender
    Other factors (specify)
10. Was the victimization disclosed before the victim reached the age of 17 years?
11. If so, what factors led to disclosure? E.g.:
    Observation by third party
    Physical injury to victim
    Venereal disease in victim
    Pregnancy of victim
    Precocious sexual activity initiated by victim
    Victim telling third party
    Other factor (specify)
12. If victim told a third party, what factors led to this? E.g.:
    To obtain protection for herself
    To obtain protection for other children
    Relief of guilt/shame
    Desire for more freedom from offender
    Resentment/anger/hostility towards offender
    Reaching puberty
    Fear of pregnancy
    Others (specify)
13. Reactions of significant others to disclosure prior to age 17 years, e.g.:
    Shock/horror
    Anger/hostility towards victim
    Anger/hostility towards offender
    Guilt over previous failure to protect victim
    Denial of victimization
    Denial of impact on victim
    Anxiety concerning impact on victim
    Anxiety concerning disruption of family
    Anxiety concerning physical violence from offender

Conflict of loyalties between victim and offender
Self-interest/self-defence/self-protection
Withdrawal from crisis of disclosure
Disbelief of victim
Attempts to undermine victim's credibility
Pressure on victim to suppress allegations
Blaming victim
Protective towards victim
Obtained outside assistance
Cooperative with outside authorities
Others (specify)

14. Consequence of disclosure prior to age 17 years, e.g.:
Investigation by social agency
Investigation by police
Medical examination of the victim
Removal of victim from home
Removal of offender from home
Prosecution of offender
Conviction of offender
Jailing of offender
Therapy for victim
Therapy for other family memers
Therapy for offender
Other consequences (specify)

15. Does current partner know about the victimization?

16. If so, what are his reactions to it? E.g.:
Anger/hostility towards victim
Anger/hostility towards offender
Guilt over previous failure to protect victim
Denial of victimization
Denial of impact on victim
Anxiety concerning impact on victim
Anxiety concerning disruption of family
Anxiety concerning physical violence from offender
Conflict of loyalties between victim and offender
Self-interest/self-defence/self-protection
Withdrawal from crisis of disclosure
Disbelief of victim
Attempts to undermine victim's credibility
Pressure on victim to suppress allegations
Blaming victim
Protective towards victim
Obtained outside assistance

    Cooperative with outside authorities
    Others (specify)

Psychosocial Adjustment of Victim

I. Problems

1. Features of victim's adjustment in past history and/or at time of current therapy, e.g.:
   Emotional
   Anxiety/phobias
   Dissociation/depersonalization/derealization
   Obsessions/compulsions
   Guilt
   Low self-esteem/'damaged goods' syndrome
   Depression
   Attempted suicide
   Anorexia/bulimia
   Sleep disturbance/nightmares
   Alcohol abuse
   Drug abuse
   Other psychiatric disorders

   Interpersonal
   Isolation/alienation from other people
   Feelings of difference from others
   Mistrust of other people
   Insecurity/anxiety in relationships
   Limited social skills, including assertiveness and communication
   Fear of men
   Anger/hostility towards men
   Overvaluation of men
   Disparagement of women
   Anger/hostility towards women
   Avoidance of long-term relationships with men
   Transient/casual/promiscuous relationships
   Oversexualized relationships
   Dissonant relationships
   Partner discord
   Oppressed by partner
   Physically abused by partner
   Fear of intimate relationships
   Homosexual relationships

Sexual
Impaired sexual motivation
Sexual phobias/aversion
Vaginismus
Impaired sexual arousal
Impaired orgasm
Dyspareunia
Sexual dissatisfaction
Victim of rape (in addition to or after childhood sexual abuse)
Precocious sexuality
Prostitution
Incest participant (after attaining age of 17 years)
Sexual victimization of other children
Deviant sexual preferences

Parenting
Inadequate parent
Physically abusive parent

Health
VD from victimization
Pregnancy from victimization
VD not from victimization
Out of wedlock pregnancy not from victimization
Poor physical health

Development/Social
Pseudomaturity
Role confusion
Running away from home
Delinquent/criminal history
Poor employment history

Other Problems (specify)

J. Prior Treatment

1. Form(s) of treatment that client has experienced prior to current therapy, and which of these included specific attention to the victimization, e.g.:
   Individual treatment
   Professionally led group treatment
   Self-help group
   Family therapy
   Marital therapy

Sex therapy
Psychotropic medication
In-patient psychiatric treatment
Others (specify)

Partner's Family of Origin

Sections C, D, E, F, and G above are repeated as appropriate in respect of the partner's family of origin.

Psychosocial Adjustment of Partner

Sections I and J above are repeated as appropriate in respect of the partner.

Belief Inventory (Revised)

NAME: ....

DATE: ....

BELIEF INVENTORY (REVISED)

Please check (√) one column from 0 to 4 that best indicates how strongly you believe each statement to be true in your own case. Please answer according to what you really believe yourself, not what you think you should believe.

	Absolutely Untrue 0	Mostly Untrue 1	Partly True Partly Untrue 2	Mostly True 3	Absolutely True 4
1. I must be an extremely rare woman to have experienced sex with an older person when I was a child.					
2. I am worthless and bad.					
3. You can't depend on women, they are all weak and useless creatures.					
4. No man can be trusted.					
5. I must have permitted sex to happen because I wasn't forced into it.					
6. I don't have the right to deny my body to any man who demands it.					
7. Anyone who knows what happened to me sexually will not want anything to do with me.					
8. I must have been seductive and provocative when I was young.					
9. It doesn't matter what happens to me in my life.					

	Absolutely Untrue 0	Mostly Untrue 1	Partly True Partly Untrue 2	Mostly True 3	Absolutely True 4
10. No man could care for me without a sexual relationship.					
11. It is dangerous to get close to anyone because they always betray, exploit, or hurt you.					
12. I must have been responsible for the sex when I was young because it went on so long.					
13. I will never be able to lead a normal life, the damage is permanent.					
14. Only bad, worthless guys would be interested in me.					
15. It must be unnatural to feel any pleasure during molestation.					
16. I am inferior to other people because I did not have normal experiences.					
17. I've already been used so it doesn't matter of other men use me.					
18. I was responsible for the abuse because I asked the offender about sexual matters.					
19. The offender abused me because he was 'sick' and therefore not responsible for his actions.					
20. The abuse was my own fault because I used sexual activities to obtain attention and/or affection from the offender.					
21. The offender abused me because he was drunk at the time.					
22. I was to blame for the abuse because I used it to obtain favours and rewards from the offender.					
23. The offender abused me because he was sexually frustrated.					

	Absolutely Untrue 0	Mostly Untrue 1	Partly True Partly Untrue 2	Mostly True 3	Absolutely True 4
24. The offender engaged me in sexual activities in order to teach me about sex and to make me a better sexual partner.					
25. The offender engaged in sexual activities with me so that our relationship would be closer and better.					
26. The offender engaged in sexual activities with me to give me physical pleasure.					

Interview Protocol for the Assessment of Discordant Relationships Between Victim and Partner*

Developmental History of Relationship

1. Partners' ages when they met.
2. How did they meet?
3. What initially attracted them to each other?
4. Courtship period.
5. Circumstances surrounding decision to marry/cohabit.
6. History of relationship since marriage/cohabitation.
7. Brief sexual history of relationship.

Current Relationship

1. Each partner's current perception of the relationship—including review and further exploration of Dyadic Adjustment Scale.
2. Each partner's description of:
   (a) current problems;
   (b) desired changes in relationship.
3. First signs of significant problems in relationship:
   (a) What were the signs?
   (b) What did the couple do about them?
   (c) With what results?
4. Immediate circumstances surrounding occurrence of current problems.
5. Global circumstances of couple's life situation (e.g. schedules, leisure, lifestyles, etc.).
6. Does the informant:
   (a) like the partner?

* This protocol assumes that the Protocol for Initial Interviews was completed earlier.

  (b) find the partner attractive?
  (c) love the partner?
  (d) feel emotionally close to the partner?
  7. In general, how does the informant feel about the marriage/cohabitation?
     How satisfied is he or she with it?
     What are some of the good things about it?
     In what ways would the informant like it to be different?
  8. How do sexual difficulties affect other aspects of the relationship?
  9. How closely do the informant and partner agree on:
     (a) the appropriate roles for the man and woman in their marriage/
         cohabitation?
     (b) who should exercise the most power and make the decisions in certain
         aspects of their relationship?
 10. How well do the informant and partner communicate with each other?
     E.g.:
     (a) talk about most things;
     (b) avoid certain topics or argue over them;
     (c) discuss their sexual problems;
     (d) speak openly and honestly;
     (e) listen, empathize, and validate;
     (f) get their points across;
     (g) resolve their conflicts;
     (h) express criticism, resentment, and anger;
     (i) express affection, appreciation, and praise;
     (j) express specific sexual preferences.
 11. How committed to the relationship is the informant?
     Has he or she ever considered separation or divorce?
 12. How much does the informant trust the partner?
     Does the informant fear that he or she may be hurt, rejected, or abandoned
     by the partner?
 13. How often do the informant and partner have arguments/rows/fights?
     What are these conflicts usually about?
     What happens during a conflict?
     How are conflicts handled or resolved?
 14. Does the informant feel angry, bitter, resentful, or hostile towards the
     partner?
     If so, what evokes these feelings?
 15. Does physical violence ever occur between the informant and partner?
     If so, in what circumstances does such violence happen?

Target Complaint Scale

TARGET COMPLAINT SCALE

Name .... Date ....

Problem: ....

....

....

....

....

....

....

....

In general, how much does this problem or complaint bother you? Check the box which best describes the amount of disturbance felt because of this problem.

couldn't be worse

very much

pretty much

a little

not at all

Assessment Interview Protocol for Assertiveness

1. *Physical Description of the Client*
   Including dress and general appearance as well as any noteworthy physical features.
2. *Observation of the Client during Interview(s)*
   Including brief description of verbal and non-verbal behavior and how she relates to the therapist.
3. *Client's Description of Assertiveness Problems and Goals in Her Own Words.*
4. *Operational Definitions of Problems and Goals.*
5. *Effects of Unassertiveness of Client's Life Functioning*
   Extent to which unassertiveness may limit the client in significant areas of her life.
6. *Consequences of Being More Assertive*
   Is client aware of these consequences and willing to risk any adverse consequences (e.g. for marital relationship)?
7. *Assertiveness in Specific Areas*
   (a) Same sex relationships.
   (b) Opposite sex relationships.
   (c) Casual relationships.
   (d) Intimate relationships.
   (e) Interactions with family members.
   (f) Interactions with authority figures.
   (g) Group situations.
   (h) Initiating social interactions.
   (i) Maintaining and developing social interactions.
   (j) Expressing positive feelings towards others.
   (k) Asking for help; letting someone know specifically what you would like them to do for you.
   (l) Refusing unreasonable requests.

(m) Standing up for one's rights.

(n) Expressing disagreement, displeasure or criticism.

8. *Estimates of Social Skill, Social Anxiety and Self-evaluations in Each of Above Areas*

9. *Inhibition of Assertive Responding by Intense Feelings*
   (a) Can client handle her own intense feelings such as anxiety or anger and still respond assertively?
   (b) Can she handle other people's anger or hostility and still respond assertively?

10. *Cognitions Relating to Assertiveness*
    (a) Client's irrational assumptions, unrealistic standards and expectations regarding social interactions.
    (b) Client's knowledge of what she is feeling in problematic situations.
    (c) Client's knowledge of what she wants in problematic situations.
    (d) Client's knowledge of her rights in problematic situations.
    (e) Client's ability to articulate her goals in social interactions.
    (f) Client's knowledge of when to be and when not to be assertive.
    (g) Client's self-evaluative thoughts when assertive behavior is not engaged in.

11. *Current Living Situation With Particular Reference to Actual or Potential Social Contacts.*

12. *Description of a Typical Day With Particular Reference to Social Contacts.*

13. *Interests and Leisure Activities.*

14. *History of Unassertiveness*
    (a) Description of onset (or note if primary).
    (b) Description of period of 'best' social functioning.
    (c) Description of period of 'worst' social functioning.

15. *Other Problems That May Impede Assertiveness.*

16. *Cultural Factors That May Impede Assertiveness (past/*current).

Interview Protocol for the Assessment of Sexual Dysfunction*

Description of Problem(s)

Nature

1. Review relevant responses on:
   (a) Sexual History Form.
   (b) Sexual Relationship Questionnaire.
   (c) Client Self-Monitoring Records.
   (e) Sexual Arousal Inventory (if applicable).
2. Check whether or not there are any problems in the following aspects of sexual functioning:
   (a) Desire/motivation.
   (b) Aversion/phobia.
   (c) Arousal.
   (d) Orgasm.
   (e) Satisfaction.
   (f) Dyspareunia.
   (g) Vaginismus (females only).
3. Description of problem(s):

Frequency

1. Does problem occur on every sexual encounter or only on certain occasions?

---

* It is intended that therapists will select and sequence items from this protocol to suit individual victims and their partners, rather than following it in a rigid or chronological fashion.

   With some couples therapists may find it appropriate to cover the sections on 'Description of Problem(s)' and 'Personal and Family Background' with both partners together, while the remaining sections are covered with each partner separately.

   Some of the information covered in this protocol will already have been gathered in previous assessment and treatment sessions but it is included again here to ensure that it is reconsidered in the specific context of the client's sexual functioning.

Timing

    1.   At what point in sexual encounters does problem occur?

Surrounding circumstances

    1. Does the problem occur in all circumstances or does it vary according to certain conditions?
    2. If it varies, what are the relevant conditions?

Duration

    1. Has the problem always been present in the client's sexual functioning or was he/she at some time able to perform satisfactorily in that particular aspect of sexual response?

Onset

    1. When did problem first begin?
    2. Was the onset sudden or gradual?
    3. What were the surrounding circumstances in which it first occurred?
    4. How satisfactory was the client's relationship with his/her partner prior to the onset of the problem?
    5. What other important events were happening in the client's life at the time the problem started (e.g. health, work, family)?
    6. How did client react to onset of problem at the time?
    7. How did partner react to onset of problem at the time?

Course

    1. Has the problem been constant since onset or has it fluctuated?
    2. If it has fluctuated, what circumstances seem to have accompanied these variations?
    3. How have the client and partner attempted to resolve the problem themselves and with what result?
    4. What previous treatment has the client undergone for the problem and what was the progress and outcome?

Personal and Family Background

Client and Partner

    1. Age.
    2. Occupation.
    3. Marital status and history.

4. Educational level.
5. Ethnic background.
6. Religion.

Children of Victim and/or Partner

1. Relationship with victim and partner (e.g. natural/adoptive/step/foster).
2. Age.
3. Sex.

Parents of Victim and Partner

1. Relationship with victim and partner (e.g. natural/adoptive/step/foster).
2. Dead/alive.
3. If dead, age at time.
4. If alive, age now.
5. Occupation.
6. Marital status and history.
7. Educational level.
8. Ethnic background.
9. Religion.

Siblings of Victim and Partner

1. Relationships with victim or partner (e.g. natural/adoptive/step/foster).
2. Dead/alive.
3. If dead, age at time.
4. If alive, age now.
5. Occupation.
6. Marital status and history.
7. Educational level.

Quality of Relationships in the Families of Origin of the Victim and Partner

1. Quality of informant's relationships with his or her parents, e.g.:
   (a) Description of parents.
   (b) Were parents emotionally distant, close, warm, cold?
   (c) Was attachment greater to one parent than the other?
   (d) How affectionate were parents towards informant?
   (e) Was affection usually verbal or physical?
   (f) Was one parent more affectionate than the other?
   (g) Would informant have liked more, less, or the same amount of affection from parents?

    (h) Was either parent competitive or in conflict with the informant?

    (i) How punitive were parents towards informant?

2. Quality of the relationship between the informant's parents, e.g.:

    (a) How affectionate were parents towards each other?

    (b) Was this affection usually verbal or physical?

    (c) Was one parent more affectionate than the other in their relationship?

    (d) Did informant get the feeling that his or her parents cared lot for each other, whether or not they were visibly affectionate?

    (e) How much anger, hostility, or conflict was there between the parents?

    (f) Were these negative feelings usually expressed verbally or physically?

3. Quality of the informant's relationships with siblings, e.g.:

    (a) How close emotionally was informant to siblings?

    (b) How much competition or conflict was there between informant and siblings?

    (c) Did informant relate better to same-sex or opposite-sex siblings?

Other Domiciles

1. Settings other than family of origin in which victim or partner lived prior to age 17 years (e.g. foster home, group home, with grandparents, prolonged period in hospital).

Sexual History

Parental Attitudes

1. What were parents' attitudes towards sex as informant grew up?

    (a) Towards each other?

    (b) Towards informant's emerging sexuality?

2. Did parents impose strongly puritanical religious or cultural standards on the family?

Parental Messages

1. What sort of messages about sex did informant receive as he or she grew up? E.g.:

    (a) 'Sex is not nice.'

    (b) 'Sex is wrong.'

    (c) 'Sex is sinful.'

    (d) 'Your genitals, body, erections, secretions, etc., are disgusting.'

    (e) 'Masturbation is dangerous/will drain you/will make you impotent.'

    (f) 'Sexual thoughts are wrong, sinful, and you will be punished for them.'

    (g) 'Nice girls don't.'

    (h) 'Don't do that to a nice girl.'

    (i) 'Men are only after one thing.'
    (j) 'S-e-x is so bad we don't even talk about it.'

Talking About Sex in the Home

1. Did informant feel free to ask questions about and to discuss sexual matters in the home?
2. How did parents respond to such questions or discussion?
3. Did informant get the feeling that his or her parents would be uncomfortable with such questions or discussion?
4. Was there a taboo on talking about sex in the home?
5. What kind of comments or jokes were made by the informant's parents about their own sexual relationship or the sexual lives of other people?

Nudity/Modesty

1. What were the standards concerning nudity and modesty in the informant's home as he or she grew up?

Vicarious Exposure to Intercourse

1. Did informant ever see or hear anyone having intercourse in the home as he or she grew up?
2. If so, what were informant's reactions at the time?

Sex Games

1. What kind of sex games did informant play as a child (e.g. 'doctor', 'postoffice', etc.)?
2. Was he or she ever caught by parents?
3. If so, what was their reaction?

Influence of Siblings or Friends

1. Did informant discuss sex with siblings or friends as he or she grew up?
2. Was sex the subject of jokes and embarrassment?
3. Did informant consider sex dirty, frightening, curious, interesting?

First Pleasurable Genital Feelings

1. At what age does informant recall having his or her first pleasurable genital feelings?
2. Were these in connection with any particular thoughts, activities, or situations?

3. Did informant define these feelings as good or bad at the time?

Masturbation

1. At what age did informant first experiment with masturbation?
2. Where did he or she masturbate?
3. How did he or she masturbate?
4. How often did he or she masturbate?
5. How did he or she feel about masturbating?
6. Did he or she fantasize during masturbation?
7. If so, what did he or she fantasize?
8. Did he or she use erotic materials during masturbation?
9. If so, what was the preferred content of these materials?
10. Was the informant ever discovered masturbating?
11. If so, what was the reaction of the person discovering him or her?

Sexual Dreams

1. (females only)
    (a) Has informant ever had sexual dreams in which she felt aroused in her sleep?
    (b) Has she ever had an orgasm in her sleep?
    (c) What were her reactions to these experiences at the time?
2. (males only)
    (a) How old was informant when he had his first nocturnal emission (wet dream)?
    (b) What were his reactions to this experience?
    (c) Had he been told about nocturnal emissions in advance. If so, by whom and in what way?

Menstruation (females only)

1. At what age did informant start to menstruate?
2. Had menstruation been explained to her in advance? If so, by whom and in what way?
3. Was menstruation discussed among her friends?
4. What terms did she use to refer to it?
5. What were her feelings in anticipation of menstruation?
6. How did she feel after menstruation began?
7. Did it influence her lifestyle in any way?
8. Did it lead to her feeling differently about herself and her body?
9. Has she ever had any menstrual difficulties?
10. Has she ever had intercourse during a period? How does she feel about this?

Knowledge of Reproduction

1. At what age did informant learn about reproduction?
2. From whom and in what way did he or she learn?
3. What was his or her reaction to this information at the time?

Dating

1. At what age did informant start to date:
   (a) in groups?
   (b) on single dates?
2. Did informant date many different people simultaneously or did he or she usually have a steady relationship with one person at a time?
3. What early fears did informant have about dating?
4. What expectations did informant have about how each person should behave when on a date?

Petting Before Current Partnership

1. What kinds of petting did informant engage in?
2. Was there any touching or manipulation of the genitals involved?
3. How did he or she respond sexually to stimulation during petting?
4. How did he or she feel about engaging in petting?
5. Any negative petting experiences?
6. Where and in what circumstances did petting usually occur?
7. With approximately how many partners did informant pet?
8. What kind of emotional relationship did informant have with a partner before becoming involved in petting?
9. How would the informant's parents have reacted if they had known about the petting?

Sexual Intercourse Before Current Partnership

1 Did informant have intercourse before curent partnership?
2. If so, under what circumstances did first experience of intercourse occur and how did he or she react to it?
3. Under what circumstances did intercourse usually occur?
4. How frequently did intercourse occur?
5. With how many partners?
6. What emotional conditions did informant need to have intercourse with someone? E.g.:
   (a) To be in love with each other.
   (b) To care for each other.
   (c) To be committed to a long-term relationship.

    (d) To be engaged.
    (e) To be married.
    (f) No emotional involvement required.
7. How did informant respond sexually during intercourse?
8. Did informant fantasize during intercourse? If so, what did he or she fantasize?
9. What feelings usually accompanied intercourse? E.g.:
    (a) Satisfaction.
    (b) Pleasure.
    (c) Guilt.
    (d) Embarrassment.
    (e) Anxiety.
10. What form(s) of contraception was used?
11. Was intercourse ever intruded upon by a third person?
12. How would the informant's parents have reacted if they had known about his or her engagement in intercourse?

Romantic Relationships Before Current Partnership

1. Has informant ever been in love before?
2. What does being in love mean to him or her?
3. Does he or she fall in love easily?
4. What kinds of person does he or she usually fall in love with?
5. How many loving relationships has he or she had?
6. How long did these relationships last?
7. In what circumstances did they come to an end and how did informant react to this?

Traumatic Experiences

1. Has informant ever had an upsetting or disturbing experience associated with sex? E.g.:
    (a) Sexual victimization prior to attaining age 17 years.
    (b) Rape or sexual assault after attaining age of 17 years.
    (c) Indecent exposure.
    (d) Unwanted pregnancy.
    (e) Abortion.
    (f) Venereal disease.
2. How did informant react to such experiences?

Erotic Materials

1. What experience has informant had with erotic materials? E.g.:
    (a) Written.

(b) Photographs.
(c) Films.
2. What is the preferred content of such material for the informant?

Homosexual Experiences

1. Did the informant have any sexual encounters with a member of the same sex?
2. If so, how did he or she react at the time?

Deviant Experiences

1. Has the informant been involved in any unusual or unconventional forms of sexual activity?
2. If so, how did he or she react at the time?

Sexual Experience With Current Partner

1. What was the nature of the informant's sexual experiences with his or her current partner?
   (a) When they were dating.
   (b) During their engagement.
   (c) On their honeymoon.
   (d) During the marriage or cohabitation up to the present time.
2. How did the informant respond sexually during these experiences?
3. What feelings usually accompanied these experiences for the informant?

Current Conditions

Sexual Practices

1. Review relevant responses on:
   (a) Sexual History Form.
   (b) Index of Sexual Satisfaction.
   (c) Sexual Relationship Questionnaire.
   (d) Client Self-Monitoring Records.
   (e) Sexual Arousal Inventory (if applicable).
2. How sexually attractive is the partner to the informant?
   How sexually attractive does the informant believe he or she is to the partner?
3. How often are the informant and partner physically affectionate with each other without necessarily expecting intercourse to follow?
   How satisfied is the informant with amount and type of physical affection he or she gets from the partner?

4. Which partner usually initiates sexual activity?

  What types of sexual advance are made?

  What are the informant's reactions to these advances?

  In what ways would he or she like the initiation of sex to be different?

5. How does the informant feel:

  (a) about seeing the partner nude?

  (b) about the partner seeing the informant nude?

6. In general, for how long do the couple engage in foreplay prior to intercourse?

  What types of sexual activity occur during foreplay?

  What are the informant's sexual responses and emotions reactions during these activities?

  In what ways would he or she like foreplay to be different?

7. How frequently does sexual intercourse take place?

  How long does intercourse usually last?

  What positions and techniques are used during intercourse?

  Does the informant fantasize during intercourse? If so, what is the preferred content of these fantasies?

  What are the informant's sexual responses and emotional reactions during intercourse?

  In what ways would he or she like intercourse to be different?

8. What do the couple do after they have had intercourse?

  What would the informant like them to do differently?

9. What form of contraception is used?

  How satisfactory is this for the informant?

  What are the informant's attitudes towards and intentions concerning the possibility of conception?

10. How frequently does the informant masturbate?

  What techniques/aids does he or she use?

  Does he or she fantasize during masturbation? If so, what is the preferred content of the fantasies?

  What are the informan't sexual responses and emotional reactions during masturbation?

  How does he or she feel after masturbating?

  In what ways would he or she like masturbation to be different?

11. Does the informant use erotic materials (e.g. written, photographs, films)?

  If so, what is the preferred content?

  What are the informants sexual responses and emotional reactions to such materials?

12. At what time does sexual activity usually occur between the informant and partner?

  In what ways would the informant like the timing to be different?

13. Where does sexual activity usually take place between the informant and partner?

What change would the informant like in these settings?

Sexual Stresses

1. In what respects does sexuality entail frustration, threat, or conflict for the informant?
   (a) Sexual anatomy or responses, e.g.:
       (i) seeing, touching, or smelling his or her genital organs or secretions, or those of the partner;
       (ii) losing control during orgasm.
   (b) Anticipation of harm, e.g.:
       (i) causing or receiving pain or injury during intercourse;
       (ii) venereal disease;
       (iii) unwanted pregnancy;
       (iv) sexual frustration;
       (v) threatening degree of intimacy or commitment.
   (c) Anticipation of failure, e.g.:
       (i) in reaching climax;
       (ii) in being able to arouse and satisfy partner.
   (d) Moral or religious contraventions, e.g.:
       (i) masturbation;
       (ii) premarital intercourse.

Stress Reactions

In what ways does informant react to sexual stresses?
1. Emotional reactions, e.g.:
   (a) Anxiety, fear, panic.
   (b) Vulnerability, helplessness, entrapment.
   (c) Disgust, revulsion.
   (d) Guilt, shame.
   (e) Anger, resentment.
2. Cognitive reactions, e.g.:
   (a) Re-experiencing traumatic events through intrusive thoughts, images, flashbacks, or nightmares.
   (b) Dissociative reactions such as depersonalization, derealization, amnesia, multiple personality disorder.
3. Physiological reactions, e.g.:
   (a) Muscle tension.
   (b) Sweating.

    (c) Rapid breathing.
    (d) Palpitations.
    (e) Dizziness, fainting.
    (f) Nausea, retching, vomiting.
    (g) Disturbances of eating, sleeping, or excretion.
4. Behavioral reactions, e.g.:
    (a) Avoidance of stressful experiences by means such as: (i) vaginismus; (ii) inhibition of orgasm; (iii) reduction of frequency of sexual activity; (iv) constriction of variety of sexual activity; (v) restriction of physical affection; (vi) cessation of communication about sex; (vii) avoidance of social contacts or other situations that might entail sexual encounters.
    (b) Aggressive acts toward partner or self.

Sexual Attitudes

1. What is the informant's attitude towards sex in general?
    (a) Good.
    (b) Pleasurable.
    (c) Dirty.
    (d) Sinful.
    (d) Degrading.
2. Does the informant believe that men and women should have distinct and different roles in sexual activities? E.g.:
    (a) Men should initiate and control sex.
    (b) It is unnatural for women to be on top during intercourse.
    (c) It is inappropriate or unacceptable for women to show a strong interest in sex.
    (d) Women should satisfy the sexual needs of their partners and not be concerned about their own satisfaction.
    (e) It is a woman's duty to have sex with a man who wants it.
3. What conflicts does the informant experience between his or her own attitudes towards sex and those of:
    (a) his or her partner?
    (b) his or her religion?
    (c) the social groups in which he or she lives?
4. What importance does the informant attach to sex in his or her relationship with a partner?

Sexual Information

1. Are there any deficiencies or inaccuracies in the informant's knowledge about sexual matters that may be contributing to a sexual dysfunction?

General Relationship

1. Review relevant responses on Dyadic Adjustment Scale and Marital Relationship Questionnaire.
2. Does the informant:
   (a) like the partner?
   (b) find the partner attractive?
   (c) love the partner?
   (d) feel emotionally close to the partner?
3. In general, how does the informant feel about the marriage/cohabitation?
   How satisfied is he or she with it?
   What are some of the good things about it?
   In what ways would the informant like it to be different?
4. How do sexual difficulties affect other aspects of the relationship?
5. How closely do the informant and partner agree on:
   (a) the appropriate roles for the man and woman in their marriage/cohabitation?
   (b) who should exercise the most power and make the decisions in certain aspects of their relationship?
6. How well do the informant and partner communicate with each other? E.g.:
   (a) Talk about most things.
   (b) Avoid certain topics or argue over them.
   (c) Discuss their sexual problems.
   (d) Speak openly and honestly.
   (e) Listen, empathize, and validate.
   (f) Get their points across.
   (g) Resolve their conflicts.
   (h) Express criticism, resentment, and anger.
   (i) Express affection, appreciation, and praise.
   (j) Express specific sexual preferences.
7. How committed to the relationship is the informant?
   Has he or she ever considered separation or divorce?
8. How much does the informant trust the partner?
   Does the informant fear that he or she may be hurt, rejected, or abandoned by the partner?
9. How often do the informant and partner have argument/rows/fights?
   What are these conflicts usually about?
   What happens during a conflict?
   How are conflicts handled or resolved?
10. Does the informant feel angry, bitter, resentful, or hostile towards the partner?
    If so, what evokes these feelings?

11. Does physical violence ever occur between the informant and partner? If so, in what circumstances does such violence happen?

Organic Conditions

1. Are there any organic conditions that might contribute to sexual dysfunction, either physically or psychologically? E.g.:
   (a) Disease.
   (b) Disability.
   (c) Surgery.
   (d) Medication.
   (e) Aging.
   (f) Menopause.
   (g) Method of contraception.
   (h) Pregnancy.
   (i) Post-partum period.
   (j) Miscarriage.
   (k) Abortion.
   (l) Drug abuse.
   (m) Alcohol abuse.

Psychopathological conditions

1. Are there any other psychopathological conditions that might contribute to sexual dysfunction? E.g.:
   (a) Depression (if may be present, review responses on Beck Depression Inventory).

Self-concept

1. Are there features of the informant's self-concept that might contribute to sexual dysfunction? (Review responses on Belief Inventory and Index of Self-Esteem.) E.g.:
   (a) Negative body image.
   (b) Impaired gender identity.
   (c) Low self-esteem.
   (d) Self-perceived unpopularity or unattractiveness in social relationships.

Non-sexual Stresses

1. Are there any non-sexual sources of frustration, threat, or conflict in the informant's life situation that might contribute to sexual dysfunctions? E.g.:

(a) Unemployment.
(b) Problems at work.
(c) Financial difficulties.
(d) Family illness.
(e) Child behavior problems.

Lifestyle

1. Are there any features in the informant's and/or partner's lifestyle that might contribute to sexual dysfunction? E.g.:
   (a) Lack of comfort, warmth, or privacy.
   (b) Couple spend little time together of;
      (i) long working hours;
      (ii) markedly discrepant working hours;
      (iii) work requiring location away from home.
   (c) Separate rather than shared leisure time.
   (d) Discrepant career plans and objectives.
   (e) Children adversely affecting marital/sexual relationships.
   (f) Low priority accorded to sexual activity.
   (g) Feeling tired, hurried, or preoccupied with things other than sex.

Extra-marital Relationship

1. During the current marriage or cohabitation has the informant been involved in a sexual or romantic relationship with an opposite-sex partner?
2. If so, how serious was this relationship?
3. How did the informant react sexually and emotionally during the relationship?
4. Did the spouse or cohabitee know about the relationship?
   If so, what was his or her reaction?

Homosexual Encounters

1. During the current marriage or cohabitation has the informant been involved in any homosexual encounters?
2. If so, how did the informant react sexually and emotionally to these?
3. Did the spouse or cohabitee know about the encounters?
   If so, what was his or her reaction?

Attitudes to Treatment for Sexual Dysfunction

1. Who made the decision to seek treatment?
2. Why was it decided to seek treatment at this particular time?

3. What are the reasons for seeking treatment?
4. How would the informant like things to be different both sexually and non-sexually after treatment?
5. What concerns or worries does the informant have about treatment and its anticipated consequences?
6. How effective does the informant expect treatment to be?
7. How willing is the informant to participate and actively cooperate in treatment?

References

Allen, C.V. (1980). *Daddy's Girl*. Toronto: McClelland and Stewart.

Araji, S., & Finkelhor, D. (1985). Explanations of pedophilia: Review of empirical research. *Bulletin of the American Academy of Psychiatry and the Law*, **13**, 17–37.

Araji, S., & Finkelhor, D. (1986). Abusers: A review of the research. In D. Finkelhor. *A Sourcebook on Child Sexual Abuse* (pp. 89–118). Beverly Hills: Sage.

Armstrong, L. (1979). *Kiss Daddy Goodnight: A Speak-out on Incest*. New York: Simon and Schuster.

Baer, J. (1976). *How to be an assertive (not Aggressive) Woman in Life, in Love, and on the Job*. New York: The New American Library.

Baisden, M.J., & Baisden, J.R. (1979). A profile of women who seek counseling for sexual dysfunction. *American Journal of Family Therapy*, **7**, 68–76.

Baker, A.W., & Duncan, S.P. (1985). Child sexual abuse: A study of prevalence in Great Britain. *Child Abuse and Neglect*, **9**, 457–467.

Bancroft, J. (1983). *Human Sexuality and its Problems*. Edinburgh: Churchill Livingstone.

Bandura, A. (1977). *Social Learning Theory*. Englewood Cliffs, NJ: Prentice-Hall.

Barbach, L.G. (1975). *For Yourself: The Fulfillment of Female Sexuality*. A guide to orgasmic response. New York: Doubleday.

Barbach, L. (1984). *For Each Other: Sharing Sexual Intimacy*. New York: Signet.

Barlow, D.H., Hayes, S.C., & Nelson, R.O. (1984). *The Scientist Practitioner: Research and accountability in clinical and education settings*. New York: Pergamon.

Battle, J. (1981). *Culture-Free Self-Esteem Inventories for Children and Adults*. Seattle: Special Child Publications.

Baxley, N. (Producer & Director) (1978). *Responsible Assertion* (Film). Champaign, IL: Research Press.

Beck, A.T. (1976). *Cognitive Therapy and the Emotional Disorders*. New York: International Universities Press.

Beck, A.T. (1978). *Depression Inventory*. Philadelphia: Center for Cognitive Therapy.

Beck, A.T., & Beamesderfer, A. (1974). Assessment of depression: The depression inventory. In P. Pichot (Ed.). *Psychological Measurement in Psychopharmacology. Modern problems in pharmaco-psychiatry*, Vol. 7. Paris: Karger, Basel.

Beck, A.T., & Emery, G. (1985). *Anxiety Disorders and Phobias: A cognitive perspective*. New York: Basic Books.

Beck, A.T., Rush, A.J., Shaw, B.F., & Emery, G. (1979). *Cognitive Therapy of Depression*. New York: Guilford.

Becker, J.V., & Skinner, L.J. (1984). Behavioral treatment of sexual dysfunctions in sexual assault survivors. In I.R. Stuart & J.C. Greer (Eds.). *Victims of Sexual*

Aggression: Treatment of children, women, and men (pp. 211–233). New York: Van Nostrand Reinhold.

Becker, J.V., Skinner, L.J., Abel, G.G., Axelrod, R., & Cichon, J. (1984). Sexual problems of sexual assault survivors. *Women and Health*, **9**, 5–20.

Beidel, D.C., & Turner, S.M. (1986). A critique of the theoretical bases of cognitive–behavioral theories and therapy. *Clinical Psychology Review*, **6**, 177–197.

Benward, J., & Densen-Gerber, J. (1975). Incest as a causative factor in antisocial behaviour: An exploratory study. *Contemporary Drug Problems*, **4**, 323–340.

Bernstein, D.A., & Borkovec, T.D. (1973). *Progressive Relaxation Training: A manual for the helping professions*. Champaign, IL: Research Press.

Blake-White, J., & Kline, C. (1985). Treating the dissociative process in adult victims of childhood incest. *Social Casework*, **66**, 394–402.

Bliss, E.L. (1984). A symptom profile of patients with multiple personalities including MMPI results. *Journal of Nervous and Mental Disease*, **172**, 197–202.

Bloom, L., Coburn, K., & Pearlman, J. (1975). *The New Assertive Woman*. New York: Dell.

Bloom, M., & Fischer, J. (1982). *Evaluating Practice: Guidelines for the accountable professional*. Englewood Cliffs, NJ: Prentice-Hall.

Boor, M. (1982). The multiple personality epidemic: Additional cases and inferences regarding diagnosis, etiology, dynamics, and treatment. *Journal of Nervous and Mental Disease*, **170**, 302–304.

Bower, S., & Bower, G. (1976). *Asserting Your Self*. Reading, MA: Addison-Wesley.

Bowman, E.S., Blix, S., & Coons, P.M. (1985). Multiple personality in adolescence: Relationship to incestual experiences. *Journal of the American Academy of Child Psychiatry*, **24**, 109–114.

Brady, K. (1979). *Father's Days: A true story of incest*. New York: Dell.

Brehm, J.W. (1966). *A Theory of Psychological Reactance*. New York: Academic Press.

Briere, J. (1984, April). *The effects of childhood sexual abuse on later psychological functioning: Defining a post-sexual abuse syndrome*. Paper presented at the Third National Conference on Sexual Victimization of Children Washington, DC.

Briere, J., & Runtz, M. (1986). Suicidal thoughts and behaviors in former sexual abuse victims. *Canadian Journal of Behavioral Science*, **16**, 413–423.

Browne, A., & Finkelhor, D. (1986a). Initial and long-term effects: A review of research. In D. Finkelhor. *A Sourcebook of Child Sexual Abuse* (pp. 143–179). Beverly Hills: Sage.

Browne, A., & Finkelhor, D. (1986b). Impact of child sexual abuse: A review of research. *Psychological Bulletin*, **99**, 66–77.

Burns, D.D. (1980). *Feeling Good: The new mood therapy*. New York: Signet.

Butler, P. (1981). *Self-Assertion for Women*. San Francisco, CA: Harper and Row.

Caldirola, D., Gemperle, M.B., Guzinski, G.M., Gross, R.J., & Doerr, H. (1983). Incest and pelvic pain: The social worker as part of a research team. *Health and Social Work*, **8**, 309–319.

Campbell, D.T., & Stanley, J.C. (1983). *Experimental and Quasi-Experimental Designs for Research*. Chicago: Rand McNally.

Chesney, A.P., Blakeney, P.E., Cole, C.M., & Chan, F.A. (1981). A comparison of couple who have sought sex therapy with couples who have not. *Journal of Sex and Marital Therapy*, **37**, 131–140.

Clionsky, M.I. (1983). Assertiveness training for corporate executives. In J.S. Manuso (Ed.). *Occupational Clinical Psychology* (pp. 147–162). New York: Praeger.

Cole, C.H., & Barney, E.E. (1987). Safeguards and the therapeutic window: A group treatment strategy for adult incest survivors. *The American Journal of Orthopsychiatry*, **57**, 601–609.

Cook, T.D., & Campbell, D.T. (Eds.) (1979). *Quasi-Experimentation: Design and analysis issues for field settings.* Chicago: Rand McNally.

Coons, P.M. (1986). Child abuse and multiple personality disorder: Review of the literature and suggestions for treatment. *Child Abuse and Neglect,* **10**, 455–462.

Coons, P.M., & Milstein, V. (1984). Rape and post-traumatic stress in multiple personality. *Psychological Reports,* **55**, 839–845.

Coons, P.M. & Milstein, V. (1986). Psychosexual disturbances in multiple personality: Characteristic etiology and treatment. *Journal of Clinical Psychiatry,* **47**, 106–110.

Courtois, C.A. (1979). Characteristics of a volunteer sample of adult women who experience incest in childhood or adolescence. *Dissertion Abstracts International,* **40**, 3194A–3195A (University microfilms No. 7926514).

Courtois, C.A., & Leehan, J. (1982). Group treatment program for grown up abused children. *The Personnel and Guidance Journal,* **60**, 564–566.

Coyne, J.C., & Gotlieb, I.H. (1983). The role of cognition in depression: A critical appraisal. *Psychological Bulletin,* **94**, 472–505.

deYoung, M. (1982). Innocent seducer or innocently seduced? The role of the child incest victim. *Journal of Clinical Child Psychology,* **11**, 56–60.

deYoung, M. (1986). 'The cloak of innocence': The concept of the participant victim in the child sexual abuse literature. *Sexual Coercion & Assault,* **1**, 189–195.

Doige, A.R. (1985). *Situation/transition group for partners of women who were sexually victimized as children or adolescents.* Unpublished master's practicum report, University of Manitoba, Winnipeg.

Dush, D.M., Hirt, M.L., & Schroeder, H. (1983). Self-statement modification with adults: A meta-analysis. *Psychological Bulletin,* **94**, 408–422.

Emmelkamp, P.M.G. (1982). Anxiety and fear. In A.S. Bellack, M. Hersen, & A.E. Kazdin (Eds.). *International Handbook of Behavior Modification and Therapy* (pp. 349–395). New York: Plenum.

Fennell, M.J.V. (1983). Cognitive therapy of depression: The mechanisms of change. *Behavioral Psychotherapy,* **11**, 97–108.

Finkelhor, D. (1979a). What's wrong with sex between adults and children? Ethics and problems of sexual abuse. *American Journal of Orthopsychiatry,* **49**, 692–697.

Finkelhor, D. (1979b). *Sexually Victimized Children.* New York: Free Press.

Finkelhor, D. (1984). *Child Sexual Abuse: New Theory and research.* New York: Free Press.

Finkelhor, D. (1986). Abusers: Special topics. In D. Finkelhor. *A Sourcebook on Child Sexual Abuse* (pp. 119–142). Beverly Hills: Sage.

Finkelhor, D., & Baron, L. (1986). High risk children. In D. Finkelhor. *A Sourcebook of Child Sexual Abuse.* (pp. 60–88). Beverly Hills: Sage.

Finkelhor, D., & Browne, A. (1985). The traumatic impact of child sexual abuse: A conceptualization. *American Journal of Orthopsychiatry,* **55**, 530–541.

Finkelhor, D., & Browne, A. (1986). Initial and long-term effects: A conceptual framework. In D. Finkelhor. *A Sourcebook on Child Sexual Abuse* (pp. 180–198). Beverly Hills: Sage.

Finkelhor, D., & Russell, D.E.H. (1984). Women as perpetrators: Review of the evidence. In D. Finkelhor. *Child Sexual Abuse: New theory and research* (pp. 171–185). New York: Free Press.

Forward, S., & Buck, C. (1981). *Betrayal of Innocence: Incest and its devastation.* London: Penguin.

Fowler, C., Burns, S.R., & Roehl, J.E. (1983). The role of group therapy in incest counseling. *International Journal of Family Therapy,* **5**, 127–135.

Frank, E., Anderson, C., & Rubenstein, D. (1979). Marital role strain and sexual satisfaction. *Journal of Consulting and Clinical Psychology,* **347**, 1096–1103.

Friedman, S., & Harrison, G. (1984). Sexual histories, attitudes and behavior of schizophrenic and 'normal' women. *Archives of Sexual Behavior*, **13**, 555–567.

Fromuth, M.E. (1986). The relationship of childhood sexual abuse with later psychological and sexual adjustment in a sample of college women. *Child Abuse and Neglect*, **10**, 5–15

Gambrill, E., & Richey, C. (1975). An assertion inventory for use in assessment and research. *Behavior Therapy*, **6**, 550–561.

Garvey, M.J. (1985). Decreased libido in depression. *Medical Aspects of Human Sexuality*, **19**, 30–34.

Gazan, M.A. (1985). *A treatment package for sexually dysfunctional women who have been sexually victimized in childhood or adolescence*. Unpublished master's thesis, university of Manitoba, Winnipeg.

Geiser, R. (1979). *Hidden Victims: The sexual abuse of children*. Boston: Beacon Press.

Gelinas, D.J. (1983). The persisting negative effects of incest. *Psychiatry*, **46**, 312–332.

Gil, E.M. (1984). *Outgrowing the pain: A book for and about adults abused as children* (2nd edn). San Francisco: Launch.

Goldfried, M.R., & Davison, G.C. (1976). *Clinical Behavior Therapy*. New York: Holt, Rinehart and Winston.

Goldstein, A.P. (1980). Relationship-enhancement methods. In F.H. Kanfer & A.P. Goldstein (Eds.). *Helping People Change: A textbook of methods* (2nd edn) (pp. 18–57). New York: Pergamon.

Goodman, B., & Nowak-Scibelli, D. (1985). Group treatment for women incestuously abused as children. *International Journal of Group Psychotherapy*, **35**, 531–544.

Goodwin, J., McCarthy, T., & DiVasto, P. (1981). Prior incest in mothers of abused children. *Child Abuse and Neglect*, **5**, 87–95.

Gordy, P.L. (1983). Group work that supports adult victims of childhood incest. *Social Casework*, **64**, 300–307.

Gottlieb, B., & Dean, J. (1981). The co-therapy relationship in group treatment of sexualy mistreated adolescent girls. In P.M. Mrazek & C.H. Kempe (Eds.). *Sexually Abused Children and Their Families* (pp. 211–218). Oxford: Pergamon.

Gross, R.J., Doerr, H., Caldirola, D., Guzinski, G.M., & Ripley, H.S. (1980). Borderline syndrome and incest in chronic pelvic pain patients. *International Journal of Psychiatry in Medicine*, **10**, 79–96.

Groth, N.A., & Burgess, A.W. (1979). Sexual trauma in the life histories of rapists and child molesters. *Victimology*, **4**, 10–16.

Gundlach, R.H. (1977). Sexual molestation and rape reported by homosexual and heterosexual women. *Journal of Homosexuality*, **2**, 367–384.

Hariton, B. (1973, March). The sexual fantasies of women. *Psychology Today*, 39–44.

Hawton, K. (1985). *Sex Therapy: A practical guide*. Oxford: Oxford University Press.

Heiman, J., LoPiccolo, L., & LoPiccolo, J. (1976). *Becoming Orgasmic: A sexual growth program for women*. Englewood Cliffs, NJ: Prentic Hall.

Herman, J.L. (1981). *Father–Daughter Incest*. Cambridge, MA: Harvard University Press.

Herman, J.L. (1986). Histories of violence in an outpatient population: An exploratory study. *American Journal of Orthopsychiatry*, **56**, 137–141.

Herman, J., & Schatzow, E. (1984). Time-limited group therapy for women with a history of incest. *International Journal of Group Psychotherapy*, **34**, 605–616.

Hollon, S.D., & Kiss, M.R. (1984). Cognitive factors in clinical research and practice. *Clinical Psychology Review*, **4**, 35–76.

Holmes, M.R., & St Lawrence, J.S. (1983). Treatment of rape-induced trauma: Proposed behavioral conceptualization and review of the literature. *Clinical Psychology Review*, **3**, 417–433.

Hoon, E.F., Hoon, P.W., & Wincze, J.P. (1976). An inventory for the mesurement of female sexual arousability: The SAI. *Archives of Sexual Behavior, 5*, 291–300.

Hudson, W.W. (1982). *The Clinical Measurement Package: A field manual.* Homewood, IL: Dorsey.

Hudson, W.W., Harrison, D.F., & Crosscup, P.C. (1981). A short-form scale to measure sexual discord in dyadic relationships. *The Journal of Sex Research, 17*, 157–174.

Jacobson, N.S., & Margolin, G. (1979). *Marital Therapy: Strategies based on social learning and behavioral exchange principles.* New York: Brunner/Mazel.

James, J., & Meyerding, J. (1977). Early sexual experience as a factor in prostitution. *Archives of Sexual Behavior, 1*, 31–42.

Jehu, D. (1979). *Sexual Dysfunction: A behavioural approach to causation, assessment, and treatment.* Chichester: Wiley.

Jehu, D., Gazan, M., & Klassen, C. (1984/5). Common therapeutic targets among women who were sexually abused in childhood. *Journal of Social Work and Human Sexuality, 3*, 25–45.

Jehu, D., Gazan, M., & Klassen, C. (1985). Common therapeutic targets among women who were sexually abused in childhood. In M. Valentich & J. Gripton (Eds.). *Feminist Perspectives on Social Work and Human Sexuality* (pp. 25–45). New York: Haworth.

Jehu, D., Gazan, M., & Klassen, C. (1987). *Therapy with Women Who Were Sexually Abused in Childhood: Part 8. Stress disorders.* Winnipeg: University of Manitoba. Psychological Service Center.

Jehu, D., Klassen, C., & Gazan, M. (1985/6). Cognitive restructuring of distorted beliefs associated with childhood sexual abuse. *Journal of Social Work and Human Sexuality, 4*, 49–69.

Jehu, D., Klassen, C., & Gazan, M. (1986). Cognitive restructuring of distorted beliefs associated with childhood sexual abuse. In J. Gripton & M. Valentich (Eds.). *Social Work Practice in Sexual Problems* (pp. 49–69). New York: Haworth.

Jehu, D., Klassen, C., & Gazan, M. (1987). *Therapy with Women Who Were Sexually Abused in Childhood: Part 1. Mood disturbances.* Winnipeg: University of Manitoba, Psychological Service Center.

Jehu, D., McCallum, J., Klassen, C., & Gazan, M. (1987). *Therapy with Women Who Were Sexually Abused in Childhood: Part 1. Description of clients.* Winnipeg: University of Manitoba, Psychological Services Center.

Jemail, J.A., & LoPiccolo, J. (1982). A sexual and marital defensiveness scale for each sex. *American Journal of Family Therapy, 10*, 33–40.

Kanfer, F.H. (1980). Self-management methods. In F.H. Kanfer & A.P. Goldstein (Eds.). *Helping People Change: A textbook of methods* (2nd eds) (pp. 334–389). New York: Pergamon.

Kaufman, L., Peck, A.L., & Taguiri, C.K. (1954). The family constellation and overt incestuous relations between father and daughter. *American Journal of Orthopsychiatry, 24*, 266–277.

Keane, T.M., Zimering, R.T., & Caddell, J.M. (1985). A behavioral formulation of post-traumatic stress disorder in Vietnam veterans. *The Behavior Therapist, 8*, 9–12.

Kegel, A.H. (1952). Sexual functions of the puboccygeous muscle. *Western Journal of Surgery, Obstetrics, and Gynaecology, 601*, 521–540.

Kelly, G. (1955). *The Psychology of Personal Constructs* (2 vols.). New York: Norton.

Kilpatrick, A.C. (1987). Childhood sexual experiences: Problems and issues in studying long-range effects. *The Journal of Sex Research, 23*, 173–196.

Klassen, C., & Jehu, D. (1987). *Therapy with Women Who Were Sexually Abused in Childhood: Part 10. Therapy with a victim in a lesbian relationship.* Winnipeg: University of Manitoba, Psychological Service Center.

Kluft, R.P. (Ed.) (1985). *Childhood Antecendents of Multiple Personality*. Washington, DC: American Psychiatric Press.

Kluft, R.P., Braun, B.G., & Sachs, R.G. (1985). Multiple personality, intrafamilial abuse, and family psychiatry. *International Journal of Family Psychiatry*, 5, 283–301.

Kolodny, R.C., Masters, W.H., & Johnson, V.E. (1979). *Textbook of Sexual Medicine*. Boston: Little, Brown.

Krause, D. (Producer) & Hirsh, M. (Director) (1983). *It's Not Like Scraping Your Knee* (Videotape). Minneapolis: Genesis II.

Kuiper, N.A., & MacDonald, M.R. (1983). Reason, emotion, and cognitive therapy. *Clinical Psychology Review*, 3, 297–316.

Lange, A., & Jakubowski, P. (1976). *Responsible Assertive Behaviour: Cognitive/ behavioral procedures for trainers*. Champaign, IL: Research Press.

Langevin, R., Handy, L., Hook, H., Day, D., & Russon, A. (1983). Are incestuous fathers pedophilic and aggressive? In R. Langevin (Ed.). *Erotic Preference, Gender Identity and Aggression*. New York: Erlbaum Associates.

Larson, D., Attkinson, C., Hargreaves, W., & Nguyen, T. (1979). Assessment of client/patient satisfaction: Development of a general scale. *Evaluation and Program Planning*, 2, 197–207.

Leehan, J., & Wilson, L.P. (1985). *Grown-up Abused Children*. Springfield, IL: Charles C. Thomas.

Lewis, I.A. (1985). [Los Angeles Times Poll #98]. Unpublished raw data.

Liberman, R.P., King, L.W., DeRisi, W.J., & McCann, M. (1975). *Personal Effectiveness*. Champaign, IL: Research Press.

LoPiccolo, J., Friedman, J., & Weiler, S.J. (Directors) (undated). *Treating Erectile Problems* (Film). New York: Focus International.

LoPiccolo, L.J., & Heiman, J.R. (Directors) (undated). *Becoming Orgasmic: A sexual growth for women* (Film). New York: Focus International.

MacFarlane, K., & Korbin, J. (1983). Confronting the incest secret long after the fact: A family study of multiple victimization with strategies for intervention. *Child Abuse and Neglect*, 7, 225–240.

Marks, I. (1981). *Cure and Care of Neuroses: Theory and practice of behavioral psychotherapy*. New York: Wiley.

Masson, J.M. (1984). *The Assault on Truth: Freud's suppression of the seduction theory*. New York: Farrer, Struass & Giroux.

Mathew, R.J., & Weinman, M.L. (1982). Sexual dysfunctions in depression. *Archives of Sexual Behavior*, 11, 323–328.

McCallum, M.J. (1987). *Group treatment of adult women who were sexually victimized in childhood*. Unpublished master's practicum report, University of Manitoba, Winnipeg.

McCormack, A., Janus, M.D., & Burgess, A.W. (1986). Runaway youths and sexual victimization: Gender differences in an adolescent runaway population. *Child Abuse & Neglect*, 10, 387–395.

McGuire, L.S., & Wagner, N.N. (1978). Sexual dysfunction in women who were molested as children: One response pattern and suggestions for treatment. *Journal of Sex and Marital Therapy*, 4, 11–15.

Meichenbaum, D. (1985). *Stress Inoculation Training*. New York: Pergamon.

Meiselman, K.C. (1978). *Incest: A psychological study of causes and effects with treatment recommendations*. San Francisco: Jossey-Bass Inc.

Millican, S. (Producer and Director) (1979). *Incest: The family secret* (Videotape). Winnipeg: Canadian Broadcasting Corporation.

Mintz, J., & Keisler, D.J. (1982). Individualized measures of psychotherapy outcome. In P.C. Kendall & J.N. Butcher (Eds.). *Handbook of Research Methods in Clinical Psychology* (pp. 491–534). New York: Wiley.

Mogul, K.M. (1982). Overview: The sex of the therapist. *American Journal of Psychiatry,* **139,** 1–11.

Mowrer, O.H. (1960). *Learning Theory and Behavior.* New York: Wiley.

Myer, M.H. (1984/5). A new look at mothers of incest victims. *Journal of Social Work and Human Sexuality,* **3,** 47–58.

Newton, D. (1978). Homosexual behavior and child molestation: A review of the evidence. *Adolescence,* **13,** 29–43.

Norton, G.R., & Jehu, D. (1984). The role of anxiety in sexual dysfunctions: A review. *Archives of Sexual Behavior,* **13,** 165–183.

Norton, G.R., Jehu, D., & deLuca, R.V. (1985). Anxiete et dysfonctionnement sexuel. *Contraception—fertilite—sexualite1,* **13,** 571–583.

Oppenheimer, R., Howells, K., Palmer, R.L., & Chaloner, D.A. (1985). Adverse sexual experience in childhood and clinical eating disorders: A preliminary description. *Journal of Psychosomatic Research,* **19,** 357–361.

Osborn, S., & Harris, G. (1975). *Assertive Training for Women.* Springfield, IL: Charles C. Thomas.

Painter, S.l. (1986). Research on the prevalence of child sexual abuse: New directions. *Canadian Journal of Behavioral Science,* **18,** 323–339.

Parker, H., & Parker, S. (1986). Father–daughter sexual abuse: An emerging perspective. *American Journal of Orthopsychiatry,* **56,** 531–594.

Persons, J.B., & Burns, D.D. (1985). Mechanisms of action of cognitive therapy: The relative contributions of technical and interpersonal interventions. *Cognitive Therapy and Research,* **9,** 539–551.

Peters, S.D., Wyatt, G.E., & Finkelhor, D. (1986). Prevalence. In D. Finkelhor. *A Sourcebook on Child Sexual Abuse* (pp. 15–59). Beverly Hills: Sage.

Phelps, S., & Austin, N. (1975). *The Assertive Woman.* San Luis Obispo, CA: Impact.

Popescul, R., & Rouillard, G. (1986). *A treatment program for women who were sexually abused in childhood.* Unpublished master's practicum report, University of Manitoba, Winnipeg.

Rachman, S. (1977). The conditioning theory of fear acquisition: A critical examination. *Behavior Research and Therapy,* **15,** 375–378.

Rehm, L.P. (1981). Assessment of depression. In M. Hersen & A.S. Bellack (Eds.). *Behavioral Assessment: A practical handbook* (2nd edn) (pp. 246–295). New York: Pergamon.

Rieker, P.P., & Carmen, E. (1986). The victim-to-patient process: The disconfirmation and transformation of abuse. *American Journal of Orthopsychiatry,* **56,** 360–370.

Rogers, C.M., & Terry, T. (1984). Clinical intervention with boy victims of sexual abuse. In I.R. Stuart & J.G. Greer (Eds.). *Victims of Sexual Aggression: Treatment of children, women and men* (pp. 91–104). New York: Van Nostrand Reinhold.

Rush, F. (1980). *The Best Kept Secret: Sexual abuse of children.* New York: McGraw-Hill.

Russell, D.E.H. (1983). The incidence and prevalence of intrafamilial and extrafamilial sexual abuse of female children. *Child Abuse and Neglect,* **7,** 133–146.

Russell, D.E.H. (1984). *Sexual Exploitation: Rape, child sexual abuse, and workplace harassment.* Beverly Hills: Sage.

Russell, D.E.H. (1986). *The Secret Trauma: Incest in the lives of girls and women.* New York: Basic Books.

Russell, D.E.H., & Finkelhor, D. (1984). The gender gap among perpetrators of child sexual abuse. In D.E.H. Russell. *Sexual Exploitation: Rape, child sexual abuse, and workplace harassment* (pp. 215–231). Beverly Hills: Sage.

Saltman, V., & Solomon, R.S. (1982). Incest and the multiple personality. *Psychological Reports,* **50,** 1127–1141.

Sank, L., & Shaffer, C. (1984). *A Therapist's Manual for Cognitive Behavior Therapy in Groups*. New York: Pergamon.

Schover, L.R., Friedman, J.M., Weiler, S.J., Heiman, J.R., LoPiccolo, J. (1982). Multiaxial problem-oriented system for sexual dysfunctions. *Archives of General Psychiatry*, **39**, 614–619.

Schwab, D. (1986). *An assertiveness training therapy group for women who have been sexually victimized in childhood or adolescence*. Unpublished master's practicum report, University of Manitoba, Winnipeg.

Schwab, D., Jehu, D., & Gazan, M. (1987). *Therapy With Women Who were Sexually Abused in Childhood: Part 5. Assertiveness training group*. Winnipeg: University of Manitoba, Psychological Service Center.

Schwartz, M.D. (1975). Situation/transition groups: A conceptualization and review. *American Journal of Orthopsychiatry*, **45**, 744–755.

Schwartz, R.M. (1982). Cognitive-behavior modification: A conceptual review. *Clinical Psychology Review*, **2**, 26–293.

Sexual Offenses Against Children in Canada (1984). Two volumes. Ottawa, Supply and Services, Canada.

Sgroi, S.M. (1982). *Handbook of Clinical Intervention in Child Sexual Abuse*. Lexington, MA: Heath.

Sharp, D., & Yantzi, M. (Producers and Directors) (1983). *Incest: The victim's perspective* (Videotape). Kitchener: Community Justice Initiatives.

Silbert, M.H. (1984). Treatment of prostitute victims of sexual assault. In I.R. Stuart & J.G. Greer (Eds.). *Victims of Sexual Aggression: Treatment of children, women, and men* (pp. 251–282). New York: Van Nostrand Reinhold.

Silbert, M.H., & Pines, A.M. (1981). Sexual child abuse as an antecedent to prostitution. *Child Abuse and Neglect*, **5**, 407–411.

Silbert, M.H., & Pines, A.M. (1983). Early sexual exploitation as an influence in prostitution. *Social Work*, **28**, 285–289.

Spanier, G.B. (1976). Measuring dyadic adjustment: New Scales for assessing the quality of marriage and similar dyads. *Journal of Marriage and the Family*, **38**, 15–28.

Spanier, G.B., & Thompson, L. (1982). A confirmatory analysis of the dyadic adjustment scale. *Journal of Marriage and the Family*, **44**, 731–738.

Spiegel, D. (1985). Multiple personality as a post-traumatic stress disorder. *Psychiatric Clinics of North America*, **7**, 101–110.

Stuart, R.B. (1980). *Helping Couples Change: A social learning approach to marital therapy*. New York: Guilford.

Summit, R.C. (1983). The child sexual abuse accommodation syndrome. *Child Abuse and Neglect*, **7**, 177–193.

Summit, R., & Kryso, J. (1978). Sexual abuse of children: A clinical spectrum. *American Journal of Orthopsychiatry*, **48**, 237–251.

Talbot, R.M.R., Beech, H.R., & Vaughan, M. (1980). A normative appraisal of erotic fantasies in women. *British Journal of Social and Clinical Psychology*, **19**, 81–83.

Torrey, E.G. (1972). *The Mind Game: Witchdoctors and psychiatrists*. New York: Emerson Hall.

Tsai, M., Feldman-Summers, S., & Edgar, M. (1979). Childhood molestation: Variables related to differential impacts on psychosexual functioning in adult women. *Journal of Abnormal Psychology*, **88**, 407–417.

Tsai, M., & Wagner, N.N. (1978). Therapy groups for women sexually molested as children. *Archives of Sexual Behavior*, **7**, 417–428.

Tukey, J.W. (1947). Comparing individual means in the analysis of variance. *Biometrics*, **5**, 99–114.

Vitaliano, P.P., James, J., & Boyer, D. (1981). Sexuality of deviant females: Adolescent and adult correlates. *Social Work*, **26**, 468–472.

Wachtel, A., & Lawton-Speert, S. (1983). *Child Sexual Abuse: Descriptions of nine program approaches to treatment.* Vancouver: United Way of Lower Mainland (pp. 157–185).

Wilbur, C.W. (1984). Multiple personality and child abuse. *Psychiatric Clinics of North America, 7,* 3–8.

Wooley, M.J., & Vigilanti, M.A. (1984). Psychological separation and the sexual abuse victim. *Psychotherapy, 21,* 347–352.

Wyatt, G.E. (1985). The sexual abuse of Afro-American and white-American women in childhood. *Child Abuse and Neglect, 9,* 507–519.

Wyatt, G.E., & Peters, S.D. (1986a). Issues in the definition of child sexual abuse in prevalence research. *Child Abuse and Neglect, 10,* 231–240.

Wyatt, G.E., & Peters, S.D. (1986b). Methodological considerations in research on the prevalence of child sexual abuse. *Child Abuse and Neglect, 10,* 241–251.

Zilbergeld, B. (1978). *Male Sexuality: A guide to sexual fulfillment.* New York: Bantam.

Zimmer, D., Borchardt, E., & Fischle, C. (1983). Sexual fantasies of sexually distressed and non-distressed men and women: An empirical comparison. *Journal of Sex and Marital Therapy, 9,* 38–50.

Subject Index